DISABILITY
AND THE TUDORS

In memory of my Dad, Robin John Vincent

DISABILITY
AND THE TUDORS
ALL THE KING'S FOOLS

PHILLIPA VINCENT-CONNOLLY

PEN & SWORD
HISTORY

AN IMPRINT OF PEN & SWORD BOOKS LTD.
YORKSHIRE – PHILADELPHIA

First published in Great Britain in 2021 by
PEN AND SWORD HISTORY
An imprint of
Pen & Sword Books Ltd
Yorkshire – Philadelphia

ISBN 978 1 52672 005 4

Typeset in Times New Roman 11.5/14 by
SJmagic DESIGN SERVICES, India.
Printed and bound by CPI Group (UK) Ltd, Croydon, CR0 4YY

Pen & Sword Books Limited incorporates the imprints of Atlas, Archaeology,
Aviation, Discovery, Family History, Fiction, History, Maritime, Military, Military
Classics, Politics, Select, Transport, True Crime, Air World, Frontline Publishing,
Leo Cooper, Remember When, Seaforth Publishing, The Praetorian Press,
Wharncliffe Local History, Wharncliffe Transport, Wharncliffe True Crime and
White Owl.

For a complete list of Pen & Sword titles please contact
PEN & SWORD BOOKS LIMITED
47 Church Street, Barnsley, South Yorkshire, S70 2AS, England
E-mail: enquiries@pen-and-sword.co.uk
Website: www.pen-and-sword.co.uk

Or

PEN AND SWORD BOOKS
1950 Lawrence Rd, Havertown, PA 19083, USA
E-mail: Uspen-and-sword@casematepublishers.com
Website: www.penandswordbooks.com

Contents

Introduction

The existence of disabled people has been woven through the tapestries and popular narratives of history. Disabled people were never seen as 'winners' or victors, so our history over time has been hidden in plain sight – ignored, untold, and viewed as insignificant. Disability history is an important topic to debate, research, and publish because such study directs its readers towards a general reclamation of our British history which rightfully includes its disabled participants.

Disability history is important to address specifically because the subject is often viewed as taboo, and as such, has, and still is often obscured from public view, understanding, and awareness. Disability studies is a field. It is considered a subject in its own right in some universities around the world, but not all. It is not adjacent to English, Sociology or History but should be considered as a subject in its own right. Disability studies deserve whole departments and dedicated faculty members, so the subject can be treated as an interdisciplinary field, rather than a cross-listed posting. Yet, academics and researchers continue to treat disability studies as a last-minute topic, something that they can 'add-on' to their research to be 'on top of the trends' in academia. Sadly, this 'trend' in studying minority histories does a disservice to those disabled people we study, research and write about. Disabled people are equally part of humanity and they give us a different perspective on what it means to be human.

Disabled people and their histories have been overlooked, and their stories so often whitewashed in the narrative of this country, yet they are vital to our real understanding of the past.

Moreover, disability narratives during the Tudor period were subtly ignored, yet hidden in plain sight. Extraordinarily, however, at the same time, a select few disabled people were on public view, because Hampton Court Palace is littered with paintings that suggest, and prove indeed, disability was very much an included part of royal life. Disabled people then, like today, were found in all aspects of Tudor society and therefore their inclusion and relevance are a vital component in our developmental history, which is why the subject needs to be addressed.

However, there is a downside to researching disability history during this period because the Tudors did not categorise disabilities, and they were only just beginning to classify and compartmentalise both physical and mental disabilities. The Tudor viewpoint towards disability is one of contrasts: deformity was thought of as a mark of the Fall, but those with low IQs, intellectual and learning disabilities were Innocents, perhaps incapable of sin. Interestingly, the Tudors also valued extremes of physical disability, such as dwarves and giants.

The use of disability in Shakespearean texts suggests that the words disability and disabled were used in three contexts during the Tudor era. First, in the legal sense 'to disable' meant 'to hinder or restrain, a person or class of persons, from performing acts or enjoying rights which would otherwise be open to them'.[1] There was the medical context of having a disability: 'a physical or mental condition that limits a person's movements, senses, or activities'.[2] Lastly, there was the conceptual context of being 'disabled' for any reason whatsoever, meaning being 'rendered incapable of action or use'.[3]

These contexts on disability, reinforce the definitions of disability within the Equality Act 2010, which states that if a person has a physical or mental impairment that has a 'substantial' and 'long-term' negative effect on their ability to do normal daily activities, then they are considered disabled. It is from this definition of disability that the research in this book is based.

Shakespeare's use of the word disability suggests that: 'The verb "disable" was first used in the legal sense in 1445, and then later in the medical sense around 1492, but the verb was not used in a conceptual sense until 1582. Disability the noun was used in the conceptual sense in 1545, in the medical sense in 1561, and in the legal sense in 1579. Disabled the adjective was used in the conceptual sense in 1598, but not in the medical sense until 1633. Additionally, "the disabled" as an adjective with a definite article referring to a class or group of people did not appear until 1740.'[4]

The definition of disability was undefined, yet the existence of disabled people was viewed as a common occurrence in everyday early modern life. Therefore, disabled people and their experiences of specific disabilities were rarely recorded, which means that case studies and anecdotal evidence for the researcher are very limited. In order to broaden the research, because the Tudors did not place disability within any category, and left disability uncharacterised, definitions of disability need to be compared and contrasted to those in our modern world.

Today, we have definitively defined disability through the Equality Act 2010.[5] Disability has also been defined over the years by medical practitioners into different types of physical and mental categories. Specifics such as these help us to understand how we can help disabled people today. To encapsulate the research, the evidence in this book is viewed through the lens of a Tudor person's ability or inability to take part in 'normal daily activities' that contemporary society considered part of everyday life. It was these expectations of people in that society and their inhibited abilities that would have rendered them disabled, without classifying them as such. It is with this dilemma that this book came into being.

Despite the voracious appetite for everything Tudor, we think we know everything there is to know about them – with English History being so familiar across the globe. Early in 2020, Henry VIII's 'ex-wives' arrived on the Broadway stage in the musical *Six*, 'Divorced, Beheaded, Live in concert!', and tourists and history enthusiasts buying 'B' pendants, sold at Hampton Court Palace, and Tudor Royal Doulton figurines, found at car boot sales. The Tudors are bigger than ever. Again. Our fascination with the Tudors and every aspect of their dynasty is satisfied and commercialised with a plethora of products. Primary sources are debated and deliberated over by historians, yet Tudor disability history is yet to be discovered, and the existence of disabled people during the Tudor period is still unfamiliar to many of us.

There were people with varying disabilities present at the royal courts of Henry VII, Henry VIII, Mary I, Edward VI and Elizabeth I, and in the household of Sir Thomas More. Disabled people played a prominent and vital role in the society of the early modern era. Once people acquire a knowledge of the presence of disabled people in Tudor

England, they presume that disabled people's experience of life during that time was one of ridicule and discrimination. This attitude is neatly summarised in our minds' eye by examples of court jesters dressed in motley, or vagrants being whipped and branded for begging, because of being physically or mentally unfit to work. The misconceptions of the status of disabled people are easy to understand because there is so very little archival evidence of how people with disabilities lived their lives. This is because the Tudors' categorising of disability was in its infancy and to understand the treatment of people with disabilities during the period, we must realise that disability was perceived as an everyday life experience, not always associated with the poor, and that disability was apparent within the echelons of the royal court.

Disability history can be told not only through royalty but through social, relational, political, religious and cultural stories which identify personal experiences of disability during the period. Contemporary uncertainties of the time naturally shape the questions we ask concerning the lives of disabled people in Tudor times. The study of Tudor society defines how disabled people lived and were treated, so our understanding of community, family, politics, and religion in shaping disabled peoples' lives is essential. Moreover, it is imperative for us in the twenty-first century to push aside our misconceptions and modern attitudes to disability to understand how the Tudors treated those less physically and mentally able than themselves.

Today, discrimination, ableism, and the institutionalisation of people with disabilities is endemic to our society and bedevil discourse. However, for matters of context, it is paramount to use the language that the Tudors used to start to define and describe disability. Moreover, the kind of terminology in the book and the glossary at the back of the book is not unique to disabled people, however, it is important to include it to aid our understanding.

In its way, such language could be considered as discrimination and bullying today, but in the early modern context, it was not. The Tudors described what they saw, therefore, the terminology used is kept within the context of the period as far as possible, and has not been included to offend. Readers should not be offended by words such as 'cripple', 'idiot', 'fool', 'dumb', 'deaf', as this is how the Tudors described disability. Fortunately, disability culture and society over the world has evolved since, and so has the terminology changed which is used to describe those who inhabit it. Our current 'social model' of disability says the main problem with 'disability' comes not from the medical condition of a person, but from a society that chooses to lock disabled people out of the mainstream. It appears from research that Tudor society tried its best to be inclusive; however, there is also conflicting evidence to the contrary. On the surface, the Tudors appear not to have any stigma towards disability; however, like today, their perceived stigma of disability flows not from disabled people, but from the assumptions, stereotypical ideas, superstitions and bigotry of non-disabled people.

To understand the lives of disabled people during the period we need to understand how they were feared through contemporary beliefs in superstition; how they carried out everyday tasks from within their communities; understand how laws affected them and also how religious beliefs and monasteries were used to support and look after disabled people both spiritually and physically, and how that implemented inclusion or exclusion of disabled people, dependent on the political and religious climate.

Politics sent non-disabled men into battle, returning home as veterans with disabilities, while hospitals and almshouses were a form of support for disabled people. Mental health issues, learning disabilities, as well as physical disabilities, were supported and treated by wise-women, barber-surgeons and physicians. Wise-women treated the infertile, or women who suffered infertility, miscarriages and stillbirths, and these midwives were thought of as witches, especially if they helped birth a disabled baby. Issues around the practice of childbirth and disability were viewed with superstition and considered a problem for any woman, but especially noblewomen, who without healthy heirs could not fulfil their roles in the families they had married into. The Tudors argued that a disabled baby was birthed because of problems with conception, pregnancy, labour and early infant death, and the worshipping of Satan.

Being born healthy and maintaining good health for a monarch was of paramount importance. A king or queen's health decided how able they were in ruling the country; any stain upon their character, physical deformity, disability, or madness, carried doubts about their ability to rule. Most Tudor monarchs at one point or another were blighted with negative stories about their health and fertility that undermined their reigns. In particular, towards the end of his reign, Henry VIII became more and more disabled from jousting accidents, weeping ulcers in his leg, and his increasing obesity which caused him mobility issues, later addressed by the use of 'walking aids', 'whistles', 'chair thrones', and 'stair thrones'.

Disabled people in high places were not always royalty; some were disabled people with learning disabilities, or possibly Down syndrome, known to the Tudors as 'fools'. Moreover, two distinctions need to be made within the category of 'fool' which can be established as the 'natural' and the 'artificial'. The natural fool was classed as a simpleton; someone considered slow, feebleminded, even an idiot in the technical sense of being severely 'subnormal'. The 'artificial' fool was one of the following, or a combination of buffoon or clown, an entertainer whose talent lay in uninhibited slapstick, a comic who indulged in extempore slick verbal wit, or a jester who offered more contrived light-hearted entertainment. Both kinds were employed at the royal court as domestic fools – as much laughed at for their mental, and even physical deficiencies, as for their antics.[6] It is fascinating that 'natural fools' would become prominent members of the Tudor court and were allowed access to the monarch when other courtiers were denied it. The fact that Tudor society was trying to define being disabled is even more remarkable when you consider how some of these 'natural fools' who lived at the Tudor court were treated.

Research suggests that in the early modern period, disabled people would have been familiar with descriptions of some limiting disabilities through the books of the old and new testaments in the Bible, but would most likely limit the definitions on disability and its experience during that era.

Comprehending the world of disabled Tudors means becoming familiar with the sixteenth century mindset and its ideas about their religious beliefs, superstitions, politics, healthcare; a mindset which is so very different from our own. When people with disabilities presented themselves in any form to non-disabled people, they discovered and felt the effects of discrimination, ridicule and fear, but they also found countrymen who were not only curious about their physical and mental differences but those who were willing to accept and support them. Most men and women knew nothing about society outside their parish boundaries, and therefore those already born within that parish who were disabled were generally accepted. Tudors often judged a person on their religious persuasion or social class, as this is generally how people interacted.

How the church treated disabled people tells us a lot about their social standing too. The country was deeply religious in which the bishop, priest or monk, held the keys to heaven or hell, through petition, prayer and penance. Religion was the foundation of daily life in Tudor England, and people's lives were dictated to by 'Books of Hours' or prayers and ritual. As a person living in Tudor England, the reality of death was difficult to ignore as there were high mortality rates for both adults and children. Life expectancy was around fifty years during this period, and life could easily be cut sooner if a person died in battle, drowned in rivers washing, or contracted an incurable disease or met some other gruesome death like an execution.

Social class directed Tudor society, much like society today, and everyone from the monarch, who at this time ruled by divine right, through to members of the aristocracy, to the nobility and gentry, yeoman and husbandmen, down to the lowliest pot-boy, farmhand and vagrant; all occupied a particular place in the social order. People with disabilities were expected to contribute to society, by being useful, learning new skills, and paying their way. The lives of disabled people during this time, it could be argued, were no more of a hardship than those Tudors who had been born into poverty, which was often the result of being at the bottom of the social spectrum in that society, not just because they had been born with, or suffered either a physical or mental disability.

It has long since been the trend that disabled people have found themselves objects of others' curiosity, and in this, Tudor society was no exception. It is through the plays and satire of writers like Robert Armin that mentally and physically impaired people were made a mockery of, as a form of entertainment.

The social standing of disabled people has changed greatly in 500 years; however, society as a whole, subjected disabled people to discrimination, which meant they did struggle, as they still do struggle, to lead fulfilling lives, to enable them to rise from their positions in society, to make a real difference. However, despite this, we see disabled people in the Tudor period achieving admirable appointments.

During the early modern era, there was a contemporary of Henry VIII, who ruled from across the Channel, a famous leader with a disability who often opposed him and whom Henry considered his 'uncle'. He was

Katharine of Aragon's despotic nephew, Charles V of Spain, who was the Holy Roman Emperor from 1519 until his abdication in 1556, and he was the ruler of the Spanish realms from 1516 until 1556. Charles V allegedly suffered from epilepsy, which although debilitating, was not considered a disability; however, epilepsy would have been considered a physical impairment that would have had a substantial, long-term and adverse effect on his ability to do normal daily activities. Charles V was said to have suffered from joint pain, presumably from gout, even though this infection was not considered a disability according to his sixteenth century doctors, it would have limited his mobility as his condition worsened. Moreover, the symptoms and infections that gout as a condition gave, meant that in his retirement, the king was carried around in a sedan chair during his time at the monastery of St Yuste.[7] Along with Charles V, Henry VIII himself was another royal ruler who would succumb to disability in his later reign, and would also become a wheelchair user.

When you research and read about these prominent people, you begin to realise that despite their disabilities, they achieved much. Consorts such as the French Queen Claude with her disabling challenges are forgotten, and disabled people like her are assessed solely on their achievements, despite their physical and mental limitations. If difference and disability should teach us anything, unlike the twistings of human nature, we might think such difference and diversity are compelling because when disabled people affirm their disability, follow their ambitions, desires, and do not allow attitudinal or discriminatory ableism to stand in their way, their achievements are limitless. In the past, disabled people have been hated, ridiculed, pitied, patronised, ignored and admired for their heroism in the face of adversity, yet despite this marginalisation, they continue to astound and inspire the non-disabled.

As impressive as some of these personalities of the period are, it is notable that the experience of ordinary, and some not so ordinary, disabled people are mainly missing from history. This gap primarily came to mind with the recent discovery of Richard III in a Leicestershire car park. The University of Leicester worked in collaboration with the Richard III Society and Leicester City Council which began one of the most ambitious archaeological projects ever attempted to discover the grave of the last of our English kings to die in battle. Incredibly, the lost grave when found, dug, and excavated, uncovered the friary of

Grey Friars church, and a battle-scarred skeleton with spinal curvature. On 4 February 2013, the university confirmed the remains were indeed those of Richard III, and his recorded disability is one topic that came out in the following discourse.[8]

Disability did not recognise class or status then, and it does not now. While it is essential to learn of these prominent figures in history, the absence of the experience of the average disabled person and their place in society is stark. So, somewhat ironically, it is at the point where one dynasty ended, and another began that we can access disabled people during the Tudor period.

———————— ⚜ ————————

The Tudor dynasty started with Henry VII's success at Bosworth field in 1485 and ended with James Stuart's succession to Elizabeth I's throne in 1603. Of the inimitable characters in history, one of the most recognisable Tudors is Henry VIII. Henry VIII has been painted so vividly into our British history, that it is an image which has not been able to be created again, before, or since.

As historians, we all have an opinion on whom we think Henry VIII was; but some of us never fail to conjure up in our minds the image of Henry in the last years of his reign as being obese, savage and cruel. Other historians concentrate on his youth, knowing the king was not always considered that way. Henry VIII, his image, health, character and reign, have always been a popular subject of historical debate. Moreover, Henry's contemporaries, for the first twenty years of Henry VIII's reign, considered that no superlative seemed too excessive in describing the king. The Venetian ambassador, Giustinian, wrote in a *Report of England*, that Henry was 'extremely handsome' and waxed lyrical on how, when the king played tennis, he was mesmerised by the sight of 'his fair skin glowing through a shirt of the finest texture'.[9] He was considered 'much handsomer than any sovereign in Christendom; a great deal handsomer than the king of France, very fair and his whole frame admirably proportioned'.[10] A courtier, a few years older than Henry, William Blount, Lord Mountjoy, enthused when writing to Erasmus on 27 May 1509: 'The heavens laugh, the earth exalts, all things are full of milk, of honey, of nectar. Avarice has fled the country. Our king is not after gold, or gems, or precious metals, but virtue, glory, immortality.'[11]

Both Henry VIII and his father were interested in immortalising their reigns, creating a great Tudor dynasty.

Henry was reported to be an affable and gracious man who would harm no one. When in his orbit, during the early part of his reign, he was considered charismatic and kind. Later towards the middle of his reign, he became a rotund figure in his middle-age, yet he was always tall, towering over all his courtiers. Henry was a traditionalist, he believed in his divine right to rule, was proud, and as his reign progressed, grew narcissistic. Hans Holbein the Younger was asked, in an act of vanity, to decorate a mural in Henry VIII's private study, his day room and privy chamber at Whitehall Palace with a super, life-sized depiction of the king. Holbein would have used a detailed working drawing on paper to transfer, with pinpricks, onto the wet plaster so that he could start work on the portrait, and because Holbein created the painting in wet plaster and oil in detail, it had to be drawn quickly to give him enough time to work on the plaster before it dried. Copies of the sixteenth century drawing, the Chatsworth Cartoon, which is a portrait of Henry VIII by Hans Eworth, after Holbein, are held in the Royal Collection, The National Portrait Gallery, as well as the Chatsworth Art Collection.[12] There is another copy in the Walker Art Gallery of Liverpool, which depicts a portrait of Henry VIII in the style of Hans Holbein, created under his tutelage.[13]

These renderings of Henry VIII are so transposed in our minds that he appears like a kind of renaissance superhero, legs splayed apart, hands-on-hips as he stares right back at the viewer, almost holding us in a trance. It is from these paintings and the shape in which the painters depicted Henry, that the king is so utterly recognisable. Henry understood the power and importance of art, which can be identified in the magnificent portraits, paintings of palaces and tapestries that he commissioned and owned. His patronage of the arts is a projection of what Henry wanted us to see, and how he wanted to be remembered.[14] Henry's description must be included here, to compare and contrast his youthful vitality to his later, immobile, and disabled bulk, in reinforcing how important the image of strength was to the Tudors, which his disability and its consequences, flew in the face of.

When we look at Henry VIII in any of Holbein's paintings, they show Henry at his most powerful but these images of strength represent the Tudor ideal in terms of physical perfection, but from the perspective of disability study, when these positive propaganda images were created Henry's health was in decline.

Henry's image in these Holbein paintings is instantly recognisable, where he stands in his sable edged gowns in cloth of gold and the carcanet around his shoulders, as he looks like a sixteenth-century 'Godfather' or gangster, staring out at you, standing defiant in his cow-mouthed shoes. The detail within these paintings is striking, as is the example of 'The Family of Henry VIII' (*c.* 1545), a compelling dynastic portrait, that depicts the king in the middle of the painting on his throne, sitting beneath his canopy of state, verged by Jane Seymour, his third wife, and their heir, Edward, later to become Edward VI. On the left of the painting, in front of Jayne Foole, is Princess Mary, later to become Mary I, the king's daughter by his first wife, Katharine of Aragon, and on the right of the painting, in front of William Somer, stands Princess Elizabeth, later to become Elizabeth I, Henry's daughter by his second wife, Anne Boleyn.[15]

In the painting, there are views through the arches into the King's Great Garden at the Palace of Whitehall. Heraldic beasts with their gilded horns sit proudly on columns, all carved in wood. These beasts are displayed prominently amidst colourful flower beds, demarked by wooden fencing and painted in the Tudor colours of white and green. Through the archway on the left part of Whitehall Palace, the Westminster Clock-house can be seen, balanced by a view through the arch on the right, which shows part of Westminster Abbey, along with one turret belonging to Henry VIII's Great Close tennis court. The two figures in the arches are members of the Royal Household, and viewers do not often notice these curious persons, standing under both arches on either side of the painting. On the left of the picture, a woman is depicted in a simple, European-style gown, and on the right, a man in a green gown wearing red trunk hose stands supporting a monkey who sits on his shoulder.[16]

Who were these two individuals, and why were they so important as to be included in such a prestigious family portrait? The woman is reputedly Jayne, who was known as 'Jayne Foole'. Jayne had initially been a member of Queen Anne Boleyn's household and the other, the gentleman, is Will Somer, the king's companion, close confidant, and advisor. The royal court considered Jayne Foole and William Somer as 'natural fools', which would suggest they both had distinct learning, or intellectual disabilities. It is with this portrait in mind, and these two people within it, that I want to examine and determine how the Tudors treated people with disabilities of all kinds, and from all walks of life.

Disabled people constituted a large part of society and were a visible part of everyday life of the peasantry, clergy, and nobility, where surprisingly, the Tudors were very adept at supporting those with disabilities. Having a disability was not always considered an extraordinary quality amongst renaissance people, and was therefore rarely documented. Very little documentary evidence exists about a general disabled community at the time, but disabled people's experiences of life have been preserved through religious texts, state papers and more recently, medical journals.

However, disability as a category of impairment was not understood with medieval and renaissance language, but in the terminology used to describe a condition, such as 'blynde', 'dumbe', 'cripple' and 'lunatic', 'lame', 'lepre', 'dumbe', 'deaff', and the 'natural fool'. Disabilities were often prevalent at birth, and people could become disabled by working on the land, such as being farm labourers, or they could be affected by different diseases, such as leprosy, and disabled by infections of gout. The terminology for different disabilities was a clear description of what sort of disability a person might be inflicted with. These terminologies are sometimes attributed to persons with physical and mental impairments today but often offend, as they are commonly used as insults. However, during the Tudor period, political correctness did not exist, which means that research, classification, and descriptions of disability in this period and terminology such as these cannot be avoided.

Attitudes to all forms of disability during the period were mixed. The Tudors believed within Catholic religious doctrine that having a disability was a punishment for sin. On the other end of the spectrum of religious belief, some considered people with disabilities to be closer to God than the average believer, and because of their disability or impairment, they were automatically suffering purgatory on earth, rather than after death, and would, therefore, enter heaven sooner. However, the idea of disability being undesirable not only stemmed from superstition but would later fuel the fascist eugenics movement that began in the early twentieth century. Scholar Henri-Jacques Stiker, the author of *A History of Disability*, argued that people living with disabilities 'were no less undistinguished at the dawn of the Middle Ages from the economically weak'.[17] Sadly, poverty and disability were often inextricably linked. Farming and agriculture were the most significant form of revenue for Tudor society, and due to the intensive labour that constituted farming during this time, many peasants and serfs would have suffered from extensive spinal and limb injuries, as well as stunted growth, malnutrition and general deformities. Many physical disabilities and deformities would have been due to accidents, as well as back-breaking work.[18]

Monarchs enjoyed dangerous sporting activities like jousting, which made them vulnerable to accidents, and injuries in battle which caused disabilities. Some monarchs were hunchbacked, with spinal curvatures, or suffered other disabilities. Lesser people with disabilities were sometimes cared for within the Tudor court and roles were created for natural and artificial fools who made the king laugh. The king trusted them to speak the truth, listen and be his confidant or court fool. When most around the king were yes-men, Henry could rely on Will Somer and other fools to speak honestly. In *In Praise of Folly*, Erasmus wrote:

> Yet in the midst of all their prosperity, princes in this respect seem to me most unfortunate, because, having no one to tell them truth, they are forced to receive flatterers for friends.[19]

The rank of court fool gave the disabled person a level of prestige. They could mock or tell the truth to a monarch, even if it displeased them to hear it. Erasmus again states:

> But, someone may say, the ears of princes are strangers to truth, and for this reason, they avoid those wise men, because they fear lest someone more frank than the rest should dare to speak to them things rather true than pleasant; for so the matter is, that they don't much care for truth. And yet this is found by experience among my fools, that not only truths but even open reproaches are heard with pleasure; so that the same thing which, if it came from a wise man's mouth might prove a capital crime, spoken by a fool is received with delight. For truth carries with it a certain peculiar power of pleasing, if no accident fall in to give occasion of offence; which faculty the gods have given only to fools.[20]

Henry VIII enjoyed the company of a 'natural fool' because of the fool's candid and outspoken manner, a behaviour that few, apart from a fool, could get away with, in the Tudor court. In times of stress, Henry would turn to his fool and companion, Will Somer. Somer always had admission to the king, especially when the king was sick and melancholy, which suggests that Henry relied on Will when he was suffering the most Robert Armin was one of Shakespeare's clown actors who was a prominent writer who moved into print culture. Armin wrote of Somer in his 1608 play *A Nest of Ninnies:*

> Lean he was, hollow-eyed, as all report,
> And stoop he did too, yet in all the court
> Few men were more beloved than was this fool,
> Whose merry prate kept with the King much rule.
> When he was sad the King with him would rhyme,
> Thus, Will exiled sadness many a time.
> He was a poor man's friend,
> And help'd the widow often in the end.
> The King would ever grant what he did crave,
> For well he knew Will no exacting knave;
> But wish'd the King to do good deeds great store,
> Which caused the Court to love him more and more.[21]

Henry encouraged William Somer to be by his side, continuously, and this was especially so when the king lost his third wife, Jane Seymour, to puerperal fever, which was then known as 'childbed-fever', having given birth to Edward, Henry's long-awaited son and heir. Henry had written to Francis I, King of France on 24 October 1537 that, 'I have so cordially received the congratulations, which, by this bearer and by your letters, you have made me for the son which it has pleased God to give me, that I desire nothing more than an occasion by the success of your good desires to make the like. Notwithstanding, Divine Providence has mingled my joy with the bitterness of the death of her who brought me this happiness.'[22]

The king was tenderhearted towards William Somer, who showed loyalty by remaining in the king's service, till the very end of Henry's life. Somer's loyalty to the Tudor crown continued beyond the rule of Henry VIII, into all the reigns of Henry's children, even into the coronation of his daughter Elizabeth, known as 'Glorianna'.

Before the king's death, and in his later years, when the king's ulcer on his leg caused him immense pain, Will Somer was the only one who could make the king smile. Henry would retreat to the privacy of his privy chamber with a handful of his doctors and only William for company, so that he could move away from prying eyes, petitioning counsellors, corrupt courtiers, and, of course, his queen of the moment. Will Somer poked fun at the Tudor court, its intrigues and gossip, however, although he carried favour with the king, this did not mean Will was protected from the king's anger.

Human beings are not too dissimilar in their vanity, folly, and cleverness, over vast periods, even though their values are different from ours. The Tudors would have thought our modern world corrupt, sensual, foolish, short-sighted, immoral, irreligious, and contemptible. We should not be amalgamating renaissance attitudes with twenty-first century attitudes, making the Tudors the same as us – we should try to understand the difference and distinction in Tudor attitudes. It is with this concept in mind that disability is esteemed, revered or despised, in its context. Henry VIII welcoming 'natural fools' into the Tudor court gives a fascinating glimpse into the mindset of the nobility and royalty of the period, in conveying their compassion for people with learning disabilities and physical disabilities, who would go on to play significant roles in the lives of the Tudor elite. Fools' perceived lack of astuteness, their directness and their sense of humour became valued as an asset, which weaved its honesty into the fabric of court life. As Erasmus deliberated, fools were believed to be closer to God and closer to the truth than other people; the 'natural fools' occupied a unique and valued position. Jayne Foole and William Somer were valued by the king and his family so much, almost as if they were members of the royal family, that they were depicted in 'The Family of Henry VIII' portrait, which hangs at Hampton Court. Jayne Foole and William Somer might not have been in the room at the time Holbein was pressing his brush to canvas, and their depiction rendered but they were nevertheless included in the scene. Disabled people, especially 'natural fools', were thought to be uniquely equipped to speak the truth, because their innocence was perceived in giving them a special relationship with God. The New Testament, in 1 Corinthians: 25, suggests that God spoke through their foolishness: 'All men are fools before God, and the foolishness of God is wiser than men's wisdom.'[23]

The humanist, and educator of Henry VIII, Erasmus, had popularised this idea with his 1509 work, *In Praise of Folly*. The unique qualities of 'natural fools' and their ability to bring mirth and truth to their relationships explains how the likes of Sexton, Will and Jayne managed to secure their privileged, revered status, which inevitably brought them both favour and authority at the court of Henry VIII.[24]

Not all 'natural fools' could preside at court; with over 2,000 members of the court and their staff, it would have been impossible to retain more than a couple of fools. As a charitable act, if natural fools could not be supported by their own families, they might be cared for by educated philanthropists. Failing that, if family life was difficult, and support was limited, the only recourse was to ask the almshouses and monasteries for assistance as far as the disabled poor were concerned. Of course, there were noble and religious men, like Thomas More, who took in 'natural fools' like Henry Patenson, who lived a pleasant life, was well nurtured, educated as far as he could be and included within the family unit.[25]

Those that could not be supported from within a family were protected by laws, which were written to help the genuinely infirm and mentally ill, and punishments were awarded to those who pretended to be disabled to receive monies and support, under false pretences.

Religion and its influence over the population was apparent in the way that religious houses deemed to look after the poor, disabled and mentally ill. Monasteries supplied free food and alms for the poor, disabled and destitute. The removal of these charitable resources for this group in society was a factor in the creation of an army of 'sturdy beggars' that plagued late Tudor England. However, the fact the poor and disabled were perceived to have been thrown out onto the streets without support is disputed by Woodward, who summarises:

'No great host of beggars was suddenly thrown on the roads for monastic charity had had only marginal significance and, even had the abbeys been allowed to remain, could scarcely have coped with the problems of unemployment and poverty created by the population and inflationary pressures of the middle and latter parts of the sixteenth century.'[26] Until the dissolution of the monasteries, support for the infirm and mad had not wholly crumbled. Lack of charitable support for disabled people caused social instability that eventually led to the Poor Laws created by Edward VI and Elizabeth I.

The subsequent dissolution of the monasteries had a resounding impact on the assistance that the infirm and mentally ill received in the community. The Act of 1539 provided for the suppression of religious hospitals which had constituted in England a distinct class of institution, endowed to care for the elderly. Saint Bartholomew's Hospital in London was an exception to the dissolution by a special royal dispensation granted by the monarch, but most hospitals closed, their residents being discharged with small pensions.[27]

Disability not only carried physical scars, but it also carried emotional ones as well. Although in Western society, infertility is not considered a disability today, some Eastern cultures believe that women not being able to bear sons or to not being able to bear children at all, is considered a disability. In the Tudor period, not being able to bear children, particularly sons, was a disability for noble and royal women of a terrible sort, especially in an age when life expectancy for women was in the mid-forties, and the child mortality rate was high. Some may argue that infertility and difficulties producing healthy children, especially males, should not possibly be considered in a discussion on disability; however, inability to bear healthy children, especially sons, destabilised women from Tudor society, and was considered a disability against the Tudor social model, and what was expected at that time, in noble, and royal circles. Moreover, an inability to bear healthy sons was probably not as essential for the poorer classes, and not considered as much of a problem; after all, recovering from pregnancy and childbirth would have been a bonus in an age where medical knowledge and intervention during labour was limited. Coming out of confinement alive with a healthy child, no matter the sex, would have been considered a blessing. However, in an age where bloodlines within the nobility and royal lines were paramount, a woman, queen or indeed, a king, being unable to secure their lineage and titles was a problem; which created inconceivable political ramifications. However, there were exceptions to that rule, as was the case of Queen Claude of France, who was disabled in numerous ways. She was engaged at six years old to François I, the Duke of Angouleme, and heir-presumptive to the French throne. Claude was a contemporary of Anne Boleyn, and Anne had served the French queen as a teenage lady-in-waiting. Claude eventually married at fourteen years old and went on to bear seven royal children, including a son who became Henry II of France.[28] However, English queens of the period did not have the same kind of success, producing children to continue the Tudor bloodline. Having complicated pregnancies, or not even being able to conceive healthy children of both sexes would have had a substantial and long-term adverse effect on a Tudor marriage, especially a noble or royal one. Complicated pregnancies and labour would have had a substantial, and long-term adverse effect on the women of the time because they would not have been able to participate in what was considered 'normal' family life, fulfilling their roles as wives and mothers, which would undoubtedly have incapacitated them, causing severe health issues and sometimes, leading to mental incapacity, and death.

The Tudors were very adept at supporting those with disabilities and no more so than when we see how 'natural fools' were welcomed into the fold of the royal court. It is such a shame that there is so little documentary evidence about the lives of Sexton, William Somer, Jayne the Foole or Thomasina; however, the evidence of their support in the society of Tudor nobility and royalty is heart-warming in an age that was tumultuous, ignominious and unpredictable.

In the medieval and early modern periods, disabled people in western society were not always well-treated and were often the victims of religious superstition and persecution. In Europe, disabled people could be associated with evil, witchcraft, and even the Devil. Just like today, being disabled meant being in the minority, because being born with an impairment that was physical, cognitive, intellectual, mental, sensory, developmental or some combination of these, suggested that during the Tudor period you were less likely to survive. If you did manage to survive, against the odds, you would often be restricted by your ability to participate in what was considered 'normal' activities in everyday society. In that respect, disability and its history have not changed much.

Disability has always been a complex phenomenon, reflecting the interaction between features of a person's body and elements of the societies in which he or she lives, and this was the same in the Tudor period. People born with a severe disability in Tudor times meant that they had no chance of survival. However, disabilities during the period covered many impairments, not just life-threatening ones. Physical impairments created activity limitations and participation restrictions, and those with learning disabilities and other health problems were affected in their everyday lives, across the spectrum of society, from the potboy, right up to and including royalty.

The person who shaped the country and the Tudor dynasty, and who is often overlooked when it comes to disability is the king himself, Henry VIII, who due to his lack of sexual prowess and inability to sire a string of healthy children, especially sons, could be considered as having a disability. To Henry, the idea of siring healthy MALE heirs was expected, and the most important act of a king's life. The ability to produce healthy male heirs as successors, an heir and a spare, was a disability in leading the life that was expected of him as a king. The lack of healthy male children reflected a king's ability to control and rule the country, with the physical and mental strengths associated with running empires.

Assistance and medical care of disabled people may have vastly improved in over 500 years, but have attitudes remained the same? From writing this book, it appears the Tudors had a well-organised society, where religion and laws, as well as convictions of conscience, dictated how the mentally and physically infirm were treated. The reader may not learn any new ground-breaking history, however, what they might learn is that despite Tudor society's limited resources, medical knowledge and materials at their disposal, the efforts of monasteries, physicians, barber-surgeons, families and the royal court, Tudor society was as progressive towards disability and disabled people as it could have been for the period.

Chapter One

Everyday Life in the Community

Just as Aristotle had considered a structured society to be the building blocks of all cities, Tudor society tended to have communities where social groupings were large and complex. Communities within Tudor society were often organised with immediate and extended family members living together, or people who belonged to the same village, town, religious order, or guild. These connections cemented relationships within local communities, counties, and, in many ways, across the nation. Such a complex set up enhanced both social and economic strength and interaction between communities. Although the disabled and infirm were very much a part of those communities, everyday life as a person with a disability was not easy.

The challenge for the historian researching disabilities and disabled people during the Tudor period is the fact that little contemporary evidence referring to disabilities was recorded; there are few, if any, autobiographical accounts of Tudor disabled people. Even the word 'disability' is an anachronism. Modern researchers, historians and Tudor specialists are disabled by access to a distinct lack of categorised sources and struggle to find materials, because they don't exist and because disabled people were not categorised as 'disabled' in the way we classify people today.

Moreover, despite Jacques Le Goff's statement in *Medieval Civilisation*, 'the medieval west was full of blind people with sunken eyes and empty pupils who would come out and stare at us in the frightening picture by Brueghel; the middle ages were full of the maimed, hunchbacks, people with goitres, the lame and the paralysed,' primary sources are scarce.[1]

The painting of his depiction of 'The Beggars', also called 'The Cripples', by Pieter Brueghel shows that the disabled were a target for ridicule. The picture is an oil-on-panel by the Flemish renaissance artist painted in 1568. The beggars are not quite ordinary, as the painting

1

depicts them wearing carnival headgear, representing various classes of society: a cardboard crown for the king, a paper shako for the soldier, a beret for the bourgeois, a cap for the peasant, and a mitre for the bishop. The work has some satirical meaning, which has so far eluded interpretation, but surely the satire was simply the carnivalesque itself. The carnivalesque was more early modern in form than medieval and the festivals were ubiquitous throughout early modern Europe, full of rich symbolic imagery and disruptive potential. Carnival was a season of excess just before, and in contrast to, the fasting and abstinence of Lent. However, there were many other carnivalesque festivities through the year, including those of May Day, Midsummer, harvest festivals in late summer, and All Fools Day in late December. Carnivals and the carnivalesque disputed and mocked the 'standard rules' of order and morality. This was the whole point of the yearly festival, and the world was turned upside down. Perhaps physical imperfections were meant to symbolise moral decrepitude, which can affect all men irrespective of class in society.[2]

The painting is dated from the end of Pieter Brueghel's career when he showed a keener interest in the natural world. Perhaps Brueghel was trying to depict the animalistic 'nature' of disabled people because, at that time, disability was considered debased and therefore a part of nature rather than separate from it. Brueghel captured the essence of nature in this painting, tiny though it is, where the landscape is seen through the opening, which is bathed in a delicate light which simmers like dew on the foliage. Modern viewers may be inclined to conclude that Brueghel intended to invoke sympathy for the plight of the crippled figures, but from a historical perspective, this is unlikely because the Europeans of Brueghel's age gave little regard to beggars. The painting provides hints that Brueghel shared this attitude because the figures are shown outside the town walls posing in ways to provoke contempt and entertainment. The foxtail seen on some of the figures was a symbol of ridicule in political caricature and real life. The woman behind them bears an empty bowl and appears to be ignoring the beggars. 'The Cripples' painting offers a conflicting view of disabled people, who happen to be beggars if we look at the art with twenty-first century eyes rather than consider the painting with sixteenth century ideas. Although the depiction of this group of disabled beggars is harsh, it is not an entirely accurate representation of how society or their communities cared for or viewed people with disabilities.[3] When this picture of 'The

Cripples' was painted, society had barely begun to categorise disability, which towards the end of the sixteenth century was in its infancy. For example, it was not until the late medieval era that legal processes and the conceptual genesis of the 'idiot' – in Latin *idiota*, someone deemed not mentally competent enough to take charge of their affairs – emerged, and legal definitions and observations of 'idiocy' were created. The medieval historian, Irina Metzler, suggests legal definitions preceded medical ones and that they introduced 'a way of thinking, ordering and rationalising, which only afterwards made its broader impact felt on society'.[4]

Although physicians did not implement the medicalisation of disability terms, lawyers created them from their justification and rationalising of illness, which did eventually, over a very long period, create an accepting environment for categorising disability.[5] It would not be until Thomas Willis fashioned the first description of mental deficiency in around 1663-64 that disability would become a 'psychiatric criteria'. Willis used the term 'stupidity' to categorise mental retardation. Today we would not dream of using such detrimental terms in the care of disabled people especially with our modern medical knowledge as such terminology is both upsetting and ableist in nature, and unfairly describes mental deficiency. Such categorisation challenges both medical professionals and patients alike because with many such cases of mental illness, there are still no definite causes or effective treatments. Nevertheless, regardless of such seemingly insensitive terms, the sixteenth century view of disability and mental retardation was very different from ideas held today and surprisingly, perhaps, more compassionate: 'Fools were considered to be marked out by God and not stricken by disease'.[6]

From the Middle Ages through to the early modern era, laws, legislation, legal matters, and jurisprudence started to pervade cultural mentalities and attitudes. Charters and other documents created binding agreements indicating that the mentally disabled, or 'idiots', were to be looked after by keepers, in a similar way to how lands and even wives were possessed. In medieval and early modern eras, this was considered a re-distribution of wealth, in a philanthropic, humanist manner, and was also considered to be morally, ethically and economically sound, as it helped and supported the less fortunate in society. However, as Irina Metzler rightly points out in her research, 'social philanthropy has always been more about the person of the philanthropist and only secondarily about the people who were meant to be helped'.[7] Concern for one's neighbour, and helping those people with disabilities was a Christian, biblical teaching, paramount in the early modern era, as there was little provision for 'welfare' or 'social security'. One way in which this was carried out was to 'keep' or look after a natural fool and was the domain of the Tudor elite, and not a common occurrence in every community, as most people with disabilities did not have philanthropists to look after them. They were expected to be looked after by their families, especially if they were unable to take up an apprenticeship or skill so they might achieve social and financial advancement. However, not all families were able to support their disabled relatives, and so a large share of resources was awarded toward domestic or household relief. Funds were awarded to individuals and families willing to accept responsibility for people considered to be incapable of looking after themselves, which shows how adept and sensible society was at that time. In our modern era, many disabled are either institutionalised, or try to lead independent lives, with community care sometimes provided by the state, but often, paid for privately by the disabled recipient. For instance, if care is unable to be provided for, provision is usually means-tested, to assess the provision needed and required by disabled individuals and their families. In Tudor times, those who were not supported by their families, or by the state, fell through the cracks and were a proportion of a vagrant population, which proved one of the chief domestic concerns of the English government.[8]

However, it was the case that under feudalism, disabled people were able to contribute, in varying degrees, to predominantly agricultural production, and manufacturing of goods. When care within families, and in the community, could not be provided, disabled people resorted to begging. Those who were severely physically impaired were virtually encouraged to beg and were included in the category of legitimate beggars. Begging was usually the last resort, as the law would come down on vagrants and beggars. Disabled people were primarily protected from the late medieval and early Tudor enforcement of begging, much like the PSBO orders of local councils today, which are chiefly motivated by a concern to prevent greedy and idle people from feigning disability, homelessness or poverty to receive support. During the Tudor period, fraudulent beggars provoked fear and hostility, so legislation was used to limit their activities. However, genuinely disabled people were not immune from criticism, and some sixteenth century authors argued that severely disabled people could, and should, find work. You could compare fraudulent beggars as a Tudor equivalent to modern, suspected benefit cheats – those who fake disability to get blue disabled badges, free parking and other concessions and benefits. Like today, there were contemporary fears about the exploitation of funds intended for the needy by the work-shy, and this has a long history.

Help from the state in the Tudor era for the disabled elderly was non-existent, and people usually only stopped work when their health was in severe decline, and they had become physically unable to work. While the wealthy and the nobility relied on their property to provide them with income, and their servants to look after their basic needs, the elderly sick of the lower classes might find themselves in a somewhat more precarious position. Children took responsibility for their parents, but support did come from guilds, charities or even former employers. Communities would argue over who should support their disabled relatives, especially those at risk of being neglected, which included widows, the infirm and former soldiers. Moreover, the infirm, elderly and disabled were obliged to work when they were no longer capable of doing so.[9]

The elderly were not the only ones to suffer disabilities during their everyday lives. Military men who had served during conflicts suffered permanent injury and physical disabilities. Men who served in the monarch's armies and navy often had to end their careers because of a disability received in battle or at sea. When the Mary Rose was raised from her slumber, in Portsmouth harbour in the mid-1980s, historians and divers were unaware of the artefacts that still existed within and around the wreck site. Those everyday objects and the skeletons of the Mary Rose's crew gave historians an incredible insight into the life of those who served honourably on the ship.

Everyone on board the Mary Rose was male, as having women on board would have been perceived to be bad luck. There were the captain and other officers, mariners, gunners, soldiers, a pilot, a purser, a surgeon, carpenters and cooks, to name only a few professions. There were more than five hundred men on board, and of these, no more than thirty-five survived.

Extensive studies have been carried out on at least 179 skeletal remains, and some were found to have evidence of disabilities. Phil Roberts, author, and member of the Mary Rose Trust explains that human remains were found on all decks of the ship. Moreover, the swiftness with which the Mary Rose sank did not allow time for the sailors to escape.[10] The state of the skeletons and the research concluded from the artefacts found on the Mary Rose that: 'some had suffered childhood illnesses, mainly from malnourishment. There are healed fractures and some battle injuries.' Phil explained to me in an interview that, 'one man's bones tell us that he was between 25 and 30 years old and 5' 7" tall. He had well-developed muscles, but his spine had signs of stress, and his right elbow was severely damaged. He had the only ivory wrist guard recovered, so he was an archer, or perhaps a Captain of archers. Another crew member was a young man who had suffered a "bowing" fracture of his right femur as a child. It is twisted, bowed and flattened, and there is matching damage on his right pelvis. There was an older man who had suffered spiral fractures in his lower right leg. These were the result of a fall. The bones were not reset after the fracture.'[11]

There were also skeletons with pre-existing conditions, such as rickets being found in teenagers from when they were children. Rickets softens the bones and allows both tibias to bow. A lack of Vitamin D causes rickets and there is evidence from one set of skeletal remains that a leg bone also showed scars from healed scurvy. On a long bone like this leg bone, extra spurs occur at the spots where the blood clots. The heads of the upper leg bones of another skeleton are flattened and his hip joints are broad and shallow, which was caused by restricted blood flow to this area in childhood. Standing upright would have been impossible, and he would have walked awkwardly.[12] Some skeletal remains from the Mary Rose had head wounds, which may have been battle injuries. There was one injury which looks like an arrow wound, but it was healed by the time the man died. The Master Gunner has been identified as being younger than thirty-five years old. He had lost many teeth, and parts of his jawbone had worn away showing that he suffered from painful abscesses.[13] There was a complete skeleton recovered of an archer, and he was found in the hold. Both his shoulders had a condition called *osacromiale*, where the tip of the bone, the acromion, on the shoulder blade had not fused. It usually fuses at the age of eighteen, but regular strain (such as archery) can prevent this. We can also tell from his tooth enamel that he was either an Englishman or a Welshman. The Welsh were well known for their fame as archers and longbowmen in late Tudor times.[14]

The cook's skeleton was virtually complete, and he was a man in his thirties, about 5' 6" tall and had dense, strong bones. Evidence from his ribs and backbone suggests he spent most of his working life bent over. At some stage in his life, he broke a rib and his left foot.[15] The 'Purser' of the Mary Rose was the person in charge of money and stores. He was a robust, muscular man and he had healthy teeth and an old head wound which had healed. The man was in his thirties and about 5' 7" tall. His leg bones and his hip joints were flat, which meant he might have walked with a rolling gait as he would not have been able to straighten his back. With this physique, he could not have been an active member of the crew, which again suggests that he was the Purser.[16] The Mary Rose Museum at Portsmouth paints a large picture of renaissance life and is primarily a memorial to all those who became disabled during their duties on the Mary Rose and to others who eventually lost their lives that fateful day.[17]

Men who served in the military who suffered disabling injuries and lost their lives, during different battles and skirmishes, or on explorer's ships, were treated by an established company of medical staff who were barber-surgeons. These barber-surgeons often served as ordinary soldiers themselves. In 1556, the Master of the barber-surgeons told the Corporation of London that if they provided qualified surgeons, members would not be forced into action and conscripted as soldiers. The Lord Mayor agreed, and it was recorded in the minutes, that barber-surgeons would not be forced to serve as privates themselves.

However, even though these barber-surgeons were exempt from conscription as private soldiers, they were still as liable for military service as everyone else, so long as they were required in their professional capacity. Surgeons were better off than their fellow officers as it was in the interest of any military company that their surgeons were looked after as their services were of vital importance, and it was never known when and if their services would be required.[18]

A military surgeon called William Clowes, born in 1543 at Kingsbury, Warwickshire, had a licence to practise as a barber-surgeon within the City of London and its suburbs.[19] He later served as a surgeon with the navy after he had been appointed to the surgical staff of St Bartholomew's Hospital, in the City of London in 1575.[20] He eventually became a full surgeon at the hospital in 1581.[21]

In the Oxford Dictionary of National Biography Murray states that Clowes 'served as Fleet Surgeon under Sir Francis Drake's Command during the Spanish Armada in 1588 and authored *The Prooved Practice for all Young Chirugeans* in 1591 while serving as the Queen's Surgeon'.[22] Clowes performed many an amputation, where his instructions offer a grim picture of how such sixteenth century surgery might have been performed:

> You shall in readiness a good strong form and a steady, and set the patient at the end of it. Then shall there bestride the form behind him a man that is able to hold him fast by both his arms. Which done, if the leg be to be taken off beneath the knee, let there also be another man appointed to bestride the leg that is to be taken off, he must hold fast the member above the place where the incision is to be made, very steadily without shaking, and he that doth so hold should have a large hand and a good grip, whose hand may better stay the bleeding ... In the manner there must be another skilful man that hath good experience and knowledge to hold the leg below, for the member must not be held too high, for staying and choking of the saw, neither must he hold down his hand too low for fear of fracturing the bones in the time it is a-sawing off. And he that does cut off the member must be sure to have a sharp saw, a very good catlin, and an incision knife, and then boldly with a steady and quick hand cut the flesh roundabout to the bones without staying ... then set your saw near the sound flesh as easily as you may, not touching it, and with a light hand speedily saw it off.[23]

Clowes finishes this stage of the extended operation by observing that the surgeon must have a good eye, a strong arm – and a stout heart.

Away from the troubles of sea battles, skirmishes, and being wounded in battle, military men came home to either die or to recover. Men disabled during their service in Elizabeth I's army were taken care of by the state. Laws were enacted to support them and were a noble attempt to help those maimed and disabled during events of the war. As such, military men were often treated in hospitals on their return to England if they had been fighting abroad.[24]

Military hospitals were a late development, and non-specialists were paid to open their houses to accommodate the ill, sick and disabled who had been injured in wars. For example, money was paid to the citizens of Dublin in 1598 to provide a hospital on the outskirts of the city, with fifty beds, bedding, nurses and a surgeon – all for 1000 pounds a year. It was established so that the pain and suffering of soldiers, who were dying in the streets for want of proper medical attention, could be alleviated. These kinds of institutions and care were encouraged so that service personnel could be rehabilitated to fight again, thus encouraging their comrades to risk their lives once more.[25]

The queen, the privy council, and parliament were deeply interested in the wellbeing of disabled soldiers. In 1593, parliament had passed the first of three acts to help disabled soldiers and sailors, and in doing so, also helped to reduce the tension that their presence in and around London created. The other acts followed in 1597 and 1601.[26] The first act of 1593 declaims that pensions to disabled soldiers were to be provided:

> Foreasmuch as it is agreeable with Christian charity. Policy, and the honour of our nation that such as have since the twenty-fifth day of March 1588 adventured their lives and lost their limbs or disabled their bodies, or shall hereafter adventure their lives, lose their limbs or disable their bodies in the defence and service of her majesty and the state, should at their return be relieved and rewarded to the end they may reap the fruit of their good deserving, and others may be encouraged to perform the like endeavours.[27]

Levies were raised from retail wine merchants, ale housekeepers, and others to pay for pensions for the disabled servicemen.

Churchwardens collected these taxes in London, as more disabled servicemen from there needed help. Wardens already collected poor relief, so it made sense for them to raise levies for pensions at the same time. The money was then paid to the high constable, who passed it on to the treasurer, while the justice of the peace paid out the pensions themselves.

Fines were put in place for those who did not abide by the new laws. For disabled soldiers to benefit from having a pension, they had to have the captain of their company sign a certificate to say they were entitled to the monies. This was not a nationwide scheme, and like those who pretended disability, the government had to decide who was entitled to such pensions. Elizabeth was attentive to the disabled soldiers who had been discharged. Cecil, Lord Burghley had stated in parliament that he would have preferred discharged soldiers to be looked after by their families and relatives and the parishes to which they had been born, and this was the premise by which the state wanted all disabled people to be looked after, so as not necessarily to be a burden on the government. Alas, nothing much has changed in over 500 years.

Recovery of men who had served in battle depended on the efficient abilities of the doctors when administering treatments, looking after the wounded's physical and emotional wellbeing, and prescribing remedies. People with disabilities that could not work, or were injured, and who obtained no support from the country, were frequently rejected by way of their families due to the fact they could not come up with the money to support and to look after them. Other disadvantaged groups such as the sick, those with leprosy, the elderly and poor, relied on sporadic donations, which were an ineffectual tradition of Christian charity and almsgiving for subsistence.[28]

If a person had contracted leprosy, for example, almshouses could provide for them. These charitable organisations put great emphasis upon cleanliness, as well as the provision of fresh, nourishing foods appropriate for those suffering from the nasal and maxillary damage characteristic of illness such as advanced leprosy. Two women would be specifically engaged to wash the patients' heads every week, their clothes twice a week and their utensils each day. Linen underclothes and unique footwear provided vital protection for those with ulcerated skin and damaged extremities. The Tudors believed that most of all, a victim of leprosy required spiritual solace. The supposal that lepers were undergoing their purgatory on earth and would, as a result, ascend directly to paradise if they accepted their fate with humility, was a process reinforced by patients hearing reassuring sermons, and being surrounded by iconography that identified their agony with that of Jesus.

Apart from the church, there was no state provision to relieve the suffering of disabled people. If family or friends could not look after them, it would be left to monks and nuns to care for them alongside strangers and pilgrims who sheltered in the monasteries. Religious definitions of those in need of charity usually included the sick, the crippled, deaf and blind, and in medieval Europe, the church influenced attitudes about illness and disability because the church was more interested in the spiritual well-being of those in their care than their physical or mental challenges. The church's interest in disabled people was based on Jesus' role as a miraculous healer and spiritual 'physician'. The monks and nuns hoped optimistically for the recovery of their charges. Care for people with disabilities was based on the Catholic Church's teachings.

When people with disabling injuries were hospitalised, they would be sent to relatively small hospitals and almshouses where the focus would be on palliative care rather than a cure. Significant changes to this essentially non-segregationist policy did not begin to be discussed or implemented until the nineteenth century. Christianity, in keeping with the other Western religions, has always acknowledged responsibility for people with disabilities and individuals with severe impairments were admitted and treated in one of the medieval hospitals in which the sick and bedridden poor could be supported. However, the ethos of these hospitals was ecclesiastical and spiritual, rather than medical; monks and monasteries were dedicated to caring for, rather than curing the sick.

Not everyone, however, was sympathetic to the infirm, crippled, blind and deaf and in Western Christendom, the appearance of the disabled in public did not always evoke understanding. Often, their presence resulted in aversion, and the law would intervene to force disabled or mutilated people to cover up their afflictions and hide their signs of disfigurement. The disabled were, and still are, a target for ridicule.

There are incidents recorded about 'natural fools', such as a visit to a nunnery in 1535 which refers to the presence of one Julian Heron, a thirteen year old, and 'an idiot fool'. Bishop Cuthbert Tunstall writing to Thomas Cromwell in 1538 identified 'an innocent natural fool' whom 'by no means we could make to grant' as he had spoken words of malice against the king. However, pension payments to a 'Julian Heron the idiot – (age blank),' were ordered to be cancelled on 3 April 1539 by Henry VIII. The source does not say why this was so.[29]

William Shakespeare's play *All's Well that Ends Well* mentions 'a dumb innocent,' woman, pregnant because she 'could not say him nay'. These instances show that people understood 'natural fools' to have a deficiency in reason or judgement and indicates they were highly visible in society. Professor Suzannah Lipscomb, in her research on court fools, argues that many nobles had fools, like the Duke of Buckingham, the Marquis of Exeter, Lady Audley and Lady Kingston.[30]

Henry VIII had many loyal courtiers and a couple of 'natural fools' around him at court and was not prone to ignoring those that were close to him and served a purpose. During the early part of his reign, none was closer to him than his advisor and friend, Thomas More, who, himself, was the keeper of the fool Henry Patenson in his household. Thomas More probably felt that the keeping of a natural fool was a Christian duty, as was likely the case when taking in and caring for his 'fool', Henry Patenson.[31] Thomas More, the philanthropist, was doing his moral duty, not really for Henry Patenson's sake, but for the sake of his own soul. Historian Noliene Hall stated that: 'Sir Thomas More was as much a man of the medieval period as of the Renaissance. The former is reflected in his acquisition of a domestic fool, Henry Patenson. The seeming paradox of this sophisticated, witty and intellectual man employing Patenson needs to be seen against the context of a still highly structured society, and in the case of More's family a strictly ordered one, medieval in character. The boisterous-type fun of the fool operated in terms of liberation and renewal, a release mechanism.' As a humanist and modern thinker, Thomas More embraced the tradition of taking in a 'fool'.

Henry Patenson was highly likely to have been a 'natural' fool. However, as mentioned in the introduction, this is difficult to establish as Tudor doctors did not diagnose and categorise disability, as our GP's do today. As a 'natural' fool, Patenson may have been a simpleton, slow and feebleminded, and he was taken in as a member of Thomas More's family, even though he was not related to Thomas More by blood. Patenson was cared for, much like Henry VIII's court fool, Will Somer.

Ultimately, it could be argued that fools like Patenson and Somer were deemed animals and to be kept in a way similar to pets. However, in the light of how Thomas More treated Henry Patenson, this argument could be totally irrational and hugely disingenuous, towards More who from the evidence, probably did not think that at all. Thomas More and his family treated Henry Patenson like one of them; like a family member. They would have brought Henry's clothing for him, and he was looked after in other ways, such as being provided with simple education, including teaching him manners, necessary life skills and the art of conversation. Educating young men at court was a pastime of Henry VIII, who enjoyed surrounding himself with young courtiers, eager to serve him. He enjoyed promoting them to be gentlemen of his privy chamber, feeding them, clothing them and paying their debts. Courtiers such as Francis Weston and the musician Mark Smeaton were all taken into the king's household at a young age, and they were supported, especially when they showed the king their loyalty and talents. Fools like Henry Patenson and Will Somer were treated in very much the same way, despite their disabilities. The only difference was that they did not hold an official position within the households to which they belonged.

Taking into consideration Thomas More's attitude to learning, Catholic religion and Christian charity, it should not be surprising to learn that Thomas More had taken a 'natural' fool to his bosom. Thomas More was a witty, intellectual man who protected Patenson, in what was a highly structured, family unit within Tudor society. More's family led a strictly ordered way of life, and having a boisterous, 'natural fool' in the household must have been somewhat of a paradox to this very religious family. However, Henry Patenson must have brought a sense of liberation and renewal to the family. Patenson's wit and conversations over the dining table, and by the fireside, would have been a release mechanism for Thomas More from the political climate that he frequented.[32]

When More was locked in the Tower of London, for not signing the Act of Supremacy in 1534, his daughter Margaret visited him, afterwards recording in a letter to Alice Allington, a family member, a conversation with her father.[33]

> Seeing her [Margaret Roper] sit very sad, he said, "How now, daughter Marget? What how, mother Eve? Where is your mind now? Sit not musing with some serpent in your breust, upon some new persuasion to offer father Adam the apple yet once again?" "In good faith, father," quoth I, "I can no further go, but am (as I trow Cresede saith in Chaucer), comen to Dulcarnon, even at my wittes end. For

sith the example of so many wise men cannot in this matter
move you, I see not what to say more, but if I should look
to persuade you with the reason that master Henry Patenson
made. For he met one day one of our men, and when he
had asked where you were and heard that you were in the
Tower still, he waxed even angry with you, and said, 'Why,
what aileth him that he will not swear? Wherefore should he
stick to swear? I have sworn the oath myself.' And so I can
in good faith go now no further neither after so many wise
men whom ye take for no sample, but if I should say, like
master Harry, Why should you refuse to swear, father, for
I have sworn myself?"

This extract of a letter shows that Margaret was trying to persuade her
father to swear to the Act of Supremacy and sign the oath, that Anne
Boleyn was Henry VIII's lawful wife, and that any children from the
marriage were the Tudor monarch's true heirs and successors. She said
that she had signed the oath and that Henry Patenson had tried to
persuade him with reason, to sign the oath, just as he himself had signed
the oath. Neither Margaret nor Henry Patenson could understand why
More refused to sign, putting his life in danger.[34]

From the source, we can see that Henry Patenson was influential
within the family of Thomas More, and he had become a permanent
part of the family circle at Chelsea around 1521, and we know he was
with the family for some time which is apparent from Holbein's portrait
of the household, generally dated 1527. The original Holbein painting
was lost, but the drawings and copy that survive, moreover, convey a
story of a truly loving family, and a politician with almost feminist
ideas.[35]

Thomas More had a forward-thinking view concerning the education
of his children, and it could be argued that More treated his sons
and daughters equally. More had educated his daughter, Margaret, a
practice which stemmed from the Middle Ages, an almost unheard-of
policy by the standards of the time, unless a family was noble or royal.
Thomas More was a charismatic, intelligent, forward-thinking man on
family matters, but stuck in his thinking when it came to politics and
religion.[36]

The depiction of Henry Patenson was an unusual addition to the Rowland Lockey portrait of Thomas More and his family, painted in the style after Hans Holbein, the Younger, in 1593. Fools were usually held in a lowly position in domestic circumstances, not often painted for prosperity. Fools were often encouraged to sleep with household animals in barns. However, from the depiction of Henry Patenson in the Rowland Lockey copy of Holbein's, 'Sir Thomas More and his Family', it could be argued that Henry Patenson had a privileged and comfortable life. In the portrait, Henry assumes neither the dress nor the stance of a servant and appears to copy the more famous poses of his monarch, Henry VIII. Within the household, Patenson appears confident of his position as 'Master Harry'.[37]

Patenson's special relationship with More and his family, as revealed by the Rowland Lockey copy, is further reinforced by the story of him in *The Confutation of Tyndale's Answer*, where the story recalls Patenson's regal 'Proclamation' issued to those who made fun of him in Bruges.[38]

The story goes that when More's embassy was at the Holy Roman Emperor's court, Henry Patenson accompanied More, and was a 'fool' in the true tradition of innocent fun, and the source substantiates this: He 'was there sone perceuyed vppon the syghte for a man of, therefore, wytte by hym selfe and vnlyke the comon sorte'. More explains how Henry Patenson was 'one to be teased to anger' because he was mocked by onlookers in the crowd. In retaliation, Patenson threw stones back at them. The rough treatment that Henry showed to his mockers by throwing stones at them suggests he had an 'artless character'. From this incident, Professor Suzannah Lipscomb has suggested that Henry Patenson provoked mixed, and sometimes conflicting responses of scorn and affection, superiority and identification. Fools like Henry Patenson, with this particular episode, caused a general social acceptance of aggressive behaviour towards 'natural' fools.[39]

The early modern playwright John Heywood, in his writing of *Witty and Witless* is particularly graphic about this. One character asks,

> Who cumth by the sott, who cumth he by,
> That vexyth hym not somewey usewally?
> Some beate hym,
> Some bob hym,

Some joll hym,
Some job hym,
Some tugg hym by the heres,
Some lugg hym by the eares.[40]

Heywood implies that it was normal for people to torment 'natural' fools. He suggests that even the most valued and highly patronised of household fools could expect a degree of casual violence. Thomas More, despite his affection and tolerance for 'naturals', confirms this social responsibility. In *The Confutation of Tyndale's Answer*, the story of Henry Patenson is an anecdote perhaps more revealing because it is not told to illustrate any point about attitudes to 'naturals'; it is instead introduced as a playful allegorical example to help explain an issue of theological controversy. The treatment of the fool is incidental, rather than central to the story. More records that, out in the streets, Patenson was observed by the passers-by in Brussels, some of whom 'caught a sporte in angryng of hym and out of dyvers corners hurled at hym suche thynges as angred hym, and hurte hym not'.[41]

In response, Thomas More writes that Patenson collected stones, 'not gunstonys, but as harde as they', and Henry Patenson proclaimed that those who had not tormented him should leave, and then threw back his stones against the crowd, inflicting some bloody injuries. Professor and historian, Suzannah Lipscomb, suggests that Patenson's stone-throwing is then interpreted as an allegory of the unjust exertion of power, based on the jest that although the fool had excused himself for his indiscriminate retaliation by warning the innocent in the crowd to leave before he hurled his missiles, he could not realise that they did not understand English.[42] Thomas More raises no questions about the tormenting of the 'natural fool' and his angry response, which form the context and background for this parable; he passes no judgement on either the crowd's or Patenson's behaviour. When retelling this story, during her talk, 'Playing the Fool', historian Suzannah Lipscomb argues that mutual aggression seems to be expected and tolerated, with people interacting with 'natural fools' the incident is not unusual and reported as a familiar incident, which does not attract a reproach.[43]

Suzannah argues: 'Apart from such everyday random violence, the household fool might also expect physical punishment, even for faults he might not understand.'[44]

Despite the incident in Brussels, Henry Patenson had a favoured place in Thomas More's family. More's simple family routine of conversations over meals, after serious discussions, would have allowed Henry Patenson to introduce a lighter atmosphere of laughter.[45]

There is plenty of evidence of real and deep affection of masters for their fools. This is attested from many quarters, and Robert Armin, the English actor and narrator, born in 1563, is explicit about the intimacy often involved. His narratives are full of phrases asserting, for example, 'he loved the foole above all, and that the household knew'.[46]

Such love was not only a personal idiosyncrasy of warm-hearted individuals, like Sir Thomas More; it is asserted in some discussions of folly as the appropriate response to the innocent. In a particular sermon, a certain preacher urges his congregation that: 'one should show [fools] goodness and love, take them in, host, clothe, feed them ... protect, shield and defend them, and not abandon them even at the time of death'.

From a twentieth-century perspective, we might well ask, though, why Thomas More would need a domestic fool. Given Thomas More's character, religious zeal and political talents, and his ordered and intellectually motivated family life, Patenson's role suggests something of an anomaly. As More was as much a man of the medieval period, out of which the tradition of fools came, as he was of the Renaissance, the answer to this anomaly lies in the pleasure derived from tactless and obscene carnival-type humour, which was very controlled and astute in its commentary on how screwed up and unfair 'normal' society was; this 'humour' was also a release mechanism from the political pressures of the day. Thomas More could well have agreed with a fifteenth century defender of fools who 'explained that wine barrels break if their bungholes are not occasionally opened to let in the air'.[47]

On the lighter side of everyday life, Thomas More was renowned for his sense of humour, he probably knew that laughter was understood to be the best medicine, as viewing comedies, plays and masques were the instruments of choice when it came to being happy and healthy in the early modern era. Moreover, the use of satire was commonplace, where vice, follies, stupidities and abuses were held up to ridicule and contempt. The human condition was attacked by ridicule in plays, verse, poetry, books, woodcuts, painting and other such mediums.

Ridicule of vice, follies, stupidities and abuses was commonplace in Tudor England and satire was used to hold these behaviours in contempt.

Comedic satire was a tool used to expose and denounce vice, folly, and abuses of evil of any kind, in any medium, not just in literature. The most pre-eminent topic of satire is and always was politics, the most rewarding, challenging and dangerous of subjects to the satirist. Women were another topic of satire during the medieval and Tudor periods. Disability as a topic did not escape from satirical comment, as the perennial topic of satire is the human condition itself. Human nature and its absurdities form man's troubled past, present and future, and satire is a way of examining this life, and how we respond to it. However, the way of satire does not lead to great works of art, but was and still is a way of responding to life through a mixture of laughter and indignation, which could be considered not the noblest of pastimes, depending on the content of the satire. Moreover, to expose, attack, or deride vices has its origins in a state of mind which is critically aggressive; a mind often irritated by the latest examples of human absurdity, inefficiency or immorality. Satire was an expression of hierarchy and a way of reinforcing the 'pecking order'. Disabled people were targets for sarcasm and satire because the satirist could express anger at a disabled persons' inefficiency while maintaining his sense of superiority and contempt over and for the disabled person. For example, there is a coloured woodcut illustrating the German translation of Boccaccio's *Decameron*.[48] In the woodcut, Masetto is pretending to be dumb, welcomed into a convent, where he seduces all the nuns. The satire in Boccaccio's polished and licentious stories uses disability in this woodcut, but the satire is aimed at the clergy rather than the frailty of women or the deaf and disabled.[49]

The easiest way for a satirist to humiliate his 'victim' was and still is, through laughter. However, the 'natural' fool and the 'artificial' fool provoked laughter with their acrobatic skills, facial expressions, voice, gestures and most importantly their verbal expression: satire, puns, wordplay, parody, and witty remarks. However, to conceptualise disabled people and those pretending disability in evoking laughter, should not be aligned with the idea of jesters, and neither should disabled people be compared to our notion of stage clowns.[50]

The early modern drama started a trend of using fools within plays, as characters and during this period there was an influx of printed jestbooks where this hero provides laughter and confusion in the satiric form to provoke readers' apprehension. However, heroes in Elizabethan drama were not always genuinely disabled but were feigning disability or pretending to be a 'simpleton' to provoke laughter. The actual clown actor, Tarlton, was often referred to in many written works and jestbooks, and books such as *Tarlton's Jests* give reports of the clown or fool in performance and print.[51]

Nevertheless, disabled characters, whether 'natural' or 'artificial' were a target for mockery, in Tudor plays and masques, and disabled people and disabilities were often examples of amusement and sometimes hatred, when they were depicted in plays and tragedies seen at the Globe theatre, and at court wherever it resided close to the capital or on progress. Many of these presentations were put on for the monarch, by a newcomer and playwright, going by the name of William Shakespeare.

The Elizabethan playwright himself made frequent references to the disabled by using descriptions such as, 'the lame,' 'the blind,' and 'the deformed'.[52] Shakespeare used the adjective 'disabled' in the medical sense in his sonnets. For example, 'strength by limping sway disabled', see Shakespeare's Sonnets 66.8.[53]

Although these were written during the Tudor period, they were not published until after James I was securely on the throne in 1609.[54]

Robert Armin promotes the model of the disabled, natural fool in his jestbook, which echoes throughout Shakespeare's writing, of which his contribution to the creation of King Lear's great fool comes to be understood as a marriage of both an artificial and a natural fool. This strategy of joining both natural and artificial fools together threatened to end the role of conventional clowns and fools in theatrical repertoires. Shakespeare's significant fools take vital roles in the growth of the English clown tradition. Once Shakespeare dies, and the jest-book declines in its readership, the creation of clowning and satire in theatrical practice becomes more synonymous with actors' activities, rather than disabled natural fools and artificial fools pretending disability for a laugh.[55]

There were many examples of jestbooks, especially during the reign of Elizabeth I. These jestbooks with an individual's name in the title, such as *Scoggin's Jests*, *Tarlton's Jests* and *Peel's Jests* established themselves in the jestbook printing business and became part of the advertising and commercial success of such works.[56]

Jestbooks were popular during the period, and these pamphlets were distributed throughout cities such as London, Norwich, Bristol and others. They were considered a form of prescription because the Tudors believed that laughter cured melancholy and depression; therefore, laughter was the best medicine. A compiler of *Scoggin's Jests*, known as the author, Andrew Boorde, wrote many guidebooks about health and well-being and linked the nature of jestbooks with good health, improved mood, and medicine. During the middle of the sixteenth century, Boorde's jestbooks exemplified the intended therapeutic aspect of the jestbook in everyday life. Jestbooks like the *Howleglas,* classical in nature, is another example of a therapeutic jestbook which ridicules the hero's stupidity.[57] *Howleglas* was first printed in Antwerp in 1519, later in London in the mid-sixteenth century and an early jestbook printer, William Copland printed copies in 1565, cementing the work in English culture. However, the Germans also printed roguish jester stories, of which *Howleglas* is a collection. The author of *Howleglas* gives the purpose of presenting his jests in his preface: 'This fable is not only to renew the minds of men or women of all degrees from the use of sadness but also to pass the time with laughter or mirth. And for because those simple knowing persons should beware if folks can see, methinks it better to pass the time with such a merry jest and laugh threat and do no sin, than for to weep and do sin.'[58] The writer is suggesting through his preface that, exposed follies can be corrected by humour; that laughter is the best remedy to calm sensitive emotions and depression and that readers will be enlightened by laughter, whoever they are. The writer is attempting to make people happy in their disappointment or grief by correcting the violation and transgression embodied by Howleglas, who has his role reversed with a 'merry jest'; the tormentor becomes the tormented.

In 1586, a physician called Timothie Bright wrote in his book *A Treatise of Melancholy* how laughter was therapeutic in curing depression. From an English contemporary medical perspective, the promotion of treating melancholy with laughter was becoming more commonplace, which is why natural fools and disabled people with learning disabilities were crucial to everyday life, both in their homes and communities and as will later be understood, at the Tudor court.[59] Laughter as therapy became a key concept to Tudor minds over time. This was essential to the boom in the printing of jestbooks over a long period and helped to promote their popularity. Melancholy was purged through the effect and function of humour and laughter which coincided with Thomas Heywood's remarks, point of view and in the proposition for fools clowning in *An Apology for Actors*, 'to moderate the cares and heauinesse of the minde'.[60] 'Heaviness' was a Tudor word for depression, natural fools and satire were the prescribed cure. The use of satire, jestbooks, plays and theatrical performances, confirms the use of the restorative power of disabled people with learning disabilities, having the ability to make people laugh, whether they were making themselves targets for ridicule, or they were suggesting the targets of their own satirical remarks. The medical and literary fields shared with Tudor and Elizabethan writers that laughter was indeed the best medicine.[61] This enthusiasm for laughter being the best medicine was significant because the positive medical effect of laughter was inexplicably linked to the jestbook, subsequently to disabled people with learning disabilities who could make people laugh, and were able to lift those afflicted with depression out of their state of melancholy. William Perkins addressed the principles of laughter as medicine 'To all ignorant people that desire to be instructed': 'That merrie ballards and books, as Scogin, Bevis of Southampton, &c. are good to drive away time, and to remooue heart-quames.'[62] Towards the end of the Tudor period and the Elizabethan age, the use of merry tales and jests is aimed at awakening doctors and the afflicted to the needs of easing hearts. These jestbooks with its scatological material discussed the daily life-giving relief of farting, where Scoggin mocks the Queen's farting, yet he saves her honour and dignity by humiliating himself, suggesting that his fart costs double what the queen's fart does: Scoggin 'girt out a fart like a horse or mare, saying, if that fart be so deare of twenty pound, my fart is worth forty pounds'.[63] Jestbooks were prized by all that read them, topics for table-talk; indecent, funny, shocking or even obscene stories in nature, which were localised in the nearby cities; they were stories which revolved around normal human relationships between members of the family, friends, merchants and townsfolk. The likes of Thomas More, his wife, daughters and sons-in-law, along with Henry Patenson might have roared with laughter, blushing at the vulgar jokes and stories that would circulate in earlier jestbooks similar to *Scoggin's Jests*. Topics such as excrement and urination in jestbooks were normal and were comically exaggerated.

These tales were written to provoke laughter and it became imperative that laughter ran alongside a licence to speak the truth. Renaissance fools, either natural or artificial were defined as clowns or fools in drama. The fool had freedom to speak with reason and wisdom as the voice of the people, as Robert Goldsmith suggests 'with the mingled feelings of awe, amused contempt, and something like pity', and he concludes that 'The merging of the professional jester with the licensed fool gave rise to a new species – the artificial fool or court jester.'[64] The traditional idea of the jester is continued in Shakespeare's witty fool. The consensus appears to be that actors who play fools are derived from artificial fools, those who feign disability and play at having learning disabilities of some kind, for money. Artificial fools took their lead from natural, or innocent fools who were allowed to criticize their masters and their keepers, much like Henry Patenson did with Thomas More. The idea of fools has changed so much starting from those disabled people with learning disabilities as natural fools, who were thought of as truth-tellers, to those clowning fools who impersonated learning disabilities and follies. However, natural fools did not have twin personalities of both jester and truth-teller, they only could speak the truth and behave similarly to a philosopher. Stage clowns were artificial fools or actors and jesters were comic characters and this is the distinct difference between natural and artificial fools within jestbooks, dramatic roles and court performances.

Tudor writers or doctors did not categorise disability in the sense that we do today. It is interesting that the prominent use of disability as a concept, i.e. rendered incapable of action or use, was used to explain the prominence of deformity over disability, and that disability, as we know the concept, is socially driven, in relation to the body and became relatively organised in the eighteenth and nineteenth centuries.[65]

Moreover, anyone perceived as different, like a disabled person with a learning disability was a target for satirists, actors and writers. As a writer, Armin has often been discussed in relation to later Shakespearean fools. It has been suggested that because Armin joined the Lord Chamberlain's Men, he influenced Shakespeare's work. Robert Armin was an unusual actor who practised his own creation of the artificial fool or clown as well as inspiring the playwright's compositions.[66] As the author of *Nest of Ninnies* written in 1608, originally titled *Fool Upon Fool* written in 1600, Armin depicted clown figures in his jestbook stories, expanding them into dramatic plays such as *The Two Maids of More-Clock*, which includes two distinctive fools, Blue John and Tutch. Armin's *Fool Upon Fool* was his own jestbook discussing natural and artificial fools. In *Nest of Ninnies*, Armin directs his readers to explain his understanding and sympathy for fools, both natural and artificial. He set up a distinction between 'artificial' and 'natural' fools which discriminated between the terms. According to Armin's definition a natural fool is a person who lacks art, ability, or skills acquired through repetitive practice, and a fool simplistic in nature, whereas the artificial fool possesses the artistic skills of dancing, singing, acting or can play a musical instrument, and reinforces the commonly held belief that fools have the power to please people. Armin also tells stories of fools like Jack Oates who is an example of a household idiotic fool, who does not amuse his master through language exchange. Oates' identity in these stories is linked to selfish and eccentric behaviour, driven by destructive urges. These stories illustrate the disparity between simple 'natural' fools like William Somer and the 'artificial' fools of Elizabethan drama.[67] In his writings, Armin defined the artificial fool as someone who had talent as an entertainer, who was not an intelligent truth-teller and who is loyal to his master or mistress. Armin defined a natural fool as a 'simple' person who did not have malicious intentions towards anyone. This is how Armin uses phrases such as artificial and natural in distinguishing fools according to their physical appearance, not their mental abilities or disabilities.[68]

In Shakespeare's lifetime, between 1564 and 1616, there were 1,660 instances in which the word 'deformity' was used, but only 214 for 'disability'. Similarly, there were 2,797 cases relating to 'deformed', but just 529 for 'disabled'.[69]

The cases of usage of 'disability' and 'disabled' in Shakespeare's works confirms that these words were often used in a conceptual sense referring to incapacity or inability to physically or mentally do something. The use of the word was in no way linked to the legal or medical sense of the word 'disabled'. Shakespeare used phrases such as 'strength by limping sway disabled' which were written as a conceptual sense of incapacity.[70]

The 'disabled' characters in Shakespeare's works are often seen to have experienced a physical, moral or economic slowdown, like in *The Merchant of Venice*. He rarely used the word 'disabled' to describe a character with a pre-existing or unchangeable or physically challenging condition. Moreover, Shakespeare uses the word 'disability' to clarify it as a temporary state, imposed on one character by another, either through actions or prejudice.[71]

23

Shakespeare liked to imply in his works that 'to be disabled' is a state that male characters 'wilfully bring upon themselves'. Overall, Shakespeare did not use the word 'disability' as we now commonly refer to it, as he did not refer to people whose physical impairments created functional and social disadvantages, but instead wrote about people who were unable to perform the tasks expected of them. Early modern playwrights like Shakespeare conveyed a social model of disability.[72]

As Shakespeare's artistic representation of Renaissance life includes examples of disability in his cultural and social depictions, it could be argued that his texts can be used to generate and support theories regarding early modern attitudes towards disabilities. His first depiction of disability is conveyed in *Henry VI*, in a familiar episode taken from the English chronicles, and the spurious miracle at St. Albans satirises the gullibility of a too superstitious King Henry. Henry VI was, essentially, mentally disabled and in reality, unable to reign as king. Shakespeare discusses this incident to disparage the person of Henry VI.[73]

Although Shakespeare would not have been familiar with the term 'disability', he used deformities and physical and mental challenges to degrade his characters. It could be argued that Renaissance writers such as Shakespeare considered 'disability' to be an identity, even if they did not use that word in that sense. Instead, they used words such as 'deformed', 'monstrous', and 'stigmatic', which abound in their works, as do more specific terms for more specific conditions, like 'blind,' 'lame,' or 'mad'. It seems the only difference is that these terms were not brought together under a single umbrella of terminology. Shakespeare addressed difference from the perspective of what was considered average during the Tudor period. In other words, through the use of stigma, which he wove into his narratives. Shakespeare was possibly one of the first writers to use the word 'stigma' in the English language and who was also obsessed with the social phenomena of discrimination, prejudice, social, mental and physical difference.[74]

He created a vocabulary of shame by dramatising his characters' abnormalities and changing their meaning. It appears that Shakespeare was the first writer in Western history to recognise that people marked off as inherently inferior, and different, such as those who suffered a physical deformity, racial minority, mental disability, radical criminality, bastardy, and idiocy, could be reinvented to cultivate memorable characters.

Shakespeare's *Richard III* is an essential example of staging disability in early modern drama. Although theorists take Richard's character as emblematic of premodern notions of disability, Richard could be a character who employs rhetorical power and performative ability to compensate for a bodily form marked with negative associations. Richard forefronts his deformed figure in ways that elevate his political power, appealing to physical disability and the infirmity he claims it entails to obscure his shrewd political manoeuvres. Understanding the dominant ends to which Richard III uses his debility allows us to think about disabled identity during the period, as a complex negotiation of discourse surrounding deformity and monstrosity, as well as revealing the instability of all bodies. Richard III, it could be argued, was used as a character to theorize the way the reader might take pleasure in representations of any and every healthy body's undoing; Shakespeare used the accounts from the battle of Bosworth, and the mutilation of Richard III's naked body over the back of a horse, to render Richard III a monster, when precise details of the king's scoliosis would not have been known, even to those at court, except perhaps those courtiers who served him in his privy bedchamber. In the play, it could be argued that Richard III shows that his physical challenges were enabling rather than disabling. Perhaps Richard III could be a standard-bearer for the possibility that difference was a powerful motivator. Perhaps because of that motivation, the character shows that most, if not all, disabled people may have the power within them to embrace all the good things life has for them, despite their challenges.

The Richard III Society, in its mission statement, believes that the traditional accounts of the character and career of Richard III are 'neither supported by sufficient evidence nor reasonably tenable'. The Society, which aims to promote, research and reassess the life and times of Richard III, is dedicated to reclaiming the reputation of this king of England who died over 500 years ago and who reigned for just over two years. Richard's infamous character and personality have been maligned over the centuries, due in part to the continuing popularity, and the belief in, the picture of disability painted of the king by William Shakespeare.[75]

It is often difficult, if not impossible in Shakespeare's plays, to gain intimate personal information about a seemingly disabled character. Before Richard III's remains were discovered by Philippa Langley, historians had been overloaded with negative information about Richard III, usually steered by the Tudors and Shakespeare. In Shakespeare's text, the writer hints and makes suggestions about possible signs of disability, but this was all best-guess on the part of Shakespeare because as Philippa Langley, the Richard III Society and the University of Leicester have since confirmed through Richard's remains that Richard was not a hunchback, and Shakespeare made assumptions about Richard III's scoliosis, without knowing the facts. Richard III, and more importantly his disability, were used as scapegoats in Shakespeare's tragedy, as a means of propaganda, to assimilate continued support for the Tudors' claim to the throne and to validate the seat of their successors.

With Richard III, Shakespeare created a villain who possessed qualities that made his character weak. In this case, Richard's 'weaknesses' were presented in a physically conspicuous way. The king cannot hide his weakness; it is constantly on display for people to see. Richard lived with this physical deformity his entire life, and as such, it influenced who he was, but it did not necessarily make him a villain. There is no evidence to suggest that Richard's scoliosis made him physically 'weak', as Shakespeare paints him. I would point out that he had to have serious physical stamina to travel the country as much as he did, let alone lead troops into battle – being one of the last English kings to ever do so. This is actually attributed to George II in 1743, who was the last king to lead in battle, but it was Richard who was the last to lead and die in battle. Richard's only weakness was that he had older brothers and nephews standing in his way of ever inheriting the crown. It is apparent through Richard's asides that Shakespeare is constantly painting these 'weaknesses' as being at the forefront of his mind as Richard says in his opening monologue:

I, that am curtail'd of this fair proportion,
Cheated of feature by dissembling nature,
Deformed, unfinish'd, sent before my time
Into this breathing world, scarce half made up,
And that so lamely and unfashionable
That dogs bark at me as I halt by them.[76]

Richard is portrayed as feeling cheated by his appearance. Shakespeare tries to show that Richard seems to think he is deserving and owed a beautiful body and tries to convey that Richard's sense of entitlement was shallow nature. The king is a melancholy character, who thinks that he is unable to participate in life, be happy, and exist peacefully just because he has a physical deformity:

> And therefore, since I cannot prove a lover
> To entertain these fair well-spoken days,
> I am determined to prove a villain.[77]

Shakespeare wants the reader to think that Richard has no choice but to partake in criminal acts to obtain the power he thinks he deserves. Shakespeare makes Richard place the blame elsewhere – his deformity has made him this way. The playwright twists Richard as a character for propaganda's sake, to have his character be physically, socially, or otherwise weak in some way, to help the reader assume that Richard was capable of evil. The reader might assume that because Richard is physically challenged, that he is weak of character, but just because Richard is not physically strong does not mean he is not capable of great mental strength and cunning. Shakespeare turns Richard's 'weakness' to his character's advantage in the play. Nobody suspects someone with a disability to act out evil deeds, as Shakespeare hints at in the tragedy.

The commentary in Shakespeare's plays and his character development link the abnormal exterior conditions, be it physical or social, of his villains to their internal motivations, which was not an uncommon practice in Elizabethan literature. As discussed in the chapter on superstitions, illegitimate children or people with physical deformities were viewed with distrust as they were considered to pose a threat to societal norms. But with the recent find of Richard III's remains, there is some tension there as to whether society's treatment of these characters and especially Richard III, is now justified. Richard was not to blame for his abnormalities, and it was the Tudor dynasty striving for legitimacy that gave rise to the unjust treatment of Richard III in Shakespeare's rendering of the character. We forget that Richard was a real person who walked the earth and unless we lived during his lifetime, spent time at court with him and knew him intimately, then we would never know the extent of his decisions, whether he was responsible for the atrocities he has been maligned for, or what his motives were for his actions if any. If we believe conjecture, rumour and propaganda, then society, indeed, faced a villain. However, Shakespeare is encouraging us to think about the relationship between one's exterior appearance and one's inner thoughts. Can we say that someone is evil because they have a curvature of the spine like scoliosis? Obviously not. Outward appearances are an inadequate way of judging others, yet people have done it for centuries.

Shakespeare was very influential in the Tudor court and therefore had the sway to establish cultural norms within the everyday society of the early modern era. The Tudors used this to their advantage by advertising and supporting Shakespeare in the development, writing and staging of his plays and tragedies. Perhaps Shakespeare is a villain for depicting disabled characters with disabilities in a derogatory way, along with people like Richard III; it could be argued that Shakespeare's motivation was his loyalty to the Tudor crown.

Throughout this book, it has been argued that disabled people in the early modern era were not considered disabled by the same standards of today. Neither Tudor society, nor Shakespeare had any recognition that the mental and social lives of people with disabilities could be determined less by the physical realities of their limitations, and more by the social attitudes, customs, and traditions that disabled people might have experienced. The disabled were not stigmatised in the same way as they are today. In the Tudor period, a general social stigma against the disabled was not a phenomenon. In a society full of illness, disease, still-births and military injuries, mental and physical abnormalities were socially typical, so it should come as no surprise that someone like Shakespeare would include such afflicted characters in his narratives.

The trouble with assessing the Tudor era and everyday life and attitudes towards the blind, lame, weak, mad and disabled generally was that conceptions of disability changed throughout the English Reformation. In many ways, they were forward-thinking in their care and support in the higher echelons of noble life, as such was the case with Thomas More and Henry Patenson, Anne Boleyn with Jayne Foole and Henry VIII with Will Somer. When it came to the unfortunate vagrants who were disabled, there was less tolerance and care. Tales of the 'disabled' were recounted by many authors: Thomas More, Richard Grafton, John Foxe, and, finally, William Shakespeare. More's opinion on disability was shaped by an understanding of mutual exchange between disabled and non-disabled persons, probably from what he had witnessed at home and within the Tudor court. The Reformation eliminated that exchange, and disability was imagined as increasingly dangerous, deceptive, and emasculating. Shakespeare expanded on contrary post-Reformation ideas about disability while the Tudors and Shakespeare simultaneously demonstrated their inability to contain disability in a period that struggled to define and regulate it.

Chapter Two

Tudor Laws and Disability

During the middle of the fifteenth century, disabled people were often grouped with the generally poor, beggars and thieves. It was a natural outcome for disabled people who were unable to work and found themselves suffering economic hardship to be grouped with the poor, but the Tudors went further by distinguishing between the 'Undeserving Poor' (normally criminal beggars) and the 'Deserving Poor', those who genuinely needed help from the state. How to look after these different groups of society, the elderly, disabled and deal with the unemployed, as well as sturdy beggars, triggered increasing public concern. The new scheme of caring for the aged, the poor, the disabled, the orphans and the unemployed was based on a series of Acts of Parliament passed during the later Tudor era. Though this had much less to do with compassion than with the need to establish order and stability, these laws imposed an obligation on every parish to take care of its poor.

While one of the outstanding achievements of the sixteenth century in most of Western Europe was indeed the assimilation of poor relief, England stood out because it developed mechanisms for administration and reinforcement where abroad there was no comparison. The Poor Law lasted for 350 years in one form or another and accounts of English, and later British social policy, tend, in consequence, to be dominated by the role of government. These policies were related to social and economic circumstances and existed because of the poverty and destitution in Tudor England in the mid-to-late sixteenth century, and beyond. The origins of the English poor laws lay in the intersection of humanist aspirations with rising economic destitution and government paranoia about the poor. As the numbers of impotent poor grew, so did attempts to implement and legislate sweeping community and political solutions.[1]

The social and economic circumstances of the unemployed, deserving poor, and disabled people often created no other options for them but to leave families who could not support them. They would then have had to leave their villages to look for work but this was an illegal practice and people who took this option were then classified as vagabonds. One in five people in the towns and cities lived in extreme poverty and in some places it has been estimated that a quarter of the population consisted of beggars. Some roamed in gangs stealing or bullying people into giving them alms. As in the early years of the period, there was no welfare state in Tudor England. Losing your job or growing too ill or old to work meant you had three main options: beg, steal or die.

Thomas More wrote in 1516 about poverty in his book *Utopia*: 'The landowners enclose all land into pastures (for sheep) ... the peasants must depart away ... And when they have wandered ... what else can they do but steal or go about begging.'[2]

The creation of the Poor Laws was influenced by the economy, population pressure, changes in public attitudes and of course, politics, with the desire to assist the poorest and disabled in Tudor society. 'The kingdom became then much more populous than in former times, and with it, the poor also greatly increased.' This is how the Elizabethan Poor Law was explained in the mid-seventeenth century, by Sir Matthew Hale.[3]

The poverty of the time was severe, especially as the population of England had been increasing since the early 1520s. Prices for goods had also increased, however food supplies and opportunities did not match inflation and real wages fell drastically to their lowest point in the late sixteenth century and early seventeenth century. In the sixteenth century, jobs were not always easy to find. Thousands found themselves wandering, looking for work, which was largely due to the breakdown of the feudal system. Feudalism was built on a hierarchal pyramid structure where everyone owed allegiance to their immediate superior where previously the nobles of the land and the Lords of the Manor were responsible for the peasants who lived on their property.

Life in the Tudor period became increasingly luxurious for the rich. For the very poor and disabled in society, however, it was as hard as it had ever been. Marjorie McIntosh argues: 'a fifth of the population lived in poverty, including the disabled, infirm and elderly, moreover, unstable economic and demographic conditions in the later fifteenth and early sixteenth centuries rendered more people vulnerable to short-term hardship.'[4]

In theory, wealthy people were expected to give help or alms to local people suffering from poverty because of their disabilities, such as being old, blind or sick. Moreover, poor and disabled people in some villages, who were dependent on aid, were well cared for while others died of starvation. The consequences of these economic issues were evident at the start of the Tudor age, and for at least fifty years before that. During this same period, illegitimacy and crime increased, as did vagrancy and it is easy to understand why the threat and fear of living in poverty affected so many of the population. Certain factions of the population merited charitable aid, and they were often the 'impotent' poor, widows and orphans, who, even though they worked, did not earn enough to cover the cost of living or support their children and families.[5]

Poor families, some of which supported their elderly and disabled relatives, especially in the 1590s during the bad harvests, were classified as 'poor, able labouring folk' or 'labouring persons not able to live off their labour'. In 1552, in London, surveys were taken which uncovered the poverty to which 'decayed householders' lived; those labourers who were poor men overburdened by their dependents were included.[6] Those also in need of charitable support were those referred to in the monastic visitation injunctions of 1535-1536 as 'those which endeavor themselves with all their will and labour to get their living with their hands, and yet cannot fully help themselves for their chargeable household and multitude of children'.[7] The financial pressure on the poor in Tudor society was brought about by economic, religious and social turmoil and was the main reason why the Poor Laws were introduced. Although there are limited specific cases of disabled people being categorised as mentally or physically challenged due to disability and indeed, being poor, it could be argued that disabled people, for lack of physical or mental ability would have been part of the labouring poor, and be paupers, because they were limited in their access to work. The poor laws were the start of state-regulated provision for the poor. There was discrimination between those deserving and not deserving of charitable relief. Disabled and destitute people were supported by institutions such as hospitals, almshouses, parochial and communal support.[8]

Tudor society questioned who should support the elderly, disease-ridden and those with disabilities, who were constant causes of dependence on their communities and ultimately their families. The Tudors began to recognise that the community, as well as the family, ought to support its more vulnerable and poor members.

Surprisingly, England was the only country amongst its Europeans neighbours that produced a system of poor relief which was financed by taxation.[9]

Previous to the sixteenth century, there had been little organisation by the state to implement support for poor and disabled people. The church had taken up the slack and been the mainstay of support for the poor and disabled, where the law had been absent.[10] Welfare was more typically developed through a combination of provisions, both voluntary and mutual, which were later supplemented by government action. Christian charity supported the poor in Europe, as it did in England, during the Middle Ages through almsgiving. The main formal organisations to implement this were the Church and the monasteries. Poor people, if they left the land and arrived in the cities were supported by charities which made it possible for some poor people to survive. However, after 1530, the government increasingly interfered, centralised and unified the poor relief system. Common inspiration for the implementation of poor relief was humanism, of which Erasmus and Thomas More were advocates. Humanist attitudes continued to influence social policy throughout the Tudor period.

Advocating social policy by humanist attitudes was only one of the ways that disabled people could be supported. Philanthropy in the form of alms being distributed on a casual basis in the city streets to organized charitable institutions supporting those less fortunate was common. Philanthropy was the main form of support in Europe and proved an adequate form of support in other countries. However, the English need to have a social-welfare system is rather unusual for the period, and says much about the attitudes towards the poor and disabled in their communities.

The law was necessary because although charity had been the mainstay behind benevolent support, these forms of support were in decline. The government wanted to remodel and reform charitable giving and set out to change this practice, by implementing the poor law. Supporting others less fortunate was a commonly praised virtue in the late Tudor period, however, almsgiving was to be abolished and donations to the poor were to be controlled, tempered and disciplined. Charitable giving shows in wills written and disimbersed between 1480 and 1660 that large and increasing amounts of money were being awarded for the relief of the poor in almshouses and other similar establishments.[11] Moreover, begging was commonplace because casual charitable giving took place on the city streets. However, these kinds of incidents of charitable giving were not measured because there was no means of doing so. Nevertheless, this practice continued.[12] Disabled and poor people were drawn into licensed begging; there was free housing offered by hospitals and almshouses, and aid given through, or by parishes. Other kinds of aid were received through essential help provided by friends, relatives, and neighbours, but because this was an informal kind of support, it is seldom documented in the sixteenth century and therefore is difficult to examine in any detail. The main purpose of the poor law was to stop the destitute and disabled from begging in their parishes door-to-door.

The poor laws had political consequences which had social repercussions for the poor. They helped to preserve political stability and offered justice. However they did differentiate the poor and disabled from the social and cultural norms of their communities. Moreover, the disabled and poor were not passive recipients of almsgiving and charitable payments, as they did have the ability to manipulate the system by entering almshouses, monasteries and philanthropists' houses when outdoor relief may have suited them better. Like our benefits system today, which is free to access at the point of need, Tudor citizens moved in and out of poverty, not defined by the status of pauper and subjected to a lifetime of receiving alms or charity. The poor law succeeded in England because the government could enforce and regulate these practical strategies to help poor and disabled people.

Up until the mid-1530s, most charitable aid was awarded only occasionally, typically to those individuals who had been struck by some particular misfortune. Poverty and its effects intensified from around 1530 until 1553, as forms of relief changed significantly. Attitudes towards the poor and almsgiving had previously been shaped by Catholic beliefs during the later medieval period, however, with the onslaught of the Reformation, humanist movements and ideas of 'commonwealth' changed ideas about whether the Christian state was responsible for the poor and disabled. With early Protestant theology lacking in how it should tackle the vulnerability of the poor, disabled and elderly, central government was expected to take up the mantle of supporting the destitute and disabled.[13]

The most important development, initiated by Tudor central government, was the introduction of parish-based aid, financed by regular payments made by wealthier philanthropists, and members of the community. During the second half of the sixteenth century, as the need of those requiring financial support increased, local towns, villages and cities, as well as wealthy benefactors and generous individuals experimented with how best to provide financial support and assistance. The elderly, poor and chronically disabled did qualify for help under these changes, and some disabled people and their families received ongoing support. Although there were some attempts to improve life for the poor, these did not always make much difference. Their suffering always increased after bad harvests. Shortages of food resulted in higher prices which meant that more impoverished families could not afford to buy food for their needs. Public concern about the suffering of the poor and disabled was escalated by bad harvests towards the closing of the sixteenth century around the 1580s and 1590s, which led to the implementation of the Poor Laws of 1598 and 1601.

The first sixteenth century poor law of 1531 was not the kind of law developed nor experienced as much by other countries in Europe. It could be argued that these Poor Laws were ahead of their times, and were the Tudor equivalent of the welfare state. However, parliament ordered vagrants to be detained and punished. Later, bills required parishes to put the idle to work, to send poor children into service, and to collect money for the elderly and disabled. The state desired a well-ordered society, and the poor law gave parishes the burden of effecting this grand design. Together, alms, work, branding, and beating were supposed to turn the frail, disabled and recalcitrant into model citizens. For three centuries, the Poor Law constituted 'a welfare state in miniature,' relieving the elderly, widows, children and those who were sick, as well as those who were disabled, unemployed and underemployed.[14]

John Simkin states that 'Since the 14th century there had been laws against vagabonds, but in 1530 a new law was passed. The old and disabled poor were to be given licences to beg. However, anyone roaming without a job was tied to a cart in the nearest market town and whipped till they were bloody. They were then forced to return to the parish where they had been born or where they had lived for the last three years. A law passed in 1536 stated that people caught outside their parish without work were to be punished by being whipped through the streets. For a second offence, the vagabond was to lose part of an ear. If a vagabond was caught a third time he or she was executed.'[15]

Henry VIII's Poor Law in 1531 was legislation designed to define English society's obligations and duties to the destitute, aged, sick or disabled people who were judged unable to look after themselves.[16] The laws also contained punitive measures aimed at non-disabled poor people deemed 'idle' or unwilling to work.[17]

On the continent, in 1531, to protect themselves from the accusations of heresy, the city of Ypres submitted its system for approval by the religious authorities of the Sorbonne. Ypres offered poor people relief, backed up by the process of inspection and control; they provided education, employment and free medical care. Charles V approved the Ypres scheme, as it was Charles V's Spanish empire who were responsible for the Low Countries.

The historian Geoffrey Elton suggests that William Marshall, who translated a report on the Ypres scheme into English, may also have been the author of the initial draft of the Tudor Act of 1536, one of the first English Poor Laws.[18] Thomas Cromwell's Act for Punishment of Sturdy Vagabonds and Beggars 1536, is in the Parliamentary records, but this is not the law he proposed, rather a compromise that the MPs would agree to.[19] Cromwell started the law between 1534 and 1535 as he gathered data. He knew parliament wanted to bring a law into being to deal with the issue of vagabonds, sturdy beggars, the poor, elderly and disabled, but he presented nothing until 1536, knowing this draft was a simple stop-gap calculator of noble intentions.[20] It all fell away after parliament rejected the plan, and the Pilgrimage of Grace erupted. All was forgotten, the vagabond laws remained pitiful for years. The Tudor government meant well in implementing the poor laws. However, many parishes ignored the law well into the seventeenth century.[21]

During the Tudor era, while the number of workers living in poverty increased, the supply of charitable assistance declined. The Tudor state tried to be a harsh taskmaster, demanding work in return for the payment of alms. The supply of alms-giving work was intermittent and often ineffective. The provision of work for alms had a poor track record, even though the idea of 'workfare' appeared a good idea. Parishes enforced vagrancy laws unevenly and irregularly, concentrating their support efforts towards the elderly, and single-parent families, who received alms when they were destitute, and poor children who were wards within families and, or given apprenticeships. Where the implementation of the poor laws declined, pension systems replaced them. Recipients benefited from relative largesse; others found provision discriminatory and punitive. However, once the poor law was established in a parish it was widely accepted by those who benefited from it. Administrators saw the poor laws as legitimate, justices of the peace enforced the laws, overseers implemented them and the poor and disabled used them.

The poor laws were even more important when the dissolution of the monasteries in 1536-40 began, followed by the demise of religious guilds, fraternities, almshouses, and hospitals in 1545-49. The Reformation 'destroyed much of the institutional fabric which had provided charity for the poor in the past'.[22] After the Reformation in England, a complicated set of institutions was developed for the care of the poor and disabled. Where the use of monasteries declined, hospitals, almshouses, workhouses and orphanages multiplied, and in England, mandatory relief was provided for poor and disabled people. There are multiple explanations for poor law provision, such as rising demand from a rising population in the sixteenth century, the ideological influence of humanism and of an activist Lutheranism, as well as the interventionist state for order.[23] All these factors worked together to poke the government to legislate procedures for action. However, real relief for the poor took place at a local level, where individual decisions were often made. Political context coloured welfare bargaining between those who would give and those who received relief. This relief was negotiated between unequals, as defined by the limits of social obligation and of communal membership in a hierarchical society.

The Tudor population tried to be self-sufficient in avoiding starvation within towns and villages, by farming animals, growing crops and increasing the wool yield, which was the significant trades of rural communities, but changes in working the land increased unemployment in rural areas and was a significant cause of poverty, especially when farming landowners changed from arable to sheep, and England began its Reformation. Henry VIII declared himself Supreme Head of the Church. The closing down of the monasteries combined created even more unemployment, as monasteries had also helped provide food for the poor.[24]

Unemployed citizens were sometimes tempted to leave their villages to look for work. The principle of a 'settlement' in a parish deterred some people, but not all, from migrating to other towns and villages. This concept of the settlement was related to feudal ideas; people were tied to certain locations. If the poor, disabled and unemployed tried to draw relief outside the parish of their birth, they could be removed, and be rejected, or physically transported to another parish. Contemporary examples of pregnant women being physically removed so that they did not give birth to a child in the parish were commonplace as this prevented the newborn baby from gaining settlement. This avoided the newborn for having a status of settlement in the parish where they would otherwise have been born. This illegal practice of trying to gain settlement meant the people who did this were classified as vagabonds.

Changes in farming practices also created vagabonds. In *Utopia,* Thomas More states that 'The landowners enclose all land into pastures (for sheep) ... the peasants must depart away ... And when they have wandered ... what else can they do but steal or go about begging.'[25] Poor vagabonds were often seen as dangerous beggars and thieves who could spread disease.

The movement of people was a regular feature of rural towns and villages during the Tudor period because many religious houses were closed, and almshouses could not deal with all the suffering. This meant that the wealth and power of the Church were significantly reduced because of a series of unsuccessful political confrontations with the monarchy. Renaissance men had not needed to wander from their villages and towns of birth before, and had, in the past, stayed put. With the lack of support and provision, it began to be noticed, in the first half of the sixteenth century, that people were moving away to look for work, because of the increasing population.[26]

The first English poor law legislation was enacted in 1536, instructing each parish to undertake voluntary weekly collections to assist the 'impotent' poor. The parish council had been the basic unit of local government since at least the fourteenth century, although Parliament imposed few civic functions, if any, on parishes before the sixteenth century.[27]

As well as poor laws being drawn up, other significant situations in how the poor were supported were affected in 1536. The dissolution of the monasteries which was famously instigated by King Henry VIII put vast sums of money into the royal coffers, saw monks and nuns made homeless and many poor people without a place of refuge. The Reformation of 1536 onwards, brought changes in religion leading to declining values and moral expectations. The abrupt chaos wreaked havoc on the close-knit religious communities of England that had adhered to the Bible instructions given to all Christians in Matthew Chapter 25 which stated that all Christians should: feed the hungry; give drink to the thirsty; welcome the stranger; clothe the naked; visit the sick; visit the prisoner and bury the dead.

The dissolution of the monasteries left many of the poorest without a safety net. There was also a steady growth in the numbers of people seeking support. This was due to several factors, including an increase in the population after a period of stagnation, depletion due to plagues, the beginnings of the commercialisation of agriculture, successive poor harvests, and an influx of immigrants from Ireland and Wales. Hence the fear of 'bands of sturdy beggars' preyed on the minds of local magistrates, who demanded a response from the central authority, namely the Crown.[28]

The leap from poverty to being reliant on the state was a large one. The money funnelled into parishes to help the poor and disabled was dished out to relatively few who needed it. Welfare was a process which emerged from complex deprivation and responsibility, which some in their communities shared and others contested. To be poor or a 'pauper' required much more than destitution. Firstly, the person suffering had to ask to be helped by charity; secondly, local government officials had to acknowledge public responsibility and decide how to proceed in supporting the applicant; thirdly, the individual receiving support had to decide whether or not they were going to accept the support offered or not. There were those who dispensed, those who received, and those who were ignored in times of need. For example, a law of 1547 said vagabonds could be made slaves for two years. Their plight was not only ignored, but it was also punished. However, a few years later in 1550 this terrible law was abolished but flogging was made the punishment for vagrancy instead.[29]

Tudor governments tolerated genuinely disabled beggars. Some people pretended to be mad or disabled to beg. However, they did not tolerate healthy people without jobs wandering from place to place. They thought such 'sturdy vagabonds' without a fixed place in society were a threat to law and order. To secure their allegiance, the Tudor monarchs were forced to make financial provision for people dependent upon charity.[30]

Monarchs tried to provide care for the disabled who ended up in London. Edward VI supplied one of the royal palaces which served as a house of correction for the poor, known as Bridewell. Here, the poor, disabled and those who were considered vagrants and criminals were to be supported and work for that support rather than be punished. They were given useful tasks to perform as part of their cure. The teenage King Edward was a progressive evangelist, and it was with his enlightened approach that houses of correction were established in other large cities to re-integrate these individuals back into society. In 1553, a letter sent by the citizens of London to Edward VI stated that 'It was obvious to all men that beggars and thieves were everywhere. And we found the cause was that they were idle; and the cure must be to make them work ... by providing work ourselves, so that the strong and sturdy vagabond may be made to earn his living. For this, we need a house of work ... And so, we ask for the king's house of Bridewell.'[31] When Edward's older, Catholic sister Mary I came to the throne, Bridewell was commonly used as a place of punishment. But during Elizabeth's reign, houses of correction once again served a useful purpose in maintaining social order and keeping vagrants off the streets.[32]

To find out how many vagrants were on the streets, Queen Mary I introduced the Poor Law Act of 1552 because the government needed to find out the extent of the problem with the poor, so they needed to be identified and the 1552 Act was passed to officially collect and record the number of poor in each Parish Register, along with the usual details of births, deaths, and marriages. A parish was the smallest unit of organisation within the Church, and every parish had its church and clergyman.[33] Of the fifteen thousand parishes in England and Wales, Parliament suggested that every parish should appoint two collectors of alms to assist the churchwardens after church services on Sunday to ask the congregation how much they were prepared to give to charity weekly towards the relief of the poor and disabled. The alms collectors distributed the money to help them register the poor of the parish. The Elizabethan problem of poverty was assessed by the information held within the Parish Registers, and this information was required by the Elizabethan government to assess the extent of the problem of the poor in England's towns and cities.[34]

These poor laws did help alleviate the problem of poverty to an extent and were started when the English defeated both the French and the

Spanish armies in battle. This left the soldiers without a job as they returned home from the war. As the soldiers arrived home, they found it harder and harder to survive and began to steal food, money and clothing. Poor people used to go to the monasteries for help, but with the destruction of the monasteries during the reformation, this made obtaining work, receiving practical and monetary support more difficult. To solve this problem parishes were built, which became the basic unit of administration. However, within these parishes, help was inconsistent as there lacked a general mechanism through which help could be enforced, and the Poor Law's operation was inconsistent between areas, despite parishes receiving taxes from the people.[35]

In 1566 Thomas Harman wrote a book about vagabonds: 'They are punished by whippings. Yet they like this life so much that their punishment is soon forgotten. They never think of changing until they climb the gallows.'[36] However, not everyone was hostile to the poor, disabled or beggars. Moreover, the practice of indiscriminate charity was one of the key issues which the Protestant reformers objected to. Several northern European cities introduced systems of organised poor relief, intended to limit the amount they had to pay for charity, to keep out strangers, and to control the poor.[37]

Poor Laws were implemented because of the growth of the population in England, and rapid inflation, caused by rapid growth in the population, and the debasement of the coinage in 1526. The debasement of coinage continued from 1544-46, as the inflow of American silver also caused problems for the economy. Towards the end of his reign, Henry VIII had debased the coinage which meant that the proportion of gold and silver in the coins was reduced. Grain prices more than tripled in the years from 1490-1509 to 1550-69, and then increased by an additional seventy-three per cent in the years from 1550-69 to 1590-1609. The costs of other commodities increased nearly as rapidly and the Phelps Brown and Hopkins price index compiled in the 1950s, states that the price index rose by 391 per cent in the years from 1495-1504 to 1595-1604.

In 1560, the Elizabethan government took steps to remedy this by replacing all debased coins with new ones, which restored England's currency to its proper levels. This was a shrewd move by Elizabeth's advisors and served to combat the problem of inflation in the early years of her reign. The cost of living rose far faster than nominal wages, which increased at a much slower rate than prices; as a result, real wages of agricultural, building labourers and skilled artisans declined by about sixty per cent over the course of the sixteenth century. These increases in the cost of living and the decline in purchasing power led to severe hardship for a significant part of the population. Conditions were unusually harsh in 1595-98 when four consecutive poor harvests led to famine.

During Elizabeth I's reign, the primary function of the House of Commons, after the granting of taxation, was to consider social and economic legislation, which occupied a great deal of time in Elizabethan Parliaments. The Elizabethan Acts in 1563 and 1572 made provision for the punishment of sturdy beggars and the relief of the impotent poor. In England, the law of 1572 was superseded in 1598. William Lambarde made a speech about poverty in England in 1594 and said that 'There were always poor lepers, aged poor, sick poor, poor widows, poor orphans, and such like, but poor soldiers were either rarely or never heard of till now ... They lead their lives in begging and end them by hanging ... They fight our wars ... enduring cold and hunger when we live at ease, lying in the open field when we are in our beds.'[38]

In 1601, the Elizabethan Poor Law was a national Act for England and Wales. (The system became law in 1597/8, but the Act that consolidated the system dates from 1601.) It provided for a compulsory poor-rate, the creation of 'overseers' of relief, provision for 'setting the poor on work'.

The parish was the basic unit of administration. There was, however, no general mechanism through which this could be enforced, and the Poor Law's operation was inconsistent between areas. Given the circumstances, the Acts of 1597-98 and 1601 were an attempt by Parliament both to prevent starvation and to control public order.[39]

Elizabethan Acts in 1563 and 1572 made provision for the punishment of sturdy beggars and the relief of the impotent poor. The Poor Law Act of 1563 was written and passed into law to curb the threat of civil disorder. Different types of poor people were categorised to determine the treatment that they might receive and they were called the 'Deserving Poor' – the old, the disabled, the young, and the sick whom parishes thought should receive help. The genuine, deserving poor were provided with 'Outdoor Relief' in the form of clothes, food, or money. Those who were willing to work were called the 'Deserving Unemployed' – but they were the unfortunate people who were unable to find employment. These poor people were provided with 'Indoor Relief' in the form of being cared for in almshouses, orphanages, and workhouses and the sick were cared for in hospitals while apprenticeships were arranged for the young. Meanwhile, the 'Undeserving Poor' – those who turned to a life of crime or became beggars, were called 'Idle Beggars' but have since been referred to as 'Poor Beggars'.[40] These terms are still common in the modern English language. Those who were dishonest people in these categories were considered criminals who turned to various forms of theft and the punishments for people placed in these categories were extremely harsh.[41] The unfortunate poor who begged were viewed and treated as criminals. The punishment of 'poor beggars' was that they would be beaten until they reached the stones that marked the town parish boundary. These beatings were given as punishments and were bloody and merciless, and those who were caught begging were often sent to prison and hanged as their final punishment.[42] There were several reasons for this increase in begging, much like the increase in working people using 'foodbanks' today. The reason for this was poverty. During the reign of Elizabeth I, the population rose from three to four million people. This increase was primarily due to a rise in fertility and a falling death rate and meant, in simple terms, that the country's resources now had to be shared by a greater number of people. Added to this was the problem of rising prices.[43]

Elizabeth's government set about tackling issues raised by vagrants, the poor, ill and disabled, by introducing a series of Acts, which were put in place to acknowledge that the care of the poor was now the community's responsibility; each citizen was expected to play his or her part, and in this respect, these socialist type values of communities helping the most vulnerable were progressive for their time, establishing a framework of support which lasted for many years, influencing later policy which would create the Welfare State in the twentieth century.

Despite England's economic problems, towns grew during Elizabeth's reign, as changes in farming led to people leaving the countryside. Before her accession, land enclosure had changed the face of the landscape. Enclosure meant that the system of traditional open fields, whereby individual peasant farmers could farm their pieces of land ended in favour of creating larger, profitable farming units which required fewer people to work on them. The wool trade was a popular way of earning a living during the Elizabethan age, which meant that land which had previously been farmed by peasants became dedicated to rearing sheep. This led to a large number of agricultural jobs decreasing and people being forced to leave their homes in search of employment in the towns.

The beautiful English countryside, with its rolling hills and flocks of sheep, did not stop the nation being hit by several poor harvests, particularly in the 1590s, which put increasing pressure on a limited supply of food. The resulting rise in food prices led to starvation amongst those who could not afford to pay. In 1563, the government further affected wages in a move to curb inflation. Upper wage limits were set by the Statute of Artificers for skilled workers such as butchers or carpenters, which meant as prices rose, wages could not reflect these increases and the standard of living dropped for many workers.[44]

Thus, many people who had lived and worked in the countryside their whole lives found themselves without any means of employment, support and, in many cases, they were evicted from their homes. Large numbers of destitute people headed for bigger towns in the hope of a better life. London was the biggest city in Europe, a colourful metropolis which contained a variety of city life. The streets were littered with alehouses, gambling dens and brothels, where the public was entertained by street performers, sat in playhouses and became fixated by spectacles such as bear-baiting. The city of London was filthy but intriguing, yet lively but dangerous. In addition to its poverty, the capital acted as a magnet for beggars, thieves, and tricksters from across the country.[45]

Several significant towns launched initiatives to try to tackle the problem of the poor and disabled. Norwich was at that time the largest city outside London, and consequently had a severe problem with poverty. A census was compiled in 1570 which detailed the name, age, and status of every citizen to provide an overview of the population of Norwich, and measure the extent of the problem of the poor. A report on a survey carried out in Norwich in 1571 stated that: 'Many of the citizens were annoyed that the city was so full of poor people, both men women and children, to the number of 2,300 persons, who went from door to door begging, pretending they wanted work but did very little.'[46]

The most significant form of support for disabled people had been private benefactors who would leave money in their wills to establish, for example, an almshouse which provided shelter for the local poor.

But as poverty worsened, it became clear that this kind of individual philanthropy was no longer sufficient, and that broader measures were called for in the form of legislation. William Cecil, Lord Burghley, one of the Queen's most trusted and able ministers, was particularly concerned that large numbers of homeless people and the unemployed could present a serious threat to law and order.[47]

Parliament introduced a series of laws in the following years of 1563, 1572, 1576, 1597 and 1601. Each Act carried a different emphasis, which often reflected the current climate. The 1597 Act, laid down stricter guidelines for people who were considered vagabonds and beggars, in response to the economic crisis of the 1590s. In the 1590s, during Queen Elizabeth's reign, a series of poor harvests occurred. The price of food increased and people were suffering from starvation. This, combined with a population increase of 25% during the Elizabethan era created a dire situation in the land. Starving and homeless people were driven to desperate acts endangering society in general.[48] Those who showed no sign of changing their ways, such as the undeserving poor, were given harsh treatment. The 1563 Act reaffirmed the policy of whipping non-disabled beggars and in later Acts, vagabonds would be burned through the right ear, if they persisted in their activities and could be imprisoned, and eventually executed. The extreme policies of ear-boring and execution remained in force until 1593. In the 1597 Act policy required each town to provide a prison for these groups of people which was paid for by local taxes. Beggars caught offending would be punished and then returned to their native parish. The Law passed by Parliament in 1597 stated that:

> Every vagabond or beggar ... shall be stripped naked from the middle upwards and publicly whipped until his or her body be bloody, and forth with sent to the parish where he was born ... If any vagabond or beggar return, he shall suffer death by hanging.[49]

The first of these Acts was introduced in 1563, which sought to minimise the danger of criminal activity due to poverty and make proper provision for the needy. These people were considered deserving of social support.

However, the decline in Christian values, and the examples set by the nuns and the monks in the Church, resulted in these charitable acts of support and mercy shown towards the unfortunate being no longer seen as a duty. The English had placed the responsibility of these people firmly on the shoulders of the Elizabethan government.

The category of people to which caused Burghley such concern was the 'undeserving poor'. Finally, the third category of poor person was recognised: the deserving unemployed, physically able who could earn a living but were unable to find work.

The Poor Law Act of 1572 was the first compulsory poor law tax imposed at a local level, making the alleviation of poverty very much a local responsibility. It was the job of the Justice of the Peace in each parish to collect taxes from those who owned land in their parish. This taxation was called the Poor Rate and the law stated that charity for the relief of the poor should be collected every week. Help could be given as cash to allow people to achieve a level of subsistence needed for survival, or in kind, such as a place in a workhouse, such as outdoor relief. The Poor Rate was used to help the 'deserving poor' with anyone refusing to pay, imprisoned. The introduction of national poor law taxes in 1572 was an important step forward in recognising that the poor were now society's responsibility. Citizens were expected to support the needy. But in the 1576 Act, each town or parish was required to provide work for the unemployed, supplying raw materials, such as wool, for them to work with. This enabled the poor to have practical assistance, whilst fulfilling a useful role for the community. The 1597 Act went even further in stating that an official should be appointed for each parish so that they could specifically supervise the needs of the poor, especially the deserving poor. Once again this located responsibility at a local level but within the structure of national legislation.[50]

Elizabeth had to find a way to combat the problem of poverty, so parliament adopted several other statutes in support of an organized system relating to the poor in the next sixty years, culminating with the Acts of 1597-98 and 1601, which established a compulsory system of poor relief that was administered and financed at the parish local level.[51]

These Acts laid the groundwork for the system of poor relief up to the adoption of the Poor Law Amendment Act in 1834. Relief was to be administered by a group of overseers, who were to assess a compulsory property tax, known as the poor rate, to assist those within the parish 'having no means to maintain them'. The poor were divided into three groups: able-bodied adults, children, and the old or non- able-bodied or impotent poor. The overseers were instructed to put the non-disabled to work, to give apprenticeships to poor children, and to provide 'competent sums of money' to relieve the impotent.[52]

The Poor Law Act of 1597 was introduced because as mentioned before, the poor harvest of the 1590s placed a significant burden on the economy. The Justices of the Peace were given authority to raise additional compulsory funds. A new position of 'Overseer of the Poor' was created and this role was created to: calculate the amount of 'poor rate' required for the Parish; collect the poor rate from property owners; dispense either money, clothes or food and supervise the Parish Poor House. The provision of Poor Relief Act of 1598 meant that local officials would supply the poor with raw materials, and this had appeared in a statute of 1576 to supplement Henry VIII's Beggars Act.[53] The present statute was re-enacted in 1601 with an extension of the tax-paying group and other minor changes. Later poor laws normally cite the revised act.[54] The poor laws of 1601 required every parish, churchwarden, and those who had 'substantial households' i.e the wealthy in the community, to serve as overseers of the poor, and they were told that the poor must be set to work whether they were married, unmarried and had no means to maintain themselves or they had no daily trade. Children whose parents could not support them were offered apprenticeships or given work alongside destitute adults. A special tax was implemented on inhabitants and occupiers of land, houses, and coal mines and wood from within the local parish forests which was used to purchase materials for manufacturing, as well as to subsidise the necessary relief of the lame, impotent, old, blind, and others who could not work.[55] When families could not support their disabled relatives, when the labour market did not offer suitable jobs and apprenticeships, the local community was ordered to step in and become the employer or the caregiver, which was often the last resort. The scheme was originally pushed by the Privy Council and was extended across the entire realm. Eventually, by the seventeenth century, elite opinion recognised three kinds of poor people: the worthy, the workers lacking jobs, and those who worked the system. The poor law accommodated them all.[56] The most problematic of this group were the unworthy poor, who deserved punishment rather than relief. 'Rogues' and 'vagabonds' marked out a subset of the Tudor population, which Elizabethan law directed should be whipped or jailed to rehabilitate them. Overseers appointed by local justices decided who was punished and who were awarded alms. Moreover, in the interests of social stability, the Elizabethan Privy Council urged an activist approach. Yet, it was not until the Elizabethan era was over that rogues and vagabonds were transported to the colonies.[57] The poor were categorised to impose order and control, and the early poor laws were used to divide the poor and disabled into the worthy and unworthy. Local authorities were vigilant and parliament forced these distinctions on the poor so they could be exhorted. However, the legitimate poor were owed relief by their local parishes, there remained destitute people who were considered unworthy of support, and their entitlement to relief was in doubt because they were minstrels, peddlers, jugglers, actors and fortune-tellers unwilling to work in settled occupations which made them suspect to the local authorities.

To fulfil the expectations delivered by the Elizabethan poor law, those in need had to meet face to face with those benefactors within their local churches and the secular authorities of their communities. The Parliamentary overseers met the local dependent poor to serve them in the church after Sunday morning services, to: 'consider some of the good course to be taken'. Overseers decided whom to give alms to, whom to give work to and whom to provide a service for. Overseers time, energy and attention were coerced by fines of dishonesty and negligence, which was tedious for them but helped the local major landlords, gentry and their tenants from having to make these important decisions.[58] Besides the overseers, others were brought into administrative duties such as town councils who set local policies. Applicants were reviewed by magistrates in individual sessions or in quarter sessions, which provided another layer of verification, oversight and action. The historian Paul Slack called the poor laws and their implementation, a 'participatory system', which forced the wealthy and the destitute to outline their expectations and obligations.[59] With the 1601 poor law, the Elizabethan Tudors thought they had categorised the poor sufficiently by separating the impotent poor from those who could, would and should work; Tudor employers assessed health, attitudes and employability as well as the place where the needy were settled when they responded to need. Eventually, the dependent poor became 'paupers'. The dependent poor had previously been categorised and identified, like disability, ill-health and old-age. These health and social issues in later centuries, were included in categories coloured with crime, disreputability, deviance and defiance.

The 1601 Act did not enunciate any radical departure from earlier medieval arrangements to support the poor, except that the Elizabethan

Poor Law was a national Act for England and this system became law in 1597-1598, but the Act consolidated any previous system from 1601 onwards. The 1601 Act provided a compulsory poor-rate, the creation of 'overseers' of relief and provision for 'setting the poor on work', however it is chiefly noteworthy because it survived as the basis of the welfare and rating system for over 300 years in England, and was not repealed until 1967, by section 117 of, and Part I of Schedule 14 to, the General Rate Act.[60]

The Poor Law of 1601 marks the first official recognition of the need for state intervention and support in the lives of disabled people.[61]

The Elizabethan Poor Law of 1601 required each parish to provide for the 'lame, impotent, old and blind'. The Poor Law Act of Relief, 1601 formalised earlier practices by making provision for a national system to be paid for by levying property taxes. The 1601 Poor Law act made provision through Justices of the Peace: To levy a compulsory poor rate on every parish; to provide working materials for the poor; provide work or apprenticeships for children who were orphaned or whose parents were unemployed and unable to support them; offer relief to the 'Deserving Poor'; collect a poor relief rate from property owners; parents and children were made to be responsible for each other, so poor, elderly parents were expected to live with their children. Overseers collected a regular amount from parishioners according to their ability to pay. Over time this evolved into a more centralised system.

Elizabethan England often conjures images of the splendid royal court with magnificent costumes, banquets, and fantastic entertainment. But for many people, especially the poor, elderly and disabled, life was very different. As the standard of living dropped for most of the population in Tudor England, the problem of vagrancy worsened, and this was to have repercussions for the country. Some vagrants faked disability to get help from the state, but they were in the minority. Historian David Turner, of Swansea University, states, 'It is also a history of distrust, in which the authenticity of symptoms has been consistently questioned.'[62]

Turner goes on to say that, 'The passage of the Elizabethan Poor Law in 1601 gave the state a role in supporting the poor. But from the outset, there was a suspicion that some people were exaggerating or faking their ailments. While undeserving recipients are held up by the press today, they were vilified as "rufflers", "palliards", or "clapperdogeons" in Elizabethan times.'[63]

When the care of disabled people passed to the state, from the first poor laws in 1388 onwards, there was a distinction made between the worthy poor and the unworthy poor. The disabled were the virtuous poor; even though it was always thought that many of them were faking it. The Elizabethan Poor Law was adopted in response to a deterioration in economic circumstances, combined with a decline in traditional forms of charitable assistance.

Poor Law Acts passed during the reign of Elizabeth I played a critical role in the country's welfare. They signalled a vital progression from private charity to a welfare state, where the care and supervision of the poor and disabled were embodied in law and became integral to the management of each town. Another sign of the Poor Law's success was that the disorder and disturbance which had been feared by Parliament failed to materialise, however, problems remained. The laws helped the destitute by guaranteeing a minimum level of subsistence, but those who scraped a living never qualified for help and continued to struggle. And, as the population increased, and the years wore on, the provisions made to care for the poor, disabled and destitute became stretched to the limit. It is, however, a tribute to Elizabethan ingenuity of the lasting success of the two Poor Law Acts, from 1597 and 1601, that endured until well into the Victorian era. A common concern present from Elizabethan England into the twentieth-first century was that any expansion or amelioration of welfare provision would engender dependency of the poor on the state. Besides, as Paul Bagguley and Kirk Mann note, there has always been a tendency to view elements of the poor and disabled as simply 'idle, thieving bastards'.[64] We do not know how many fraudulent beggars there were in Tudor England, but the number today is as low as 3 per cent of benefit claimants. However, we English are renowned for our charitable giving and helping others less fortunate than ourselves. Moreover, these early Renaissance Acts of Parliament brought about much sought-after State help, to those who were worthy of financial and practical assistance and were the fore-runners to the Victorian 1834 Poor Law act, and the much-loved formation of the 'Welfare State', and the National Health Service brought about by legislation, after the Second World War, of Clement Atlee and his Labour cabinet. Without the insight and thinking of successive Tudor monarchs, we might never have had the help that the disabled, and their keepers and carers, so rightly deserve.

Chapter Three

Superstition and Disability

For those living in the early modern era, under the Tudor dynasty, England could be a terrifying and confusing place. For the population to make sense of it, there were certain principles, superstitions, beliefs and values to which people held. For the twenty-first century observer to understand them, it requires a vast stretch of the imagination for our modern minds. Moreover, without grasping these superstitions, it is impossible even to begin to comprehend the mind of the ordinary folk of the period, and to comprehend how disability may have been perceived during this era.

Predominantly, this was a world that believed in the existence of a divinely created order, by a supernatural God. However, superstition was also rife during the Tudor age.[1] At the turn of the fifteenth century, the majority of the English population held a belief in the certainty, and the formidable power, of all things supernatural.[2] A belief in magic and religion permeated every aspect of daily life, from the lowliest peasant to the highest of nobility including the monarch. Superstitious and religious beliefs created order, which was reflected in society by rank, status, sexuality and hierarchy, and days that were governed by Books of Hours, religious ceremony, Masses and religious conviction.

However, although linked, supernatural beliefs and religious beliefs differed because religious belief included God as the divine, a being who could not be manipulated because he was, and is, understood to be omnipotent and omnipresent in all things. Whereas supernatural forces in people's lives and supernatural forces in magic meant these elements could be controlled, manipulated, conjured and changed. People believed in the supernatural, because, like God, they believed such forces affected every aspect of their day to day existence. During the Tudor period, a whole range of beliefs existed encompassing the supernatural, which included witchcraft. A belief in witchcraft had been around for centuries before the Tudors. Witches were understood to be malevolent people who held mysterious powers to heal or harm others, which could include the way they looked at a person, thinking evil thoughts about someone, or speaking curses against a person. Their abilities might be benign, or could carry good luck – through talismans, using herbs, or hiding shoes in chimney breasts. These kinds of practitioners were known as 'cunning' folk.

At the opposite end of the spectrum, there was a belief in learned natural magic, almost akin to a primitive form of early science, where people believed there were forces in the natural world that could be harnessed and manipulated such as the influence of the stars. Astronomers and astrologers, who were usually learned people, conducted their research in Latin or Greek. A whole range of beliefs was not confined to ordinary people but often included the reigning monarch.

People were inspired by literature. The Bible became a life guidance tool for all when it was finally translated from Latin and Greek into English, made accessible by European printing presses, which enlightened the ignorant, luring them away from their old superstitions and folklores. However, old superstitions did not entirely vanish. There was still a fashion for visiting astrologers, who would foretell events by studying the position of the stars, and would sell information to help people with all kinds of human enterprise. An element of the population looked to astrologers, cunning folk, and wise-women for help, and carried on believing in superstitions to encourage and help them in uncertain times.

During this time, Italian astronomer, mathematician, philosopher and rebel, Galileo was arguing for heliocentrism; John Napier invented logarithms; Rene Descartes, the French philosopher, mathematician and writer was birthing his ideas on analytical geometry; John Dee, a British astronomer and philosopher, was predicting the future of monarchs while Francis Bacon, philosopher and statesman, established empiricism.[3] The astrologer John Dee researched the unexplainable. He was an Elizabethan courtier and a mathematician at Cambridge University. Dee was a learned expert who believed he was communicating with angels via mediums like Barnabus Saul and Edward Kelly. Dee interpreted the constellations and astrology was a common belief during the Tudor period. Elizabeth I consulted astrologers such as John Dee during times of crisis. An idea that the stars influence the affairs of humankind had existed since the very earliest of man's conception when people looked up to the sun, moon, and planets and wondered what their movements might signify. It reached a peak in the Elizabethan period and was widely contemplated by all strata of society. As a rich source of symbolism, it has continued to inspire some of the world's most significant works of art and remains a vehicle for self-exploration and understanding. The early modern period was a mixture of declining superstitions, established religious belief and reformation, and growing scientific knowledge.

The Tudors believed in a range of fantastical ideas and superstitions. The definitions of superstition are contradictory, as the term superstition derives from classical antiquity, implying a 'bad' as opposed to 'good' or correct belief or practice in the realm of religion. The definition can refer to a belief or practice resulting from beliefs that were very different from our own, such as a fear of the unknown, trust in chance, or a false conception of causation, or an irrational attitude toward the supernatural, nature, or God resulting from superstition. Today, 'superstition' is a derogatory term when, in fact, the root of the word itself means 'to stand over something in awe'. It does not mean that the 'something' in question is unworthy or of little importance. It would be wonderful to consider that they held disabilities in awe, and the Tudors did, to a certain extent, especially when we consider how disabled people were viewed in the Tudor court in later chapters.

With the invention of the printing press, the Tudor equivalent of the internet, superstitions slowly began to dwindle, as a popularised knowledge enlightened society's ignorance, yet did not entirely alleviate the period from the superstitions of an earlier age. These beliefs continued in an aggravated form, be it belief in a variety of fetishes, love spells, luck-bones, folk-remedies, herbal remedies and evil magic. Despite all these conflicting beliefs and superstitions, religion and faith prevailed, and during the reign of Henry VIII, most of the population in England were Roman Catholic Christians, until the winds of the Reformation began to blow from across the Channel and Tyndale's Bible began to be smuggled from Antwerp, and beyond. There had always been strong religious beliefs held in the teachings of the Latin Bible, which told of biblical characters influenced by God and the Holy Spirit. The supernatural and divine being of God as creator has always been the crux of all Christian belief and was the opposite of the majority of superstitious belief.

53

As the English Reformation took hold, a reformation of belief in magic and the ideas surrounding witchcraft began. Ideas around religious reformation and change sparked by the writings of Martin Luther and William Tyndale were a catalyst for a whole movement of radical and spiritual transformation in England. The Lutheran Reformation began to eclipse the imaginative Catholic superstitions of the Bible and ultimately changed Tudor society. In a virtually secular society, it is almost impossible for us today to appreciate the extent to which at the beginning of the Tudor period, many in the community were God-fearing people who could not understand the Latin of the Catholic priests unless the scriptures were interpreted for them. People's lives were affected by their religious beliefs, but their ideas about magic, and the world of spirits, and superstition continued, and the use of magic or witchcraft was not considered serious before the Reformation. However, after the Reformation, using magic became a crime which was punished by the state. Belief in magic and the ideas around it become narrower and was thought of as satanic, immoral, treasonous and evil. By the end of the sixteenth century, magic was equated with witchcraft.[4] Use of the dark arts was considered a spiritual crime in such a religious age. Being accused of meddling in the dark arts became a nasty accusation which taunted a traitor for life. This medieval legacy of magic was continued into the Tudor period in England when witchcraft became a crime in 1542, a statute renewed in 1562, and ratified in the House of Lords in 1563 – *The Bill for Punishment of Invocations of Evil Spirits, or exercising Inchantment, Witchcraft, or Sorcery.* and listed as an *Act Against Conjurations, Enchantments, and Witchcrafts,* in the parliamentary rolls on 20 March 1563.[5] The association of magic and superstition is a point of continuity into the Tudor period.[6]

What has the belief in magic and superstition to do with disability in the Tudor period? The Tudors continually looked to intellectuals and wise women, healers and herbalists to relieve them from sickness and help them to heal themselves, so midwives were often singled out as practitioners of magic and were often linked with witches in a society that demonised practices which were considered unreligious. Young, single women and widows were easy targets for accusations of being witches because their status in society meant they could not be controlled by men.

If cunning women, healers or magical practitioners could not heal sickness or disability, then a sickness was identified as witchcraft or caused by witchcraft.[7] It was easy to blame someone else for calamities and tragedies that might befall others; men rarely took responsibility for their mistakes, in a world run by men, and would never blame themselves.

Historian Tracy Borman writes in *Witches,* 'In an increasingly unstable and volatile society, people clung ever more tightly to their deeply held superstitions – even those who claimed to have embraced the new religion. The Kingdom of Darkness was as real to them as the Kingdom of Heaven, and ordinary people everywhere believed in devils, imps, fairies, goblins and ghosts, as well as legendary creatures such as vampires, werewolves and unicorns'.[8]

A witch was a person who the late-sixteenth century commentator George Clifford defined as: 'one that woorketh by the Devil, or by some devilish or curious art, either hurting or healing'.[9] William Perkins, a contemporary of George Gifford, agreed with him when he said that, 'A witch is a magician, who either by open or secret league, wittingly and willingly, consenteth to use the aide and assistance of the Devill, in the working of wonders'.[10]

A witch was defined in pamphlets of the time as a hag, who made pacts with the Devil through his persuasion and inspiration so that the witch could bring all manner of evil down on nature, and animals. They could fly, be lustful, lewd and monstrous.[11] Assumptions were therefore made that witches caused all kinds of disability and physical and mental deformities.

Historian Ronald Hutton, suggests in his book, *The Witch* that in studying the history of witches, we must consider the idea that, 'If the term "Witch" will be reserved here for somebody believed to be using magic for harmful purposes, what of the many individuals who have claimed to be able to use magic for the benefit of others, and have been believed by others to have this ability?'[12] In looking at superstitions and witches, we cannot just presume that witches were out to do evil against others, many who were labelled 'witches' considered themselves 'healers' who might have tried to cure a persons' disability, or at least try to improve the person's quality of life through divination, spells, medicine and spiritual healing, much like those today who claim to be new-age healers, or reiki-healers. However, disabled people were usually made scapegoats, and associated with sinners or evil people, who were thought to bring disasters upon society. It was, therefore, a belief that monasteries looked after a disabled persons' spiritual, as well as their physical and emotional needs, to combat such attitudes. If communities lacked the support offered by monasteries to look after the sick, a cunning woman was consulted for her remedial medicines.[13]

In his book, *A Brief History of Discrimination and Disabled People*, Colin Barnes writes that 'the association between disability and evil was not limited to the layman. Protestant reformer Martin Luther proclaimed that he saw the Devil in a profoundly disabled child. If these children lived, Luther recommended killing them. They were the focus of a mixture of emotions which embodied guilt, fear, and contempt.'[14]

Witches were blamed for almost everything unexplainable.

Religion and superstition were woven through society like a silken thread which linked disability and illness through the Roman Catholic ceremonial practice of healing and the laying on of hands – not just any hands, but royal hands, specifically, known as 'the king's touch'. Specific cures prescribed for particular ailments, particularly physical healing and prayer, were considered to be treatments. French and English monarchs laid hands on their subjects and prayed for them regardless of the social classes that divided them, with the intent to cure them of various diseases and conditions. The monarch, having been anointed at their coronation as a divine ruler, reinforced the point that through them God could heal those afflicted with scrofula.

Henry VIII was reportedly the earliest English monarch to preside over 'services for healing the sick'.[15] The royal touch originated in France during the eleventh century, and healing services were practised intermittently until it became a royal prerogative.[16] In England, the origins are less specific, but by the thirteenth century, the ceremony had been assimilated into English royal custom by the Plantagenet kings.

The monarch's touch was most commonly applied to people suffering from tuberculous cervical lymphadenitis (better known as scrofula, or the 'king's evil'), and the practice was exclusive to cures of scrofula in the sixteenth century onwards. It was called the 'king's evil' because kings could heal it, and touching for scrofula was the key aspect of sacral monarchy, whereby the sovereign was anointed and performed this religious duty.[17] The practice of services treating scrofula was started in the eleventh century by Edward the Confessor and ended in England with the death of Queen Anne in 1714. Henry VII revived the practice of the royal touch after which it was performed by all the Tudors, although the evidence for Edward VI is weaker than for the others. Mary I also adopted this ritual of healing scrofula through the 'royal touch'.[18] The numbers touched to heal scrofula by the Tudors are small though when compared to Edward I, Edward II or Edward III, or the Stuarts.

Nevertheless, the Tudors continued the ceremony, which became a permanent part of English royal ritual during the sixteenth century.[19] The ceremony reinforced the idea of the monarch as a divinely appointed agent of God, and the monarch would touch the infected person, hang a gold angel on a ribbon around their neck and say specific prayers. European monarchs of the medieval and early modern periods practised the healing rite to cure their subjects of scrofula – a tuberculosis infection of the lymph nodes. Fortunately, scrofula rarely resulted in death, entering remission of its own accord, giving the impression that the king's touch had cured it. The claimed power of healing was most notably exercised by monarchs who sought to demonstrate the legitimacy of their reign and their newly founded dynasties.[20]

During the early reign of Henry VIII, six shillings and eightpence were the equivalent of a gold coin weighing slightly more than five grams.[21] This coin was called an angel because it bore the image of St Michael, the archangel. The angel became the coin specifically used under the Tudors for giving to those who received the royal touch. The idea was that the transformation of a coin, when giving to those suffering, would turn into something of a prize and used as a lure, to encourage those to come forward to receive the royal touch, when they might not have otherwise. Sufferers who sought the royal touch were seeking to be cured, and many believed that this ritual allowed the gift of miraculous healing.

Like the angel coins, rings were also used and distributed because like relics, they were considered to have miraculous properties and if worn or touched by the monarch, also had the power to heal and guard against epilepsy. Miracles were often linked with religious relics and shrines, which were religious beliefs rather than superstitions. In the end, these cramp rings replaced coins as conduits for healing, although coins worth twenty-five shillings were exchanged for the rings. Usually, the highest-ranking lord would present the plate of rings to the king for him to hand out to those suffering before an offering was made. The royal touch was a central belief of early modern England, a juncture at which politics, medicine, and religion met.

In the late sixteenth century, Protestant monarchs had mixed feelings about a practice so Roman Catholic in nature, but the ceremony was an essential opportunity for royalist propaganda, that helped confirm the legitimacy of a Tudor monarch's rule in the face of opposition, for example after the Pope excommunicated Elizabeth for taking the middle way on religion, and not wishing to 'make windows into men's souls'. When James I ascended the throne, he did not have faith in the superstitious rite and spoke out against it. Eventually, he gave in to pressure from his English counsellors and took up the ceremony of the king's touch. Monarchs attempted to emphasise the role of prayer and personal faith or imagination, rather than magic, within the ceremony, but the nature of the 'miracle', and whether it ever actually occurred was still ambiguous.[22]

Ritual, religious belief and superstition were important to people throughout the Tudor period, but, as time went on, the power of superstition and magic became less critical, until James Stuart, king of Scotland wrote his book on witches, highlighting the use of magic, spells and the crime of accusation and suspicion in everyday life. Popular myths linking the causes of disability with witchcraft have grown since the medieval and Tudor periods, and these myths are ones of barbaric darkness, where people with disabilities have, invariably over time, been demonised.[23] Medieval historian Dr Irina Metzler believes that modern stereotyping of disabled people comes from interpretations of the work of Kramer, *Malleus Maleficarum*, which translates as 'The Hammer of the Witches' and the people to be hammered were *maleficae* or female evil-doers. However, nowhere in Kramer's writing does it mention that the blind, lame or epileptic, or any person with a physical or mental impairment, were accused of being witches. These myths have found recent momentum through various sources on the internet, which link the phenomenon of superstition and witches with disability.[24]

Kramer's work was far from universally accepted in his own time, which is peculiar when you consider that his infamous book was a massive influence in later periods, and Kramer's writings were, and are, still being blamed for the ideological foundations on which the witch-crazes and witch-hunts of the early modern period and James VI rested. Witches and disabled people were used as scapegoats by the rich and powerful, who wanted to persecute and prosecute the innocent because they did not match up to the idea of perfect human beings, often based on the way their beliefs were regarded, how they lived their lives and, importantly, by the way they looked. Throughout all the allegations, persecutions, convictions and executions that took place, the disabled themselves hardly mattered; not as accused perpetrators based on the guidance provided by the *Maleficarum*, nor as victims of other supposed malefactors.

Witches and their craft became an obsession for James VI of Scotland and the accounts of the surviving witches were written in the witchcraft pamphlet 'Newes from Scotland'.[25] James ordered the pamphlet to be printed as part of his attack on witchcraft. It contained a description of three women accused of witchcraft who were tried before the Scottish king. To show how strongly James felt about the 'detestable, slaves of the devil', he wrote a book in the form of a dialogue, called, *Daemonologie* which resulted from James' research, detailing his opinions on witchcraft.[26] *Daemonologie* consists of three sections, one magic, the second on sorcery and witchcraft, and the third on spirits and ghosts; James VI said the purpose of the book was to, 'so farre as I can, to resolve the doubting harts of many, both that such assaultes of Sathan, most certainly practized'. Here, James's opinion, without any question or doubt, is that witches existed in their multitudes in Scotland and that they were Satan's minions, warning readers to take heed and believe his words The books states that witches are real, that they should be prosecuted by the authorities and that anyone who does not believe it, is at best fooling himself and at worst, is in league with the devil. The book was popular and was republished twice. The reader could be in no doubt that James VI was hellbent in taking on the Satanic surge. However, his book *Daemonologie* was not just trying to whip up fear of witch hatred, as the *Malleus Maleficarum* does, rather, he was making a case by rational argument rather than mere superstition. *Daemonologie* sanctioned forms of evidence and torture that institutionalised murder in England.[27]

For common disabled folk, in Tudor times, superstition, magic and witchcraft, was very much involved in creating misconceptions of the disabled, and inevitably why people were considered disabled in the first place. Superstition was the catalyst that helped to create suspicion around the blind, lame or epileptic. *The Hammer of the Witches* or *Malleus Maleficarum* can be blamed for original stereotyping of the disabled that perpetuated the view that disabled people were treated as witches, outcasts, devil's children, or that witches themselves were disabled or inflicted disability on others.

The *Malleus* does discuss the 'falling sickness', now commonly known as epilepsy. Epilepsy is mentioned three or four times in the book, and only in the context that the 'falling sickness' is one of many illnesses that can be caused by sorcery and witchcraft. Witches were believed to cause epilepsy, and epilepsy was not a disorder that witches themselves would have. Epilepsy is discussed by the *Malleus* in Book II, part 1, chapter 11, detailing how magic can inflict illness, but this point is extremely brief. The author of the *Malleus*, Kramer, uses the example of epilepsy to point out that epilepsy, and indeed leprosy, are disabilities and illnesses that are defects of the internal organs, which only commonly arise through long-standing, underlying physical issues. Moreover, Kramer has to concede to the idea being that there were 'natural causes' for disabilities such as epilepsy and leprosy; he reluctantly wrote that malicious manoeuvrings of magic rarely caused such disabilities, however minor.[28]

Stereotypical writings in books such as the *Malleus Maleficarum* declared that deformed, disabled or lame children were the product of the mothers' intercourse with Satan. Therefore, it is not surprising that historical fibs, folklore and stereotypes follow Anne Boleyn, and many consider it fact that she must have been a witch. These allegations were never based in fact but were based on writings of the Catholic propagandist, Nicholas Sander, made years after her death. He surmised she had given birth to deformed stillborns, and she had physical deformities. However, the only reference to Anne Boleyn being associated with witchcraft comes because Spanish Ambassador Chapuys wrote that Henry VIII told one of his courtiers that; 'this King had said to someone in great confidence, and as it were in confession, that he had made this marriage, seduced by witchcraft, and for this reason, he considered it null; and that this was evident because God did not permit them to have any male issue, and that he believed that he might.'[29]

While Anne was never formally accused of witchcraft directly, it is a clear link between Tudor perceptions of witchcraft and the supernatural, and it's connections to disability. Where political aspirations, religious beliefs, superstition and a lack of medical understanding collided, it is not surprising that Anne's inability to give birth to a healthy child and her supposed 'physical deformities' all contributed to this suspicion of witchcraft.[30] Anne Boleyn's predicament is a primary example of how superstition and stories of witchcraft combined with ingrained fears to achieve political agendas by political operatives – a way to manipulate public perception; fear-mongering.[31]

The *Malleus* was all about fear-mongering and explained how witchcraft became misconstrued linking Kramer's superstitions with disabled people, over stretches of time. During the 'Great Witch Hunts' of 1480-1680, the *Malleus* explains how witches were identified by their impairments, by 'evidence' of them creating impairments in others, or by them giving birth to disabled children.

Nowhere in *The Hammer of the Witches* does Kramer mention blind, lame or epileptic people being witches. Witches causing disability or suffering disability is a popularised myth. Witches supposedly being disabled is unsubstantiated for the Tudor period, and these legends around the *Malleus* add to later folklore of both witches, and the disabled. The *Malleus* and Kramer's work was far from accepted, in his own time, and it was not until a later period that this text, in particular, became an infamous influencer of suspicion and superstition surrounding the disabled or those considered disabled.

Along with misconceptions when reading and rereading the *Malleus*, suspicion, superstition and ignorance further castigated the disabled creating stereotypes about them, which to this day are continuously perpetuated. Superstition, magic and witches are heavily associated with both mental and physical disability. In early modern Europe, disability was often associated with superstition, persecution, and religious attitudes as well as rejection, with evil, witches and witchcraft. Illnesses and disabling conditions such as madness, and epilepsy in society, as well as the plague, were linked traditionally to supernatural causes such as God's divine providence and will; fate, the Devil, and witchcraft. This belief eventually began to decline from the late seventeenth century and contemporary links between illness, disability, and divine providence did not arise when veterans of war and the elderly benefited from help from the state. Disabling injuries experienced in military service were the work of other men and not God, and it was accepted that the elderly were more susceptible to disabling conditions.[32]

Illnesses such as epilepsy, and narcolepsy had had previously been assigned supernatural causes until Thomas Willis studied the pathology of the brain in the early to the mid-seventeenth century, and the nature of the nerves, when he developed ideas about the physical origins of these conditions.[33] Over the course of the early-modern period, developments in science, philosophy, and medicine had a significant impact on understandings of disabling illnesses. This was the case concerning mental illness. Philosophies such as Cartesian mind/body dualism challenged previous opinions that mental illness was caused by disturbances in the immortal soul or the mind. Moreover, it gradually became accepted that such illnesses were caused by material and corporeal problems within the body and brain.[34]

Religious and superstitious attitudes towards disability did not help. They were ideologies that were intertwined, yet separated by a divine God at one end of the spectrum and magic at the other, and were inextricably linked because disability and deformity were seen as a punishment for a disabled person's parents being involved with the dark arts. Deformed and disabled children were thought to be deformed by the Devil, an outcome of the disabled person's parents involvement with the black arts or sorcery.

The 1487 *Malleus Maleficarum*, or *The Hammer of the Witches*, declared that these children were the product of their mothers' intercourse with Satan, and reinforced the idea that any form of physical or mental impairment was the result of divine judgement for wrongdoing, an argument which became pervasive throughout the British Isles in this period.[35]

Tudor perceptions of impairment and disability were coloured by a deep-rooted psychological fear of the unknown, the anomalous and the abnormal. Every type of disability from idiocy to insanity, to diabetes and bad breath, were sources of amusement. 'We jest at a man's body that is not well proportioned,' said Thomas Wilson, 'and laugh at his countenance ... if it be not comely by nature.'[36]

Disabilities evoked superstitious beliefs even though disability was just as much a highly visible presence during everyday life in Tudor

England. People could be born with a disability, the same as today, or become disabled from many kinds of diseases or years of backbreaking farming work or physical labour. Attitudes to the disabled in society were mixed, and what was not understood, was often belittled and misunderstood. Myths have built up over time to suggest that anyone born with some sort of physical or mental abnormality or disability meant that disabled people were, to a degree viewed with superstition and treated as witches, outcasts, and devil's children, or their deformed bodies and mental disorders were the product of the child's parents consorting and worshipping the devil. Superstition and suspicion, as well as religion and ignorance probably made the everyday lives of disabled people of every class in Tudor England exceptionally difficult, compounded by misconceptions, and ignorance.

Chapter Four

Religion, Reformation, and Disability

In recent years we have seen and live in an age of religious extremism; an age of terror and violent slaughter – a bewildering ideological battle with religious fundamentalism, a war against terror, which the Tudors similarly, would have experienced due to the break with Rome, with Lutheran and Catholic factions fighting each other; sending faithful, Christian men from both sides to their deaths. We have those same struggles today, with terrorists killing innocent people in the name of faith; for example 'The Troubles' in Northern Ireland before the peace process. Religious fundamentalism has been with us in some form or another across the centuries, and more often than not, takes most of us by surprise, as it seems so contradictory to our own, easy-going and 'get on with it' style and British way of life. But these fundamental ideologies are not new, or strange, and the Tudors would have been very familiar with them.

Following the arrival of Luther's Christianity, the Tudor era witnessed the most sweeping religious changes in England, which affected every aspect of national life and every aspect of one's personal life. The year 2017 marked the 500th anniversary of one of the most significant events in Western civilisation: the birth of an idea that continues to shape the lives of everyone today; the breach within Christianity which tore Europe, England and the Church into two. It was the same kind of apocalyptic violence that we see today with religious terrorists. This Tudor religious epoch whipped up passion, with a political intensity; England's very own jihad – a religious and cultural revolution called the Protestant Reformation.[1]

This early modern revolution eventually transformed an entirely Catholic nation into a predominantly Protestant one. All Tudor governments shared was a desire for national 'uniformity' in matters of religious belief and practice. Before Henry VIII's break with the papacy in the 1530s, the Roman Catholic Church remained all-powerful in England. Only a small, persecuted minority questioned its doctrines. Even the early years of Henry's reign saw traditional religious practices, such as pilgrimages, saints' holidays and religious plays, enthusiastically observed; churches continued to be built and embellished in the Catholic style.[2]

The Protestant Reformation threatened to sweep away the most powerful institution in the Western world, the Catholic Church, and orchestrate its possible destruction, following the pope's refusal to sanction Henry's divorce from his Spanish wife.[3] Henry's desire for an annulment was essential, firstly because Anne Boleyn, whom he was obsessed with, had refused to become his mistress, and refused to marry him until separation from his first wife was concluded; secondly, Henry did not want England to lose its independent status if his daughter Mary married a foreigner. Therefore, Henry was anxious to produce a legitimate son who would be undisputed as the next in line; thirdly, Henry was convinced his marriage to Katharine of Aragon, who had previously been his brother's widow, was sinful because he believed he had broken the laws concerning affinity laid down in Leviticus in the Old Testament. Chapter 20:Verse 21. It was for these main reasons England would be catapulted into religious reform including that by 1532, it was pointed out to Henry that the English monarchy had enjoyed an unlimited authority over the church within its realm for centuries. Reform meant the sweeping away of institutions that symbolised medieval Catholicism – the monasteries, in particular, became the primary focus of the king's initiative to bend the country to his will and to fill the royal coffers.[4] When the Reformation hit England, it led to a hard Brexit, sixteenth century style, when Henry broke with Rome and then declared himself Supreme Head of the Church of England, in 1533.

This split with Rome, and the destruction of the religious monastic ethos of the Catholic Church in England, profoundly affected disabled people, because those who were not supported by their families or communities tended to turn to the Church for support. With this support slowly devolving in England because of the stripping of the altars, and monks being turned out of the Orders, disabled people began to be let down by the Church, excepting those disabled people who were living in religious communities run by stricter orders like the Carthusians. These monasteries had become property-owning corporations – some very rich – with few inhabitants. Rievaulx Abbey, North Yorkshire, for example, had about 650 monks during the medieval and early modern period, but only about twenty by the 1530s. The massive Castle Acre Priory in Norfolk had dwindled to just ten. The suppression of the monasteries was accepted mainly in the south, primarily by those who acquired monastic lands. But in parts of the north, it provoked the 1536-7 Pilgrimage of Grace, the most significant peacetime revolt in English history.[5]

Henry may have rejected papal authority, but he remained doctrinally a Catholic and burned Protestant 'heretics'. Real religious change only began to speed up under his radically minded son, the Protestant Edward VI, before being reversed when Henry's eldest daughter, the Catholic-minded Mary I, tried to restore the old order, burning nearly 300 Protestants in the process.[6] The rapid changes for ordinary worshippers, disabled people looking for divine healings, and the poor, were bewildering, as shrines, images of saints and other trappings were destroyed, removed or whitewashed over. However, once Mary I ascended the throne, these images were renewed and colour restored by royal command, only eventually to be removed once more when the Protestant Elizabeth I succeeded in 1558.[7]

The Reformation resulted in striking changes to religious practice and in time, belief. The Bible became accessible to all literate people through English translations. Instead of being simply spectators at Latin Masses, congregations became participants in English-speaking services that focused on sermon-preaching, and these Bible readings were revolutionary in their set forms of prayer. The year 1549 saw prayer normalised in the hugely influential *Book of Common Prayer*.[8]

The Church of England effectively became the product of the religious compromises promoted by Elizabeth I, but how far this changed the outcomes of disabled peoples' lives is impossible to measure. The red-headed queen declared that 'I would not open windows into men's souls.'[9] All that concerned 'Good Queen Bess' was that her subjects remained loyal and as long as their beliefs were kept private, she would not, in theory, challenge them. Elizabeth's church was nevertheless Protestant and crises of national security after the execution of Mary Queen of Scots meant the persecution of Catholics, particularly after the arrival of the Armada in 1588, was inevitable. Catholics who had been free to worship in private were hunted out, fined, imprisoned or executed. Priest-holes were built in many Catholic homes to provide hiding places. Elizabeth's religious settlement did not go far enough to 'purify' the old Catholic practices.

Following rituals and religion was the lifeblood of Tudor England; a pulse in the events of daily life, and these rituals would have been essential for those disabled people with learning disabilities who might cling to routines and regulations. Despite the Roman Catholic Church being uprooted in England in the mid-sixteenth century and being replaced by the Church of England, for many, especially the poor, unless a disabled person was denied community or charitable support, life carried on in much the same way as before. Sinners clung to the idea of Christ being the prime physician, an ideology that had been widespread in the Middle Ages and that continued through the Tudor era, despite institutional changes. Monks believed that to heal a disabled person, this meant curing the soul, first, and then secondarily, the body. Their ideology was perceived as an essential aspect of medical care. For disabled women, and Catholics in general, the Virgin Mary seems to have had associations with medicine that went beyond her more recognised associations with intercessory healing and with childbirth.[10]

The sick, the disabled and other disadvantaged groups, such as the elderly and the poor, sought supplication from the Church, especially when they were rejected by their families in the Tudor period. Despite disenfranchising the poor, sick and disabled from religious ceremonies, Christianity, in keeping with the other major western religions, always acknowledged responsibility for disabled people. Individuals with severe impairments were often admitted to one of the tiny hospitals where the sick, disabled and bedridden poor were cared for. However, the ethos of these hospitals was ecclesiastical rather than medical; they were dedicated to 'care' rather than 'cure' demanded by law. The Church responded to disability and disabled people with an odd mixture of doctrinal problematics and exclusion, practical kindliness, and rather grim-faced care, the balance often being tipped heavily like a see-saw, towards one side or the other. The extent to whether help was felt positively or negatively by those on the receiving end of this Christian charity and involvement is very hard to determine.[11]

The Christian church inherited the Jewish scriptures, which provided some basis for both exclusion and inclusion of the disabled. For example, Levitical prescription says that the priest, in the public role of representing the people before the Almighty, should not have any visible blemishes; yet, the same man was entitled to benefits as a member of the priestly hierarchy, regardless of any disability.[12]

The Western Church inherited and absorbed the accounts of Jesus healing chronically sick or disabled people, sometimes by command, sometimes by touch. Jesus sometimes commanded the sickness to go when at a distance, and sometimes he prescribed treatment instantaneously, or through stages, often 'out of compassion'. He retold these miracles as part of theological discourse, with apparent ease, and sometimes with difficulty in the face of disbelief. Jesus' experiences of ministering to the disabled and mentally ill often linked miracles of healing with the exorcism of demons, by tapping into the faith of the recipients of such healings. These examples in scripture meant that there were a range and variety of reports, that was enough to indicate that almost anything could be demonstrated from them, and almost anything could be reasoned into or out of those healings.

However bold these stories were during biblical times, the practice of prayer and requests for healing, and a 'laying on of hands' has continued throughout Christian belief and history; this practice continues with many evangelists today, who have witnessed God's miraculous healings of the disabled in their congregations and parishes.

However, a person's physical appearance could cause him or her to be rejected because a physical disability was thought to be reflective of one's character; they were looked at as objects to be treated and improved upon, rather than as human beings who could still be independent and learn to handle their disability.[13]

Traditions and beliefs have come and gone, some have stayed within the church, but the major upheaval of the Protestant Reformation was caused primarily by one man, Martin Luther, who sparked a revolution that would reform the Catholic Church.[14]

Luther despised the Catholic practice of buying indulgences; a way for people to buy their way out of purgatory and receive a place in heaven. Indulgences were sold to finance church schemes, such as rebuilding St Peters in Rome. The Catholic Church appeared to have forgotten Christ and had become fixated on accumulating wealth. But nowhere in the

Bible does it discuss the ability to buy your way into heaven as a genuine possibility. To Luther, this was an abomination and on 31 October 1517, he publicly denounced the buying of indulgences by marching through the town of Wittenberg, Germany, to the great doors of All Saints' church and hammered up a document so everyone could read it; his ninety-five theses were points of contention of the church's teachings on sin and penance. Martin Luther, the revolutionary, who like a political student activist, pinned his agenda, written in Latin, to a university notice board. This protest would plunge Europe into a magnitude of two centuries of religious war, which would unleash bloodshed and brutality across the Continent, all in the name of God.

In 1517, Luther was an unlikely revolutionary, a thirty-three year old monk and professor of biblical theology at the University of Wittenberg in a small German-speaking state called Saxony. Saxony was just one piece of a jigsaw, a small state which helped to make up the country of Germany. Each state had its ruler, all of whom were overseen by an elected monarch called the Holy Roman Emperor who, in turn, was crowned by the Pope. All were subject to taxation and papal authority. Luther wanted to stir up debate on reformation of the practice of indulgences, faith and grace, and to do this, he employed the early modern equivalent of the internet, the printing press – Guttenberg had developed his printing press in the late-fifteenth century, which would turn Martin Luther into Europe's most published author. This piece of technology metamorphosized Luther from a lowly monk into a wanted man, because when he wrote his academic thesis, he showed himself as fearless. Luther had commented that the printing press was the gift of God for the spreading of his teachings and that the nature of print itself posed serious threats to the 'establishment'. Luther was aware of those outside university audiences and he condensed his ideas by writing a German tract of twenty points on indulgences and grace. It was printed and distributed throughout Germany, and the tract could be read aloud in ten minutes. It was reprinted throughout Germany in 1518 and sold several hundred thousand copies. Luther spread his ideas, in print, not in Latin but in his own language. Those who received copies of the books and pamphlets were capable of reading them in their native tongue, and once they had read them, they passed them on to their family and friends.

His tracts on indulgences would evolve into the fundamental doctrine of raising the power of personal faith above the remedies offered by the hierarchy of the Catholic Church. He believed that humans could only be saved by faith and not through prayer, fasting or indulgences, and looking to faith in Christ, as told in the New Testament. He believed that Rome was an obstacle to such faith. A Papal Bull *Exurge Domine* by Leo X was issued on the 15 June 1520 against Luther, when state control or regulation of printed content commenced, which condemned the writings of Luther and ordered their confiscation and burning. Martin Luther had to either recant or be excommunicated; he was given sixty days to make his decision. His response was to produce a manifesto to reform the German Church – a form of German nationalism. On 10 December 1520, he burnt the papal bull and in January 1521, he was excommunicated by the pope in Rome. Everywhere Luther went, he was hailed as a figurehead for taking on the power of the church in favour of an anti-establishment movement against taxation and foreign interference in Germany, yet Luther was ordered by Charles V to renounce his heretical writings.[15]

An English scholar, lawyer and theologian, Cuthbert Tunstall, was the first Englishman to understand Luther as a threat to the Catholic Church. Tunstall in his dispatches of 29 January 1521 warned Cardinal Wolsey to never allow Luther's writings into England. Tunstall saw Luther as a mortal enemy of the Church and offered suggestions for what had to be done to stop the reformist ideals of Luther spreading to England. He recommended that Wolsey, 'must', he said, 'call before him, the printers and booksellers and give them a straight charge that they bring none of Luther's books into England, nor that they translate none of them into English, lest thereby might ensue great trouble to the realm.'[16]

Wolsey was galvanised into actioned and ordered a ceremonial burning of Luther's books. On 12 May 1521 at St Paul's Cross, Wolsey and the Bishop of Rochester presided over the event and this was to be one of many book burnings across Europe after the Pope had condemned Luther. However, Lutheran books continued to flood surreptitiously into England and at one point, the Bishop of Rochester, John Fisher, gave a two-hour sermon declaring Luther a heretic, as books were burned before him and Wolsey, who branded Lutheran books in his hands, waving them around, condemning the writings before a vast crowd. And again, on 12 October 1524 London booksellers were summoned by Bishop Tunstall of London and warned against: 'importing into England books printed in Germany or any other books whatever containing

Lutheran heresies, or selling or parting with any such books already imported under pain of the law; and further he warned them that should they import new books into England or buy books already imported, provided that these were newly composed and made, they were not to sell or part with them unless they first showed them either to the Lord Cardinal, the Archbishop of Canterbury, the Bishop of London or the Bishop of Rochester'.[17]

It is against this backdrop that religious doctrine was dictated. In the early sixteenth century, religion shaped every aspect of human life. In Rome, the Pope ruled a spiritual world bigger than the Caesars. The Catholic Church was a wealthy, bureaucratic machine at the very heart of Europe. It controlled education, media, family-law and had a private language, Latin.

The clergy, whatever their nationality, swore allegiance to the pope, whose toe, even kings dropped to the ground to kiss. The Catholic Church's greatest power was over men's minds. Church buildings themselves were dominated by huge paintings of the Last Judgement, when Jesus as judge, sentenced each soul to the joys of heaven or the eternal torments of hell. These paintings were terrifying visions. The Church mitigated its stark horror by the doctrine of purgatory; this was an intermediate state between heaven and hell where people considered not too sinful were purged of their soul's offences, which would make people feel that when they were dead, they had been made fit to enter paradise. You could reduce the amount of time you could spend in purgatory by doing good works; saying prayers; going on pilgrimages and giving to the poor, or you could draw on the good works of Jesus, the Saints, and the Virgin Mary, whose transcendent goodness had endowed the church with the treasury of merit. The pope dispensed in return, for consideration, of course, this treasury in the form of spiritual I.O.U's, known as indulgences. These were printed bits of paper that, in return for cold, hard cash, absolved the soul of its offences, and acted as its passport to paradise. However, any disability was viewed by some as the afflicted already suffering purgatory on earth but this possibly never made disabled people exempt from paying a penance, or not having to place their coin on the offerings plate for indulgences.

The Catholics dictated who got into heaven by the amount of gold that passed into the preacher's palm. This ideology of indulgences was paramount, regardless of a member of the congregation being disabled, or not. Up until the mid-sixteenth century, Catholic doctrine was the spiritual backbone of Britain, and this doctrine and the Protestant Reformation, that began to change spiritual and religious thinking about disability, was bound to affect ordinary disabled people in their lives in Tudor society.

Superstition and scripture influenced the doctrine of the association between disability and evil, which was not limited to the layman.[18] It was the ecclesiastical interest in 'monsters' and their alleged origin or association with witchcraft and demonic activity that linked these ideas to disabled people. In some aspects of religious doctrine, disabled people were treated as second-class human beings who were unfinished and deformed. The clergy pushed these ideas, reasoned with these attitudes and make them acceptable because they thought that deformity and disability of any kind were either due to past sins or a cheat of nature. Invisible, and mental disabilities must have made individuals aware of their limitations. Social attitudes towards many disabled people in this era must have been tormenting.[19]

Luther may have created a Protestant revolution, but general attitudes towards disabled people did not appear to change that much. Moreover, he initially spread doom and gloom with his depressing ideas about the disabled in Germany, as he was probably influenced by the writings of Henricus Kramer and his book, the *Malleus Maleficarum*, which we have already learned, claimed that witches should be pursued and eradicated, starting in Northern Germany, because Henricus had written that he believed these cunning women worked in the service of the Devil.

Even though Martin Luther was just a child when the *Malleus* was published, as we have seen, eventually, he would become an influential mouthpiece for changes in Christian doctrine throughout the Western world.

As we have discovered, the *Malleus* sets out various doubts as to whether anyone was obliged to believe in witches or warlocks, or in their power to effect real harm. In more modern times, the denunciatory thrust of the *Malleus* has often been taken as representative of sixteenth century thought; yet its pattern of question and answer, or proposition and attempted refutation, suggests as discussed in the chapter on superstitions, that there were a good many questions and doubts about the attitudes towards disabled people, in the minds of the educated public in early-sixteenth century Germany.

Martin Luther's views on disabilities of all kinds have been widely misunderstood, from a few items in a dubious edition of shorthand notes of conversations. His arguments, both written and spoken, from 1517 to 1546, are concerned with childbirth and infancy, devils, superstitions, changelings, prodigies, folly, disablement, deafness, participation in Christian sacraments, and exegesis of Biblical texts on disabled people. They give a more reliable and interesting guide to his views, in the context of Luther's involvement with sickness, disability and practical care. Historically, European social and religious developments contained a broader range of views on disability than is commonly supposed, with some challenges for twenty-first century thought and practice.

To begin with, it appears from historians' writings that Luther aligned himself with the writings of the *Malleus* and there is evidence to suggest that he proclaimed that he saw the Devil in a profoundly disabled child. If these children lived, despite their abnormalities, Luther had initially recommended killing them. During the sixteenth century, Christians such as Luther and John Calvin indicated that the mentally retarded and other disabled people with disabilities were possessed by evil spirits. Thus, theologians and other religious leaders of the time often subjected people with disabilities to mental and physical pain, or both, as a means of exorcising the spirits. This was the early modern era's equivalent to the experiments that doctors like Joseph Mengele in Nazi Germany would carry out on the mentally and physically disabled. As Coleridge, a scholar on disabilities, states, 'Hitler was not the first to advocate getting rid of disabled people: in medieval Germany, Martin Luther strongly endorsed the killing of disabled babies as "incarnations of the devil".'[20]

Children who appeared to learn very little, and very slowly from infancy, and whose behaviour was far behind the informal norms for their age, were seriously unacceptable to their families or villages they came from – so much so that they were often vilified, as their physical and intellectual disabilities puzzled early modern Tudors as well as their contemporaries in Europe. Ignorance sadly breeds contempt. Such derogatory reports on Luther's ideology relating to the disabled, and what Martin Luther himself wrote and said about disablement, especially in children with severe congenital impairments, has widely been assumed to be obnoxious, insensitive and terse. However, Martin Luther's views on disability have been widely misunderstood based on a few conversations with Luther on the subject. Importantly, Luther's varying views on disability were likely amassed from his involvement with sickness, disability and taking practical care of disabled people around him. His written and spoken arguments span thirty years of his religious life and his interpretations were concerned with the sacraments, and of Biblical texts on disabled people.

The reasoning behind Luther's arguments was that congenital foolishness in children was viewed as a result of 'original sin'. When he became a father, he was more concerned with the spiritual side of a child's life and believed that babies born healthy or with a disability, should be baptized, regardless. Talking of the baptism of the deaf, he said: 'They deserve the same things that we do. Therefore, if they are rational and can show by indubitable signs that they desire it in true Christian devotion, as I have often seen, we should leave to the Holy Spirit what is his work and not refuse him what he demands.'

The identity is known of one deaf person at Eisenach, the daughter of Christian Cotta, who personally influenced Luther, as he is known to have maintained cordial relations with the Cotta family of Eisenach, long after the death of the deaf girl called, Ursula Schalbe Cotta, in 1511. The family had made Luther welcome in the Cotta home when he was a schoolchild and, thus, from this very personal experience, Luther believed that it was only fair, proper and righteous to admit deaf people to communion.[21] He was said to comment that, 'It may be that inwardly they [deaf people] have a better understanding and faith than we, and this no one should maliciously oppose.' When drawing attention to Luther's remarks about deaf people's faith, Rudolf Mau, the German theologian concludes that 'the idea that a person, because of a disability, regardless of what kind, would be denied his God-given human worth has no place in the thought of Luther'.[22]

Besides communion and baptism, Luther believed that disabled people should be allowed to follow other religious sacraments, such as marriage, which from the early days of the Reformation he believed should be open to disabled people. Luther slowly begins to sound like a disability advocate as his religious career progresses, when he endorses such practices.

Luther had practical, everyday contact with disabled people. He suffered from disabling ailments, such as ear infections, tinnitus, giddiness, headaches, kidney stones and bowel disorders, which periodically rendered him incapable of work and sometimes reduced his extraordinary work rate.[23] Sources exist detailing Luther's long-term, close relationship with a mildly disabled man, his personal assistant named Wolfgang Seberger, who joined Luther's household in 1519 and continued there after Luther's death in 1546.[24] One writer and editor of Luther's life and his work suggested that Wolf was 'weak-minded' and 'half-witted'.[25] Another thought Wolf was 'perhaps even lame'.[26] Luther seemed to tolerate his disabled assistant and because of Wolf's weaknesses, viewed his faithful assistant as a 'family dependent' as much as a 'living-in assistant'.[27] In April 1535 he wrote to pastor Augustin Himmel at Colditz expressing his pleasure that an official allowance to Wolf had been increased, and suggesting that 'I should like a little house to be bought for my good Wolf, into which he might retire after my death, as he has a weak arm, and needs a roof of his own, so that he may not have to seek refuge in an institution, poor and forsaken.'[28] Wolf must have had some acumen to be included in Luther's household, and despite Wolf's weak arm, must have been of some service to his master. It seems that Luther exercised his Christian duty and charitable love by supporting Seberger in his household.

Historically, European social and religious developments contained a broader range of views on disability than is commonly supposed, with the likes of Thomas More taking in Henry Patenson and treating him like a member of the family and Martin Luther taking in the likes of Wolf Seberger. This thought and practice was new and challenging in the Tudor period and considered even more shocking as disabled people were the focus of a mixture of emotions which embodied guilt, fear and contempt. The teachings of the *Malleus* spread this idea of guilt, fear and contempt by having specifically pertinent references to witches and impairments in children. For example, in the *Malleus* Part I, Qn.1, a Canon 'clearly says that creatures can be made by witches, although they necessarily must be very imperfect creatures, and probably in some way deformed'.[29]

Then in the *Malleus*, there is an opposite argument in Part I, Qn 18 that discusses whether or not afflictions necessarily come through witchcraft: 'submit that they are similar to natural infirmities and defects and may therefore be caused by a natural defect. For it may happen through some natural defect that a man becomes lame, or blind, or loses his reason, or even dies; wherefore such things cannot confidently be ascribed to witches'.[30]

However, this argument is duly dismissed as in Part II, Qn.1, Ch.11 doubt is again raised: 'although greater difficulty may be felt in believing that witches can cause leprosy or epilepsy since these diseases generally arise from some long-standing physical predisposition or defect, none the less it has sometimes been found that even these have been caused by witchcraft'.[31]

Several pages of examples are given in the *Malleus* to bolster the hypothesis that witchcraft caused disease or disability, and several pages also refute the theory. Ideas around this were amplified by the fact that the Devil was 'a frequent figure in everyday speech, in slogans, curses, epithets, and aphorisms'.[32]

Such familiarity does not necessarily translate that there was a strong belief in the Devil's actual power and immediacy; indeed, the reverse might be argued. Religious teachers of the early-modern era could not reconcile scripture to the likes of the *Malleus*, as these medieval beliefs were on the opposing ends of a theological spectrum. Luther's ideas towards the disabled were forward-thinking and challenging and fought against the ideologies of the Middle Ages where disabled people were looked upon with superstition, rejected and persecuted.[33]

Martin Luther was both influenced by and had some influence upon, the teaching of the Bible and the *Malleus* regarding disabled people. Midelfort points out that when dealing with people in the flesh, Luther could be more moderate in his attitude.[34]

In early-modern Europe, the fields of law, medicine, and theology were particularly rich for studying folly in general, with focus on the natural fool and the mentally disabled person taking place.[35] The theologian Thomas Aquinas provided material for a substantial catalogue of fools and their characteristic activities, such as: 'Cataplex, credulous, fatuus, grossus, idiota, imbecillus, insensatus, insipiens, rusticus, stolidus, stultus, stupidus, tardus, turpis, vacuus, and vecors,' or otherwise confused, idiotic or reckless.[36] St Augustine, a fourth-century theologian whose works greatly influenced writers and thinkers in the Middle Ages, allowed congenitally disabled infants, including the 'born fool', a brief appearance in a gloomy argument for original sin: 'Indeed, if nothing deserving punishment passes from parents to infants, who could bear to see the image of God, which is, you say, adorned with the gift of innocence, sometimes born feeble-minded since this touches the soul itself ?'[37] Parents of disabled children were inevitably smeared by the association and believed that whatever folly preachers denounced in society, was a result of their sin. Augustine confirmed that feeble-mindedness was an evil to be long lamented, quoting Ecclesiasticus 22. In a different debate, however, he cited that a simpleton who revered Christ could bear no insult to the holy name, though indifferent to injuries to himself. In this particular example, Augustine refutes believers in reincarnation who thought all feeble-minded persons had been especially sinful in previous lives.[38] With these spiritual and religious ideas about disability in play during the early modern era, is it any wonder that disabled people were maligned and made fun of? [39]

From the opposite extreme of the intellectual spectrum, the sixteenth century Dutch Humanist Erasmus could perhaps afford to be more relaxed and forgiving about folly as is shown in his work of 1509, *Encomium Moriae*, or *In Praise of Folly*.

Brant, a late-fifteenth-century commentator and scholar, had a slightly different view to Erasmus and assumed that man's folly was ridiculous and sinful. While Erasmus believed that feeble-mindedness and folly were absolved only through divine grace, he also took man's situation with gaiety and assumed that he has sufficient vitality himself to digest all his experience eventually into some usable form. Therefore, Erasmus believed that however simple a natural fool's view of life, he could always be blessed and enjoy and appreciate life.

Tudor attitudes and making fun of fools did begin to change with the writings of Erasmus. In *In Praise of Folly* he points out that Paul said, 'all men were fools before God, and the foolishness of God was wiser than men's wisdom', 1 Corinthians 1:25. Fools could be considered holy, possessors of essential goodness and simplicity that meant they were incapable of sin and conduits of the divine. Their folly was wiser than wisdom. So, fools were holy, and possessors of essential goodness and simplicity which meant they were incapable of sin and therefore conduits of the divine, who gave great pleasure to God.[40]

Studies on fools of the Tudor court have shown that, in England, the disabled, too, were often honoured, for their purity of spirit, and because they were seen to be suffering purgatory on earth through their physical or mental disability.

There were those in the Roman Catholic and later, English church who supported disabled people, and provision and support for people with disabilities came not from the state, but religious institutions. During this period, a nationwide network of monasteries used as hospitals had begun to emerge. These hospitals were usually based in or near villages with monasteries, nunneries and other religious establishments. These hospitals were formed from the idea of Christian duty, which was to give shelter to pilgrims and strangers.These religious institutions evolved slowly into the hospitals caring for the sick and infirm, which would become the basis of hospitals we recognise from a modern perspective.

The type of people needing help from the monasteries would be people suffering from leprosy, blindness, deafness and those unable to speak, or people who were considered natural fools – anyone with a learning difficulty. Others requiring help would be those who were crippled, lame and those considered a lunatic and suffering from acute mental health issues. Individuals with disabilities were placed in the care of family members and would not be on their own. The majority of the time, if they could be, disabled people were not cared for in monasteries or society if their care could be maintained from within their own families.

A compassionate attitude began to grow from within the communities of disabled people as religious teachings began to change and develop with the Reformation. Lutheran religious teaching began creating a more compassionate argument for disabled people which eventually filtered through to all levels of Tudor society. These ideas, based on scripture, upheld the view that many in religious houses wanted to support those with both physical and mental disabilities, thus giving the impression that in some, but not all cases, religion in the Tudor age was the backbone of spiritual, and at times, medical support to those with physical and learning disabilities. During the Tudor age, the changing religious landscape – and the politics that ran alongside that – affected the very real, day to day lives of disabled people, and how they were treated and cared for.

Chapter Five

Almshouses and Hospitals

Almshouses and hospitals in Tudor times were very different from what we know today. Illnesses and diseases were rife in the sixteenth century and were caused by a lack of understanding of the importance of hygiene, as well as the filthy living conditions endured by most the population. As all the houses in Tudor times were built very close together, it was typical for illnesses and diseases to spread quickly.[1]

Physicians failed to recognise that many Tudor diseases were spread by the lice, fleas and rats which infested the streets, houses and people. Doctors were also unaware of the dangers presented by the open sewers which ran through the streets of London, or of the pollution and disease caused by the dumping of rubbish in the streets, rivers and waterways. Doctors and physicians had no idea about germs and how they spread, so Tudor medicine was basic in the extreme, and not equipped to deal with the diseases of the time, the simplest of which could result in the death of the patient.

Hospitals did exist, but as a form of welfare, paid for by wealthy benefactors in return for prayers assiduously made by inmates, for the salvation of their benefactors' souls and some poor patients would forfeit meals if they failed in their daily devotions.[2]

By definition, alms were charitable donations of food, clothing or money made to the poor or those considered unable to look after themselves. They were usually offerings of money received from a congregation during a religious service and presented at the altar by the minister and donated to these hospitals, hence the name 'almshouse'. In essence, an almshouse was a privately financed home for the poor.[3]

Almshouses were homes built from the medieval period onwards primarily to shelter elderly, disabled or other people considered unable to look after themselves, and in Tudor times almshouses became the answer – along with the implementation of the Poor Laws, to establish a kind of Tudor welfare system. Lazar House was a medieval term for specialist institutions housing lepers, derived from the name of the Biblical character Lazarus.[4] They were also known as a *Maison Dieu* – literally 'Godly house', an alternative term for an alms-house.[5]

Bedlam and Bethlem were famous names used by the public for the Royal Bethlehem Hospital in London, the first English institution for people with mental illness.[6] Bridewell, also in London, was originally a type of hospital, first established in the sixteenth century for the improvement of the 'idle poor'. Eventually, it became a house of correction for beggars and petty criminals. In London, there was also Christ's Hospital for children, Bridewell for vagrants, and the two hospitals for the sick, St. Thomas' and St. Bartholomew's. A minimum of 1,300 hospitals and almshouses were founded in England between the very late-eleventh century and the 1530s and dominated the approaches to most villages, towns and cities, although now almost all have entirely disappeared from the landscape.[7]

St Leonard's in York is a lasting monument to the importance of almshouses and hospitals, which ran from 1137-1539. There are many examples of almshouses throughout England. One example is Jesus Hospital, Rothwell, Hospital Hill, Northamptonshire. It is a fantastic example of a Tudor almshouse, which has now become old peoples' flats. The original building was built in 1593 for Owen Ragsdale, with late-eighteenth-century and late-nineteenth-century additions. Jesus Hospital was initially established as almshouses for twenty-six men.[8]

The destruction and loss of so much evidence of early Tudor almshouses, both documentary and architectural, largely due to the devastation caused during the English Reformation, means that the use of these almshouses is widely misunderstood. Professor Carol Rawcliffe suggests that 'medieval hospitals were primarily religious institutions, whose form and function was very different from what we today might expect in the way of institutional care'.[9] Therefore, our modern mind dismisses almshouses and their use as being 'backward' or 'superstitious'. Patrons were not guaranteed professional care either considering that hospitals did not employ the services of trained physicians, surgeons and apothecaries.

Rawcliffe states that it was not until after Henry VII's death that the recruitment of professionally qualified practitioners was introduced.[10] As hospitals were founded for the care of the sick poor, rather than the rich, who would have been treated in their own home, only the wealthy could afford the services of university-trained physicians and surgeons; and, although successful practitioners were expected to undertake charity work, few members of society would ever have consulted a physician. The poorer in society would have relied upon a combination of domestic medicine, provided by female relatives, and recourse to a range of herbalists and local healers, many of whom were also women.[11]

English hospitals were segregated according to patients' needs. Many inmates of almshouses suffered from leprosy and the earliest endowments were leper hospitals, which accounted for approximately a quarter of all foundations, and almshouses. As well as the foundation of hospitals and *leprosaria*, the gifting of pious bequests to these houses was a popular form of charity, which features regularly in wills into the sixteenth century, when the general populace feared that infections were on the increase. In the National Archives, a primary source shows how people supported hospitals for lepers. Joan Frowyk, included bequests in her will to each of the London *leprosaria,* which included St Giles by Holborn, and the Loke in Southwark, alongside houses in Hammersmith and Knightsbridge, for lepers to pray for Joan's soul.[12]

These types of hospitals and institutions were on the immediate outskirts of a town or city and it was never intended to segregate lepers to remote hospitals, far from human habitation. Some were mixed establishments, which contained a combination of leprous and elderly inmates who needed care.[13] However, strict rules were sometimes imposed on *leprosaria*, in a similar style to monastic foundation hospitals and almshouses, which ensured a contemplative life among its patients. Residents remaining chaste in a leper hospital was a primary concern to those who ran them, and to combat such problems, some *leprosaria* had different accommodation established for men and women, while other leper houses might require vigilance amongst its staff and the other residents; there were strict punishments for those who disobeyed the rules, like being expelled from the hospital.[14] Places were avidly sought in almshouses, hospitals and *leprosaria*.

As leprosy was such a debilitating disease, the emphasis was on the provision of long-term support for people who were chronically sick, who might initially be mobile enough to undertake light gardening, animal husbandry or horticultural work, but who would eventually need intensive nursing as their condition deteriorated. As was also the case in almshouses for the elderly, gardens and outdoor activity offered a valuable kind of therapy, while also providing a regular supply of fruit, vegetables and medicinal herbs.[15]

Care was needed across all levels of society, so that not just the elderly, but the disabled and pregnant women were provided with sheltered accommodation and basic nursing in almshouses.[16]

There were 'open wards' or 'common hospitals' much like a general hospital, whose patients suffered from acute diseases or who were in the throngs of death and so meant their stay would only need to be accommodated for a short period of time. Other inmates were malnourished and exhausted and simply needed nourishment, a warm bed and some home-from-home comfort, while others were transient paupers, vagrants or pilgrims in search of welcoming overnight accommodation. Women, especially pregnant ones, were housed separately from the men. In this way, they were provided separate facilities away from the main infirmary, and in cases of death in childbirth, their orphaned babies were taken in and cared for.[17]

The onset of regular outbreaks of plague and, specifically the Black Death, which gripped the country from the fourteenth century onwards, had a dramatic impact on standards of living. Although after the plague, life expectancy increased – with a smaller population, food and housing were plentiful and there was much more to go around. Nevertheless, the plague took its toll on the younger generations who otherwise would have looked after their elders. As such, there were many foundations which required a government response to the problem of people living to an older age. The Tudor equivalent of a retirement home became this response.

Certainly, care was made accessible to more than just pregnant women as along religious pilgrimage roads across the country, hospitals were founded on the edge of English towns and cities. The 150 almshouses around England reflected the towns and cities they were built to serve. There were larger houses, situated on the outskirts of towns and cities, which accommodated 100 beds and they differed in sizes like the great houses of York and London, compared to mid-range provincial hospitals with thirty beds such as St Giles's, Norwich.[18]

Establishments and hospitals such as St James, Horning, in the middle of the Norfolk Broads, on the roads between the healing shrines at Bury St Edmunds and Walsingham, were smaller.

Great lords and merchants were often responsible for some of around 700 almshouses that sprang up all over England. They were grand, prodigious foundations, built by lords like Richard Whittington, while other almshouses were tiny and housed only a couple of people. Most medieval towns and renaissance cities featured these almshouses, which became a ubiquitous feature of the period.

For example, in 1534, the Mayor and Corporation of Bristol granted a presentation to the hospital of St. John the Baptist in Redcliffe Pitt, at the request of Queen Anne Boleyn, to Sir Edward Beynton and Dr Nicholas Shaxton, of the queen's household, and David Hutton, a grocer of Bristol. Their nominee was Richard Bromefield who surrendered the hospital in March 1544. So, hospitals like the Hospital of St. John the Baptist, in Redcliffe were patronised at the request of a queen. It is encouraging to find such primary sources, which shows a woman and queen, much maligned by history, was so prevalent at assisting others less fortunate than herself.[19]

King Henry VIII and Queen Anne Boleyn were patrons of the arts and learning and were interested in humanism, so it is not surprising that ideas on human physiology had been adopted during this period from the Greeks, like Galen and Aristotle, and concepts like female and male humours that were so prevalent in the Middle Ages. However, these ideas were augmented to distinguish them from Christian theology and agenda. Like Christ, who did not shun, but healed the lepers, renaissance doctors and healers chose to care for those with leprosy, and 'common' hospitals and almshouses were used for such a purpose, but the quality of care and the facilities in these almshouses and hospitals varied immensely from area to area. As was paramount in Christian belief, the body and soul were inextricably linked. Moreover, all but the poorest institutions and hospitals adopted this holistic approach.[20]

Leper houses, hospitals and institutions, for instance, aimed to provide food that was nourishing and appropriate for the sick. Often, medical and health problems during the period stemmed from physical exhaustion and malnutrition.[21] Hospitals and almshouses tried to be self-sufficient, like the monasteries. Hospitals were beacons of compassion as cooked food would often be distributed at the gates to poor people in the vicinity. The founder would also show compassion by allowing the poor and disabled to eat their meals by the fire, when the English winters were harsh.[22] The residents drank home-brewed ale and ate fresh bread, cheese and eggs produced on the premises and hospitals' pigs provided bacon for soup, or savoury porridge, known as potage that was a crucial part of the lower classes' diet, which was supplemented by a small inclusion of seafood from time to time. Medieval and renaissance diets varied between the classes as the nobility and royalty believed that eating meats was healthier than the poor, whose diet was centred upon consuming vegetables. Fruit was grown in local orchards in the precinct, milk from the cows in the meadows and herbs and vegetables from the gardens.

Almshouses were built resembling barns with beds as a provision designed to encourage the circulation of air and thus to prevent a build-up of miasmas or disagreeable smells, that were believed to spread disease.[23] Caregivers paid considerable attention to sweeping the wards clean, washing linens and the shifts, kirtles, doublets and hose that the patients arrived in. Several hospitals, like St Giles's, Norwich, boasted piped water supplies, and effective drainage systems to flush away waste. Cleanliness was all very good, but the renaissance and medieval Christian believed that confession of sins, and spiritual cleansing of the soul, as well as cleanliness of the environment, were fundamental in dealing with curing the poor of their ills. Additionally, good food, warmth, cleanliness, security and comfort, diminished the anxiety that the ancient Greeks and their successors believed caused many types of illnesses.[24]

The design of almshouses provided a clear view of the altar where Mass was celebrated at least once a day, and the body of Christ was regarded as the most potent source of both physical and spiritual health and healing. For the most part, in an age of religious piety, the poor, disabled and sick probably considered themselves privileged, expiring in such a sacred environment, after having received the last rites. The significance of this event meant that their souls would be dispatched rapidly, through the fires of purgatory. Masses were sung to lift the spirits, ease the soul and take patients' minds off their physical pain and focused them on the spiritual. Music therapy was a notable practice in the treatment of the sick during the renaissance period and was employed to moderate the pulse and raise the spirits, just as it had been an important part in ancient Greece and medieval practices. The Masses, recited with music, were a constant feature of the larger hospitals, such as St Giles's, Norwich, where masses and other services were sung throughout the day. This provided the sick with a therapeutic accompaniment to their recovery in an age where prayer was usually the only comfort.[25]

The Tudors had to decide who would benefit from the care given in these hospitals and almshouses and they were astute when it came to financial matters. Officials had to discriminate between the 'deserving' and 'undeserving' poor. Disabled people with physical and intellectual impairments were among the 'deserving poor', there was little attempt to separate them from the rest of the community. The apothecary was the person to buy medicines from. They were mostly herbal in nature, though the church did also provide the poor with herbs for medicines from their gardens. The first point of call for medical assistance for a great proportion of the population was the local 'wise woman', who was a woman with a good knowledge of herbal lore and healing methods. Although the medical profession was obliged to treat everyone for 'free', as mentioned earlier, only the rich could afford qualified treatment – this does not mean there was no treatment for the poor, but that it was provided either by monasteries or the local wise-woman and for obvious reasons, very little recording of this treatment remains.

To secure the allegiance of local magistrates, the Tudor monarchs were forced to make financial provisions for people who were dependent upon charity. There was a general suspicion of those claiming alms. However, charity had already been established with the statute of 1388. Moreover, every effort was made to keep the poor, elderly and disabled within the local environment. Although there was some variation in the actual level of benefit they might receive, there was a degree of regulation in the way disabled people were treated.

The government increasingly accepted that they needed to take responsibility for the care of the sick and needy. One such institution was called Saint Mary of Bethlehem, originally a priory which by the early-fifteenth century had become a hospital for the mentally insane; its name, shortened to Bedlam, gives a clear idea of the scene that must have met the visitors who went there. Henry VIII ended the abrupt control of the church over such hospitals at Bethlem in 1536 and with the start of the English Reformation, he ended the tradition in England and Wales of the control of the monastic houses over the health and wellbeing of those in its community.[26]

With the Reformation, monasteries and hospitals that belonged to the church became the property of the Crown, and the state took over their administration.[27] Usually, hospitals were parcelled up and

85

sold off as private land, but even though Bethlem was seized by the king's administration during the Reformation, he did not have it decommissioned and it kept its function as a charitable institution so that the hospital remained the only one of its kind in England.[28]

Bethlem or Bedlam was threatened with closure during the English Reformation, but rather than destroying it, before his death Henry passed it to the Corporation of London. With Bethlem in state hands, the king was pressed by the Corporation of London to give them overall control; this proposition lay dormant until January 1547, when the 'custody, order and governance' of Bethlem was transferred to an elected body in the Corporation of London called the Court of Alderman. Despite Henry's death two weeks later, the Court of Aldermen stayed in charge of Bethlem hospital, and the monarchy retained the right to make decisions regarding Bethlem's management.[29]

In 1574, the Court of the Aldermen was still running Bethlem, but not very successfully. It recognised that running a mental hospital was harder than they expected, and members had neither the time nor experience. This situation began to change during the early Stuart period when court physician Helkiah Crooke became the first doctor to be appointed as Keeper of Royal Bethlehem Hospital. The appointment of a medical expert as manager was a huge step toward enlightened attitudes about treating the mentally ill, but alas, this came too late for those of the Tudor period.[30] This meant that Bethlem's management was consequently handed over to Bridewell hospital.[31] Bridewell was an institution that acted as a place of punishment for 'lewd' women, and Bridewell had long been a part of London's urban stories, like Bethlem, and was a place to be both feared and admired.[32]

St Thomas's and Christ's hospitals shared Bethlem and Bridewell's management structure and were how the aldermen organised themselves. Governors ran Bridewell with a court of forty-two overseers who administered work to the hospital's senior officers. The job of a governor was an honoured position and the decisions they took defined the outside world's view of the hospitals. To become a governor of such a place was achieved by donating to either hospital, which almost certainly was met with approval after the submission of an application. Management decisions were taken by senior officers, who controlled its financial matters.[33]

A grand court would meet once a year, usually, before Easter, attended by half of the governors who were convened to deal with emergency issues raised in times of crisis and to confirm senior staff appointments.[34] The Corporation of London was Bethlem's controlling body and the governors related to this body because Bethlem acceded to Bridewell. Many of these governors were aldermen within the City of London who were senior members of mercantile guilds. Eventually, landed gentry, MPs, artists, doctors and lawyers became governors of Bethlem hospitals, those amongst them, the brother of Queen Anne Boleyn, Viscount Rochford, George Boleyn.

Why did the public visit hospitals like Bedlam and Bethlem? Professor and historian, Suzannah Lipscomb, argues that it was not necessarily to see relatives or to offer charity. The sight of mentally disturbed patients became a spectacle, a form of entertainment, much like going to see an execution at the Tower. Tudor society found madness, and mental illness, entertaining.[35]

Being foolish and speaking out was different from madness. Madness, like a disease, the Tudors believed was the result of an imbalance of the four humours: the Greek physician Hippocrates described the four temperaments as part of the ancient medical concept of humourism, when four bodily fluids may affect human personality traits and behaviours. Though modern medical science does not define a fixed relationship between internal secretions and personality, some psychological systems use categories similar to the Greek temperaments. The four-temperament theory is a proto-psychological theory that suggests that there are four fundamental personality types: sanguine, choleric, melancholic, and phlegmatic.[36]

Most formulations include the possibility of mixtures between the types where an individual's personality types overlap and they share two or more temperaments. For example, if there was an excess of the choleric humour the person was manic; the choleric humour is perceived by the fire element. The fire element, in general, symbolised energy, dynamism and expression, and was associated with the colour red, which correlated to the choleric humour, dynamic and expressive component of the blood. If a person was too melancholic, the person was depressed. These individuals tended to be analytical, detail-oriented and were deep thinkers and feelers. They were introverted and tried to avoid being singled out in a crowd.[37] A melancholic personality leads to self-reliant individuals, who are thoughtful, reserved, and often anxious.[38] They often strove for perfection within themselves and their surroundings, which led to tidy and detail-oriented behaviour.

Madness was seen as especially disturbing because, in defiance of the natural order, humans became like beasts when, in their intellectual and emotional turmoil, they lost their power of reason. Care of the disabled, the mad, the old and sick took on many forms that just does not resonate with us because to us, they do not constitute proper treatment. Therefore, procedures should be assessed in the context of the social, and indeed spiritual, needs of the time, rather than by the standards of our highly medicalised and technologically advanced society.

Physicians to the wealthy would have received their training at university, as well as through attending the Royal College of Physicians. Physicians would charge ten shillings, a gold coin, for a home visit, which placed their services well out of reach of most the population. Tudor surgeons, on the other hand, were not as well qualified as doctors. Known as 'Barber-Surgeons' they would pull rotten teeth and perform bleeding for a patient.

Physicians carried out treatments to the best of their ability and knowledge and dressed for the procedures they were to perform. Part of the attire of the Tudor physician might have included a face mask, which prevented him from inhaling most germs from airborne diseases. Many images of physicians and doctors of the time show them wearing masks which had a beak-like shape on the front of it. These masks were especially worn during the outbreak of diseases such as the bubonic plague or Black Death as it was known. The end of the beak held some sweet-smelling oils or herbs such as bergamot, which would mask the smell of death and decay. The practitioner was also covered from head to foot in long clothing, which was believed to keep him safe from infection. Tudor doctors were superstitious, not understanding the nature or cause of most Tudor diseases. Physicians would wear boots, thick gloves and long gowns to protect them from infection from flea bites, vermin and other infestations; but it was still a dangerous job. The medical profession moved on in Europe, and by the early sixteenth century, anatomical texts were being published. However, backward England took some time to integrate anatomical medicine into the learning of medicine. John Caius was a Galenist physician who had been primarily responsible for founding the College of Physicians.[39] Tudor surgeons adapted their skills as their knowledge increased.

Hospitals in Tudor times were very different from the NHS we know and love today. Medical treatment of the population was surprisingly organised for the majority from all walks of life and in studying research on almshouses and hospitals, it has been encouraging to find that Tudor society was compassionate and caring, and far from being negligible in supporting the sick, disabled and dying. Despite their limited resources, materials and medical knowledge at their disposal, almshouses and hospitals were as progressive as they could have been for the time.

Chapter Six

Physicians, Surgeons, Barber-Surgeons and Healers

Living conditions during the Tudor period for the common people were often squalid, and the dwellings of the court and aristocracy also lacked hygiene and sanitation, which is why the court constantly moved from one palace to the next every three months.[1] The provision of pure water, bathing facilities and the disposal of excrement, the features of Roman Britain, now barely existed. In the towns and cities, the rich had the conveniences of commodes, but that did not stop the contents of them from being emptied into the streets every evening. Houses were filthy, the same as the streets. The humanist Erasmus, who was a frequent visitor to England, and a friend of Thomas More, described the floors 'as made of clay and are covered with layers of rushes, constantly replenished, so that the bottom layer remains for twenty years harbouring spittle, vomit, the urine of dogs and men, the dregs of beer, the remains of fish, and other nameless filth'.[2]

People in Tudor society were no better in their personal hygiene practices; bathing was rare unless you were wealthy. The changing of linen undergarments, which helped people to avoid bodily odour, and infection, was only done frequently if you had the money to purchase or make several linen shifts or shirts which could have been changed daily. Child mortality was appalling and the expectancy of life was short. There was a family called the Colets, where the mother bore her husband eleven sons and eleven daughters, but only a son called John, survived infancy. John would later go on to become the Dean of St Paul's.[3]

Boils and abscesses were caused by the lack of skin cleanliness, due to infection. Other infections virilant were scarlet fever, puerperal fever, which likely killed Queen Jane Seymour after giving birth, and other bacterial infections were prevalent such as cholera, dysentery, and typhoid fever. The lack of pure drinking water and the disposal of excrement and urine made diseases common. There was another disease called the sweating sickness, affecting all classes of Tudor society, including members of the royal family and their courtiers. The sweating sickness was a mysterious illness which appeared in 1485 and disappeared in 1551.

Diagnoses of illness and concepts of disabilities and disease were based on assessing humours during the early modern period and were collectively known as Humourism. Humourism was a holistic system of medicine, which detailed the makeup and workings of the human body, which ancient Greek and Roman physicians and philosophers adopted.

The theory of the four humours corresponded with the teachings from the ancients and to the four elements, which were earth, water, fire and air.[4] An excess or deficiency of any of four distinct bodily fluids in a person, known as humours, were thought to directly influence a persons' temperament and health. Hippocrates advocated the humoral theory, which was adopted by Greek, Roman and Islamic physicians, and became one of the most commonly held views of the workings of the human body among European physicians until the advent of modern medical research in the nineteenth century.[5]

Assessing the four humours was the Tudor way of diagnosing illness, apart from observing the patient, looking at the colour of a patients' urine, checking their body temperature by feeling the tackiness of the forehead with the back of a hand, and, perhaps recommending bloodletting treatments with leeches. The Tudors believed that disease arose from imbalances within the body humours and was corrected by bleeding, purging or blistering, which meant barber-surgeons tried to withdraw a humour in excess.

The theory was that within every individual, there were four humours, or vital fluids, which consisted of black bile, yellow bile, phlegm, and blood. Various organs produced these in the body, and they had to be in balance for a person to remain healthy. An abundance and over-production of phlegm in the body, for example, was thought to have caused lung problems; and the body tried to cough up the phlegm to restore a balance within the humours. The balance of humours in humans was considered to be achieved by diet, medicines, and by blood-letting through the use of leeches. The four humours were associated with the four seasons, black bile–autumn, yellow bile–summer, phlegm–winter and blood–spring.

Physicians and surgeons of the Tudor age formed this prevailing view of how the universe worked. Everything in the cosmos fitted into the scheme of the four seasons, the four ages of man, and the four elements of fire, water, earth and air. The system dominated the physicians' understanding of how they believed the body worked and determined their diagnosis of an illness. The Tudors believed that disease occurred when the humours in the afflicted body became unbalanced.[6] So what physicians would do is get rid of some of the excesses of a humour by bleeding a patient with the use of leeches, or by giving them something that would act as a laxative or make them vomit. These would be extensive and disgusting treatments which might make patients have diarrhoea. These were real, physical interventions to rebalance the body, which is what sixteenth century medicine was all about. The polemic approach allowed doctors to define the temperament of each patient and treat them accordingly. The College of Physicians rigorously upheld the teachings of Galen, and the physicians' influence was enormous because members drew their authority directly from the monarch.[7]

Physicians treated their patients using remedies and herbs which had certain 'signatures', i.e a mottled leaf called *pulmonaria* resembled the human lung and was thought to cure pulmonary diseases. Some fruits resembled the human uterus called *Aristolochia,* and this may have been used to treat women with gynaecological problems. These kinds of incidences were the extent of Tudor medical knowledge, apart from the wise woman who might have concocted herbal remedies. There were many healers, and these healers did not usually have professional qualifications.

There were categories of physicians, surgeons, and healers; physicians were an elite group who possessed a doctorate of medicine and this elevated their status beyond all other medical practitioners of the time, however, they were not renowned for their healing practices. During the Tudor period, the medical profession was based upon university qualifications which scarcely existed, and there were few with medical degrees. They studied the ancient Greek medical texts, and had extensive knowledge of anatomy, geometry, rhetoric, logic and grammar, along with astrology. They believed that the status and position of the stars and the earth at the birth and time of treating a patient was crucial. When the planets were favourably placed, this is when physicians would gather the herbs they required for treating their patients, and they did not often physically see their patients, but prescribed remedies from the patients' clinical history or from viewing the patients' urine. The implement for examining urine was the symbol of the physician; a flask. Physicians such as Andrew Bourde practising in the early to the mid-sixteenth century, would look at the colour of the patients' urine and examine the shape of any mucous deposit within the urine, which then directed his attention to any imbalance in the humours of his patients. Bourde wrote extensively on the practice of uroscopy and was a leading practitioner.[8]

Physicians like Bourde would instruct and prescribe to surgeons and apothecaries, and as well as examing urine samples, bloodletting was performed by some surgeons, not physicians. As the physicians once belonged to a holy order, the spilling of blood was not allowed. This was voted in by the fourth Lateran Council in 1215 (canon 18), as part of a general prohibition that clerics should not shed blood, and particularly included the practice of surgery.[9]

Surgeons were from a lower social order than physicians because they had little education, however, they had a much wider and practical experience which they had gained during apprenticeships. Bleeding was the most common practice carried out by surgeons in civilian practice, who would carry out treatment procedures prescribed by physicians.

Barber-surgeons were in the lower orders of surgeons, which meant they had restrictions on how they could practice and the remedies they prescribed.[10] Barber-surgeons were permitted to tooth draw but they were not allowed to do minor surgery or to blood-let a patient. Barber-surgeons had formed guilds and companies in provincial towns and in the city of London. They were numerous in number, and it was in London that some of them served the Tudor monarchs. Barber-surgeons were also resident on large household estates and in monasteries. These surgeons started as ecclesiastical priests, and barber-surgeons would create the tonsure, by clipping and shaving the hair on the monks' heads. As we have seen in the use of almshouses, all diseases, disabilities and illnesses were cared for but not necessarily cured. Barber-surgeons cared for the sick and eased their suffering, but didn't always have the ability or the knowledge to heal a patient and bring them back to full health. Many surgeons would go on to become experienced, wealthy and serve large lists of patients.

It was the apothecaries who harvested, prepared and stored the herbs which surgeons might use and physicians would prescribe. They would go on to become indispensable as a profession.[11] Apothecaries were called on by the common people to administer medical attention when required. Most yeoman and townsfolk could not afford the fees of a barber-surgeon or a physician. Apothecaries would provide medical advice, and remedies, however, they were not allowed to prescribe any medicines. The unqualified were the largest number of practitioners working during the Tudor period. Apothecaries were not educated, unlike physicians, however, they were versed in the healing practices. They were of both sexes and some of the women would be married to surgeons or apothecaries. These apothecaries applied their practice to domestic animals as well as to local families and friends. They used simple, herbal remedies, lanced boils and applied poultices. Legislation would later be written to protect the physicians, surgeons, barber-surgeons and apothecaries, rather than their multitudes of patients.

Physicians, barber-surgeons, apothecaries and healers dealt with all kinds of disabilities, ailments and diseases such as physical and mental disabilities which were common during the Tudor period and were just as common as they are in the modern-day. Crookedness was suffered by many and was an early English term to describe people seen as misshapen in their bodily form. There were some famous Tudors who suffered from crookedness and curvature of the spine or scoliosis like Richard III, King of England, as we have previously discussed. In the early sixteenth century, in France, the wife of François I, Queen Claude, was a sufferer of scoliosis, amongst other disabilities. A member of the English nobility who suffered from scoliosis was that of Charles Brandon, 1st Duke of Suffolk, 1st Viscount Lisle, who was friend and brother-in-law to Henry VIII. When he was married to Anne Browne, before his marriage to Henry VIII's sister, Mary Tudor, the widowed Queen of France, he had a daughter, Lady Mary Brandon, Baroness Monteagle who reportedly suffered from scoliosis.[12] It should be of no surprise that with several known cases of scoliosis within the royal line that Prince Andrew, Duke of York's youngest daughter, Eugenie has also had scoliosis, but has fortunately been treated for the condition.[13]

Tudor common-folk suffered from other disabilities such as deafness, and those who were 'deaff' were most likely cared for by those in their family. Likewise, those unable to speak and struck 'dumb' would have also been cared for in family surroundings. Otherwise, deaf and dumb people would have been cared for in religious settings like monasteries. Common disabilities in Tudor times were epilepsy, which was, and still is, a physical disability in modern times. It was described as the 'falling sickness', an early English term for epilepsy.

In the mid-sixteenth century, Catholics edified a woman with a mental disability without perhaps realising; in fact, that she had epilepsy or a disability. Her unperceived illness was seen as a demonstration of spirituality. Elizabeth Barton was known as the Holy Maid of Kent, and revisionists think she could have suffered from blackouts and even epilepsy. According to Barton's biographer, Diane Watt, she had made predictions for over five years: 'During this period of sickness and delirium, she began to demonstrate supernatural abilities, predicting the death of a child being nursed in a neighbouring bed. In the following weeks and months, the condition from which she suffered, which may have been a form of epilepsy, manifested itself in seizures (both her body and her face became contorted), alternating with periods of paralysis. During her death-like trances, she made various pronouncements on matters of religion, such as the seven deadly sins, the ten commandments, and the nature of heaven, hell, and purgatory. She spoke about the importance of the mass, pilgrimage, confession to priests, and prayer to the Virgin and the saints.'[14]

Elizabeth Barton reported visions of 'wondrously things', and she attained 'a great reputation for holiness' and widespread acclaim until she opposed King Henry VIII's Great Matter and his desirous marriage to Anne Boleyn.[15] In October 1532, Henry VIII agreed to meet Elizabeth Barton. According to the official record of this meeting:

> She [Elizabeth Barton] had knowledge by revelation from God that God was highly displeased with our said Sovereign Lord (Henry VIII) ... and in case he desisted not from his proceedings in the said divorce and separation but pursued the same and married again, that then within one month after such marriage he should no longer be king of this realm, and in the reputation of Almighty God should not be king one day nor one hour, and that he should die a villain's death.[16]

Henry made sure she was held prisoner.

In November 1533, the Spanish Ambassador Chapuys wrote in a letter to King Charles V of Spain that King Henry VIII, 'has lately imprisoned a nun who had always lived till this time as a good, simple, and saintly woman, and had many revelations. The cause of her imprisonment is that she had had a revelation that in a short time this King would not only lose his kingdom, but that he should be damned, and she had seen the place and seat prepared for him in Hell. Many have been taken up on suspicion of having encouraged her to such prophecies to stir up the people to rebellion'.[17] Elizabeth Barton was condemned for her prophecies, that she had committed treason by condemning the king with her treacherous words and was executed on 20 April 1534, when she was hung and then beheaded. Her head was then impaled on a spike at London Bridge as a warning to others.[18] Whether she had a condition pertaining to epilepsy or even mental illness, where she went into a trance-like state and that was interpreted as having prophetic abilities is unclear, but if she did suffer a debilitating condition such as epilepsy, then it did restrict her from leading and taking part in everyday life in Tudor England.

Barber-surgeons and doctors did treat the sexes differently, in terms of diagnosis and treatment. The lines were sometimes blurred between physical and mental disabilities; especially where the female sex was concerned. The Tudors determined madness with criteria, based on assumed causes of insanity, the prevalence of insanity in families and on the sex of the afflicted. Tudor England thought that females were more prone to madness because they believed that hysteria was a disease originating from the uterus. The Tudors inherited the notion from the ancient Greeks and Romans that the womb could move around in the body. This 'wandering womb' theory of mental illness persisted for centuries.[19] The Tudor era assumed causes of madness were associated with environmental conditions. They believed that, for women, fragrant or fetid odours might cause a 'wandering womb'.[20]

Physicians assumed that the movement of the womb might also be due to dehydration. Hysteria was also connected with giving birth when what really should have been diagnosed was postpartum depression.[21] The Tudors recommended the cure for a wandering womb and hysteria was pregnancy, probably because a woman being constantly pregnant was society's way of controlling women.[22] Women could not meddle in religion or politics if they were always in the birthing chamber. Women were kept in their place by the confines set upon them by men;

if women did not adhere to these rules, then they were deemed wanton, or considered a whore or worse, and might even be considered mentally ill or insane.

For both sexes, Tudor era criteria for determining madness are not dissimilar to those of today. These included the person being 'raving and furious' and 'likely to do harm and mischief to themselves or others'.[23] Insanity is a general term, still in use but not as widely as in the past, to denote mental illness, and it tends to be associated with criminal or highly irrational behaviour rather than lower-level illness. The term 'lunatic' or 'lunatick' was an early term to broadly describe the mentally ill. Lunatic is not a term we often used today as its current usage is pejorative or abusive. Tudor physicians developed their treatments for madness, and created institutions for housing those deemed to be mad like the hospital named Bethlem, an institution that by 1574 admitted only those who fit the criteria. Bethlem housed around twenty residents which suggest that Tudor society encouraged families to take care of their own.[24]

Nevertheless, regardless of the medical care from physicians and barber-surgeons, depression and melancholy, with symptoms including 'grotesque hallucinations,' were widespread by the end of the sixteenth century.[25]

Madness was often called 'foolishness', and the term 'fool' was an early English word usually used to try to categorise a disabled person whom we would recognise today, as having a learning disability, and sometimes the term might be used to denote a person who was mentally ill. Professor Suzannah Lipscomb suggests that physicians believed some disabled people were born 'foolish'. The latter term was used to make a distinction from 'lunatics', seen as people suffering a temporary impairment due to mental illness.[26] The 'natural' fool was someone who was by nature, by birth, foolish; today, we would say mentally disabled. Poor nutrition in diets and inadequate health care produced a much larger number disabled people with mental illness than we are accustomed to in today's society, and some of those with intellectual disabilities were lucky, or clever enough to make a living from their disabilities.

Another disease that stopped people engaging in everyday activities during the period was a disability that people had suffered with, in biblical times, called leprosy. Leprosy is now known as Hansen's disease to remove the stigma with which it has often been linked; the condition has a long and complicated history, from the ancient world to the present-day.[27] Leprosy is an extremely complicated disease, comprised of several strains, has historically presented in multiple ways, over different timescales, from benign cases being not outwardly visible, through to extremely severe manifestations. Leprosy has been subject to many popular misconceptions, originally brought about by lepers from biblical stories, and the medieval leper, who is shunned by society and forced to live in rigidly policed and controlled isolation, to protect the general healthy population who live close by. However, in reality, individual reactions to people afflicted with leprosy were complex and contradictory. The period between the Norman conquest and the Black Death saw hundreds of *leprosaria* or leper-houses, established across England, in line with new religious foundations and hospitals. *Leprosaria*, much like hospitals, were built on the outskirts of towns and cities, however, this was not to isolate those with the condition, but to decongest urban centres and use space outside of these areas to hospitalise and treat them. For those who had leprosy, it was a highly prevalent disabling condition wide-spread throughout England and the rest of Europe. Physicians suggested that lepers should be treated within monasteries and almshouses explicitly set aside for those with leprosy.[28]

Another common disability that physicians and barber-surgeons came across was where people were deemed lame, or suffering from lameness, which was an early English term meaning that the person was restricted in the use of one or more limbs. This term applied to the limited use of arms as well as legs. Lameness was also referred to by the word 'cripple', meaning someone unable to walk, through the failure of the use of a limb or limbs. These Tudor terms are now held as derogatory in meaning in modern society. When directed at a disabled person, they are deemed insults, but because disability was not categorised in the early modern era, the term seems archaic to us. Moreover, they were suitable descriptions for lameness and physical disability in the sixteenth century.

Another disease causing lameness, and an inability to walk was gout. Tudor nobility and royalty survived on diets heavy in protein and fish, whereas, peasants subsisted on fruits, vegetables, and legumes; the upper classes suffered higher cases of heart disease, gout and chronic illness whereas the poor suffered fewer cases of such problems.

The earliest textbook of surgery printed in English was by Thomas Gale. On the front piece of Thomas Gale's *Certain Works of Chirurgerie,* there is a depiction of an amputation being carried out in the sixteenth century.[29]

Surgeons made minimal provision for treating the mad and would treat such cases with bloodletting. Roy Porter points out, 'Through the Middle Ages and well beyond, crazy people had rarely any special, formal provision made for them.'[30] As mentioned previously, the medical care for madness was non-existent and treatment, if you could call it that, could only be afforded by those who could pay physicians and surgeons.[31] Care of people with a mental health condition was left to the religious houses of the day, institutions such as Bethlem. The only alternatives were 'refuges specifically for lunatics', but these were mostly unheard of. Healers such as Richard Napier, as Jonathan Andrews, in the Oxford Dictionary of National Biography, explained:

> The combination of astrology and medicine helped Napier to build up a prodigious and popular practice, tending to the bodily and mental ills of tens of thousands of patients. The afflicted came to him from all social ranks, although the majority of his clients were derived (and remained) from the lower middling, artisan, farming, and labouring classes. Even the poorer folk sought Napier out, no doubt encouraged by the fact that his fees were on the modest side, and that he would often forgo charging the poor, although the extent of his charity may have been exaggerated by some of his hagiographical biographers.[32]

Richard Napier's empathy for the mental travails and ills of some of his patients may have been enhanced by the fact that he was evidently 'afflicted with mopish melancholy'.[33] For both rich and the poor, the Tudors resorted to treatments based on superstition and prayer, which were ineffective therapies related to theories about bodily humours, and folk remedies were considered the conventional treatment for madness. Richard Napier dispensed a mixture of orthodox medicinal remedies, religious-moral counsel, and astrological, quasi-magical intervention. Again according to Jonathan Andrews:

> From purgation and bleeding to mutual prayer, horoscope casting, the provision of amulets and charms, and ritual

exorcism. Astrology informed Napier's entire practice, from the content and style of consultation and diagnosis to record-keeping and the timing and nature of treatments. Yet the stars were not his only otherworldly guides for, allegedly (according to Lilly and Aubrey), he also discoursed regularly with the spirit world, calling upon the angel Raphael for advice about his patients. However, there are (perhaps deliberately) scant signs of such angelic consultations in his notes, while even astrology remained merely a tool in his medical practice. It was a more earthly and more regular medical assessment of signs and symptoms on which Napier relied most.'

However, Richard Napier combined both his astrological and Protestant beliefs in his medical practice. Physicians and surgeons whose practices smacked of magic faced a severe threat in this period. Practices like conjuring or necromancy were capital crimes. Nevertheless, while Napier was attacked and abused by some as a conjurer or witch, he was able to chart a relatively safe course socially and professionally through a steady assertion of moderate, conforming Protestant beliefs. Napier would argue against Catholic doctrines, and champion unity in the church. Jonathan Andrews notes that Napier was clever in submerging and diffusing the more esoteric arts within a thorough grounding in mainstream Anglican theology, as well as the right kind of classical and medieval learning, which he states must 'have further contributed towards Napier's avoidance of hazardous controversy'. Richard Napier was intelligent enough to decline to broadcast his magical interests and practices openly.

For these and other reasons Napier has been portrayed somewhat as one of the last of the Renaissance magi but also as a crusader for Protestantism, and he was a significant figure in a world when astrological and magical traditions, once permissible, had gradually transitioned, which helped some practitioners lose credibility and legitimacy. Andrews states that Napier is worthy of note because his medico-astrological practice can be understood in detail from the prodigious amount of his private manuscripts that have survived.[34]

The more fortunate in Tudor Society were cared for by their families as well as physicians and barber-surgeons. For a prosperous patient with estates, wealth, or businesses to manage, a Court of Wards might mandate that the administration of one's affairs be passed to a responsible person. Thus, the care and treatment of the mad was a family or community matter and occasionally a legal one, but not typically a medical one.[35]

Many of the illnesses, disabilities and diseases that were rife in Tudor times were caused through childbirth, and most of the population endured battle scars, poor diet as well as hereditary issues and a lack of understanding of the importance of hygiene, and filthly living conditions. Physicians, surgeons, barber-surgeons and healers tried to treat their patients as best they could with the limited medical knowledge available to them. Living, and even trying to survive in the Tudor era was an unhealthy time, even for the nobles who could afford the most delicate foods and best medical care the age had to offer.

Chapter Seven

The Health of a King and his Decline into Disability

Despite Henry VIII's reign being plagued with marital difficulties, and his preoccupation about providing England with a male heir who would be his successor, his achievements in ruling England were significant.[1] Henry was pro-active when it came to the medical profession, and he enacted legislation for medical licencing that sufficed for several hundred years.[2] The amount of detail within the legislation indicates that Henry was fascinated by the disciplines of medicine, was concerned for the medical care of his subjects and he was moderately knowledgeable in pharmacy.[3]

Many of the disabilities, illnesses, and prevalent diseases Henry and his friends might have experienced for themselves were mostly due to a lack of understanding concerning germs, knowledge of childbirth needs, the importance of hygiene, and the filthly living conditions which were notoriously dangerous, especially in London, and other larger cities. The Tudor era was an unhealthy period to live in for most of the population; this was the case even for nobles, who could usually afford the finest foods, cleanest linen undergarments and best medical care the period had to offer.[4]

Moreover, the medical profession needed standardising, and England had started this process during the reign of Henry V in 1421. However, it was not until the reign of Henry VIII that the required legislation became enacted. It took seven acts of parliament to ratify; however, the legal aspects of medicine remained unclear until 1858 with the Medical Act, which was the only significant legislation made since the Tudor period.[5] London was a teeming metropolis over 500 years ago, and the city was one of the most densely populated in Europe, and it was a constant challenge for physicians, surgeons, barber-surgeons, healers and apothecaries to help the English population maintain a reasonable and healthy quality of life.

Physicians had a mammoth task on their hands, as death stalked the streets, fettered streams and open sewers seethed with potential risks of infection and disease during a time when there was no concept of germs; it was easy to see why people became ill and died, and there were little physicians or surgeons could do to save their patients. Infection was understood to be a corruption of the air; a miasma that exuded from the earth. London was a sick city, because the population contracted all kinds of diseases caused by poor water, overflowing sewage, and a poor diet. Fevers, dysentery and epidemic diseases would seep through the city, killing up to twenty per cent of the population. Life in all of England's major cities during the period was very similar. Life was cruel, brutish and life expectancy was low, and only the rich could afford the practising physicians and barber-surgeons who charged very high fees. The poor were forced to use an underground army of illegal practitioners, which was not an ideal scenario in the world of medicine during the sixteenth century.[6] The royal Tudor court and its monarchs enjoyed staying outside of London, as much as possible to avoid the miasmas, disease and illness circulating in the larger cities. Palaces such as Richmond, Hampton Court, Nonsuch, and others on the outskirts of the City of London were popular with the royal court because the air seemed fresh and the Thames became cleaner as barges carried their passages upstream further away from the waters of the polluted capital. The closer into the countryside the court stayed meant that life improved, and good health might be restored because of taking constitutional walks within the surrounding parks, along with the court's appetite for hawking in autumn, and hunting in winter, meant enjoying exercise in more amenable air.

An example of the court removing itself from contagious disease was when the sweating sickness broke out in June 1528. As noted by the physician John Caius, Henry feared contagious disease.[7] Caius was a humanist and he looked back to the last years of Henry VIII's reign as a golden age. In his monograph, *A boke, or conseill against the disease commonly called the sweate, or sweatying sicknesse*, he noted that Henry who was paranoid about illness 'took off on a flight from safe house to safe house' once the sweating sickness had broken out.[8] The king was so terrified of infectious diseases that he introduced the first quarantine laws to combat the bubonic plague in 1518. There was an epidemic between 1499-1500 that killed the equivalent of half of the capital's population, which was approximately 30,000 people.[9] There were further outbreaks which occurred between 1509-10, 1516-17, 1523, 1527-30, 1532, 1540 and 1544-6. It was those who lived in penury who suffered the most, as their living conditions were so unsanitary.[10]

To give Henry the best possible chance of not contracting any illness, disease or disability, he would remove himself from any contagion, often retreating to his network of residences; Windsor Castle, palaces such as Richmond, Greenwich, Whitehall, Bridewell, and amongst others, Hampton Court Palace; a house originally built in 1514, by Henry's advisor and chancellor Thomas Wolsey, who knew that his palace would create such a glorious footprint on the history of England. Palaces such as Hampton Court with its tall twisted chimneys, and spiral red-brick design, are memorable and create a unique skyline, and were meant to be a place for recreation and entertainment. Hampton Court was a palace where Wolsey had initially invited the king and the royal family, along with foreign dignitaries. It is often argued that Henry was jealous of Wolsey's riches and status and that he envied his cardinal's houses and furnishings; however, Henry wanted Wolsey, as his chief minister to receive all deference due to him as Lord Chancellor, archbishop and finally, papal legate.

Moreover, it was not until Wolsey fell from grace in 1529, that he surrendered Hampton Court Palace to the king on 22 October. Henry made extensive alterations to the building, adding the Great Hall; but it was not a favourite residence. Henry's premier residences were Whitehall and Greenwich Palace.[11]

Hampton Court was accessible from the city, and Henry enjoyed staying at the palace due to its distance from the capital. He considered it a place to showcase his court, and like Wolsey, before him, he would entertain visiting ambassadors. However, the royal court was not static and moved around from palace to palace, every three months or so, so that after the court had left, each palace could be cleaned after accommodating a few thousand courtiers, their visitors, and everybody's servants. Tudor palaces were architecture where power and protocol presided and catered for everyone within the Tudor court; the non-disabled, disabled people, visitors, and of course, royalty visited, stayed and worked there. With every move across London and its outskirts, a myriad of kitchen staff, household servants, cleaners, groomsmen, gardeners, and courtiers battled illness and disease regularly, which is why they moved from palace to palace so often.

During the Tudor period, the practice of medicine within the court, and the country, was always changing. To combat potential disease, Henry VIII was closely involved in advances in medicine, medical law and its practice because he was concerned for his health and those of his close companions, as well as the population as a whole. However, ordinary people's views of medicine were complicated and kept changing, especially when breakthroughs raised expectations in medical practice. The medical aspirations of the barber-surgeons and the Tudor court's inhabitants never stood still.[12] Physicians to the king and his wealthy courtiers would have charged in the region of ten shillings, a gold coin, for a doctor's visit, which priced their services out of reach of most of the population.[13]

Henry VIII was fastidious about all medicinal matters, including cleanliness to prevent illness, but he was only fastidious as far as his knowledge and the knowledge of his barber-surgeons allowed.[14] It is well-documented that Henry VIII paid great attention to his medical care and what his physicians prescribed for his ailments. He was also keen to make sure that his residences, his courtiers and servants remained disease and illness free.[15]

Palaces like Hampton Court and Whitehall housed, fed, entertained and looked after over two thousand young courtiers, as well as the staff that ran each palace, which was no small task. Making Hampton Court safer and healthier for all its inhabitants became a project for Cardinal Wolsey, when in 1526, he wrote a set of ordinances under Henry's watchful eye to reduce incidences of illness and disability, as well as accidents that could have disabled, maimed, scolded or killed servants and courtiers alike. When Cardinal Wolsey wrote the Ordinances, he commanded the palace's kitchen boys no longer to go naked in the heat of the fires, so that the sparks from the fire would not burn the boys' skin. 'Spitboys' (young men who turned the meat on the spit over the flames of the great fires in the kitchens) were not permitted to wear garments of 'such vileness', in other words, dirty linens and shirts were understood to cause a health hazard. The servants and palace staff all had their allotted vocations and did struggle to keep the palace clean, which is why the court moved every three or four months.[16] For example, the transcript of the Ordinance, which is thirteen pages long, states, 'To keep the king's bedroom pure and clean and to stop people disturbing the king, no one is allowed to enter it except the Marquis of Exeter, who is a relative of the king and was brought up with him from a child, six waiters, two ushers, four grooms, the barber and a page; in all 15 people.'[17]

The spread of disease was such a concern that as soon as the residents had left for another palace, the former palace they had occupied was cleaned, floors swept adequately, kitchens restocked, and larders replenished, as well as any general maintenance carried out, as required.[18]

Moreover, some courtiers and members of the royal family reviled putrid odours, both from the garderobes, and from each other and were fastidious about personal cleanliness, especially, Henry. We know this because, from the vertiginous roof of the East Front of Hampton Court Palace, the conduit which fed into Henry's bathtub can be traced across the park. On the first floor of Henry's new privy rooms, Henry's bedchamber had an en-suite bathroom. According to architectural historian Simon Thurley, 'The baths were circular and wooden.'[19] He goes on to say that the bath was 'filled by a great tap with hot water from a boiler in the next room; the water came from a cistern on the floor above.' Parts of these privy chambers were said to have survived up until the 1950s when it was agreed to demolish it to make way for a lift shaft; which is now used for visitors with mobility issues to access the Royal School of Needlework. Towards the end of Henry's reign bathrooms were not small like the panelled bathroom previously described and built at Hampton Court in 1530. Henry's private bathrooms became large, luxurious and Turkish in style, containing sunken pools. Whitehall Palace had a bath that was walked down into using three steps. The Whitehall site was excavated during the 1930s and showed that the bath had been tiled.

Large, glazed ceramic stoves heated the water in these large baths and were stoked with coal. Historians like Simon Thurley know this because as he states, 'The remains of one of these stoves were excavated at Whitehall near the sunken bath and many of the panels bore the royal arms.'[20] There were large bathrooms at Whitehall, Beaulieu and Greenwich. Windsor had a bathroom which was panelled with mirror glass and, Whitehall according to Simon Thurley, 'an upstairs bathroom at Whitehall had a shell grotto with a water fountain'.[21]

Henry commissioned the making of Turkish baths in many of his residences, but hot water piped throughout any of the palaces would have been a luxury, only his bath had running water. We only have evidence that Henry had a Turkish bath; however, that does not imply that all courtiers or his wives did not like to bath regularly. There is also the contradiction that the Tudors were said not to have liked bathing, because they believed that when water entered the pores of the skin, it brought disease and infection. However, as we can understand from the evidence, bathing and cleanliness were essential to the Tudor nobility, and it could be argued that they desired to bathe regularly to keep disease and illness at bay.

Moreover, if courtiers and servants, or ordinary folk, did not have access to a bath, then there was another way in which courtiers and their servants could keep clean and avoid disease and infection. They would sew or purchase a wardrobe full of freshly laundered linens, which they changed regularly, allowing their skin to perspire, without damaging their outer garments. Using and changing linen undergarments, shifts for women and shirts for men meant they did not expose the open pores in their skin to the air, which Tudor physicians believed might allow potential diseases to enter the body.

It is not difficult to understand or imagine how the Tudors believed disease entering the body might happen considering the sky often filled with wood smoke, and river fog hung in the air as servants wandered around the different palaces trying to get on with their allotted tasks. They may have been coughing, suffering perhaps from common irritable asthmatic and bronchial conditions brought about by the great fires in the kitchens and the small log fires in the courtiers and monarchs' private apartments. Arthritis was widespread too, brought about by the damp of being situated so close to the river Thames. Imagine how bone-chilling the cold weather would have been without central heating. Fireplaces stacked with firewood kept the palace heated, and emphysema from smoky rooms was also a problem and may have contributed to the famous 'weak lungs' of the Tudor family. Chimneys became popular additions to homes around this time, but there would still have been much smoke from the candles, braziers and incense.[22]

Tudor palaces had amenities to combat disease and infections such as the garden in Chapel Court at Hampton Court, which would have produced a wide variety of medicinal plants. The garden still grows plants used for curative recipes by the food archaeologists working in the palace kitchens. Beekeeping was therapeutic too, and sixteenth century honey was consumed as a dietary supplement to aid supple joints. It also alleviated common skin complaints, never mind its use to sweeten savoury food. Lavender was grown and it prevented moths from nibbling at precious, ornate garments, as it may have been worn inside a pomander carried on a girdle belt. Lavender was also as a sleep remedy, helping to relax courtiers anxious about the vicious gossip and political backbiting at court. Women wore pomanders hanging from their girdle belts, filled with sweet-smelling waxes, or oranges, to ward off foul smells and lavender oil was used on a pillow to ease a headache. Willow bark was also taken as a medicinal cure for a headache as willow bark was a form of aspirin.

The Tudor medical regime was holistic, and physicians and barber-surgeons believed that a proper diet, regular exercise and a positive mental attitude were the first line of defence against ill-health, before medication.[23] Before physicians prescribed any medication, they had to be skilled in storytelling when symptoms were baffling to them, and they did not have answers for a cure so they would talk their patients back into health, or a natural fool like Will Somer or Jayne might spend time with courtiers to cheer them up.

Most Tudor households, as a social unit, cared for its members during life's meandering patterns, and the royal household would not have been an exception. The physical labour of the work may have been hard for the servants, but noble and royal households and palaces were also social spaces that created a sense of belonging. Few people were left alone for long, whether they were non-disabled or disabled; everyone had a part to play in life whether they were part of large families or were part of the royal court.

Life at court had become impeded with many issues that could provoke disease and illness. For hygiene reasons, Henry probably ordered that the only dogs that could be kept at court were ladies' spaniels. Here is the regulation of the Ordinance: 'No one is allowed to have greyhounds or other dogs at court, except for a few small spaniels for ladies.' Many of the dogs brought to court were not house-trained and left messes on the floors and furnishings, which was a source of parasites. Worms, fleas and other parasites likely afflicted many of the members of the court. However, that is not the only health problem their lifestyles presented.[24]

Diet would have presented many problems as many of the dishes served at those lavish court banquets contained sugar, which was a sign of wealth in the era, and courtiers would then wash the courses of food down with sweet wines. Tooth decay was a severe problem, and to try and avoid infections, nobles cleaned their teeth by polishing them with a tooth cloth, but that was nowhere near as useful as modern toothbrushes and dentistry.[25] Most people had lost several teeth by the time they reached their fifties if they even lived to what was considered old age. Some used 'cheek plumpers' to avoid the sunken look in their features. To combat bad breath, the Tudors had recipes for mouthwashes, some more effective than others. Elizabeth I notoriously ate sweets, misbelieving that they would 'sweeten' her breath. Their dental problems were probably aggravated by a vitamin deficiency, especially in the winter.[26]

When Tudor nobles ate fruits and vegetables, they would be reduced to absolute mush inside pies and as such, most of the vitamins and nutrients were leached out. Vitamin deficiency caused loose teeth, and pain in the joints, which were common complaints. While lack of vitamins was problematic, what they were unwittingly putting into their bodies was much worse. Most of them probably had high levels of heavy metals in their blood as lead was commonly used in food containers, cosmetics, pottery glazes, paints, and medicines. Mercury was another deadly substance used in medications and ointments. Minerals like zinc, alum, borax, silver nitrate and copper were also prescribed for various ailments.[27]

The king was obsessive about his health, was fastidious when prescribing medication for his ailments, and was keen to outlaw quacks, superstitions and religious oversight from medical practice, which he hoped would combat the lack of medical knowledge and expertise, basing his beliefs firmly in the emerging principles of scientific discovery. Monarchs and courtiers alike were trendsetters in medicine during the Tudor period, trying to improve pain relief, by commissioning new scientific research on the human body. Henry hoped to combat disease, disability and illness by elevating the profession of barber-surgeons to regulate the medical profession, a regime which would lay the foundations of not only our modern National Health Service but of a modern health care system that would be rolled out across the world over the coming centuries. Henry created this regime when he formed and founded the Royal College of Physicians in 1518, amalgamating the Barbers Company of London and the Guild, or Fellowship of Surgeons to form the Company of Barber-Surgeons in 1540. His administration passed seven separate Parliament Acts aimed at regulating and licensing medical practitioners; incredibly, the legislature would require no further amendment for 300 years. Guided by Sir Thomas More, the under-sheriff of London, Henry presided over significant improvements in public health; installing municipal water supplies and sewers, and implementing segregation and crude disinfection during epidemics of plaque and sweating-sickness.[28]

Henry VIII was proactive within the Company of Barber-Surgeons, by setting up an Act concerning Physicians and Surgeons, An. 3 Henry VIII c.11 (1512/1513).[29] This Act contained twenty-four dispositions, which concerned both physicians and surgeons. Bill 18 was sponsored by members of the Privy Council, such as Thomas Wolsey and Thomas Linacre. Surgeons were prohibited from practising as physicians or surgeons without a licence from either the Dean of Saint Paul's or the Bishop of London.[30] The Church was given the responsibility of overseeing which physicians and surgeons were licensed throughout the realm. Licensing of physicians ensured that practitioners were of good moral character, who had to be honest and respectable. The act was an essential permit for practice, which was rapidly accepted across the country. The groups of the Surgeons Company and the College of Physicians indicates the probable number of London surgeons at that time, which were fewer than sixty fellows, at any one time paying and annual fee, and licensed to practice, until numbers increased in the Georgian era.[31] Other Acts were brought into law such as an Act concerning physicians, An. 14 Henry VIII c. 15 in 1523, which defined the powers and responsibilities of the College of Physicians.[32] There were further Acts concerning physicians and barber-surgeons including An. 23 Henry VIII c. 40 in 1540, which defined the powers and privileges granted to physicians.[33] The act concerning barber-surgeons, An. 32 Henry VIII c. 42 (1540) was a comprehensive review of the functions of barbers and surgeons. The two companies were to be united into one Company of Barbers and Surgeons.[34] A painting was commissioned to commemorate the union between the Company of Barbers and the Guild or Fellowship of Surgeons in 1540, and it was displayed to celebrate this act of union which is traditionally known as 'King Henry VIII and the Barber-Surgeons'. The Holbein is oil on 11-12 oak panels, in a late seventeenth century gadrooned giltwood frame, painted in 1542.[35]

In the painting, the king sits on a throne wearing state robes and the Order of the Garter, and he is holding the Sword of State. He is shown handing a charter with the Great Seal to Thomas Vicary, in the presence of his barber-surgeons on his left, and his physicians and apothecary on his right; the majority are named. The charter and seal shown are artist's licence, as this Act of Parliament established the union. In the foreground is a Turkish carpet on rush matting and in the background a floral tapestry wall hanging on which a cartouche is superimposed contained a Latin inscription which translates as follows:

> To Henry VIII, best and greatest King of England, France and Ireland, Defender of the Faith and Supreme Head of the English and Irish Church, the Company of Surgeons with vows in common consecrate these lines: Sadder than ever had the plague profaned the land of the English, harassing men's minds and besetting their bodies; God, from on high pitifully regarding so notable a mortality, bade thee undertake the office of a good Physician.
>
> The light of the Gospel flies round about thee on glowing wings; that will be a remedy for a mind diseased, and by thy counsel men study the monuments of Galen, and every disease is expelled by speedy aid. We, therefore, a suppliant band of thy Physicians, dedicate to thee with reverence this house; and mindful of the gift with which thou, O Henry, hast blest us, we wish the greatest blessings on thy rule also.[36]

The Act specified that no surgeon could perform haircuts, or shave another and that no barber could practice surgery; the only everyday activity was to be the extraction of teeth. The barber pole, featuring red and white spiralling stripes, indicated the two crafts, surgery in red and barbering in white.

The first enrolled Master of the Company of Barbers and Surgeons was the superintendent of St Bartholomew's Hospital and royal physician, Thomas Vicary. Vicary was an early English physician, surgeon and anatomist, born in Kent, in about 1490. He was described as 'but a meane practiser in Maidstone, that had gayned his knowledge by experience until the King advanced him for curing his sore legge'.[37] Henry VIII promoted him to the position of sergeant-surgeon to the royal household, and he became one of the leading surgeons in the City of London, becoming the first master of the Company of Barber-Surgeons and again on three further occasions. On Henry VIII's death, he continued to serve the Tudor monarchs as a physician.[38]

Other members of the company were surgeons like John Gerard, who was a botanist and herbalist. He maintained a large herbal garden in London. Gerard was an author of a large illustrated book called *Herbal, or Generall Historie of Plantes*.[39] First published in 1597, it was the most widely circulated botany book in English. Gerard's *Herbal* is primarily an unacknowledged English translation of Rembert Dodoens's herbal initially published in 1554.

It was this developing medical backdrop which saw the most well-known Tudor monarch come to the throne in 1509. As a teenager, he was young, fit and healthy. The king was a fascinating character: initially blessed with good looks and stature; with great sporting prowess; Henry was a renaissance scholar revered by his subjects and given the affectionate name of 'Bluff King Hal'.[40] On 24 June 1509, Henry was crowned King of England in a ceremony at Westminster Abbey, alongside his Spanish wife, Katharine of Aragon, whom he had married several weeks earlier. The seventeen-year-old sovereign succeeded to the throne with enormous popularity, a phenomenon caused in part by his good looks and charisma, but also by the profound unpopularity of his late father's twenty-four year reign, during which Henry VII had continuously raised taxes and fended off violent challenges to his rule. At the beginning of Henry VIII's reign, hopes were high and his reign full of potential, and it was the start of an expectant 'Golden Age'. A promising young lawyer Thomas More had watched Henry and Katharine's coronation procession ride through Cheapside. On 23 June 1509, which was the eve of the coronation, the majestic couple set out from the Tower of London and made their way through London's city streets to Westminster. It was an exercise in opulence, designed to impress the crowds and show off the magnificence of the new King of England. Henry was decked out in shimmering cloth of gold and jewels, sitting proudly on horseback, leading the parade, while Katharine was sat in a litter some way back, bedecked in jewels with her long red hair hanging down her back. Everyone came out from the side streets of Ironmonger Lane to get a glimpse of the spectacle.

On 8 July 1509, King Henry VIII wrote to Cardinal Sixtus de Ruvere, 'To inform him of the events which have taken place since the death of the King, his father.' The Cardinal informed the Vatican that, 'taking into consideration the high virtues of the princess Katharine, daughter of the King of Aragon, has espoused and made her his wife, and thereupon had her crowned amid the applause of the people and incredible demonstrations of joy and enthusiasm'.[41]

The men of the Mercer's company, the Guild of London's Merchant's, had sponsored More to compose and deliver a poem, 'Coronation Ode of King Henry VIII' to celebrate the new king. More would become one of Henry's most trusted friends and advisors:

> If ever there was a day, England, if ever there was a time for you to give thanks to those above, this is that happy day, one to be marked with a pure white stone and put in your calendar. This day is the [end] of our slavery, the beginning of our freedom, the end of sadness, the source of joy, for this day consecrates a young man who is the everlasting glory of our time and makes him your king – a king who is worthy not merely to govern a single people but singly to rule the whole world – such a king as will wipe the tears from every eye and put joy in the place of our long distress.[42]

In using the descriptor of a 'Golden Age', Thomas More was referring to the works of the ancient Roman poet, Virgil. More was schooled in the humanist tradition, which was an emerging intellectual movement that looked back to the ideologies of ancient Rome and Greece. Henry would have realised what Thomas More was referring to as the art of chivalry; a concept which involved protecting the weak, when required, with violence. These ideologies were paramount to Henry VIII, and the country was optimistic about this new age that Henry's reign would bring.

There was much rejoicing which greeted the new king, and it reflected the country's relief that after nearly a century, the monarchy had returned to the stability which, as an institution, it was supposed to guarantee. This change was caused in no small part by the appearance of Henry VIII, who at 6'2", with golden hair, a muscular frame, and all the towering good looks of the York kings, from whom he descended on his mother's side, created much admiration. In the first few halcyon days surrounding his accession, Henry sought to secure his public image, so he ordered the execution of his father's two closest advisers, Richard Empson and Edmund Dudley. The two courtiers had languished in the Tower ever since their royal master's death, and as these were councillors most clearly associated with Henry VII's unpopular taxes, their executions significantly increased the popularity of the young king.[43]

Henry VIII was, in 1519, reported to be 'affable and gracious'.[44] During the initial years of his reign, Edward Hall the chronicler described Henry with:

> The features of his body, his goodly personage, his amiable visage, princely countenance, with the noble qualities of his royal estate, to every man known, needs no rehearsal, considering that, for lack of cunning, I cannot express the gifts of grace and of nature that God has endowed him with all.[45]

It is with this backdrop of vitality and good health that Henry's medical history was well documented within the State Papers of the period. However, not by his physicians or surgeons, who did not keep records, probably for their safety, as to imagine the king's death was treason. Furthermore, it was usually the dispatches sent from the English court by foreign ambassadors that reported the state of the king's health to their respective governments.[46] The health of Henry VIII was not just personal, but a matter of state and a political issue. For our government, Henry's health was used as a propaganda tool, because the matter of the king's health tied in with the political strength and health of England.

Medical science during the Tudor period was less advanced than it is today; diagnostic skills of Henry's physicians and surgeons were imperfect, apart from diagnosing the bubonic plague, smallpox, syphilis or the sweating sickness, because they were all too familiar with these diseases and illnesses of the time. Few letters and papers of his physicians survive because it was considered dangerous to divulge information of a monarchs' medical condition. It, therefore, fell to his courtiers and foreign ambassadors, who were not medically trained, to pass on or record royal health and medical matters.[47]

These medical reports from the period, give us a reasonably accurate picture of the health of Henry VIII over his lifetime. Moreover, these ambassador's reports would have been based on pronouncements by the king's physicians and surgeons, along with eyewitness reports. For example, at the beginning of his reign, Henry contracted a fever in December 1513, considered at the time to be a viral infection caught from the air; a case of smallpox, which according to a Venetian ambassador, caused his physicians to say they, 'were afraid for his life'.[48]

In his younger years, the dashing and sporting prince showed his ability to recover from illness. Pietro Pasqualigo, a Venetian ambassador in England, wrote in his dispatches on 30 April 1515 describing Henry thus:

> The King is the handsomest potentate I ever set eyes on; above the usual height, with an extremely fine calf to his leg, his complexion very fair and bright, with auburn hair, combed straight and short, in the French fashion, and a round face so very beautiful that it would become a pretty woman, his throat being rather long and thick. He was born 28th of June 1491, so he will enter his twenty-fifth year the month after next. He speaks French, English and Latin, and a little Italian; plays well on the lute and harpsichord, sings from book at sight, draws the bow with greater strength than any man in England and jousts marvellously.[49]

One of the Venetian Ambassadors to England wrote in his dispatches on 3 May 1515 that:

> The King tilted against many, stoutly and valorously. According to their own observation and the report of others, King Henry was not only very expert in arms and of great valour, and most eminent for his personal endowments, but so gifted and adorned with mental accomplishments, that they believed him to have few equals in the world. He spoke English, French, and Latin, understood Italian well, played on almost every instrument, sang and composed fairly, was prudent, sage, and free from every vice, and so good and affectionate a friend to the Signory, that no ultramontane sovereign ever surpassed him in that respect.[50]

Another entry in the Calendar of State Papers relating to English affairs in the archives of Venice, Volume 2, 1509–1519 dated 6 June states that:

> The preparations for the joust being at length finished, the King made his appearance in very great pomp. On his side

were ten noblemen on capital horses, all with housings of one sort, namely, of cloth of gold with a raised pile. The King's warhorse was caparisoned in the same manner, and in truth, he looked like St. George in person on its back. The opposing party consisted of ten other noblemen, also in rich array and well mounted. Never saw such a sight. They jousted for three hours, to the constant sound of trumpets and drums. The King excelled all others, shivering many lances, and unhorsing one of his opponents. Did not expect to find such pomp. The King exerted himself to the utmost for the ambassadors' sake, and more particularly on account of Pasqualigo, who returns to France today, that he may be able to tell King Francis what he has seen in England, and especially of his Majesty's own prowess.[51]

Henry loved participating in sport, and it was his physical activities in the early part of his reign that kept him healthy and robust enough to recover until he contracted malaria or 'tertiary fever' in 1521, which was endemic in the English marshlands. Few marshes were drained at the time, so mosquitos which can carry the disease, flourished. Sources tell us that on 20 May 1521:

He [the king] had just caught a fever, which shortly grew to two tertians. Owing to the long continuance of paroxysms in cold and heat, with no interval between to enable him to take his meals, the physicians were fain to give him his meals before the end of his paroxysms. The disease is now gone, and for five or six days, he has been fresh, merry and well at ease; much better than before.[52]

Henry ruled at a time when the image and health of the king set the tone for the whole nation. Henry was image-conscious, and at every opportunity, he enjoyed showing off. There was no better way for Henry to showcase his strength and manhood than by competing in such public displays as in the sport of jousting. 'In archery, in wrestling, in joust, Henry was a match for the best in his kingdom. None could draw the bow, tame the steed or shiver a lance more deftly than he.'[53]

As Henry VIII approached his thirties, ambassadors and foreign observers such as Sebastian Giustinian were writing from England that Henry appeared to be accomplished in every way; not only was he good-looking, but he reported:

> King Henry was 29 years old and much handsomer than any other Sovereign in Christendom,—a great deal handsomer than the King of France. He was very fair, and his whole frame admirably proportioned. ... He was very accomplished and a good musician; composed well; was a capital horseman, and a fine jouster; spoke good French, Latin, and Spanish; was very religious; heard three masses daily when he hunted, and sometimes five on other days, besides hearing the office daily in the Queen's chamber, that is to say, vespers and compline. He was extremely fond of hunting, and never took that diversion without tiring eight or ten horses, which he caused to be stationed beforehand along the line of country he meant to take. He was also fond of tennis, at which game it was the prettiest thing in the world to see him play; his fair skin glowing through a shirt of the finest texture.[54]

However, his most favourite of pastimes was jousting and this was a dangerous sport; Henry put his life on the line every single time he appeared in the lists. Henry was thirty-two years old, when on 10 March 1524, he appeared in a joust, riding in a new design of armour with his visor raised. However, the crowd shouted to him to put his visor down, but Henry thought onlookers were cheering him on, so he continued charging his opponent, which was Charles Brandon, his brother-in-law, the first Duke of Suffolk. Brandon could not hear the crowd shouting either, and visibility through his visor was poor, so the aim of his lance splinted above Henry's right eye, giving him a very nasty knock. The king was fortunate not to break his neck or fracture his skull; instead, Brandon had bruised Henry badly. Determined to carry on regardless, Henry ran another six courses but would suffer from this point on, complaining of terrible migraine headaches. The resulting migraines would plague him for the rest of his life.

The chronicler Edward Hall recorded the following account of the incident:

> The 10th day of March, the king having a new harness [armour] made of his own design and fashion, such as no armourer before that time had seen, thought to test the same at the tilt and appointed a joust to serve this purpose.
>
> On foot were appointed the Lord Marquis of Dorset and the Earl of Surrey; the King came to one end of the tilt and the Duke of Suffolk to the other. Then a gentleman said to the Duke, "Sir, the King is come to the tilt's end." "I see him not," said the Duke, "on my faith, for my headpiece takes from me my sight." With these words, God knoweth by what chance, the King had his spear delivered to him by the Lord Marquis, the visor of his headpiece being up and not down nor fastened so that his face was clean naked. Then the gentleman said to the Duke, "Sir, the King cometh".
>
> Then the Duke set forward and charged his spear, and the King likewise inadvisedly set off towards the Duke. The people, perceiving the King's face bare, cried "Hold! Hold!", but the Duke neither saw nor heard, and whether the King remembered that his visor was up or not few could tell. Alas, what sorrow was it to the people when they saw the splinters of the Duke's spear strike on the King's headpiece. For most certainly, the Duke struck the King on the brow, right under the defence of the headpiece, on the very skull cap or basinet piece where unto the barbette is hinged for power and defence, to which skull cap or basinet no armourer takes heed of, for it is evermore covered with the visor, barbet and volant piece, and so that piece is so defended that it forceth of no charge. But when the spear landed on that place, it was great jeopardy of death, in so much that the face was bare, for the Duke's spear broke all to splinters and pushed the King's visor or barbet so far back by the counterblow that all the King's headpiece was full of splinters. The armourers for this matter were much blamed, and so was the Lord Marquis for delivering the spear when his face was open, but the King said that no-one was to

blame but himself, for he intended to have saved himself and his sight.

The Duke immediately disarmed himself and came to the King, showing him the closeness of his sight, and swore that he would never run against the King again. But if the King had been even a little hurt, the King's servants would have put the Duke in jeopardy. Then the King called his armourers and put all his pieces together and then took a spear and ran six courses very well, by which all men might perceive that he had no hurt, which was a great joy and comfort to all his subjects there present.[55]

The crowd were alarmed by the incident because the speed Brandon was riding combined with the impact of the lance could have killed the king instantly.

Henry nearly died in another incident in 1525, where he almost drowned while using a stave to vault over a water-filled ditch when out hawking in Hertfordshire. The pole suddenly snapped, and the king landed unceremoniously head-first, into the clay marsh. The chronicler Edward Hall retells of the incident: 'if Edmond Moody, a footman, had not leapt into the water and lifted up his [the king's] head which was fast in the clay, he, [would] have drowned'; the king was pulled out safely, feet first.[56]

Henry was proud of his sporting abilities, despite them putting him in danger and being life-threatening; he continued to take part in all kinds of activities to show the court and ambassadors how full of vitality he was. Henry was inordinately proud of his physique, especially his beautiful calves, displaying them by use of a garter which the king usually had fastened around his leg just below the knee. However, his propensity for vigorous sport led to a variety of injuries to those calves, of varying severity. Henry built the first tennis court at Hampton Court Palace for the game which was a mixture of squash and court tennis. In 1527 Henry wrenched his left foot playing tennis at Whitehall, and the resultant swelling led him to adopt and wear a single loose black velvet slipper, to ease the pain while walking, because of a weak ankle tendon. He ended up wearing the slipper for several weeks, and this prompted a new fashion in footwear for most of his courtiers who then copied him.

Henry remained relatively healthy between 1527-1536, despite the violent religious and political upheaval. However, there were reports of the king being confined to bed at Canterbury in 1527-1528 with a 'sore leg' which refers to an ulcer on his thigh. Henry was still a relatively young man at aged thirty-six. The infection was believed to be a varicose ulcer on his left leg, caused by the constrictive garter he wore beneath the knee, which restricted his blood flow, and made it difficult for the blood to return to his heart due to bad circulation; or possibly a traumatic injury sustained during jousting.[57] A local surgeon was summoned to treat the king, and the ulcer healed, earning Thomas Vicary the position of sergeant-surgeon, and an annual salary of 20 shillings, along with the king's thanks. Henry was the true renaissance prince and was interested in medicine and invented a host of cures and ointments for several ailments and the king created his own ointment to cure his ulcers called the 'King's Majesties own plaster'. It contained over twenty-five ingredients and may have included lead, which is highly poisonous.[58]

The doctors would prepare most of the medicines they prescribed for the king, and they also examined all the fluids that came out of the king's body, like his spit, his urine and his stools. They would inspect the colour of the king's urine and even taste it, if necessary. If any of the humours were out of balance, they would rebalance them with bloodletting, placing leeches on fifty-seven points of the body. Each of Henry's blood-letting sessions might have lasted a couple of hours, and he was bled regularly as a preventative measure, supposedly to cure his many ailments.

Despite Henry's keen interest in medicine, and all physical sports, which he still enjoyed participating in, as he grew older, the king became increasingly interested in debate and making political decisions, which for the first few years of his reign he had previously left to Cardinal Wolsey. Evidence of Henry slowly changing his attitude to his role as king is recorded in 1529, by the humanist Desiderius Erasmus, who described Henry as 'a man of gentle friendliness, and gentle in debate; he acts more like a companion than a king'.[59]

During this period, Henry became preoccupied with who would follow him in the line of the succession, as Henry had decided to rid himself of his first wife, Katharine of Aragon, to marry a lady-in-waiting of the court, Anne Boleyn.[60] Henry began to pursue an annulment of his marriage because his only surviving legitimate heir was female.

Therefore, this meant that his realm was open to losing its independent status if his daughter married a foreign prince.[61] Through nearly three decades of his reign, Henry's inability to sire a healthy male heir ran like a trail of poison through his veins. For a king, this meant that his inability to produce a surviving male heir could be argued a disability because, as a king, the inability to secure the succession meant that he was failing to secure his realm.

Although Katharine suffered a terrible natal record of six pregnancies between 1510-1518, which resulted in the miscarriages of two female babies, one stillborn male and three live births – one being Prince Henry Duke of Cornwall, where, in the Letters and Papers of Henry VIII, administrators record the event: "The christening of Prince Henry, first son of our sovereign lord King Henry the VIIIth." 'On New Year's Day, Wednesday'... '1 Jan., about _(blank) a.m., 1510, 2 Hen. VIII., at Richmond in Sowthrey, was born Prince Henry.'"[62] Consequently, on 15 January, Andrea Badoer, wrote from England, that, 'On the 1st the Queen was delivered of a son.' He then goes on to write about the christening: 'A son born to the King on 1 Jan.; and christened, on Sunday the 5th, in presence of ambassadors of the Pope, France, Spain and Venice, who afterwards visited and congratulated the Queen. The son is named Henry.'[63]

Sadly, the little prince lived for just fifty-three days, and in the records of 27 February is a list made for black cloth and other items required for the heir's funeral procession:

> Th'entierment of Prince Henry son of King Henry the viijth. Lengths and prices of black cloth received from merchants (named) to a total cost of 379l. 14d. Payments for making gowns, banners hearse, including 50l. to the abbot of Westminster for twelve palls and a canopy, to John Browne, Ric. Rowndangre, John Whytyng, John Wanlasse and John Hethe, painters, for banners, 974 lbs. of wax for the hearse at Westminster and 4,327 lbs. in torches. Expenditure at Richemounte, 25 and 26 Feb. 2 Hen. VIII., in divers offices of the Household, about the funeral, and at Westminster on Thursday, 27 Feb.[64]

Another prince was born in September 1513. However, unfortunately, he died a few hours later and then finally Princess Mary, born 18 February

1516, where the queen notified those of the 'birth of Princess [Mary]. Under her signet, at Greenwich'.[65] Fortunately, the child survived. However, as the child was a daughter, Henry squarely laid the blame at the feet of his wife for her inadequacy to produce a male heir. Henry pinpointed the verse in Leviticus and cited God's judgement against him for marrying his brother's widow, as an excuse in not producing a surviving, healthy male heir. Katharine had no problem falling pregnant; clearly, fertility was not the queen's problem. Antenatal care was not fantastic in Tudor times, and even someone in the royal household only had the care, and midwives, that their limited knowledge allowed. The lack of sanitation may explain Katharine's lousy childbirth record.

Moreover, Henry's despondency did not come to an end with his first marriage, as on marrying Anne Boleyn, she produced a daughter called Elizabeth in September 1533. On 10 September 1533, in the Harley MS, it is recorded that Elizabeth was born 'On Sept 7, between three and four o'clock p.m., the Queen was delivered of a fair lady, for whom Te Deum was incontinently sung.'[66] The following year she suffered a phantom pregnancy, and in 1536 she miscarried a male foetus of fifteen weeks gestation on 29 January 1536, the day her rival Katharine of Aragon had been laid to rest in Peterborough Abbey.[67] On 10 February, Spanish ambassador Chapuys wrote to Charles V informing him that 'the Concubine [Anne Boleyn] had an abortion [miscarriage] which seemed to be a male child which she had not borne 3½ months, at which the King has shown great distress.' He goes on to say in the same dispatch that, 'Some think it [Anne having a miscarriage] was owing to her own incapacity to bear children...'[68]

Like Katharine before her, Anne was blamed for her inability to produce a healthy male heir that grew to full term and survived. Spanish ambassador Chapuys strangely wrote in his dispatches, a few days before Anne's miscarriage that he had:

> Heard some days ago from various quarters, though I must say none sufficiently reliable, that the King's concubine, [Anne] though she showed great joy at the news of the good Queen's death, [Katharine of Aragon] and gave a good present to the messenger who brought her the intelligence, had, nevertheless, cried and lamented, herself on the occasion, fearing lest she herself might be brought

to the same end as her. And this very morning, some one coming from the lady mentioned in my letter of the 21st of November ultimo, and also from her husband, has stated that both had heard from the lips of one of the principal courtiers that this King had said to one of them in great secrecy, and as if in confession, that he had been seduced and forced into this second marriage by means of sortileges and charms, and that, owing to that, he held it as nul. God (he said) had well shown his displeasure at it by denying him male children.[69]

This dispatch to the Emperor from Chapuys was written on 29 January 1536, the day that Anne had miscarried, and Chapuys mentions that he had heard rumours some days before, that Henry was already contemplating that he had been seduced into his second marriage and that he believed he would probably not have a male heir by Anne. Henry would never consider that his infertility issues might be the cause of his problems. He would use his wives as scapegoats for his shortcomings. However, Henry's ability to father children has been speculated on by many historians, and it is a topic of conjecture to suggest that his infertility issues render him disabled. However, his inability to produce many healthy legitimate male heirs was a problem for Henry, because as a king, this is what was expected of him.

Moreover, Henry's health would, over time, dictate the stability of England; a physical symbol of the realm's authority and power.[70] Furthermore, it could be suggested that Henry had not failed in producing healthy children, as it ignores, of course, Henry's success in fathering his illegitimate son the Duke of Richmond, Henry Fitzroy, Princesses Mary and Elizabeth and Prince Edward.

Fertility issues could have stemmed from Henry; some historians think there might be an explanation for Henry's reproductive problems, namely syphilis. Syphilis arrived in England in 1497 and was referred to as 'the French pox'.[71] Tudor physicians were familiar with treating syphilis and referred to it as 'the Great Pox', which distinguished it from smallpox or chickenpox; Tudor physicians quickly recognised the symptoms so they could treat the infection.[72] The symptoms for syphilis would begin with a small painless genital ulcer, then a fever, rash, and muscle pain in the night. Abscesses would appear on the body, which was large, foul-smelling and painful and such abscesses would destroy the nose and lips. According to Erasmus, syphilis was the most destructive of diseases, when he recorded in 1520: 'which for years had been raging with impunity ... What contagion does thus invade the whole body, so much resist medical art, becomes inoculated so readily and so cruelly tortures the patient'.[73] The belief that started the rumour that Henry had syphilis was his 'sore leg', however, there is no evidence that the king was ever treated for syphilis; in fact, neither Henry nor his wives developed any manifestations of untreated secondary or tertiary syphilis, unlike their counterpart and Henry's 'brother' King François I of France who was reputed to have suffered from syphilis.[74]

Life at the French court may have been licentious; however, the English court remained one of spectacular excess itself where the consumption of food was concerned. Henry was a *bon-viveur* renowned for his appetite, which steadily increased his weight, despite the king's love of sport, and his raw athleticism.

Although Henry was not as athletic at forty-four as in his youth, he was in good enough health to continue his favourite sporting pursuits, especially jousting. Entering the lists was an opportunity to continue to display his masculinity or 'manhood' and the perfect way to demonstrate this was through physical strength, courage and violence. The tiltyard was the prime place for demonstrating his manly courage and physical strength; an essential element of magnificence, good lordship and kingly honour. The joust was all about impressing foreign ambassadors in a show of the wealth and prestige of the monarch of the country. However, on the occasion of 24 January 1536, at Greenwich, the king was unseated from his horse in the joust and crashed to the ground with his fully-armoured horse landing on top of him. Henry probably only survived because he was wearing armour. According to one report, he lay 'for two hours without speech', possibly through a severe concussion or bruising of the cerebral cortex. When news of Henry's jousting accident was relayed to his second wife, Anne Boleyn, by her uncle, the Duke of Norfolk, she went into shock over the potential severity of his injuries and days later, she miscarried a male child. The son and heir Henry had so desperately needed. There are three main contemporary reports of Henry's jousting accident of 1536. The first account of the jousting accident is a report which reinforces the idea that this was a devastating event, with serious consequences. The report was written by Pedro

Ortiz, to the Empress on 6 March 1536: 'Has received a letter from the ambassador in France, dated 15 Feb., stating that he hears from England that the King intends to marry the Princess to an English knight. The French king said that the king of England had fallen from his horse and been for two hours without speaking. "La Ana" was so upset that she miscarried of a son.'[75] Henry was reported as 'without speech' for two hours and suffered a head injury which may have caused his brain to rattle around in his skull. The difficulty with this report of the king being unable to speak suggests that the king was unconscious; however, this report was third-hand hearsay, as Ortiz who reported it, was abroad in Rome and did not witness the event. Moreover, he heard the news from the French ambassador, who had heard it from François I, whom himself was not present at the joust, and must have heard it from one of his ambassadors who were there in England. Two accounts afflict with the account of Henry being 'without speech', and they were written by people who were at the English court, watching the joust.

The chronicler Charles Wriothesley, writing of Queen Anne Boleyn's miscarriage on 29 January, recorded that, '[...] it was said she [Anne] tooke a fright, for the King ranne that tyme at the ring and had a fall from his horse, but he had no hurt; and she tooke such a fright with all that it caused her to fall in travaile, and so was delivered afore her full tyme, which was a great discomfort to all this realme'.[76]

The Imperial ambassador, Eustace Chapuys reported that 'On the eve of the Conversion of St. Paul, the King being mounted on a great horse to run at the lists, both fell so heavily that everyone thought it a miracle he was not killed, but he sustained no injury.'[77] However, there were reports that Henry's legs were crushed in the fall when his horse fell on top of him, which may have opened the varicose ulcer he had from 1527-8.

Professor Suzannah Lipscomb attributes an acute deterioration in Henry's behaviour to the head injuries sustained during the joust of 24 January 1536. Suzannah suggests this was an accumulative process, which was 'greatly accelerated by the events of 1536'.[78]

This prolonged period of the king being unconscious due to the head trauma could have damaged his frontal lobes, which would have affected his moods and caused a personality change, affecting his emotions, making him erasable and unpredictable, and as Suzannah writes, 'now contrary, secretive, dogmatic, and unpredictably changeable'.[79] The 1536 jousting accident was a blow to Henry's ego, as well as his body, and he could no longer take part in sports as he had done before.

Henry's 'annus horribilis' was 1536: his sporting injuries, the loss of his potential heir, accusations of Anne Boleyn's treason and adultery, and the untimely death of his illegitimate son the Duke of Richmond, made the king increasingly unpredictable, irascible and cruel, which, with all these events cumulated together, meant that he had reacted more brutally to events in that year than any other, up unto this point in his reign. The effect of chronic pain on his temperament is well-recognised and the actions of King Henry VIII in dispatching his wife, and his closest courtiers and friends, during this year could have been linked to his physical misery. Henry began to suffer from chronic headaches, and although the wounds Henry sustained to his legs initially healed, ulceration reappeared shortly afterwards, being particularly unpleasant and painful to manage from 1536 onwards. His ulcer must have been irritated by the continual wear of garters about Henry's calves. However, history does not record how tightly Henry's garters were bound around his upper calf, and he had several injuries to his legs because of his sporting activities, both of which represent risk factors for deep vein thrombosis.

Henry's health was in rapid decline in 1537, with evidence of ulcers now on both of Henry's legs. Tudor physicians knew how to diagnose familiar health issues such as bubonic plague, smallpox, syphilis and sweating sickness. However, physicians were wise not to record the details of the health of the king, as possessing information on the king's health was dangerous, and disclosing his personal information would lead to accusations of treason. In March 1537, and a few weeks later on 30 April, it was reported by John Husee to Lord Lisle that 'The King goes seldom abroad because his leg is something sore.'[80] In June of the same year, Henry wrote to the Duke of Norfolk, explaining why he could not visit the north and wanted to leave the progress until the following year. Firstly, 'the Queen being now quick with child, she might be in danger from rumours blown abroad in our absence, and it is thought we should not go further than 60 miles from her.' Secondly, 'to be frank with you, which you must keep to yourself, a humour has fallen into our legs, and our physicians advise us not to go so far in the heat of the year, even for this reason only.'[81]

Henry's chronic leg ulcers could be attributed to recurring osteomyelitis, which can develop in the bones following an injury, and

126

affects those with blood conditions such as diabetes.[82] Modern doctors today would treat leg ulcers with antibiotics and by draining the pus from the diseased bone but these twenty-first century treatments and knowledge were not available to Henry's sixteenth century physicians.

The Marquis of Exeter and Lord Montagu were put on trial during the Exeter Conspiracy, and witnesses testified that the traitors had disrespectfully discussed Henry's health saying of the king that 'he [the king] has a sore leg that no poor man would be glad of and that he [the king] should not live long for all his authority next to God' and claiming that 'he [the king] will die suddenly, his leg will kill him, and then we shall have jolly stirring.' After such treasonous comments, both traitors were beheaded; execution for treason which would be carried out either by hanging, eviscerating, beheading, burning the traitor at the stake or even boiling them alive. These kinds of capital punishment were to become increasingly commonplace in the latter part of Henry's reign. The king was responsible for ordering all these deaths and it subsequently gave him a reputation for brutality. Henry was feared by all for his cruelty.[83] Henry's health remained a matter of speculation as his legs continued to be persistently severely ulcerated, but his spirits rallied by the birth of his son, Edward VI, and were then dashed by the unforeseen death of his wife, Jane Seymour, twelve days later from puerperal sepsis. Some medical historians believe that Jane was 'feigned to be ripped', based on MacLennan's reports that a caesarean section was performed.[84] While mourning the loss of his third wife, Henry piled on the pounds as can be seen from his expanding girth, easily imagined from the measurements, by the comparison and change in the size of his armour displayed at the Tower of London.

The king's increasing weight and the ulcers on his legs would be the cause and the start of the king's immobility and disability; the ulcers would become renowned for their smell, purulent and seeping, and superficial healing of the skin probably led to episodes of sepsis and bouts of fever.

On 14 May 1538 Castillion wrote to Montmorency: 'This King has had stopped one of the fistulas of his legs, and for 10 or 12 days the humours which had no outlet were like to have stifled him, so that he was sometime without speaking, black in the face, and in great danger.'[85] Henry's physicians attempted to keep these fistulae open to allow drainage of the 'humours', often lancing the ulcers with red-hot pokers;

a therapy unlikely to have improved the king's ill-temper. Courtiers and ambassadors were aware of the king's medical problems and would report these instances to their monarchs, especially if these instances indicated that the king was lucky to survive.

On 15 May 1539, John Worth writes to Lord Lisle explaining 'This present Holy Thursday eve the King took his barge at Whitehall and rowed up to Lambeth. He had his drums and fifes playing and rowed up and down the Thames for an hour after evensong. On Holy Thursday he went in procession about the Court at Westminster in the Whitehall. My lord Cobham bore the sword before him with a multitude of other nobles. The high altar in the chapel was garnished with all the apostles upon the altar, and mass by note and the organs playing, with as much honour to God as might be devised. I was told by those of the King's chapel and by Kellegrew that upon Good Friday last the King crept to the cross from the chapel door upwards devoutly and served the priest to mass that same day, *his own person kneeling on his Grace's knees.*' For Henry to creep to the cross from the door of the Chapel Royal, and to serve others during Mass on his knees, doubtless in agony from the pain in his legs, was some feat.[86] Not only did Henry suffer from the ulcers in his legs, his growing waistline and constant migraines, he also suffered from a bad case of constipation in September 1539. This incident with his health was undoubtedly due to his poor diet which mostly consisted of red meat and a lack of fibre and vegetables in his diet. However, despite his struggles with his health, the king was never cowardly or feeble, and he tried to maintain his dignity and a pretence of regal formality.

Moreover, due to all his medical complications, in the last seven years of Henry's reign, the affable and gracious prince vanished as he fought and lost against the geriatric decay of disease and disability that plagued his body, making him unpredictable, irrational, paranoid and bad-tempered.[87] Furthermore, with declining health, Henry became obsessed with the relentless risk of disease, infection and sudden death, especially as he approached old age. Only ten per cent of the population lived beyond their forties; the average life expectancy of the male Tudor population was thirty-seven years old. To live to any age beyond that was considered a blessing.

By 1540, Henry married his fourth wife, Anne of Cleves, who became queen consort of England from 6 January to 9 July 1540. At this time, Henry's health was deteriorating, and he was putting on more weight; his waist measured fifty-four inches. We know this because we can study and measure the measurements of his suits of armour, the majority of which are on display in the Tower of London. Henry was eating a lot, and not taking any exercise, and because he was in constant pain from a running sore in one of his legs, he had become somewhat of a hypochondriac. He suffered from migraines, ulcerated and varicose veins, obesity, fatigue and the inability to get around because he had become physically disabled. The king was now using a staff to support him when walking. Around the same time, Sir John Wallop, King Henry's ambassador to France reports that 'Their father [Francois I] delights in them [his children] and is himself more lusty than he has been for 12 years past. He dances every night except at this last banquet, when, having been "pricked in the leg [by a sword] with Mons d'Orleans' sword lacking a chape," he walked with a staff.'[88] Wallop added that 'I wished myself that I had one of your highnesses' staves to have presented to him [Francois] in your name. If it shall please your majesty to send him one … he would take it very gratefully.'[89]

Henry owned at least two staves or walking sticks, which he was forced to use to aid him in walking and help him keep his balance and mobility. They are described in his inventory. 'One of them [walking stick] having a cross upon the upper end of black horn with a whistle at either end of the nose' and the other 'having a whistle of white bone at the upper end.' There is a third interesting entry in the inventory, what we would now compare to an elderly person's twenty-four-hour personal alarm in case they fell over when alone at home, used to summon help. Henry owned two kinds of Tudor device for 'shouting', rather like a loud megaphone or hailer, which were called 'trunks', one was covered in black leather, and the other one was 'painted green with metal gilt at both ends'.[90]

It is difficult to imagine that Henry was ever left alone, especially in his old age, as he would always have had attendants around him. However, he would probably have been very afraid of falling, and not being able to get back up on his own again, which meant that he needed to summon help in case of such a fall. Whistles on the end of his walking sticks were the easiest way for Henry to alert an attendant to his plight. You could just imagine Henry bellowing through one of his megaphones in a panic, to get the attention of one of his servants after he had taken a fall. His bulky frame may have needed more than one anxious attendant to help raise him back on his feet and would probably have been a blow to Henry's fragile ego and cause him untold embarrassment. Henry was no longer this virile, omnipotent monarch admired by all, but an old man, broken by disability who was undoubtedly pitied and feared. Henry was no longer an imperial king full of majesty, but a faded and a rather pathetic figure of a man crushed by ill health.

In the same year of 1540 Henry went on to suffer another bout of malaria, which became a chronic problem, as another bout followed in 1541, and Henry lived in permanent fear of catching a disease.[91]

In 1540, the king was reported 'somewhat troubled by a tertian [fever]. The extremity is past and his highness [is] clean rid…and out of all danger'.[92] These bouts of malaria set off a paranoia about his health, and he became obsessed with catching any infection. His obsession with his health and his attitude toward illness affected the whole court where it was not unheard of to be dragged out of bed if an illness was contagious, and an example of this recorded about an incident at Windsor in 1540, saw courtiers and servants carted outside the town's precincts and left to die in outlining fields to reduce the danger to the king and his court. On 8 October 1540, the Privy Council ordered the Dean of Windsor and the town's mayor:

> To cause the inhabitants of the infected houses with their families and household stuff to void the town to some good distance and from such other places as where the king's highness resorts, signifying unto them that the king would bear the charge of their removing.[93]

The portraits by Holbein, completed during Henry's later reign were propaganda and lies, depicting Henry as he had once been in his youth. Now, the king had transformed into someone unrecognisable from these earlier paintings. His osteomyelitis and the ulcers in his legs forced him to use a walking stick, his weight had soared, he had become more unpredictable and irascible than ever, struggling to cope with his infirmities, disability and old age. However, there is one portrait which clearly shows the deterioration of the king due to his health, and this is the image contained in the King's Psalter of psalms, which can be found in the British Library.[94]

The psalter is bound in red velvet, written on vellum in 1540 by John Mallard, and the image of Henry is one found within its

176 pages; a poignant miniature showing the king hunched up on a coffer, seated with his legs crossed, strumming the strings of a harp. He wears a heavy, furred gown, which pronounces his hump, making him look old and frail, his features wrinkled with lines, and distinctly depressed.

Some historians believe that Henry's deterioration was not entirely down to his obesity; suggesting that it was Henry who had syphilis, rather than François I.[95] In the last six to seven years of his life, Henry's symptoms suggest that he could have been suffering from an endocrine abnormality known as Cushing's syndrome. This potential diagnosis was first considered by Clifford Brewer, in *The Death of Kings*.[96] The disease centres around the excessive levels of the hormone cortisol, secreted over long periods by the adrenal glands. The syndrome makes your torso obese, increasing deposits of fat in the neck and creating a hump on the sufferers back. It is the cortisol which causes the body to store excessive amounts of excess fat. Other characteristics of Cushing's syndrome is a round face caused by fatty deposits; the skin becomes thin, fragile and prone to bruising easily, while wounds take a long time to heal. Any excessive exercise weakens the bones, and in serious cases causes backache and fractures. The onset of mild diabetes is another characteristic caused by high levels of sugar in the blood, along with high blood pressure. All these symptoms, it could be argued were characteristics of Henry's problematic obesity, along with the bouts of depression, anxiety, mood swings and insomnia, which he reportedly suffered with. In reviewing the portrait of Henry in the psalter portrait, it is easy to see how the conclusion of Cushing's Syndrome, might be an appropriate one. The jousting accident of January 1536, not only caused the ulcer in Henry's ley to reopen but the brain injury he may have suffered due to the fall can be attributed to causing problems affecting the neuro-endocrine system, which in turn, causes Cushing's Syndrome to be contracted. If Henry did contract Cushing's Syndrome, due to the jousting accident, then this is a very compelling argument as to why Henry's character and personality, as well as his physical body transformed for the worst after January 1536.[97]

It is interesting to note that King Henry had been suffering from headaches and depression, an important characteristic of Cushing's Syndrome, since the jousting accident. Henry was very particular as he entered the Tudor equivalent of old age in whom he surrounded himself with; during this period, Henry's long-standing companion and 'natural' fool, William Somer was never far from Henry's presence. Will Somer is depicted with Henry in that particular psalter portrait, and the reason why William was convincingly painted into the portrait suggests that Henry was dependent on William, for the benefit of his health, and it reinforces the notion that Will was never far from Henry's presence, especially as the king entered old age.[98] Henry knew that for his health, laughter was the best medicine and this concept is so important because Henry believed this was the purpose of a 'natural' fool, like William Somer, to take Henry's mind off his worries; to lift his depression or melancholia, and to make him laugh. In Henry's experience, and the minds of the Tudor court, (and in Tudor society), disabled people spoke truths, cured depression with laughter, and lightened the mood within the royal court; this was one of the main reasons why William Somer never left Henry's side.

> But this Will Summers was of an easie nature, and tractable disposition, who ... gained not only grace and favour from his Majesty, but a general love of the Nobility; for he was no carry-tale, nor whisperer, nor flattering insinuater, to breed discord and dissension, but an honest plain down-right, that would speak home without halting, and tell the truth of purpose to shame the Devil; so that his plainness mixt with a kind of facetiousness, and tartness with pleasantness made him very acceptable into the companies of all men.[99]

From an English contemporary medical perspective, the promotion of treating melancholy with laughter was becoming more commonplace, which is why 'natural fools' and disabled people with learning disabilities were crucial to everyday life, both in their homes and communities and at the Tudor court.[100] Erasmus had suggested in his book, *In Praise of Folly*, that 'Folly is the one thing which can halt fleeting youth and ward off the relentless advance of old age.'[101]

As King Henry advanced in age, he increasingly became a challenging patient for his surgeons to treat, so William Somer often relieved that burden for them. Moreover, throughout his thirty-eight year reign, Henry underwent a dramatic personal metamorphosis to become a despotic, cruel and tyrannical sovereign, vile of temper and cursed by his deteriorating health and his 'sorre legge'.[102] Henry's changing health and character undoubtedly mirrored the personal pressures and political machinations of the day. It is interesting to reflect on how the surgeons would have treated an infection that disabled him in later life and the impact that persistent ulceration would have had on his life, personality and political administration.

Henry VIII was proactive of his care, working tirelessly with his doctors to develop a new type of bandage for his ulcerous legs. The king was fascinated in the treatments of the day, and the king had a book of prescriptions for treating ailments, concocting some of his remedies, which he prepared. These treatments took the form of compounds, made from salves, ointments and ground pearls and white lead, which he not only used for himself, but also for the treatment of his closest friends. In the book, a prescription for the treatment of ulcers reads 'An Oyntment devised by the kinges Majesty made at Westminster. And devised at Greenwich to take away inflammations and to cease payne and heale ulcers called gray plaster.'[103]

In February 1541, Henry was suffering again with the ulcers on his legs and by 3 March, French Ambassador Marillac, wrote to François I, that 'this King [Henry] talked of visiting his castles and palaces on the South coast towards France, to have the ramparts which had fallen remade, particularly the port of Dover. Henry travelling was prevented by an illness which happened to him at Hampton Court, in the form of a slight tertian fever, which should rather have profited than hurt him, for he is very stout, but one of his legs, formerly opened and kept open to maintain his health, suddenly closed, to his great alarm, for, five or six years ago, in like case, he thought to have died. This time prompt remedy was applied, and he is now well, and the fever gone.'[104]

On the same day, Marillac writes to Montgomery saying:

> With regard to his letter to the King, this King's life was really thought to be in danger, not from the fever but from the leg, which often troubles him because he is very stout and marvellously excessive in drinking and eating, so that people worth credit say he is often of a different opinion in the morning than after dinner.[105]

Henry was over six feet tall, and in his twenties weighed about fifteen stone with his waist measuring 32 inches and his chest was 39 inches, but by his fifties, his waist had increased to 52 inches and, by the time of his death in 1547 at the age of 55 years, he is thought to have weighed about twenty-eight stone. As Henry's grew older, his weight increased and he became obese, his risk of high blood pressure and Type II diabetes must have been high. Without exercise, Henry was to become a binge eater and suffer from constipation. His doctors repeatedly urged him to reduce his tremendous consumption of meat and wine, as he had a penchant for high cholesterol foodstuffs as was documented in the Ordinances of Eltham. Henry regularly ate three meals a day. Amongst his favourite meals were galantines, game pies and haggis. He would consume copious amounts of wine, beer and gin. The Tudor table displayed birds slaughtered for consumption: larks, stork, gannet, heron, snipe, bustard, quail, partridge, capons, teal, crane and pheasants and pies with birds in were all digested, and a favourite on the court menus.

Salted and fresh fish followed the meat course and favourite marine life and fish were: cod, herrings, eels, salmon, porpoises, dolphin and ling. Fresh fruit was a limited food on menus as it was believed to cause stomach aches, diarrhoea and fever, however, the king did enjoy eating cherries. Green vegetables were considered peasant food and were to be avoided at court because they were thought to cause flatulence and caused depression. However, first courses were made up of cucumbers, lettuces and herbs. Henry enjoyed most meats such as pork, lamb, chicken and beef, to peacock, swan, rabbit and venison. His diet consisted of over five thousand calories a day, which makes his obesity no surprise. He would drink ale, red wine with sugar instead of water and copious amounts of white bread. His organs must have been surrounded by subcutaneous fat and he may have suffered from high blood pressure, poor circulation and an enlarged heart.

Despite his growing ill health, the king married for a fifth time. After the political match with Anne of Cleves made by Thomas Cromwell was dissolved, Anne was rapidly divorced and removed to the country. Henry then followed his heart into a fateful liaison with the pretty and young Catherine Howard. Unfortunately, they were married only a short while, when Henry ordered Catherine to be dispatched to the Tower on accusations of adultery and treason. Condemned by a bill of attainder, she was executed on 13 February 1542.

Some interpreted his final marriage in 1543 to Catherine Parr as acquiring a convenient nursemaid in the final years of his life. In March 1544, the scourge of his infectious legs returned and the ulcers that plagued him flared up again, confining him to bed with a fever. His sudden and terrible rages would send his courtiers fleeing, and none but his wife could calm him. When Henry was up and about supported by his walking stick, the stench of his infected ulcers could be identified three rooms away, often heralding the monarch's arrival.

Henry's legs tortured him for the last two decades of his life, described on 18 May 1544 by Chapuys, the Spanish Ambassador, when writing to the Queen of Hungary that:

> The King will not act prudently in attempting the journey, for, besides his age and weight, he has the worst legs in the world, such that those who hare seen them are astonished that he does not stay continually in bed and judge that he will not be able to endure the very least exertion without danger of his life, yet no one dare tell him so. It is clear that his presence might he very useful if health permitted it, but as he now is it will be a danger.[106]

The king would have been in constant pain. However, Henry was always concerned with his duties, mindful of the threats facing England from its immediate neighbour, France. He refused to rest, extensively visiting ports and cities around his kingdom, and by June he was well enough to personally lead an invasion into France.

From around the same time in 1544, Henry's eyesight was beginning to fade, and he was slowly going blind. To read paperwork involving government business, he had ten pairs of wire-framed spectacles to use at his disposal, which had been sent over from Germany. He probably ordered so many at a time because the design clipped onto the bridge of his nose and he was always losing them. In the royal expenses records of October 1544, it records, '10 pair of spectacles at 4d. the pair'.[107] Henry's poor eyesight, coupled with a distaste for letter-writing and administration, compelled him to use a 'dry stamp' from September 1545; this was a device which stamped state papers with the royal autograph. The signature block was made of wood, with a raised royal signature, used to impress onto every document, witnessed by members of the Lord Privy Seal Department. Every use of the stamp was recorded in an individual ledger by a Clerk to prevent fraudulent use. The king would then examine the ledger at monthly intervals.[108]

By the spring of 1546, Henry's activities had been seriously limited although he continued to travel to his estates in the southern counties of England, and even to hunt in between periods of ill-health, refusing to rest despite the advice of his physicians. Henry's mobility was completely impaired and 'king's trams', rather like sedan chairs, were purchased to carry him around the royal apartments of Whitehall, because he was unable to walk as his grossly swollen legs could not bear his weight. These tram-like contraptions probably resembled a kind of Tudor-style wheelchair. Professor Suzannah Lipscomb in conversation with historian Dan Snow, suggests that Henry's many illnesses incapacitated him in later life, stopped him taking part in the sports he enjoyed rendering him disabled, so much so that he had no choice but to be pushed or carried in a contraption that resembled a wheelchair.[109] Henry VIII undoubtedly used a wheelchair, which was a two-shafted car, upholstered in tawny silk with a double rose embroidered as an emblem on the back.[110]

The original records do not state whether the trams had wheels on them, so Henry would have had to have had at least four body-builder type attendants to lug the king from room to room, and through gallery to gallery, in his palaces. Moreover, his use of a wheelchair and his disability was never depicted in any portrait, as this would have broken the concrete Tudor propaganda machine that was Holbein. However, van der Delft, Spanish ambassador, mentioned that he saw Henry 'passing in his chair' at Windsor Castle on 7 October 1546.[111]

Henry's ownership of two 'wheelthrones', is confirmed in a transcript held in the British Library. Entry 11798 states:

> Item Twoo Cheyres called trauewes for the Kinges Majestie to sitt in to be carried to and fro in his galleries and Chambres couered with tawney vellat all over quilted with an acordaunte of tawney silke with a half pace undernethe euerie of the saide cheyres and twoo fotestoles standing vppon euerie one a rose of venice golde and frengid rounde aboute with tawnye silke.

Above left: Henry VIII Chatsworth cartoon. Workshop of Hans Holbein the Younger, 1536. (Walker Art Gallery)

Above right: Queen Mary I touching the neck of a boy for the King's evil (scrofula). Watercolour by M.S. Lapthorn, 1911, after a watercolour, sixteenth century. (Wellcome Library, London)

'Newes from Scotland', Declaring the damnable life and death of Dr. Fian (woodcut), English School, (sixteenth century). (Lambeth Palace Library, London, UK/Bridgeman Images)

The Beggars or *The Cripples*, oil panel by Flemish renaissance artist Pieter Bruegel the Elder. (©RMN-Grand Palais, Musée du Louvre)

The Family Of Sir Thomas More by Rowland Lockey (*c.* 1565-1616) after Holbein, 1592, in the Lower Hall at Nostell Priory, Yorkshire. The original version of this painting by Holbein, painted about 1527, is now lost. The image shows Henry Pattenson in the yellow, who was Thomas More's fool. (Nostell Priory, by kind permission of Lord St. Oswald & the National Trust. (©National Trust Images/John Hammond)

Exterior view from the north-east showing the former Maison Dieu almshouse, Ospringe, Kent. (With kind permission of ©Historic England Archive)

Above left: Portrait of Queen Claude, wife of King François I of France. (©RMN-Grand Palais, Musée du Louvre/Michèle Bellot 2021)

Above right: Portrait of Anne Boleyn by Hans Holbein the younger, inscribed in gold over red 'Anna Bollein Queen'. Black and coloured chalks on pink prepared paper. (Royal Collection Trust/©Her Majesty Queen Elizabeth II 2021)

Below: Anne Boleyn portrait medal. Work in progress. Lucy Churchill's wax reconstruction and the tools she used, shown with an image of the original coin. (©Lucy Churchill, 2021 used with kind permission.)

Above left: Lucy Churchill's reconstruction, cast in bronze resin. (©Lucy Churchill 2021, used with kind permission.)

Above right: Lucy Churchill's annotated sketch. This shows the notes that Lucy made at the British Museum on the line drawing of the original 'footprint' of the medal, with observations regarding depth and details apparent when viewing the original, but not in the BM's stock photo of the medal. (©Lucy Churchill 2021, used with kind permission.)

Above: John Laurence, cook, to the Lords of the Council, petition, SP 1 version, Gale/Cengage State Papers Online, MC4301701136, ref. SP1/100 f.60 (@The National Archives, reproduced with kind permission.)

Left: John Laurence, cook, to the Lords of the Council, STAC 10, Star Chamber miscellaneous. ref. STAC10/4/128 (@The National Archives, reproduced with kind permission.)

Entry 1179 states:

> Item an other Cheyre called a Trauewe serving for theafforesaide purpose couered with russet vellat all ouer quilted with a cordaunte of russet silke with a halfe pace vndrenethe the same Cheyre and twoo fote stoles standing vppon the same halfe pace embrawdred vppon the backe and the toppe of the two highe pomelles a rose of Venice golde fringed rounde aboute with russet silke.[112]

Not only did Henry own and use two wheelchairs, he also owned and used a primitive style 'stairlift', which assisted members of Henry's Yeomen of the Guard to hoist him up and down the twenty-six stairs to his sixteen-thousand square foot privy apartments, on the first floor of Whitehall Palace. This stairlift may have been a kind of hoist, used to carry him from the ground floor of his palaces, to avoid using stairs. Access to his apartments was insurmountable without the use of this 'stairlift'. When I attended a talk on 'A Monarchy of Misfits?' by the historian David Starkey, at the Allendale Centre in Wimborne Minster on 18 May 2019, in a conversation with him, he kindly verified that Henry did indeed own a Tudor style stairlift. David told me it was 'a kind of lift, with a system of ropes and pulleys, much like one used on the Mary Rose warship.'[113]

The fact that Henry owned a stairlift to carry him around, is also confirmed by an entry in the 1542 inventory of royal possessions at Whitehall Palace. The entry describes a:

> Cheyre couered with purple vellat allouer quilted with a cordaunte of purple Silke standing yppon a falfe pace couered with like vellat likewise quilted with twoo fote stoles vppon the same all frengid with purple Silke enbrawdred vppon the backe and pomelles with a rose of venice golde the same cheyre did serue in the kinges house that goeth vpp and downe.[114]

The details of the item show that Henry would have rested his feet, supported by an attached footstool, while he was transported up and down by his burly guards.

Professor Suzannah Lipscomb writes in her brilliant book, *The King is Dead, The Last Will and Testament of Henry VIII*, that the king was:

> Fifty-five years old, grossly overweight, and had been plagued by a decade by a terrible running sore on his leg that had recently caused him into the Tudor equivalent of a wheelchair and stairlift.[115]

Being carried or wheeled around in a mobility contraption would have heightened Henry's vile temper, which was undoubtedly influenced by his clinical situation. The king did not bear his suffering with fortitude, and the later years of his reign were characterised by frequent tempestuous outbursts and cruelty, viciously turning on those that he had once patronised. He was courageous in his refusal to do as his physicians suggested and lie a-bed, preferring to struggle, and tried to continue the façade of being the valiant prince he used to be.

In December 1546, even though Henry did not want to think about his impending death, he was not well. He made plans with his secretary Sir William Paget to prepare for death, and in doing so, plans to provide care for his heir, Edward. According to Paget, he had recalled, that Henry said 'that he felt himself sickly, and that if ought should come to him but good, ... that he could not long endure'.[116]

Further bouts of fever and complications with his leg ulcers followed, and he deteriorated rapidly. Henry spent his last days bedridden, and the stench of his putrefying leg ulcers must have been foul. His doctors probably feared to tell him he was dying, as to do so was dangerous. The treason law forbade anyone speaking or predicting the king's death. However, it was Henry's Groom of the Stool, Sir Antony Denny, who had the unenviable job of warning the king of his approaching end. Henry lay in his nine-foot long four-poster bed decorated with crimson hangings, within his blood-red bedchamber, which must have felt almost as silent as the grave. The king looked as comfortable as he could have been under the circumstances, propped up against his carved walnut headboard, with plain white linen pillows piled up behind his head and torso for comfort. The white linen sheets which covered him were decorated with Venice gold silk.[117]

His breathing was laboured, as Denny nervously spoke to him. Sir Antony urged Henry to prepare for death, and to remember his sins, just as good Christian men should. The king asked for Dr Cranmer to be summoned so Cranmer could advise him on the matter, but that first, he should like to sleep. According to accounts, those were the king's last spoken words, and he sank into unconsciousness.

Archbishop Thomas Cranmer was summoned from his palace at Croydon, Surrey, riding to London through a chilly and frosty night. He eventually arrived after midnight, where he had to fight his way through knots of Privy Councillors, who were congregating outside the royal bedchamber, plotting and whispering with one another, while waiting for news of the king. Archbishop Cranmer entered the inner sanctum, the king's bedchamber, with Antony Denny and others looking on. As Thomas Cranmer scrambled to Henry's bedside, he tilted his head close to Henry so that he could whisper into the king's ear. Cranmer wanted some sign from Henry that he still put his trust in Christ and the Christian faith and wanted to receive God's mercy and grace, knowing that his death was imminent. The room was silent; Henry was unable to speak. However, Henry was able to 'wring his [Cranmer's] hand as hard as he could' in a gesture to show that he understood his old friend.[118]

Henry died in the faith of Christ, undramatically, in the early hours of 28 January 1547 at the age of nearly fifty-six in a period when life expectancy for men was said to be around fifty, yet other courtiers would live longer. It is more than likely that the king died of all his ills, had diabetes and suffered heart and kidney failure at his end.

The funeral cortege consisted of a stately gilded chariot, with a life-size effigy of the king laying on top of the coffin for its twenty-four mile journey. There were hundreds of mourners, from nobility to foreign ambassadors, to courtiers. Mourners were dressed in black apparel.[119] Amongst the contingent of mourners in the queen's household was Henry's faithful companion and friend, the natural fool, William Somer, listed in the account of the funeral as 'the fool'.[120] Henry's funeral procession followed his cortege from Whitehall to Syon Abbey; the only stop overnight on the way to Henry's final resting place. The chariot arrived at Syon Abbey in the afternoon of 13 February and his coffin was placed before the high altar, guarded by an overnight watch. However, a horrific account later told of putrid matter leaking from the king's coffin while it lay in state overnight, when stray dogs wandered into the church after Henry's body had imploded, leaving his blood to filter out and leak on the ground. The dogs then licked up the putrefied blood that had seeped from the cracked elm coffin.[121] The story of dogs licking up Henry's blood upon his death came from the vile prediction of the Franciscan friar and preacher William Peto, who had predicted years before in 1532, that if Henry continued to defy the Pope and the Catholic Church, dogs would lick up his blood just as they had in the biblical story of Ahab. In the morning, once the coffin was repaired, Henry was taken from Syon Abbey to Windsor Castle in a procession, where he was eventually buried in the chapel of St George at Windsor, with his third wife, Jane Seymour.

Henry's rule started with high hopes, as Thomas More commented, of a 'Golden World', almost like 'Camelot', but with Henry's decline into disability towards the end of his reign, it is difficult not to feel sorry for the ageing king, feeling embarrassed by the putride smell oozing from his leg ulcers, to the fear of being discovered by foreign ambassadors as he was pushed around the private passageways of his palaces in one of his wheelchairs, to his privy chamber servants hoisting him up the stairs at Whitehall Palace in his chair throne. Henry VIII should have been proud of the fact he had survived the threat of so many unsuitable wives, plotting courtiers and political intrigues and to have entered old age with the assistance of mobility contraptions which enabled him to reign to the best of his abilities, even with mental and physical disabilities right up to the end of his life.

Chapter Eight

Disabled People in High Places

During the Tudor period, there were mentally and physically challenged disabled people who were close to those in positions of power, or were in positions of power themselves. These disabled people were observed, but were rarely written about; but from the portraits, and accounts that survive of disabled people in the Tudor period, we can understand that many of them thrived. Mostly, disability was washed over, or it was hidden in plain view. One of the most notable, said to be physically challenged, was King Richard III, whose death by the forces loyal to Henry VII at the Battle of Bosworth Field in 1485, created the Tudor dynasty. So, it is where we began, that we start to end this study of disabled people during the Tudor era.

During the reign of the last Tudor monarch, Queen Elizabeth I, Shakespeare portrayed Richard III as twisted in both body and mind. Little did the playwright know whether or not Richard III was deformed, or the exact nature of his assumed deformity. Scoliosis was not understood as a disability in medieval or Tudor times. Moreover, Richard's physical condition was not proved until Philippa Langley commissioned the search for his remains, which were eventually discovered in a Leicester car park in 2012. Furthermore, Richard was physically able to fight in three battles and numerous skirmishes, led an invasion force of 20,000 into Scotland and defend his throne, but Shakespeare was determined that Richard would succeed as a villain. John Rous recorded that, 'let me say the truth to his credit: that he bore himself like a noble soldier and despite his little body and feeble strength, honourably defended himself to his last breath, shouting again and again that he was betrayed, and crying 'Treason! Treason! Treason!'[1] It could be argued that Shakespeare had been writing about his contemporary, Robert Cecil, and not Richard III. Cecil was known to be short in stature and having a curvature of the spine.[2]

This distorted and inherently negative view of people with physical or mental challenges and disabilities is evident in numerous sources of literature and art, both classical and famous, which has always been produced. William Shakespeare's *Richard III* illustrates attitudes experienced by someone born into a world which placed a high premium upon physical normality:

> Cheated of feature by dissembling nature,
> Deformed, unfinished, sent before my time
> Into this breathing world, scarce half made up,
> And that so lamely and unfashionable
> The dogs bark at me as I halt by them.[3]

However, from a metrical account of the family of Richard, Duke of York, written between 1455 and 1460, and quoted in *History of the Life and Reign of Richard the Third*:

> John aftir William nexte borne was
> Whiche bothe be passid to Godis grace.
> George was nexte,
> and aftir Thomas Borne was, which sone aftir did pace
> By the path of dethe to the hevenly place.
> Richard liveth yit; but the last of alle
> Was Ursula, to Hym whom God list calle.[4]

This account could be argued to suggest that Richard was a sickly child, when in fact, it is stating that, of the Duchess of York's last six children, only George and Richard were still living. Moreover, further contemporary descriptions of Richard III, do not mention any sickness or physical abnormality, except to record that Richard was 'short in stature'. Archibald Whitelaw, the Archdeacon of Lothian, who came to Richard's court at Nottingham with an embassy from James III of Scotland in 1484, stated that 'Never has so much spirit or greater virtue reigned in such a small body'.[5]

In Richard's day, his scoliosis would not have been considered a disability; however, his scoliosis was used as a topic of propaganda by the Tudors to discredit him when it is evident from the contemporary accounts that Richard had been more than capable on the battlefield. As Duke of Gloucester, and as King, Richard led an active life as a competent administrator and military commander. He rode on horseback in full body armour and wielded a sword, battle axe and lance in battle, demonstrating that scoliosis does not limit physical capability. There is no contemporary evidence that Richard III was disabled, with any visible physical problems. A surviving description of the king is provided by a Silesian ambassador of the Holy Roman Emperor Frederick III, Nicolas van Poppelau, who spent time at Richard's court in 1484 and described the king as lean, with slender arms and legs and that he was 'three fingers taller' than Poppelau himself. Also, that the king had a 'great heart'.[6]

I have been fortunate to discuss with Philippa Langley, MBE, the findings from the discovery of the remains of Richard III and the supporting evidence that had been researched during and after excavation. The skeleton showed that Richard was 5'8" tall and suffered from scoliosis, a sideways curvature of the spine which would have the effect of giving him one shoulder higher than the other. In Richard's case, his right shoulder was higher than his left. The imbalance of his shoulders was recorded after the king's death in a contemporary source by John Rous, an antiquary and chantry priest at Warwick, who probably saw Richard during his visits there. Rous's account of the king following his death in battle is openly hostile, saying that Richard was 'retained within his mother's womb for two years and emerging with teeth and hair to his shoulders. He was small of stature, with a short face and unequal shoulders, the right higher and the left lower'.[7]

Rous was unsure which shoulder was the higher as he left a gap in the text for this information to be inserted. Whether this was completed by Rous later, or by another writer, we do not know, but the information was correct.[8]

Another contemporary account comes from John Stow, a London antiquary, who had talked to those who had seen Richard and he stated that 'He [Richard] was of bodily shape comely enough only of low stature.' Another contemporary source, this time from Polydore Vergil, who was an Italian cleric and scholar, commissioned to write an official history of England for Henry VII, which was first published in 1534, stated that: 'He was lyttle of stature, deformyd of body, the one showlder being higher than the other, a short and sowre cowntenance, which semyd to savor of mischief and utter evydently craft and deceyt.'[9] Despite these descriptions, Richard's skeleton revealed that his arms were of average length; he had straight hips and legs, and usually walked with no gait; the king was not lame.

Despite the circumstantial evidence from visible battle wounds, the skeleton, on initial examination, appeared to have suffered significant perimortem trauma to the skull consistent with an injury received in battle. A bladed implement, perhaps a sword, appears to have cleaved part of the rear of the skull, and a curvature of the spine known as scoliosis, was visibly apparent when the remains were unearthed. The Tudors insisted on embellishing Richard III's physical challenges, painting a defamatory picture, for propaganda purposes, and from what Philippa and the team in Leicester discovered about the remains, we now know that Richard was not 'hunchbacked', as Shakespeare had described him in his play. The university of Leicester archaelogists argue that Richard's curvature was not kyphosis, which Tudor sources attributed to Richard III, along with a 'withered arm' and limping gait. These latter deformities such as a 'withered arm' were not in the least apparent in the remains. The skeleton found in the choir area of the buried ruins of Leicester Abbey had spinal abnormalities, indicative of the individual having had severe scoliosis.

When King Richard III was unceremoniously stripped of his clothes after he was slain on the battlefield at Bosworth, his corpse was thrown over the back of a horse. His body so exposed in this manner, and displayed to the victors, would have revealed that his spine was crooked. To add insult to Richard, it seems they further injured him after death, by thrusting a dagger into his upper back on the right-hand side. A physical insult to his body, to probably attack and draw attention to his deformity emphasised the suspicion that if he had a curved back, to the Tudors at least, Richard's mind must have been crooked also. In the Tudors' thinking, if his mind was crooked, then he could not rule the realm and was, therefore, never entitled to be king. This was the beginning of the Tudors' inception of the dark legends surrounding King Richard III. It was only after his death that vindictive propaganda of Richard III began to be embroidered with descriptions of various disfigurements.

A paper entitled 'Perimortem Trauma in King Richard III: a skeletal analysis' concluded that Richard's injuries were consistent with those created by weapons from the later medieval period. The team could not identify the specific order of the injuries, because they were all distinct, with no overlapping wounds. Three of Richard's injuries – two to the inferior cranium and one to the pelvis – could have been fatal.

The wounds to Richard's skull suggest that he was not wearing a helmet. The rest of his body must have been armoured, as there was an absence of defensive wounds on his hands and arms.[10]

Therefore, the potentially fatal pelvis injury that Richard's remains show, was probably received post-mortem, meaning that the most likely injuries which caused his death, are the two to the inferior cranium.[11]

This paper formed the basis for the television documentary, *Richard III: The New Evidence*. This intriguing documentary, shown on Channel 4, set out to investigate just what Richard III would have been capable of, given his scoliosis of the spine. Using the latest scientific evidence from the examination of his skeleton and the services of a 'body double' with scoliosis, the programme demonstrated Richard's fighting abilities and physical state after becoming king. Dominic Smee volunteered to act as Richard's double, taking part in experiments specifically designed to test his mobility and strength. He rode a horse and was fitted with medieval-style armour and took part in hand-to-hand combat. His armour, fitted by a Swedish expert, was personally tailored due to his condition, but once he was fully dressed, like Richard III, his condition was not visible. Dominic Smee recreated Richard III's last 1,000-metre cavalry charge at Bosworth. The medieval-style saddle, with solid supports back and front helped Dominic, being more secure for him than a modern saddle. He made the charge successfully and hit the waiting quintain, thus proving that when fully armed and mounted on horseback, Richard would have been a formidable warrior. Once dismounted, however, like all medieval knights, he would have been more vulnerable.

In conclusion, the programme proved that Richard III's scoliosis would not have prevented him from being a compelling force on the battlefield. He would have had to be very fit and had probably been trained for battle since childhood. The contribution of Dominic Smee in this documentary, helped the scientists bring to life King Richard's likely capabilities.

Shakespeare's portrayal of a hunchback was incorrect as there is no evidence for kyphosis, or the withered arm and limp, or that Richard was disabled, or his physicality prevented him from being a king in both a political and military sense. It seems we now know that sadly they are the inventions of those trying to blacken Richard's image, to aid the Tudor propaganda machine. To dispel many of the myths of Richard III, the Richard III Society was formed to promote a balanced, view of Richard III's life, reign, military career and a detailed account of the remains discovered in the car park and their scientific evaluation. They have changed much of what we know, or thought we knew, about this critical historical figure.

The Tudor dynasty had members of royalty, relations and counterparts who suffered disabilities. In neighbouring France, one such member of the French royal family suffered from several disabilities which were debilitating and did prevent a normal and healthy life. Claude de Valois, Queen of France, was an unusual ruler who faced numerous disabling challenges. Claude of France was born on 13 October 1499. The Chronicler of Anjou stated that Claude was, 'A pearl of a woman … goodness without sin'. Claude's parents were Anne of Brittany and King Louis XII and due to her standing at birth, Claude would be married off for diplomatic and political reasons.

Like most royal children of the period, Claude was raised by a governess, and Claude's parents were very protective of their daughter, who grew up in the palatial, royal Château of Blois. King Louis adored Claude who was a happy child. He continued to enjoy her company as she grew older, and despite her deformities and disabilities, he encouraged Claude to go hunting with him. Claude was brought up religiously and was pious, and her reading primer contained the alphabet and a selection of prayers and Bible stories. Her piety would stand her in good stead because she was an essential pawn in the marriage market. Even though she was a paramour of virtue, intelligent, witty and religious, due to French law, women were not allowed to inherit the throne and rule. Claude's mother had no surviving male heirs, so Claude became heiress to the Duchy of Brittany. The Crown of France, however, could only be inherited through its male heirs, according to Salic Law.[12]

For the French throne to be passed down to a male heir, it was to be passed to Louis' relative, François d'Angoulême who was brought up by his mother, Louise of Savoy in Amboise. Louise and François had a guardian called Pierre de Gié, who strongly advocated for a marriage between Claude and François.[13]

Different factions surrounded Claude, especially prominent where those vying for her marriage to a husband, would be of the most benefit in unifying the duchy of Brittany with one of her European neighbours. Eventually, after much political negotiations, Louise of Savoy had obtained from the king a secret promise that Claude could be married to François.[14] Claude was an advantageous match for François, who was an unbelievably wealthy woman and was considered to make an excellent royal consort.

Claude's mother, Anne of Brittany, died on 9 January 1514. Louis XII, despite being devastated at the news, remarried quickly, choosing Henry VIII's more youthful sister, Mary, as his next spouse. Claude became Duchess of Brittany; and just four months later, on 18 May, she married her cousin François at Saint-Germain-en-Laye. With this union, it was considered that Brittany would remain united to the French Crown if the third marriage of Henry VIII's sister Mary and Louis XII would not produce the long-awaited heir. According to Robert de la Marck, Francis I's companion said Claude 'was greatly distressed, for her mother had been dead only a short while, and she was now obligated to serve her [Mary Tudor] as she had formerly served the Queen her mother'.[15] Despite her misery, Claude put on a brave face and did not neglect to demonstrate her respect for Louis XII's new wife, who was only three years older. Sadly, the marriage between these newlyweds did not last long and finished when Claude's father Louis XII died on 1 January 1515. His marriage to Henry VIII's sister Mary was childless: Louis XII had been reputedly worn out by his exertions in the bedchamber.[16]

After her father's death, Claude's husband, François, as the king's nearest male relative, inherited the French crown, and as the English chronicler Raphael Holinshed explained, François 'was preferred to the succession of the kingdom before the daughters [Claude and Renée] of the dead King by virtue and disposition of the Salic law, a law very ancient in the realm of France, which excluded from the royal dignity all women'.[17]

Her parents' deaths had sent Claude into a tailspin of grief and she was in tears throughout her entire wedding ceremony. François had brought a poster-bed, a bolster and coverlet and Claude had contributed silk hangings. François' mother did not attend but she noted in her journal that the couple were married in the morning at ten o'clock, and they retired to bed together that evening. Claude was considered the best dynastic match for François, but some courtiers opposed it based on Claude's fragile health. Some chroniclers were universal in their praise of Claude as the epitome of the ideal queen, while others opposed her because of her looks, suggesting she was 'strangely corpulent', 'small and badly lame in both hips' and sadly, not thought of as 'beautiful'.[18] By the time of his marriage to Claude, François was already a known womaniser, and on the morning after his wedding, he left to go hunting and seek the company of one of his mistresses. Sadly, François never valued fidelity and saw his marriage as his duty to France.

To make matters worse for Claude, Pierre de Rohan, Marshal of Gié, told Louise of Savoy that he would rather see François 'married to a simple shepherdess of this kingdom than to Madame Claude because the misfortune is such that Madame Claude is deformed in body and unable to bear children'.[19] Their Tudor counterparts in Europe had similar superstitious ideas around disability, as they thought that if a woman was disabled in any way, then her chances of bearing children were slim, to nought.

Moreover, this idea is reinforced by the Austrian ambassador who describes Claude as retiring with a pale complexion, thin, a little sickly, slightly hunchbacked and somewhat unattractive. He goes on to say she was petite with a strange corpulence and her grace in speaking, compensated for her lack of beauty. There is another description of Claude in *The Travel Journal of Antonio De Beatis* and he offers a back-handed compliment that the queen is young, and though small in stature, is plain and severely lame in both hips. However, he says she is cultivated, generous and religiously pious. Due to her disabilities, it was hard for Claude to compete physically with her husband. Claude's thoughts touching the preferment of her husband's claim to the French crown over hers are not recorded but we may assume that she was content with the role of royal consort because she had been groomed to become a queen consort from birth. If she had been crowned as a monarch in her own right, her reign may have been maligned, as firstly, she was a woman, and secondly, she was physically disabled, which meant that her ability to rule her nation would have been questioned. Her disability would have ruled her out from reigning alone, in her own right.

On 10 May 1517, Claude was crowned Queen of France at the Basilica of Saint-Denis by Cardinal Philippe de Luxembourg, who 'anointed her in the breast and forehead'.[20] Claude was aware that as Duchess of Brittany in her own right, she looked to accept her political role. However, Claude likewise realised that because of her significance as Louis XII's heir, and now she was the Queen of France, she was expected to demonstrate her value in being the best dynastic match for

François, and she showed her strength of character by never trying to factionalise the court and enduring the control and coercive behaviour of her in-laws with dignity and grace.

It was essentially her wifely duty to ensure that France had a healthy male heir. However, some courtiers opposed the match, and the marriage, based on Claude's frail health. Claude of France was ridiculed unkindly at court due to her 'small size, and her ugliness,' but her good qualities were acknowledged, and as such, it seems that, despite her limitations and appearance, Claude triumphed. She had been, from her birth, the pawn of much dynastic manoeuvring, which was expected, considering her pedigree. Yet she was a pious and formidable character, even though she was short in stature and had scoliosis, which gave her a hunched back. Claude also had one leg shorter than the other, walked with a limp, was apparently in pain and had an eye condition called strabismus, affecting her left eye. Strabismus was also called 'crossed eyes' or refers to having a squint; it is a condition in which the persons' eyes do not align correctly with each other when looking at an object.[21] Strabismus may be present for the patient occasionally or continuously. If the condition is present during a large part of childhood, it may result in amblyopia or loss of depth perception. Adults with the condition may also have double vision.[22] Strabismus is caused by an episode of trauma, muscle dysfunction, an issue of farsightedness, and perhaps a problem in the brain, or an infection. Risk factors include instances of premature birth, cerebral palsy, and a family history of the condition. Types of strabismus include esotropia where the eyes are crossed; exotropia where the eyes diverge; and hypertropia where they are vertically misaligned. The condition is classified today by whether the problem is present in all directions a person looks or varies by direction. Diagnosis is often made by observing the light reflecting from the person's eyes and finding that it is not centred on the pupil.[23]

Claude probably struggled with many health issues which would have been challenging in an age when medical knowledge and care was in its infancy, even for royals. Moreover, with every successive pregnancy, Claude became more unhealthy, and this made her appear continuously plump and with her back hunched with scoliosis, she attracted unkind attention and ridicule at court. Foreign ambassadors noted her 'corpulence', claudication, the strabismus affecting her left eye, her small size, and her ugliness. However, they also acknowledged her good qualities. She overcame being a political pawn, by doing her duty, leading a pious and uncorrupt life in a licentious court, despite her deformities and disabilities and she influenced many, with her excellent qualities, kindness and sensibilities.[24] Comments about her disability did not help Claude's reputation, and her physical disabilities did not endear her to some at court. Moreover, when Claude became pregnant, most courtiers assumed that she would die while giving birth. According to the Bishop of Worcester in a letter to Cardinal Wolsey, rumour had it that even the pope alleged that 'the French asserted the present Queen would die in childbed'.[25] Despite the defaming comments, Claude admirably fulfilled her wifely duties in producing children, refuting her critics, bringing forth seven children during the period from 1515 to 1524. Historian Simone Bertière determined that Claude was pregnant sixty-three months of the one-hundred and twenty-two months of her reign, having been pregnant at least seven times in eight years, which is incredible considering the disabilities she had. Five of Claude's children survived into adulthood. François was born in 1518, then a year later the future King Henri II was born, and Charles followed in 1522. A daughter Madeleine came in 1520 and would fall in love with and marry King James V of Scots. Another child was born in 1523, a second daughter Marguerite, who would go on to marry Emmanuel-Philibert of Savoy. Sadly, another two daughters died young: Louise at the age of two and Charlotte at the age of seven.

These continuous pregnancies negatively affected the Queen's delicate wellbeing and she could not go to François' court and assume her role as regularly as decorum dictated. Claude did go on a religious pilgrimage to southeastern France in 1515 to pray for a son. She travelled to Brittany in 1518 where she was received with enthusiasm as the Duchess of Brittany, rather than being Queen of France. Moreover, because of her many pregnancies, and the difficulties they caused for her health, she was not consecrated as queen until 1517.

It has regularly been suggested that Queen Claude lived in some deliberate seclusion from the court, and spent most of her time participating in strict religious observances and that her philandering husband did not give her enough respect. However, while the facts confirm that François I was a famous adulterer who kept a few courtesans, he was fond of his wife.[26] One eyewitness commented that he held Claude 'in such honour and respect that when in France and with her he has never failed to sleep with her each night'. Being always pregnant or in confinement, it is not surprising that Claude made very few public appearances during her reign. Her many pregnancies, and labours caused her health to suffer, making it challenging to travel and fulfil ceremonial duties. However, Claude officially attended the summit of the Field of Cloth of Gold in June of 1520 along with Katharine of Aragon, Henry VIII's queen. Nevertheless, both ladies were self-effacing, and Claude's mother-in-law, sister-in-law and her husband's official mistresses presided over the tournament to fulfil their formal roles.[27]

Moreover, Claude delighted in taking particular care over her appearance and clothes to keep up with the courtiers at court. She dressed elegantly, frequently amazing foreign ambassadors with the amount and size of gems she wore, and the quality of fabrics and silks she chose for her gowns. She additionally showed enthusiasm for beauty preparation, accepting three containers of scented hand cream from the popular Isabella d'Este. However much she tried to improve her appearance, Queen Claude was to became more obese and incapacitated. Her limp, caused by her deformed hips and scoliosis, became more pronounced. She became increasingly private, withdrawing to Blois where she occupied herself with her ladies-in-waiting, living in relative piety in comparison to other ladies within the royal family. Her last years were isolated and melancholy, especially as she became immobile and disabled. The birth of her previous daughter Marguerite in 1523 had sapped all her strength, and it became increasingly clear to the court she would not live long.[28]

Claude of France fell seriously ill in October 1523, and the King's sister, Margaret, nursed Claude and asked her companion Guillaume Briçonnet, Bishop of Meaux, 'to visit the Queen, who is gravely ill'.[29] The Queen passed on 26 July 1524 at the Château de Blois, at the tender age of just twenty-four. A few historians express the view that Claude died on 20 July; however, this is a mistake that previously began because of the nineteenth-century release of Robert de la Marck's memoirs.[30] The contemporary *Journal d'un Bourgeois de Paris sous le Règne de François Premier* fixes the Queen's passing at 26 July 1524.[31]

No one is certain how Queen Claude of France died. The exact cause of her death is disputed amongst historians: some alleged she died in childbirth, or after a miscarriage, others believed she died of exhaustion, or after suffering from bone tuberculosis combined with her frail body and her disabilities. However historians such as Brantôme accused Claude's philandering husband François, of infecting her with syphilis, a sickness that 'shortened her days'. Though many French historians reject Brantôme's case as conjecture, reports of Claude experiencing 'the French pox' as syphilis was famously called in the sixteenth century, flourished during the months before her demise. Numerous ambassadors composed that the youthful Queen 'was said to be dying of the [great] pox'. In August 1524, François I was likewise supposed to have been treated for this disease.[32]

François' reaction to his wife's demise was a mixture of shock and grief. Despite François having had several mistresses during his marriage, he nevertheless had strong feelings for the mother of his children. In a letter to Guillaume Briçonnet, François' sister, Margaret, wrote about François' reaction to his wife's death:

> Perceiving that it could not long be averted, he mourned exceedingly, saying to Madame [Louise of Savoy, their mother]: 'If my life could be given in exchange for hers, willingly would I surrender it. Never could I have believed that the bonds of marriage, confirmed by God, were so difficult to sever'. And so in tears, we separated. Since, we have had no news how he fares, but I fear that he is burdened with heavy sorrow.[33]

François arranged an impressive funeral for his wife; however, he was preparing to go to war, which meant that he was unable to return for the ceremony. Claude was embalmed and temporarily laid to rest in the Saint-Calais Chapel in Blois. An air of sanctity surrounded the late Queen, and she was buried in the Basilica of Saint-Denis on 6 November 1526. 'She was very much beloved by her husband, and well treated, and of all France, and much regretted after her death, for her admirable virtues and good-nature.'[34]

Many years after her death, chroniclers and historians talked of Claude's good character. The historian Brantôme wrote:

> I must speak about madame Claude of France, who was very good and very charitable, and very sweet to everyone and never showed displeasure to anybody in her court or of

her domains. She was deeply loved by the King Louis and the Queen Anne, her father and mother, and she was always a good daughter to them; after the King took the peaceful Duke of Milan, he made him declare and proclaim her in the Parliament of Paris the Duchess of the two most beautiful Duchies of Christendom, Milan and Brittany, one from the father and the other from the mother. What an heiress! if you please. Both Duchies joined in all good deed to our beautiful kingdom.[35]

Queen Claude was an incredible woman, who despite all the physical challenges and disabilities she faced, managed to fulfil her duties as a queen, wife, and as a mother. She appeared uncomplaining, humble and pious, despite the pain she must have had to cope with from her limp, having one leg being shorter than the other, her hips also being out of alignment, and claudication, which was mild to extremely severe. Claudication is a condition that is most common in the calves, but it can also affect the feet, thighs, hips, buttocks, or arms, and the definition of *claudication* comes from the Latin term *claudicare* meaning 'to limp'. It could be that along with the curvature of her spine, her hunchback, her limp, her irregular hip alignment, and one leg being shorter than the other, along with her strabismus, meant that her diagnoses could be argued to be a very mild form of cerebral palsy. Her conditions would class her as disabled had she lived today.

Queen Claude of France influenced many ladies-in-waiting around her and she was served by a young woman who knew and admired her. The young woman joined Claude's court after serving the Dowager Queen of France, Mary Tudor (Henry VIII's sister), who later become the Duchess of Suffolk. The young woman was English, but by the time she left France at the end of 1521, early 1522, she had become like a French woman born.

There was a strong connection and admiration between these two women. Both England and France would come to know the young lady who, whilst in France, had become sophisticated and educated. Cavendish states merely that 'mistress Anne Boleyn, being very young, was sent into the realm of France, and there made one of the French queen's women.'[36] Anne Boleyn became a member of Claude's household in 1515 and it is assumed that Anne served as the queen's translator whenever English visitors arrived at the French court; such an occasion would have been at the Field of Cloth of Gold, from 7 June to 24 June 1520. Whilst in the household of Queen Claude, Anne would have witnessed for herself the challenges that Claude had to physically overcome; she undoubtedly would have admired the queen for her determination, religious piety and modesty. Anne would have also noticed how tenacious Claude was, especially in a man's world, and this would have indicated to Anne that despite all that was levelled at the queen because of her ill health and disability, Claude still managed to fulfil her duties. Anne Boleyn would eventually leave Claude's service, returning from France to England to her family estate in late 1521.

Twelve years later, on 25 January 1533, Anne Boleyn would become King Henry VIII's second wife. He would wait seven years, set aside his wife, Katharine of Aragon, of twenty-four years and have the Roman Catholic Church excommunicate him to have Anne as his new wife. However, within ten years, Anne would be found guilty of treason for imagining the king's death. Much has been written about Anne since then, very few indisputable facts about her life remain. her date of birth and her appearance are the subject of continued debate and speculation. We do not know for certain what Anne Boleyn looked like, however, a source suggests Anne 'was remarkable for the exquisite turn of her neck and her glossy throat. She was a little, lively, sparkling brunette, with fascinating eyes and long black hair, which, contrary to the sombre fashion of those days, she wore coquettishly floating loosely down her back, interlaced with jewels'.[37] 'She is young, good-looking, of a rather dark complexion, and likely enough to have children,' says Grynæus, who saw her on 10 September 1531. A less favourable witness says, 'Madame Anne is not one of the handsomest women in the world. She is of middling stature, dark complexion, long neck, wide mouth, not prominent bust, and in fact she has nothing but the English King's great appetite, and her eyes, which are black and beautiful, and produce great effect on those who once served the Queen (Katharine) when she was in her prosperity.'[38]

The only contemporary likeness we have is a medal struck in 1534 to commemorate her coronation. The medal was made in lead showing a three-quarter bust of Anne Boleyn and a English gable hood. A cross hangs from her necklace and her dress is low-cut, witha mantle over her shoulders. In the field, are carved the initials, AR.[39] However, it is safe to say that she had dark red/brown very long hair and dark eyes, an olive or sallow tone to her skin with a few moles and that she was of medium build and had small breasts; an asset her future husband admired.

The stone carver, Lucy Churchill, recreated a medal made in 1534 of Anne Boleyn, which is known to be a good likeness of her and a contemporary source. It is interesting that in the medallion, Anne is wearing a gable hood, which was a status symbol of headwear which showed she was queen. I discussed the medal with Lucy, Anne Boleyn's appearance and Anne perhaps having a goitre or mild scrofula. Lucy herself told me that, 'I think it's highly plausible given the visual similarity. Of course, there is no proof.' Lucy Churchill continued to say: 'If you look at the BM medal you can see a small circular patch which is slightly lighter than the surrounding area. It is ever so slightly raised. Whether this represents a swelling, or merely an attempt to give a three-dimensional representation of her throat, I couldn't say for certain.'

Professor David Starkey has said that 'Lucy Churchill's reconstruction of The Moost Happi portrait medal is the best image we are ever likely to have of Anne Boleyn.' The late, Professor Eric Ives, Anne's biographer, and author of *The Life and Death of Anne Boleyn: The Most Happy* said that 'Lucy Churchill's brilliant achievement has brought us as close to the real Anne Boleyn as we shall ever be able to get.' Alison Weir states: 'Through meticulous research, Lucy Churchill has created an authentic replica of the medal of Anne Boleyn, as it would have looked originally. A must for anyone interested in Anne Boleyn.'[40]

The reason for writing about Queen Anne Boleyn, in a book to do with Tudor disability, is that rumour still abounds about a sixth finger, as well as wens or warts on her neck and other blemishes. Could the marks on her neck have been to do with scrofula? Could Anne have been marked with unnatural blemishes? Would the king have still set his heart upon her had she had any form of disability?

Dr David Starkey believes that any deformity on Anne's neck was a goitre, which is an abnormal enlargement of the thyroid gland.[41] The swelling of the thyroid gland causes a lump to form in front of the neck. The bump will move up and down when swallowing. The size of a goitre varies from person to person. In the majority of cases, the swelling is small, which does not cause any symptoms. However, if Anne suffered from a goitre, was this a sign she was suffering from some serious medical problem? It could have been an overactive thyroid gland or (hyperthyroidism), an underactive thyroid gland, or hormone changes during pregnancy, or the menopause, or something as simple as there not being not enough sea or plant foods, which would have given Anne iodine in her diet. Or was this a growth? Something like an inflamed thyroid gland or (thyroiditis), or perhaps a benign cyst, or something more severe like thyroid cancer? With a physicians' lack of knowledge and ability to diagnose in Tudor times, we will never know if Anne did suffer from a goitre, we can only speculate by looking at the only contemporary likeness we have of Anne Boleyn.[42]

Anne Boleyn's identity and whether she had any discriminating marks or disability is always up for debate, and historians John Rowlands and Dr David Starkey wrote an interesting article, 'An Old Tradition Reasserted: Holbein's Portrait of Queen Anne Boleyn' for *The Burlington Magazine*, in which they stated that identifying Anne was always a problem.[43] A Windsor drawing by Holbein which David Starkey has suggested, without question, is Anne Boleyn, shows the sitter with few signs of beauty, much like the portraits of King Henry's other Queens.[44]

> Madam Anne is not one of the handsomest women in the world; she is of middling stature, swarthy complexion, long neck, wide mouth, bosom not much raised, and in fact has nothing but the English King's great appetite, and her eyes, which are black and beautiful, and take great effect on those who served the Queen when she was on the throne.[45]

David Starkey suggests that Anne was, 'a strident and intelligent mistress and the drawing [Windsor Portrait] suggests the sitter has a strong will and intelligence, from the way she is depicted and from how her contemporaries had commented'.[46] Rowlands suggests that in 'the Windsor drawing, you can see that her double chin is so pronounced, which, it could be argued, suggests a swelling of the throat glands, which is partly hidden by a high neckline'.[47] If the sitter is Anne, she appears in a state of undress and this shows that Holbein enjoyed intimate, friendly patronage from Anne Boleyn, because she permitted him to take her likeness while her toilette was incomplete.

Holbein was commissioned by several male sitters who appear in his works in similar stages of undress, yet Anne Boleyn was the only woman to do so. Was Anne trying to prove her chaste and humble character?

The viewer of the drawing could argue that because she was in a state of undress, the opposite would appear to be the case. However, liberty such as this, in court circles, would only have been made by a woman of the very highest rank.[48] The king showed relaxed behaviour in front of his attendants, the gentlemen of his privy chamber, so the sitter's behaviour in the Windsor portrait is not unusual. However, the extraordinarily free-and-easy atmosphere in the queen's privy chamber provided Cromwell and Anne's other accusers' ammunition against her, providing them with 'evidence' for the multiple charges of adultery and incest that were used to destroy her and her faction in May 1536 (evidence which was properly dismissed as 'bawdy and lechery' by one of the judges in his notes on her trial).[49]

A state of undress in privy apartments, on full view of courtiers, might have been acceptable for Henry VIII but he enjoyed breaking the rules he set for others. He would dress in casual attire, much like Holbein's sitter. In 1530, he received a visitor in the same dishevelment, when after spending some time shooting at the butts, the king had gone into the palace to change. Then Henry Norris, the Groom of the Stool, and the king's most intimate personal attendant summoned George Cavendish, Wolsey's biographer and sometime gentleman usher into his presence. He found the King standing behind 'the garden posterne gate' clad 'in a nyght gown of Russett velvett furred with Sabelles'.[50] There was always one rule for Henry and one rule for everyone else. He was the king after all.

There is the inscription, 'Anna Bollein Queen', as identification on the drawing and according to the Lumley Inventory, 'subscribed' by Sir John Cheke, Secretary to King Edward VI.[51] The significant evidence and writings on the Windsor portrait are the observations made by historian David Starkey about the comments made by the anonymous French contemporary who noted, 'an anonyus and scurrilous account of her entry into London on Saturday, 31st May 1533, the day before her coronation'. The writer describes her as scrofulous and adds that therefore she wore her dress fastened up very high on the throat, in the fashion employed by the goitrous people. In the drawing, Anne's double chin is so pronounced as to suggest such a swelling of the throat glands, which is indeed partly hidden by a high neckline. Her high neckline could have been worn to hide the usual signs and symptoms and appearance of a chronic, painless mass in the neck, which could have been persistent and would usually grow with time. The mass could be referring to as a 'cold abscess', as the skin with scrofula is not accompanied by any local colour or warmth and the overlying skin acquires a violaceous, bluish-purple colour. Could Anne have been hiding an infection such as scrofula with her high shifts and dressing gowns?[52]

The Holbein sketch of Anne Boleyn shows the sitter with a pudgy looking chin, which is somewhat strange, especially as Spanish ambassador Chapuys referred to her as that 'thin old woman'. Could Anne have had an infection under her chin in the region of the thyroid? She may have suffered from a thyroid malfunction. Or perhaps at the time of sitting for this portrait, she suffered from a goitre, brought on by a thyroid malfunction. If the goitre causes hyperthyroidism which means too much thyroid is being produced, apparently this can cause fetal tachycardia when the woman becomes pregnant which might explain Anne's miscarriage in January 1536. Anne's miscarriage was not the only reason for her eventual downfall from grace, even though the historian Retha Warnicke built a fascinating hypothesis on the basis that she had given birth to a deformed foetus. Perhaps this is a slightly provocative theory, but could Anne have been suffering from an infection that caused her miscarriage in 1536?

Anne suffering from a thyroid infection, which is shown as a lump under her chin in the Windsor portrait, would explain why Anne was sometimes called a 'goggle-eyed' whore, as those who suffered from a thyroid malfunction sometimes suffered with their eyes slightly bulging as a result. The scrofula infection does not show other notable constitutional symptoms but scrofula caused by tuberculosis is usually accompanied by other symptoms of the disease, such as fever, chills, malaise and weight loss. It was reported that Anne had grown thinner towards the end of her reign. Was this a symptom of tuberculosis and the onset of scrofula? Can this portrait be evidence of these theories, or will they forever remain conjecture considering we are examining these issues at a distance of nearly five hundred years? Perhaps poor Anne was afflicted by this infection and tried to hide it from those closest to her. Perhaps this infection was the cause of the malicious and slanderous comments made by Nicholas Sanders, the Catholic Propagandist, eighty years after her death. Oddly enough, scrofula was known as the king's evil, and in the Middle Ages, it was believed that the 'royal touch', the touch of the sovereign of England or France, could cure diseases due to the divine right of the monarch through the laying on of hands and prayer. It is a shame Henry and Anne's relationship had cooled by the early part of April 1536 and did not enjoy such an intimate relationship as they had done previously, towards the end of Anne's reign, as her husband might have been able to cure her if the rumours and assumption of the scrofula infection and the reasoning behind her relaxed style of dress were true.[53]

Nicholas Sanders was a Catholic rumour monger who hated Anne and wrote of her in his book, *Rise and Growth of the Anglican Schism*:

> Anne Boleyn was rather tall of stature, with black hair, and an oval face of a sallow complexion as if troubled with jaundice. She had a projecting tooth under the upper lip, and on her right hand six fingers. There was a large wen under her chin, and therefore to hide its ugliness she wore a high dress covering her throat. In this she was followed by the ladies of the court, who also wore high dresses, having before been in the habit of leaving their necks and the upper portion of their persons uncovered. She was handsome to look at, with a pretty mouth, amusing in her ways, playing well on the lute, and was a good dancer.[54]

Combined with all the salacious rumours and the alleged allegations in the indictment against Anne made by Secretary Cromwell, is it any wonder that Sanders wrote such lies about her?[55]

Myths need to be dispelled and many credible historians do not believe Sanders' writings on Anne to be accurate because he was Catholic and would have wanted to paint Anne in the most gruesome of lights, to show that she was the instrument by which Henry broke from the Church in Rome. Nicholas Sanders was a Catholic recusant and wrote *De Origine* while in forced exile during the reign of Elizabeth I, a woman he also hated. *De Origine* has been applauded by some as 'an excellent, popular account of the period', from a Catholic point of view, in the New Advent Catholic Encyclopaedia.[56] Sanders was described as 'Dr Slander, the most violent of anti-Elizabethan propagandists … an enemy agent and no bones about it, an emissary from the Pope to a rebel army.'[57] While acting for the English exiles in Spain in the 1570s, Sanders urged Philip of Spain to attack Protestant England, believing that 'The state of Christendom dependeth upon the stout assailing of England.'

To Sanders, Anne Boleyn was a 'she-wolf', the kind of woman whom you would never have expected to catch Henry's eye. Anne had been pursued relentlessly by Henry, and he had written seventeen love letters in quick succession, to show his adoration. Writing was an occupation Henry hated and putting quill and ink to vellum was an occupation he tried to avoid. The letters were stolen by a supporter of Katharine of Aragon during Henry's 'Great Matter' and are now housed securely in the Vatican library. Henry wanted to find a woman to fall in love with to give him a son and heir, so considering how superstitious people were during the Tudor period, it is surprising the king of England would be attracted to a woman who was afflicted with many deformities. Henry would have recoiled at the thought of an extra finger, or hereditary disease being passed on to his precious heir.

Nicholas Sanders' reports were venomous and successful libels against Anne, who had been a long time dead when he started his campaign of hate against her; he had made use of every 'scandalous story' going around at the time and wanted to blacken the name of Elizabeth I, by sullying the reputation of her mother, because both she, and her mother were evangelicals and Elizabeth was a Protestant. For this reason, Sanders probably considered Elizabeth an illegitimate queen, wanting to make her cause as queen, even more disreputable and impossible. He planted these rumours and half-truths, to grow his mountain of lies making them believable using contemporary descriptions of Anne Boleyn and then embellishing them to blacken her name, and that of her daughter Elizabeth I.

The Venetian ambassador described Anne as 'not one of the handsomest women in the world; she is of middling stature, swarthy complexion, long neck, wide mouth, bosom not much raised ... and her eyes which are black and beautiful'.[58] Reformer, Simon Grynée wrote that 'she is young, good-looking, of a rather dark complexion, and likely enough to have children'.[59] Sanders relied on a hostile account of Anne's coronation to deepen the rumours blacken her reputation and malign her appearance. The extracts of an account of the *Coronation Of Anne Boleyn* were unfavourable to her, and they were once in a catalogue of papers at Brussels:

Her dress was covered with tongues pierced with nails, to show the treatment which those who spoke against her might expect. Her car was so low that the ears of the last mule appeared to those who stood behind to belong to her. The letters H. A. were painted in several places, for Henry and Anne, but were laughed at by many. The crown became her very ill, and a wart disfigured her very much. She wore a violet velvet mantle, with a high ruff (goulgiel) of gold thread and pearls, which concealed a swelling she has, resembling goître.[60]

This contemporary account of Anne having a wart is the only one that historians know of but, as Professor Eric Ives pointed out, Anne's coronation robes would have covered her neck, if her carcoat and mantle were similar in manufacture to her predecessors and those of her daughter's coronation robes. Ambassador Chapuys never mentions a wart or wen on her neck; it is the mystery account from Brussels which mentions a swelling on Anne's neck at her coronation. Sadly, because the original account is in a bundle of lost letters, the identity of the author is lost to researchers. Therefore, a wen, goitre, or wart is not mentioned by any contemporary report apart from this, and, contrary to Sanders's account, Anne has only ever been depicted wearing a high necked dressing gown, in the example of the Windsor portrait. Although one historian has quoted George Wyatt, grandson of poet Thomas Wyatt and author of *The Life of Anne Boleigne*, as saying that Anne had a pronounced wen, Wyatt doesn't mention it in any of his writings.[61]

Lancelot de Carles, the secretary to the French ambassador, wrote that Anne was 'belle et de taille elegante', beautiful, with an elegant figure, and he had no reason to lie. Would de Carles have described a woman with a projecting tooth, six fingers, yellow skin and a wen as 'belle'? I very much doubt it.[62] Some contemporaries were rumoured of accusing Anne as being 'a thin, old, and vicious hack'. Other descriptions of Anne are often given as a reason for King Henry losing interest; one such description comes from a translation of Chapuys' words in 1536, where he called Anne a 'skinny, old and nasty ring' when translated. It may be that Chapuys was saying that Henry VIII wanted to replace a thin, old, nasty wedding ring with a more agreeable one, i.e. Jane Seymour – a reminder of John Heywood's, *The Play of the Weather*, where Heywood compares Katharine (the old moone) to Anne (a new moone). The 'new moon' speech contains some important, if not very subtle references to Henry's marital affairs, where we find Merry Report's explanation to The Gentlewoman as to why Jupiter (probably Henry VIII) cannot see her:

> Merry Report: By my fayth, for his lordship is ryght besy
> Wyth a pece of work that nedes must be done.
> Even now is he makynge of a new moone:
> He sayth your old moones be so farre tasted
> That all the goodness of them is wasted;
> Whyche of the great wete hath ben moste mater,
> For olde moones be leake, they can holde no water.
> But for this new mone, I durst lay my gowne
> Except a few droppes at her goynge downe,
> Ye get no rayne tyll her arysynge
> Without yt nede, and then no mans devysynge
> Coulde wyshe the fashion of rayne to be so good:
> Not gushynge out lyke gutters of Noyes flood,
> But smale droppes sprynklyng softly on the grounde:
> Though they fell on a sponge they wold gyve no sounde.
> This new moone shal make a thing spryng more in this while
> Than a old moon shal while a mile go a mile. (793-809)

Merry Report's speech fills the space of the court with bawdy, uncomfortable and insulting, misogynistic jokes, not only about the 'tightness' of the new moon compared with the leakiness of the old moon but also with references to Katharine's miscarriages, meaning that the old moon cannot contain its water but instead lets it gush out in too great quantities before its time.

The speech also refers to Henry's sexual prowess, 'the new moon will make a "thing" spring', where the reference to Jupiter [the king] making a new moon, maybe a reference to Anne's pregnancy, with the shape of the new moon relating to her pregnant body. It is possible that in this speech Merry Report is telling the court that Anne is pregnant, and confirming with its misogynistic overtones, Katharine's complete downfall. The play was first performed at Hampton Court but, unusually, not in front of Henry during Christmas 1532-33, as Henry and Anne were away on a matter of European diplomacy in Calais, trying to secure King François' support for their impending nuptials. The courtiers remaining in England must have been anxious during this period over the king's absence, and Heywood was probably trying to sway support for the resolution to the king's 'Great Matter'.[63]

Controversies still surround Anne Boleyn's appearance, especially the rumour of an extra finger. It is impossible to say precisely what the blemish or deformity may have been on her hand, but there was some truth to the rumour, as George Wyatt, grandson of Sir Thomas Wyatt, the poet and one of her admirers, describes her in the fantastic language of the sixteenth century as having:

> A beauty not so whitely as clear and fresh above all we may esteem, which appeared much more excellent by her favour passing sweet and cheerful. There was found, indeed, upon the side of her nail upon one of her fingers some little show of a nail, which yet was so small, by the report of those that have seen her, as the work-master seemed to leave it an occasion of greater grace to her hand, which, with the tip of one of her other fingers, might be and was usually by her hidden, without any least blemish to it.[64]

In the footnotes of that source, with Wyatt's comment, it reads:

> The story that Katharine had her to cards, the better to expose this defective finger to the King, is a mere malignant invention. In the first place, card-playing never seems to have been one of Katharine's amusements; in the next place, it is very doubtful whether Anne Boleyn was ever permanently attached to the Queen's household. That is the statement of Cavendish, but no mention of her name occurs on the lists of the Queen's household, and in details of this kind Cavendish must not be implicitly trusted.[65]

Moreover, the digging up of Anne's remains may not have shown an extra finger and would have been even more unlikely to prove that she had a 'show of a little nail' protruding from one of her fingers.[66]

Furthermore, Thomas Wyatt's grandson retells family tales that were retold like Chinese whispers down the generations, that Anne Boleyn did have some physical abnormality on one of her hands. In the 1590s,

George Wyatt wrote: 'There was found, indeed, upon the side of her nail, upon one of her fingers, some little show of a nail, which yet was so small ... albeit in beauty she was to many inferior, but for behaviour, manners, attire and tongue she excelled them all ... she was indeed a very wilful woman ... but yet that and other things cost her after dear.'[67] Wyatt elaborates on Anne's appearance, saying that Anne had 'certain small moles', but goes on to write of her rare and admirable beauty. Wyatt saw this 'little show of a nail' as a minor deformity small enough for Anne to have been able to conceal.

Although George Wyatt was not a contemporary of Anne Boleyn, he explains in his biography that his information came from a lady who attended on Anne before and after she was queen. It was probably Anne Gainsford, 'a lady of noble birth, living in those times, and well acquainted with the persons that most this concerneth, from whom I am myself descended', so George Wyatt had obtained verbal, first-hand accounts from those who had known Anne, his grandfather Thomas Wyatt included. With a distance of nearly 500 years, and few contemporary accounts, it is impossible to say with any certainty what blemish or deformity was on the finger of Anne's left hand, but there was something, as George Wyatt recorded.[68]

With such half-truths and passed-down accounts circulating about Anne Boleyn and her appearance, from both her supporters and her enemies, it is easy to understand how religious and political propaganda, during and after her lifetime, created such myths of associations of witchcraft and a sixth finger on both hands. In an age of such superstition, it is easy to conclude that if had Anne had more deformities other than a few 'moles' and 'the show of an extra nail' on the index finger of her left hand, it is safe to say that Henry would never have been as besotted and beguiled by her.

Although historians and propagandists throughout history have implied Anne Boleyn may have had deformities and disabilities, the only one we now know to be accurate is that Anne certainly had the show of a second fingernail on her left index finger, but no other deformity, apart from her enlarged black pupils. This has been suggested by detailed research into Anne Boleyn's recently discovered personal portrait, as cited by Art Historian Graeme Cameron. It remains to be seen if the portrait is indeed, Anne Boleyn. This portrait, is suggested by Cameron to be her final Whitehall Palace portrait dated 1536, painted prior to

Anne's May execution and also has verso her newly created 'Personal Coat of Arms' reflecting her family's 'Bullen' origins in the French Style. A later 1570s portrait of her daughter Elizabeth copied many unique features of Anne's 1536 portrait. In both portraits, the stance is similar, as is the similarity between both sitters dress, shirt, hands, jewellery chain and gloves, which he has also cited. It is heartbreaking, yet respectful, that Elizabeth wanted a copy of herself 'as' or in the same pose as her mother's portrait. It would have been impossible for the 1570s artist who painted Elizabeth in the same style to have known in such detail the unique features of Queen Anne Boleyn's 1536 portrait – the shape of her dress, jewelled shirt, jewellery and rosary chain, pose, hand positions and gloves to have so faithfully copied them without the presence of the 1536 portrait to refer to. As art historian Graeme Cameron argues, Anne Boleyn was England's most coveted and enigmatic Queen – beautiful, worldly and could justifiably be deemed 'England's Mona Lisa'.[69]

It is also a point to make that as Anne Boleyn had been a lady-in-waiting to Queen Claude in France, she had seen how stoically Claude had coped with being disabled. If she did have any such deformities as alleged, she would have thought nothing of getting on with her life despite them, as her contemporaries did. In an age when any abnormality in appearance created fear and superstition, it is surprising how accommodating the Tudors were regarding people with disabilities. Attitudes and actions contradicted themselves in a period where society was at loggerheads with itself.

Anne Boleyn's sister-in-law, Jane Boleyn, Lady Rochford, was held in the Tower of London after aiding Henry VIII's fifth wife, the teenage Catherine Howard, in her affair with Thomas Culpepper. During Jane's stay at the Tower and before her brutal execution there are theories that Jane feigned madness to avoid the executioners' block. Jane Boleyn, Viscountess Rochford, was a royal lady-in-waiting who married George Boleyn, brother of Henry VIII's second wife Anne Boleyn. When Queen Anne was accused of adultery, Jane's husband who was Anne's brother, was accused of incest with the queen and was beheaded. The widowed Jane returned to court and eventually became a lady-in-waiting to Catherine Howard. Jane was a trusted favourite of Queen Catherine Howard, and she arranged liaisons with Catherine's lover, Thomas Culpepper. When Jane's role in the affair was revealed, she was imprisoned in the Tower of London. It was there that the symptoms of her supposed madness surfaced.

An ambassador at Henry's court wrote 'she went mad', on her third day at the Tower. She was soon pronounced insane.[70] However, the historian Gareth Russell asserts that her insanity began years earlier: 'The black legend of Lady Rochford says that she was driven mad with jealousy [by] the bed-hopping [of] George Boleyn.'[71] No list of her symptoms survives, but manifestations of what might today be called a 'mental breakdown' include dizziness, trembling, hyperventilation, hallucinations and paranoia.[72] Jane Boleyn likely suffered many of these, unless she was feigning madness to save herself. Under English law the insane could not be executed for treason; however, Henry wanted Jane dead for her role in his queen's adulterous affair. He dispatched his physician to cure Jane, without success. Proceedings against her began and a new law superseded the one protecting the insane from the death penalty. Gareth Russell wrote that the king 'push[ed] a bill through Parliament allowing the execution of the medically insane for the first time in English history'.[73] Author Danielle Marchant notes in her blog that, 'The fact that Henry had got his doctor to nurse her back to health and had passed a special law maybe does indicate that her madness was genuine.'[74]

Nevertheless, on the day of her execution, Jane Boleyn, the supposed madwoman, ascended the scaffold 'with calm dignity' and behaved graciously toward her executioner.[75] Her last words, which historian, Gareth Russell calls 'a long and rambling speech', seem nevertheless not to be the ravings of a madwoman, so perhaps she was feigning insanity after all: 'I have ... offended the King ... so my punishment is just ... All ... who watch me die should learn from my example. ... I now entrust my soul to God.'[76] A recent biographer of Jane Boleyn, Julia Fox, said that 'After a single blow of the axe, Jane's head, which may or may not have housed a mad brain, was held aloft for all to see, then buried with her body at the Tower.'[77]

A year before Jane's sister-in-law, Anne Boleyn, was executed, there is an account of a cook to the Privy Council, named John Laurence, who served at the time of Queen Anne Boleyn's reign. John Laurence petitioned the King with a personal story of being overworked and suffering a growing disability from the nature of that work: He had cooked for them for more than twenty-four years. He was paid 2s 4d per day for his services but he suggested, due to his disability, that his pay was not a sufficient reward. He said that he, and his servants and his pans were worn out. He had 'passed into age' and was 'sore troubled with the gout' to the point that he was almost lame. Laurence petitioned the king requesting a life annuity or other reward in lieu of the fact he could no longer work because he was lame.[78] There is no record of how the king responded to the petition.

There were famous courtiers at court who were disabled. The sister to Queen Jane, the 'Nine days queen', or Lady Jane Grey, was Lady Mary Grey, and she had a spinal disability.[79] In *Crown of Blood* by Nicola Tallis, the historian and author states:

> There was something slightly unusual about Mary, for as she grew, it became clear that she had a spinal deformity that made her appear hunchbacked. She was also small, and in later years was cruelly described by the Spanish ambassador as "little, crooked-backed and very ugly".[80]

Leanda de Lisle states that Lady Mary Grey's family 'were unaware that there was anything wrong with her. But Mary was never to grow normally.'[81] The later suggestion that Mary's birth amounted to a disaster is an exaggeration, however, her deformities were the subject of conjecture because it was speculated that Mary Grey was a dwarf. Moreover, for besides the unkind comments of the ambassador, Mary's condition drew no other comment from her contemporaries, and especially not from her family, who made no record of her disabilities.

Lady Mary Grey, or Lady Crookback, as she was known, was born around 1545 at Bradgate Park near Leicester. Their father Henry Grey was the son of Thomas Grey, 2nd Marquess of Dorset and Margaret Wotton. Their grandfather, Thomas Grey, was the grandson of Queen Elizabeth Woodville, by her first marriage to Sir John Grey of Goby. Mary's mother, Frances Brandon, was the eldest daughter of Charles Brandon, 1st Duke of Suffolk and Mary Tudor, who was the younger sister of King Henry VIII. Little Lady Mary was not a renowned beauty like her elder sisters.[82]

The Grey sisters derived their claim to the English throne through their Tudor maternal grandmother, which was the line of Margaret Tudor who was Queen Consort of Scotland, and who had been the elder sister of Henry VIII. This line of succession was later represented after

1542 by Mary Stuart, Queen of Scots. However, King Henry VIII had excluded the Stuart line in his will, and from the English succession, placing the Grey sisters next-in-line following after his children, Edward, Mary and Elizabeth. In 1553, as the young King Edward VI lay on his deathbed, the boy king and John Dudley, his chief minister, intended to exclude Edward's staunchly Catholic sister, the Princess Mary from the succession in favour of Mary Grey's Evangelical elder sister, Lady Jane. According to letters patent issued on 21 June 1553, 'Edward VI's Devise for the Succession', Edward states in his own handwriting the plan by which the dying king, aged sixteen, seeks to exclude his half-sisters Mary and Elizabeth from the succession in favour of his cousin, Lady Jane Grey.

In the document, Mary was declared third in the line of succession behind her elder sisters and their heirs' male. With the Grey sisters next in the line of succession under King Henry VIII's will, and Edward VI when he wrote his will, and his 'Devise for the Succession', he planned to disinherit his illegitimate half-sisters and 'to create a new dynasty, one founded upon the true faith'.[83] The original draft stipulated that the Crown would descend through the male heirs of Frances, Duchess of Suffolk, and the male heirs of her children if Edward died childless. The problem was that there were no male heirs yet, so when Edward made a turn for the worse he decided to change the Device to read: 'To the Lady Fraunceses heirs males, if she have any such issue before my death to the Lady Jane and her heirs' males.'[84]

Jane's accession to the throne failed due to a lack of popular support. She, her young husband Guildford Dudley and the Duke of Suffolk, the Grey sisters' father, were executed by Edward's elder sister and successor Mary I in February 1554. Queen Elizabeth I, Mary I's younger half-sister and successor decided to appoint Mary Grey as one of her Maids of Honour and granted her a pension of £80 a year.[85]

Some historians argue Mary was born with the congenital scoliosis of her ancestor Richard III as there are references to her diminutive stature suggesting that she was, aside from her spinal distortion, remarkably small, possibly a dwarf. Lady Mary was a young woman with significant disabilities, and yet one who inhabited the highest echelons of the court. In early modern Europe, superstitious and medieval belief still held sway, that physical flaws equated to sin, as demonstrated effectively in Shakespeare's evil characterisation of that 'lump of foul deformity'

Richard III. But Mary, with her deformities and disabilities, had not been a child who was hidden away like a shameful secret or defiled and defamed in literature. On the contrary, the historian Susan Doran suggests that Mary was educated alongside her sisters, and is thought to have been educated like her eldest sister Jane and spent many years at court, a place where dwarfs and fools held special sway, having a hallowed status.[86]

Moreover, Mary already had a hallowed status, not just because of her disability and 'crooked-back'. She was different: she had royal blood flowing through her veins and so her position was more complex than the dwarf, Thomasina, who was treated as a kind of pet. The dint of her stature and the fact she held a position in line to the throne would have held her in a revered position. Mary inhabiting a place of ambivalence may have prevented her disability from being dehumanised in the eyes of others, and her presence was probably not considered a threat. Lady Mary Grey was probably empowered by her intelligence.

Despite this standing, her life was a difficult one, as roles for aristocratic women of the period were limited, especially concerning marriage and the bearing of children, something impossible for Mary, probably caused by her disability. Lady Mary Grey lived an endless life lived out in limbo at court where, as the daughter and sister of traitors, she would have been watched closely. But the most remarkable thing about Lady Mary Grey, which truly demonstrates her extraordinary character, is that she refused to be bound by her disability and the expectations of her situation. A true heroine of her times.

A gentleman of the king's court, Robert Cecil, would have known Lady Mary Grey. He was a man who suffered kyphosis, which is a curvature of the spine that causes the top of the back to appear more rounded than usual. It could be argued that Shakespeare had been writing about his contemporary in his plays. Robert Cecil, who was an English administrator and politician was the younger son of William Cecil, 1st Baron Burghley. Robert was small in stature, and hunchbacked, in an age which attached much importance to physical beauty in both sexes, and he endured much ridicule as a result: Queen Elizabeth called him 'my pygmy', and King James I nick-named him 'my little beagle'. Nonetheless, his father recognised that it was Robert, rather than Thomas, his eldest son, who had inherited his political genius. While Lord Burghley was fond of both his sons, he is said to have remarked that

Robert could rule England, but Thomas could hardly rule a tennis court. Cecil went on to become Lord Privy Seal, in office from 1598-1612. He ruled under both Elizabeth I and James I. He became Chancellor of the Duchy of Lancaster and was in office from 8 October 1597-1599 and was later Secretary of State. Even with his kyphosis, Robert Cecil aimed high at the machinations of the Elizabethan court.

Throughout the Tudor period, extraordinary, disabled people overcame their physical and mental limitations, to contribute to society, to influence policy, to support their monarch and sometimes to be accused of trying to overthrow or usurp their monarch. Despite their deformities, disabilities, mental and physical health, disabled people were often close to those in positions of power, or were in positions of power themselves. These disabled people were survivors in a period where even the elite struggled to thrive.

Chapter Nine

Disability in the Tudor Court

When we think of disabled people in Tudor society, inevitably, we are drawn to the biggest stereotype of the period, that conditions for disabled people must have been more challenging than today. The further back we go in time, we think life experience must have always grown worse for disabled people. However, evidence exists to the contrary.

When we think of the Tudor court, we think of courtiers inhabiting palaces such as Richmond, Whitehall, Nonsuch, Oatlands, Greenwich, Westminster and Bridewell amongst others. One of the most magnificent palaces that still stands is Hampton Court Palace; that impressive home of Cardinal Wolsey, where he had acquired the land to build his house in 1514. As the first spade went into the ground to start the building works, Wolsey knew that such a property would put him on the map of political and social Tudor hierarchy, creating a glorious footprint on the history of England. The palace today represents a visitors' gateway to England's Tudor past.

Hampton Court is an extraordinary building because it survives like no other palace of that period, and as a visitor, you can share the space that kings, queens. courtiers and natural fools once knew, and where they lived. As we follow in the footsteps of people who occupied Hampton Court Palace, our imaginations inhabit those same halls and passageways, which is why the building has a rapour with us, because as a visitor, we feel as if we are occupying a space between the past and the present. It is with that experience in mind that we come to examine the lives of a handful of extraordinary occupants of the Tudor court. History shows us that 'natural fools' had an unmistakable, special and crucial task to carry out at the Tudor court. Disabled people with certain learning or physical disabilities had opportunities open to them that were unique.

Court fools, disabled people with learning disabilities, were considered 'natural fools'. The term natural fool was the terminology

171

used to describe learning disabilities, and learning disabilities were understood by a difference of degree, not by the different and distinct kinds of learning disability we define today. In 1516, Nicholas Breton characterised people with learning disabilities as, 'Abortive of wit, where Nature had more power than Reason'. The legal term 'idiota' was interchangeable with 'natural fools', who were characterised as incapable or insensible of their actions. By looking at disability in the Tudor period we see that the Tudors had distinct perspectives on disability which informed them how they treated disabled people at different points during this period, at different levels in their society.

For example, a report from a visitation of a nunnery in 1535 to Thomas Cromwell, records the presence of a boy, Julian Heron, thirteen years old and 'an idiot fool'; the petition states that the nunnery 'Desire also to know whether Margaret Fitzgared, 12 years of age, being dumb and deaf, and Julian Heron, 13 years, an idiot fool, shall depart or no' from the said nunnery or whether they were continued to be allowed to stay there so they could be looked after and cared for.[1] However, pension payments to a 'Julian Heron the idiot – (age blank),' were ordered to be cancelled on the 3 April 1539 by Henry VIII. The source does not say why this was so.[2] Bishop Cuthbert Tunstall when corresponding with Thomas Cromwell in 1538, identifies 'an innocent natural fool' whom 'by no means we could make to grant', that he had spoken words of malice against the king. Perhaps this Julian Heron had spoken a truth, which may have been interpreted by others as 'speaking out of turn', which is why the grant for him was possibly denied. Evidence of natural fools such as these indicates that fools were disabled people understood to have a deficiency in reason or judgement, and from the evidence, they were highly visible in society.[3] While Tudor terminology of disabled people is dissimilar to our own, it is clear that the Tudors were trying to categorise learning disability. Disability was defined far more fluidly in the Tudor period and we can tell a lot about Tudor society by how they supported the disabled population. Moreover, to add to this narrative, the historian Professor Suzannah Lipscomb of the University of Roehampton has been one of the first, and few historians, to research Tudor court fools specifically.[4]

Previously, disabled people of the period have so often been ignored, for their second-rate counterparts, the court jester. The prevalent misconception about court fools and one that some historians have perpetuated is, that they were simply jesters pretending to be foolish or disabled to amuse onlookers. However, historical research proposes that many – maybe all – court fools in the early Tudor period were disabled people, with learning or physical disabilities, which clarifies much about their conspicuous position.

Suzannah Lipscomb researched experiences of natural fools to see whether there was any truth in the history of fools, not necessarily being jesters. Remarkably, through their difference, disabled people with learning disabilities, or natural fools, were considered closer to God, made and born that way by God, because it made them stand out from everyone and they could do God's work on earth; talk to power – to royalty. The Tudors believed that the innocence of natural fools was understood to be God-given, something good, and disabled people were believed to be able to achieve salvation. They were seen as human, but also seen as holy people, part of Christianity and not entirely excluded. However, a natural fools' story was never relayed from their point of view, always from the view of their carer, or keeper. Natural fools generally came from a lowly, or poor social background, and were reliant on the monarch for the cost of their care. Having any form of learning or physical disability meant that these natural fools were dependant on their keepers, and ultimately the monarch held the Privy Purse-strings. Tudor courtiers and royalty in positions of power, deliberately chose disabled people as court fools because they were thought to have spiritual powers directly from God and could be used as conduits for spoken truths, and honesty. Fools were not considered a threat to those in power, and therefore, became close companions to members of the royal family, which gave them the ability to become unofficial advisors, able to change the king's mood for the better. For example, William Somer was one who had uncompromising access to Henry VIII, was quick with words and considered a wit, which implies he had a learning disability and could also infer that he was on the autistic spectrum.

William Somer was well thought of because, with his quick wit, he could improve the king's disposition, which ultimately meant he could influence the spirit of the country. Helping to restore the king to good health, and keeping him in good health both mentally and physically, was of paramount importance. If Henry VIII, for example, suffered from melancholy at any time, or if he was ill, he was prescribed mirth as therapy by his physicians. From an English contemporary medical perspective, the promotion of treating melancholy with laughter was becoming more commonplace, which is why 'natural fools' and disabled people with learning disabilities were crucial to everyday life, both in their homes and communities and at the Tudor court.[5]

Suzannah Lipscomb's research was in preparation for *All the King's Fools*, a dramatised, ground-breaking performance, shown at Hampton Court in February and October of 2011. The production, devised by The Misfits, a company of actors with learning difficulties from Bristol, worked with English Heritage National Jester, and director, Peet Cooper of Foolscap Productions, to produce a piece of creative performance that showed how jesters performed in Henry VIII's court.[6] This research and a group of re-enactors putting on these performances were forward-thinking and inclusive; this group were commendable in bringing disability history to the forefront of public consciousness, in showing the visitors of Hampton Court how natural fools might have behaved. Foolscap Productions, along with the research Suzannah Lipscomb has undertaken, has brought to life this neglected area of Tudor history, showing and explaining how natural fools lived, and how they were treasured during the early modern era.[7]

However, viewing disabled actors re-enacting members of the Tudor court through our twenty-first century prism and experience is problematic. When watching re-enactors, we are watching them with modern-day misconceptions and categorisations of disability, rather than trying to compare and contrast them to contemporary Tudor 'natural fools' who were known as 'innocents'. Furthermore, for clarification, viewers can glimpse a couple of Tudor disabled contemporaries who were once occupants of Hampton Court, rendered in contemporary depictions, such as one seen hanging on the wall of the Haunted Gallery. Hidden in plain sight, amongst this well-known family group of Henry VIII are two disabled people shown on the periferary of the canvas, painted alongside Henry VIII, they stand conspicuously into the background.[8]

The painting is adjacent to the entrance of the Chapel Royal when walking from the Processional Gallery. The picture is known as 'The Family of Henry VIII' in the style, after Holbein the Younger, and is an early, contemporary representation of courtiers with learning disabilities. The painting is an exquisite rendering of two such disabled people, included in this family sitting, which dates from 1545. The delineation shows Henry VIII almost at his most virile and vigorous best, with third wife, Queen Jane Seymour, who has been already dead for over a decade, on his left. To the king's right hand is Henry and Jane's son, Edward, his long-awaited male heir, whose birth caused his mother's death in 1537. Completing this perfect Tudor idyll are the princesses, Mary and Elizabeth. Being daughters, and with both of their mothers' long since dead, the girls were bastardised and legitimised so many times they had no real idea as to their high status in society. In defiance of her father, Anne Boleyn's daughter Elizabeth wears an 'A' cypher pendant in remembrance of her executed mother. The immediate Tudor royal family of Henry VIII assemble in a fantasy gathering, save for Henry's sixth wife, Catherine Parr, who was the reigning queen at the time the picture was painted. The family portrait portrays Henry as a perfect husband and father, in an alternative truth to please him.

Henry VIII's immediate members of his family are not the only ones who are shown in the painting, however, as framed by the two archways in the wings, which sit on either side of the picture, there are two other figures. One is a man in a pair of crimson hose, he wears his red hair short and is dressed in his green 'clothe coote', with his velvet purse hanging from his belt. His pet monkey obligingly picks lice from this natural fool's hair, while the monkey balances, poised, on the man's shoulder. This gentleman is no ordinary fool, but the King's fool, William Somer.[9]

The other figure opposite William Somer, in a mirroring archway, is a likeness of a woman, believed to be of Jayne, another 'innocent'; a natural fool connected with the royal court. Jayne stands under the archway on the left, hiding her shaven head under a coif, she is wearing a Dutch-style gown, consisting of a red-stripped kirtle, which had an upstanding collared partlet, worn over a simply styled gown, which had probably been stiffened with buckram. The fabric used in her outer clothing was often parti-coloured and expensive, crimson velvet, purple damask, and green satin. Her attention is not on the viewers who might be considering the painting; her focus is gripped by something out of frame.

We know very little about Jayne – there is no record of her date of birth, where she was born, or how she became a natural fool in Anne Boleyn's household, or at what age she joined Anne's household. What we do know is that after Anne's execution, Jayne was cared for by Princess Mary and then, Catherine Parr.[10]

The painting suggests that these two 'natural fools' included in this royal, sentimental and dynastic setting, had distinct, privileged and vital roles to play within the Tudor court of Henry VIII. The presence of these royal fools implies that they were considered on intimate terms by the Tudor royals, in what is considered a very personal portrayal of Henry's family, which can only point to their significance.[11]

At the start of the reign of Henry VII, onwards, to the English Civil War, Privy Purse accounts, state papers, ambassadorial dispatches, plays and portraits record the presence of natural fools, 'innocent' disabled people with learning disabilities in the Privy Chamber, the monarch's most private apartments. During the early modern era, fools were prized entertainers who often held favour and authority with the king. They described disabled people with learning disabilities as 'foolish' and 'lacking judgement', yet disabled people's perceived directness and humour was greatly admired. The 'foolish things of the world' delighted and uniquely influenced the Tudor elite.[12]

These persons were Tudor court fools, who provided company and entertainment to the royal family and their courtiers. The performances that were given by 'fools' gave them unique access to not merely the corridors of power, but the opportunity to build an intimate friendship with the king himself. Natural fools became licensed truth-tellers and candid counsellors, they punctured the hypocrisy of court with their brazen, mocking honesty, and there was a practical reason for this, based on politics, power and medicine.[13]

Historians Professor Suzannah Lipscomb, and Lauren Johnson, acquaint us with the notion that owning a fool, 'aided in making their owner well'. A familiar old wives' tale of saying that 'laughter is the best medicine' comes into play.[14] Research suggests that laughter in the company of others raises the pain threshold, and enhances well-being, which implies improved physical, medical, emotional and mental states.[15] The Tudors believed this too. The Tudors were far more intelligent than we have given them credit for, as the Tudor mind believed that everything to do with well-being was linked; every function of the body had to balance, in a holistic way, connecting 'mind, body and spirit'. Therefore, if the king was depressed, it was terrible for the politics of the day. It was believed by the Tudors that and suffering from depression, hastened the onset of death. The king needed to be kept in good humour and often required a 'good laugh', to turn his mood around and therefore, turn the atmosphere of the realm around. When the king was depressed, this affected social, and political outcomes in his court. If Henry was depressed, this affected his decision-making process and his courtiers and ministers lived in fear of his changeable, melancholy moods. Henry VIII revived the use of fools in court to help turn around his state of mind, create positive perceptions and to help him improve the state of his kingdom.[16]

The awareness of the relationship between a person's physical well-being and their emotional and mental state was a vital feature of the holistic nature of Tudor medicine. Sir Thomas Elyot, a contemporary of Henry VIII and one of his registered barber-surgeons, claimed that 'there is nothing more enemy to life than sorrow – also called heaviness'.[17] he also wrote 'For it exhausteth the body and does extentuate both natural heat and moisture of the body, and does extenuate, make the body lean, darkeneth the spirit, dulleth the wit, lefteth the use and judgement of reason and oppressive memory by heaviness, death is hastened.'[18]

To the Tudor mind, the body politic, and man's physical body were linked inextricably; so it stood to reason that if personal sorrow was 'bad' for the king's body, it was bad for politics, and therefore the governing of the country. If how the country was governed was affected by the state of the king's mind and health, then the well-being of the king's health was of vital importance to the realm. When the monarch fell ill, either mentally or physically, Henry's enemies, both at home and abroad, might be found wringing their hands, waiting for a moment to pounce and to take advantage of the king politically.

The king's health became carefully guarded, and Henry's physicians barely recorded bouts of illness. To alert foreign ambassadors to the king's ailments could be a treasonous act, and lead to political problems. There was also the issue that King Henry was a hypochondriac, and to report untruths about his health would also have been considered treasonous. As understood in a previous chapter, and through the study of the contemporary records of Henry's health, we know an enormous amount about his jousting accidents, and that he suffered from headaches and melancholy. Henry hated writing letters because concentrating on the skill caused him headaches, and pain. He also complained to his closest companion and 'groom of the stool' of his constant constipation, which he endured due to an abundant, meat-heavy diet. Henry suffered from the continual reopening of an old wound from the ulcer on his thigh, as already discussed. As Henry neared his death, he lurched from paranoia, depression and heaviness, to fits of anger; so much so, that his courtiers were afraid, as they never knew what kind of mood their master would be in from the start of the day until the end. Henry's sixteen personal physicians, apothecaries and surgeons could not always cure his ailments, and could only do so much, as noted in previous chapters. It seemed that the only cure for his gnawing symptoms was a good laugh, which is where the court fool, William Somer, came in.

In England, writers of the Doomsday book recorded details of royal fools. In contemporary accounts for the reigns of Edward II and Edward III, both kings had natural fools called 'Robert'.[19] Henry VIII must have studied the history of his ancestors as a boy when he was at Eltham, living with his mother and sisters, and was accustomed to the company of court fools from when he was just a prince. His father, Henry VII, took a fool on progress with him in 1492 to Sittingbourne, called the 'the folyshe Duke of Lancaster'. This fool was a 'fool double'.[20]

Years previously, at the start of the Tudor dynasty, when Henry Tudor defeated Richard III at Bosworth Field in 1485 and succeeded to the throne as Henry VII, thus ending of the Wars of the Roses, he brought a period of stability and economic prosperity in England. Under the banner of the pink rose, the result of joining the red rose of Lancaster with the white rose of York, through the marriage of Henry VII and Elizabeth of York, with the 'Cousins' War' over, it became possible to develop the lighter side of English court life, as the fighting and quarrelling subsided.[21]

In Henry VII's reign there are records of inquisitions which mention natural fools:

> Margaret, late the wife of Thomas Schaa, holds the under-mentioned lands, late of Thomas Schaa, her husband, for life, the reversion belonging to Robert Schaa; The said Robert is a natural fool and incapable of managing his lands.

Another record from September of the same period states:

> John Dryver, late of Almaly, died seised in fee of the under-mentioned messuage, which on his death descended to Richard Dryver, his son and heir, who entered therein and

was and still is seised thereof in fee. The said Richard is, and has been since birth, a fool and natural idiot, and is not capable of managing himself or his lands and goods. So the custody of him and his lands &c. pertains to the king by reason of his royal prerogative.[22]

In another inquisition record on 6 January is the death of a Francis Metcalf:

He [Francis Metcalf] is and has been since birth, an idiot and natural fool, incapable of managing himself or his lands. He and Joan his wife, late daughter of Everard Seyton, esquire, were seised in fee of the under-mentioned lands, in right of the said Joan. From 5 February, 20 Edward IV, until 20 June, 21 Henry VII, during which period the said Francis and Joan were so seised of the premises, Thomas Metcalff and James Metcalff received all the issues and profits thereof.

This record shows that despite his learning disabilities that Francis had married a lady called Joan, and that land belonging to Joan, which was in her name and not in her husband's, because of his idiocy, was seized and given to other family members. This source shows that common, disabled people tried to live fulfilling lives within society but were often not awarded the same benefits as their able counterparts.[23]

In another inquisition record on the death of a William Porter, during the reign of Henry VIII, the record states that William's estate cannot pass to his son and heir, John, because he is a natural fool incapable of looking after himself: 'He died [William Porter] seised in fee of the under-mentioned messuages &c. on 10 May, 12 Henry VII. John Porter, aged 26 years and more, is his son and heir, and is, and has been since birth, a natural fool, incapable of managing himself or his property.'[24]

The young Prince Henry, Duke of York, even at the tender age of ten, would have been aware of 'natural fools' from his father's dealings with them, and was not considered too young to keep a fool of his own, called, 'the Duc of Yorkesfole'. In March 1502,' John Goose, my lord of Yorkes fole' was sent by Henry with a gift of carp to his mother, Queen Elizabeth.[25] 'Goose' was a new court fool, nicknamed by the young prince, and was one of the first in a series of 'innocent' fools, both silly and intelligent, to have received patronage when he became Henry VIII.

Court fools enjoyed a long career in Tudor England, but the role also carried many dangers. Natural fools laughed with, but also laughed at the king; an ingenious, if not a troublesome balancing act, that could, if a wrong word was uttered, or overheard, lead to their downfall. However, we must not confuse disabled people who were natural fools or people who had learning disabilities, with the artificial fool, which was a term that seems to have been synonymous with 'jester'. A jester was said to mimic the 'foolishness' of a natural fool. The juxtaposition is that we should also not confuse learning disabilities with learning difficulties, which are succinctly very different. Therefore, a natural fool was one with learning disabilities, rather than learning difficulties. Moreover, disabled people with learning disabilities were commonplace, as is evident from visits to monasteries, written accounts, letters, and statutes, which suggest that these natural fools, as we have seen in previous chapters, were widely present in Tudor society. Disabled people were highly visible in society, and understood to be distinct from those with mental illnesses, such as those who were considered mad, or insane. Bouts of madness were deemed to be curable and therefore not a disability, whereas being an 'idiota' or 'fool' was not treatable and was considered a disability. It is challenging to understand disability categorisations of the past. Before modern medicine, physicians had failed to compartmentalise disability.[26] It is a very difficult challenge to research developmental and learning disabilities, especially when they were understood at the time so differently.

Due to the lack of categorisation of disability, it is difficult to say if natural fools were likely to have been people with permanent disabilities, like Down syndrome, cerebral palsy or other different types of physical or learning disabilities. It was firmly believed by many, that 'Holy Innocents', as natural fools were also known, were disabled people who suffered from what we might now identify as autistic. However, the Tudors did not categorise them as disabled, as we might today. Natural fools were people with reduced intellectual disabilities, with a lack of everyday life skills, who were unable to develop new life skills without the support of a carer, or what the Tudors called a 'keeper'. Keepers cherished the natural fools they looked after, for their directness, and above all, for their innocence. The notion that disabled people were highly honoured, and favoured is heart-warming, in such an age of violent brutality. Disabled people being looked after and holding a privileged status at the Tudor court shows a degree of foresight and emotional intelligence within the echelons of Tudor society.[27]

The account books reveal that natural and artificial fools were plentiful under the Tudor monarchs. Henry VII, who was famous for his tight-fisted monetary policy, did not hold back when it came to providing natural fools for his court. In the expense accounts of Elizabeth of York, there are records from 1502 and 1503 of regular payments to her fool, and there are notations of gifts given to natural fools of great noblemen. Phyp oversaw the natural fools of the court, and was given the title 'Keeper of the King's Fools'.[28] Henry VII even made provisions in his funeral expenses for two hooded gowns to be prepared for the king's fools; Mr Martin (who attended the king on progress and who even rode a horse supplied by the king), and Mr John, and a new coat for the queen's fool.[29] Phyp is recorded as Mr Martin's master being explicitly mentioned in a letter from the king to the Keeper of the Wardrobe as 'Kepar of oure foole'.[30] In 1509, Thomas Cliffe was kept, and given 'a gown of tawny medley furred with lamb for Thomas Cliffe'. Two years later, Cliffe's keeper was replaced by a Thomas Taylor and given a warrant for a delivery of a fustian coat to Cliffe. There were regular provisions made for natural fools, and they were kept well fed and finely dressed by their keepers.[31]

In the Exchequer Accounts, there is mention of the 'King's Fools' and commissioning of gowns on 12 December 1509, which states 'Warrant to Great Wardrobe to deliver Wm. Worthy, "keeper of our fool," Tawney medley for a gown, Tower of London. 12 Dec. 1 Hen. VIII. Signed.'[32] Henry VIII was very fond of the natural fools in his care and made every provision for them to have a comfortable and happy life.

Henry's wives were not immune to caring and making provision for the natural fools who lived amongst them at the Tudor court either. Arrangements were made for a woman called Jayne, who was a natural fool living in the household of Anne Boleyn, then Catherine Parr, and afterwards, Lady Mary. As mentioned above, in the family portrait of Henry VIII, Jayne Foole appears, and she seems to have slightly distorted facial features in the dynasty portrait, which has led to some speculation that she may have had Down syndrome. Natural fools like Jayne were at the mercy of their keepers. However, from primary accounts, it is clear to see that many were well looked after, because like today, some disabled people were, and are, still incapable of looking after themselves, because of the physical and mental challenges they face. The Tudors understood that looking after someone incapable of looking after themselves was their Christian duty, and they considered the use of a 'keeper' or carer as a way of integrating disabled people into society in a compassionate manner. Due to the religious nature of renaissance men and women at court, natural 'innocents' were revered, thought to be sent by God, and cared for accordingly.

There are several indications that natural fools were very important at Henry VIII's court. The first is their inclusion in the dynastic portrait of his family. The second is that William Somer and Jayne Foole were not dressed in the multi-coloured motley of medieval fools, but attired in luxurious fabrics. Moreover, motley was the traditional costume of the court jester, fool, or the harlequin character in commedia dell'arte. The word motley definition in the Oxford English Dictionary as a cognate with medley, and as a noun, it can mean 'a varied mixture'. As an adjective, it is disparaging; a motley collection describes an uninspiring pile of stuff; motley crew. The word motley originated upon the birth of Hemmers in England between the fourteenth and seventeenth centuries, which referred to a woollen fabric of mixed colours, the characteristic dress of the professional fool.[33]

During the reign of Elizabeth I, motley fabric design served the vital purpose of keeping the fool outside the social hierarchy, which meant that they were not subject to class distinction. Since natural fools were outside the sumptuary dress laws, fools could wear what keepers deemed right for them. Their dress reflected the natural fools' status, and motley did not have to be chequered or one pattern, with different coloured threads running through it. However, it is interesting to note that William Somer and Jayne Foole, in the family portrait of Henry VIII c. 1545, were not dressed in motley, but fabrics and colours far more prized and expensive, thus showing their pronounced status.

A third reason and evidence for natural fools being relevant in the court of Henry VIII was that fools were given to courtiers, sometimes as gifts. As natural fools were looked after by keepers, they did not receive wages directly for the service they provided to Tudor society, which suggests that natural fools like William Somer, were unable to care for themselves. Natural fools did not have the wherewithal, nor did they have the funds, nor the ability to order and pay for their own clothes. Their keepers did this for them. Henry looked after those keepers who looked after, or you could say, adopted natural fools such as Sexton, William Somer, and Jayne Foole, which showed the esteem in which Henry held disabled people of his court. Above all, natural fools, like Sexton, possibly nicknamed 'Patch', and William Somer, both held in high esteem, were always the ones to whom Henry would turn when he was melancholy or sick, particularly Somer.[34]

Through the research of the household accounts, we can argue that 'Patch', William Somer, and Jayne needed keepers, or carers to look after them. The severity of their disabilities meant they did not have the 'life-skills' nor the conventional sense, or finances to care for themselves. Given the notion that in the twenty-first century we are progressive, it seems clear that the popular myth perpetuated by Enid Welsford, that the purpose of fools was to act as 'clowns aping foolishness' for a laugh, is untrue. Moreover, it could be argued that the Tudors were progressive because the roles of natural fools at the court of Henry VIII were not the same as the roles of fools or jesters at other courts. Many courts in Europe had dwarves, and the idea of dwarves at court was to amuse. Dwarves being the butt of jokes and being amusing to others because of the limitations of their height played havoc with the social order.

In an anonymous pamphlet, talking about Geoffrey Hudson, who was a dwarf at the court of King Charles I, the author wrote in 1636, 'That those who desire to approach near princes ought not to be ambitious of any greatness, but ought to acknowledge that all their courtly lustre is but a reflection of the beam of royal sun that is their master.' These disabled courtiers were there to serve as a reminder to royal subjects of the social hierarchy. By the end of the sixteenth century, there was a distinction between natural fools and artificial fools. Over time, the term 'fool' has been used synonymously with the term 'idiota', meaning someone characterised with limited capacity or sensibility, or who were incapable or insensible of their actions.[35]

Natural fools spoke their minds and at the same time, were supposed to be funny. Natural fools were essential in creating lively entertainment, which meant laughter, but also amusement, good company, lively conversation, music-making, and being merry with one another. Being in the company of a 'natural fool was more important than being around an 'artificial fool' because artificial fools were making up jokes, and making jokes of others, whereas natural fools spoke honestly, from the heart and from their own life experience which is why they were considered so important; 'natural fools' spoke with directness and honesty, which is why they were highly valued.[36]

While the terminology used to discuss natural fools and disabled people during the Tudor period is dissimilar to our own and can seem offensive, the Tudors were attempting to categorise learning disabilities. These instances of permanent and life-long illnesses showed that natural fools were considered different from everyone else. These conditions were unlike madness or being mentally insane, which the Tudors considered temporary and curable. Folly or disability was deemed by Tudor society to be permanent, and distinct from the illness of insanity.

Learning disabilities were different from learning difficulties, as learning disabilities reduced intellectual ability and those who suffered from them had trouble coping with everyday life, tasks and managing money. As well as struggling with daily activities, sufferers would have problems dealing with situations many able-bodied and mentally-well take for granted. Like many disabled people today, disabled people of the Tudor period suffered for the whole of their lives. And, like today, people with learning disabilities during the Tudor period needed help to develop new skills, to understand complicated information, to socialise and to interact with other people. They struggled and needed support, especially if they suffered from conditions such as Down syndrome, autism, Williams' syndrome, Asperger's syndrome and cerebral palsy. But with some distance of over five hundred years, it is challenging and problematic to surmise how far the Tudors categorised these conditions, and because of the veil of time and understanding, historians do not like applying retrospective diagnosis to disabilities of the past, and it is problematic to try to diagnose natural fools such as William Somer and Jayne Foole.[37]

When we view William Somer, and Jayne Foole in the family portrait hung in the Haunted Gallery at Hampton Court, we speculate and try to categorise them. Many historians disagree about the disability status of William Somer, in particular.[38] Historians like Roy Porter suggest that 'real idiots are invariably absent from inverted ceremonials. Court jesters, after all, tended to be professional comedians.'[39]

Contemporary accounts indicate that court fools were natural because, in the play by John Heywood, *Wit and Witless*, intended for performance at court, William Somer is described as 'sot Somer', meaning William Somer was drunk.[40] Natural fools were easily a target for derision.

Sarah Carpenter, from the University of Edinburgh, in her paper, 'Laughing at Fools' argues that 'the naturals were rarely capable of the conscious or sophisticated verbal wit of the artificial fool, although some of the high-functioning natural fools like Will Somer were valued for their repartee.'[41] A compelling piece of evidence that William Somer was a natural fool is a warrant from 1551 approving payment of 40 shillings to William Seyton 'whom his Majesty hath appointed to keep William Somer'. This source implies, as has been said before, that Somer needed a keeper, who is named, to care for him, much as people with learning disabilities might need a carer today.[42] William Somer was an 'innocent' who was unable to comprehend the basics of living.[43]

Despite a natural fools' incomprehension, many fools did offer verbal comedy or even wisdom. Oral entertainment tended to be of one of two types. A natural fools' words might reveal their laughable lack of comprehension of social and intellectual skills, or as a natural fool was valued for being honest, their inability to use words to deceive, to flatter, or to lie. John, a natural fool who lived at Christ's Hospital and was personally known to Robert Armin, 'was of this humour: aske him what his coate cost him, he would say a groate: what his cap, band or shirt cost, all was a groate, aske what his beard cost, and still a groote'. Laughter seems to be prompted by the apparent naivety and lack of understanding such words betray.[44]

Some people associated with the many palaces of the court suffered from a wide variety of medical conditions when they lived, worked or visited the various royal households, during the Tudor period. Among those who had achieved such status as to live at prominent royal palaces such as Hampton Court, was Cardinal Wolsey's fool, Philip Sexton, or 'Patch' as he was known, whom Wolsey seems to have cherished. There is no reliable biographical information for him, yet 'Patch' seems to have been a nickname which meant 'fool', like a patch on clothing fools the viewer into thinking it's whole.

'Patch' was probably a 'natural fool', and the king had allowed Cardinal Wolsey the custody of any man who had been proved legally insane. This legal arrangement may explain why Wolsey was able to treat 'Patch' as chattel and dispose of him against his will. 'Patch' is first found in the records around 25 November 1529. In sources such as

Cavendish's *Life and Death of Cardinal Wolsey*, we are eloquently told of the mutual bond between a natural fool like Sexton, alias 'Patch', and their guardians or 'keepers'.

The circumstances surrounding 'Patch' given to the king as a present stem from when Wolsey was on his way from Putney to Westminster and his train was intercepted by Henry VIII's Groom of the Stool, Sir Henry Norris. Norris gave Cardinal Wolsey the gift of a ring from the king, passing a message on, that with the ring, Wolsey should be 'of good cheer, for he was much in his highnesses favour as ever he was or so shall be'. When Wolsey heard this, the cardinal alighted from his mule and knelt on both knees in the mud, 'holding up his hands for joy'. With that, Norris bowed and withdrew, but Wolsey called him back. In an attempt to win back the favour of the king, Wolsey offered his fool to the king: '"I am sorry," quod he, "that I have no condign token to send to the King: but if ye would at this my request present the King with this poor fool, I trust his highness would accept him well. Surely for a nobleman's pleasure, he is worth a thousand pounds".'[45] Henry Norris took 'Patch' with him. Cavendish goes on to say that, 'my lord was fain to send six tall yeomen with him to conduct and convey the fool to the court; for the poor fool took on and fired so in such a rage when he saw that he must needs depart from my lord. Yet notwithstanding they conveyed him with Master Norris to the court, where the king received him most gladly.'[46]

For Sexton to have to be removed by six yeomen meant he must have been a large, strong man. This transaction was said to have taken place towards the end of 1529, either late October or early November, as 'Patch's' first recorded appearance at court was on 25 November 1529. Despite, the esteem in which Wolsey held "Patch' and the displeasure at which 'Patch' himself showed at being hoisted away in such a transaction, Wolsey was still prepared to sacrifice his fool to curry favour with the king. Wolsey must have been so desperate to stay in favour with the king that in his mind, he knew that Sexton would be assured of a safe and secure future, even if Wolsey knew his days of prosperity might be over, for all of Henry's reassurances.[47]

In a Spanish account, Sexton appeared to have an insight, or a 'hunch' if you like, about Wolsey's fall – he saw it coming. The report says that Wolsey took a fool with him to see a sepulchre which he was having made for himself. Sexton turned to Wolsey and said, 'My lord, why are you striving and spending so much money on this? Do you think you will be buried here? I tell you, when you die, you will not have enough to pay the men to bury you.' The tomb had been real enough, but unfinished, and Wolsey was later buried in Leicester Abbey where he died.[48]

John Heywood is an authority on Sexton. The contemporary writer knew that Sexton had begun his career as a fool to Cardinal Wolsey, and was known at that time by the nickname, 'Patch', through an epigram, not printed until 1562 during Elizabeth I's reign, that belongs to a time before Wolsey's fall from favour in 1529.[49]

> A saiying of Patche my lord cardinals foole
> Master Sexton, a parson of knowne wit,
> As he at my lord Cardinals boord did sit,
> Gredily raught at a goblet of wyne:
> Drinke none (said my lord) for that sore leg of thine,
> I warrant your grace (quoth Sexton) I provide
> For my leg: For I drinke on tother side.[50]

This exchange, in the circumstances of the moment, as a spontaneous riposte to public criticism, would have raised raucous laughter amongst the cardinal's guests. When the cardinal was stripped of the Great Seal, at the mercy of the Duke of Norfolk, and Duke of Suffolk, parliament, and ultimately the king, the cardinal would eventually give Sexton to the king on receiving the king's assurance on a degree of protection. The king would then pay a carer, or 'keeper' to look after Sexton. *The Life and Death of Cardinal Wolsey*, written by George Cavendish, is one of the few accounts which speaks of the mutual affection between fools and their patrons. Sexton never received any wages, bonuses or rewards, and he always had keepers to look after him, which proves like Will, Sexton had a distinct learning disability.[51] Sexton had three keepers, Greene, Sexton's servant, Skinner, who waited upon him and Epsom, his attendant. They supplied Sexton's clothes, food, ale, laundry, shoes and posite of beer. Sexton's keepers were given money to buy his food and do his laundry, as Sexton had no use for money himself.[52]

The king had ordered a royal livery coat for Sexton, which the royal embroiderers had decorated with Henry's monogram. He also received an additional doublet and hose of worsted, linked with sarcenet (a light, silken material), as well as a wig, which was known as a 'perwyke', a later provision of a 'myllain bonet' and several nightcaps. The cost of his new wardrobe came to a total of £5 12s 9d. Sexton was provided with quality items of clothing, on a par with gentlemen of the privy chamber.[53]

Clothes were ordered and made for Henry's fools, so they were set apart from other courtiers. However, this did not mean that they wore a 'motley' design, usually reserved for artificial fools. Moreover, like the young, male courtiers whom King Henry supported, like Francis Brereton, and later, the musician Mark Smeaton, they were afforded clothes to denote their status, and London tailors were approached to make clothes for them.[54]

The household accounts of Henry VIII have recorded all the clothes commissioned for Sexton (Patch), Somer, Jayne and other courtiers who needed to be supported. Sexton must have been well turned out and would have looked splendid in his doublet of woven worsted hosen and silks. He reputedly had a bonnet from Milan, and nightcap, along with a coat of kendle, a gown of green woollen cloth and a doublet of cotton and flax.[55]

Sexton was popular with Wolsey, and Wolsey had been in despair of having to hand 'Patch' over to Henry. Wolsey had nothing left to give; Wolsey had previously handed over his beloved Hampton Court, as suggestions of clouded allegations from opposing factions at court had begun to accumulate. Way before Wolsey fell from favour, Sexton had been popular among Wolsey's ministers because he reportedly had had a rhetorical wit. He was the first fool recorded as being 'of the Privy Chamber'. Sexton was baudy and had a humorous and spontaneous way with words, whose humour, and 'banter' as a fool was renowned for lifting Henry out of the foulest of moods.[56]

It was not long before another 'innocent' from Shropshire would join 'Patch' at court. Thomas Bedyll wrote to Cromwell about Sexton on the 26 January 1536:

> As he has hitherto had occasion to write of sad matters, now writes of a merry one. The King hath one old fool, Sexten, as good as might be, which by reason of age is not like to continue. I have espied a young fool at Croland, much more pleasant than Sexten ever was, not past 15, who is every day new to the hearer. Though I am made of such heavy matter that I have small delectation in fools, he is one of the best

I have heard. He is very fit for the Court, and will afford the King much pastime, which he shall make both with gentlemen and gentlewomen. Begs he will send for him to the abbot of Croland.

The source does not state whether this is about William Somer, or indeed another natural fool.[57]

There are no references to Sexton in the Privy Purse expenses or State Papers after December 1532, however, he did remain at court with the king for another two and a half years. His relationship with the king had never been as close as it had been with Cardinal Wolsey, but for Henry to keep Sexton in his service for so long, meant that Sexton must have given reasonable satisfaction in keeping the king in a good humour. Ambassador Eustace Chapuys, writing in a report home in July 1535, about Henry VIII's harsh treatment of his eldest Princess Mary whose escape from England he was trying to arrange, added a postscript, written in cipher, attached to his letter: 'Le roy d'Angleterre a cuyde tuer son fol, quest ung innocent, pour ce quil disoit et parloit bien de la Royne et Princesse et disoit Ribalde a la concubine et bastarde a sa fille et a este banny de court et la recelle le grand escuier.' Translates as: 'He [the king] the other day nearly murdered his own fool, a simple and innocent man, because he happened to speak well in his presence of the Queen and Princess, [Katharine of Aragon and Mary] and called the concubine "ribaude" and her daughter "bastard." He has now been banished from Court, and has gone to the Grand Esquire, [Sir Nicholas Carew, Master of the Horse] who has sheltered and hidden him.'[58]

The name of the natural fool who spoke these words in the presence of the king is not recorded, but on this occasion, this fool was speaking the truth, as Catholic factions of the court perceived events at the time. However, his words would not be excused nor ignored. In 1539, like so many of Henry's contemporaries, Carew would be arrested and sent to Tower Hill, like so many before and after him. A letter dated 26 January 1536, from one of Thomas Cromwell's commissioners for the visitation of abbeys, suggests that Sexton was still in the king's service at that time. 'The King hath one old fool, Sexten, as good as might be, which by reason of age is not like to continue. I have espied a young fool at Croland, much more pleasant than Sexten ever was, not past 15, who is every day new to the hearer. Though I am made of such heavy matter that

I have small delectation in fools, he is one of the best I have heard. He is very fit for the Court, and will afford the King much pastime, which he shall make both with gentlemen and gentlewomen.' The records are silent on what happened to Sexton, and this young, natural fool of 15, mentioned in this letter was a non-starter.[59]

William Somer, Henry's next well-known natural fool, is of unknown parentage and place of origin, who according to James Granger, 'was some time a servant in the family of Richard Farmor, Esq. of Eston Neston, in Northamptonshire'. Richard Fermor was a Merchant of the Staple at Calais, who brought him to Greenwich to present to the king.[60] Impressed by William Somer's sense of humour, Henry promptly offered William Somer a place at court and he was in Henry VIII's service by 28 June 1535.[61]

It was at Greenwich Palace that William Somer, the court fool to Henry VIII, was chiefly domesticated. He used his influence with the king in a way that few court favourites – not being classed as 'natural fools' – have done before or since. He tamed the royal tyrant's ferocity, and occasionally, at least, urged him on to good and kind actions, himself giving the example by his kindness to those who came within the humble sphere of his influence and act. Robert Armin, in his *Nest of Ninnies*, published in 1608, describes William Somer as a philosopher:

> A comely fool indeed, passing more stately; who was this forsooth? Will Sommers, and not meanly esteemed by the king for his merriment; his melody was of a higher straine, and he lookt as the noone broad waking. His description was writ on his forehead, and yee might read it thus:

> Will Sommers, born in Shropshire, as some say,
> Was brought to Greenwich on a holy day;
> Presented to the king, which foole disdayn'd
> To shake him by the hand, or else ashamed;
> Howe're it was, as ancient people say,
> With much adoe was wonne to it that day.
> Leane he was, hollow-ey'd, as all report,
> And stoope he did, too; yet in all the Court
> Few men were more belov'd than was this foole,
> Whose merry prate kept with the king much rule.

When he was sad the king and he would rime,
Thus Will he exil'd sadness many a time.
I could describe him, as I did the rest;
But in my mind I doe not think it best.
My reason this, howe'er I do descry him,
So many know him that I may belye him;
Therefore to please all people one by one,
I hold it best to let that paines alone.
Only thus much: he was the poore man's friend,
And help'd the widdows often in the end;
The king would ever grant what he did crave,
For well he knew Will no exacting knave;
But wisht the king to do good deeds great store,
Which caus'd the Court to love him more and more.[62]

It is a comfort to think that Henry VIII had at least one honest and kind-hearted counsellor; it did not matter that William was considered a court fool, or indeed a disabled person; as William had so much to offer the king in terms of raising his spirits, improving his mood, dispelling his melancholy, giving advice and emotional support.

William Somer stayed with Henry throughout his reign, acting as Henry's entertainer, playing rhyming games, being a companion to the king and engaging him in conversation. At the time of joining the court, William Somer, was a young man, in his late teens or early twenties, who hung around the Tudor court making merry with the younger gentlemen of Henry's privy chamber. As an 'innocent', William added to the revelry of court life, entertaining those under the blue and gold vaulted ceilings of the court, fulfilling no other purpose than to lift the courtiers' spirits.. Will Sexton and William Somer were permitted familiarities without regard for deference, and Somer possessed a clever wit, which he exercised both on Cardinal Wolsey and the king.

We can learn much from the portraiture of Henry's ministers and courtiers from the renditions of their likenesses, in the many paintings by Holbein the Younger, and there are several portraits of William Somer with his master, King Henry VIII. These pictures give us an excellent indication of William's appearance. There is a depiction of him in the 'The Psalter of Henry VIII' and is a rare example of a sixteenth century illuminated manuscript that belonged to Henry. It is now in the British

Library under the title, 'Henry VIII with William Sommers, from the Psalter of Henry VIII'.[63]

The king commissioned his prayer book during the early 1540s from Jean Mallard, a French illustrator, who had worked for Francis I. The psalter contains eight miniatures, amongst them, scenes which show William Somer, with his likeness facing the viewer directly. William is dressed in a 'grene cloth cote recognisable from the descriptions in the Privy Purse accounts. Behind him, Henry sits, playing the harp. The string instrument is an allusion to Henry as King David. In the psalter, Henry is depicted in his old age, and is probably lamenting his sins and setting them to music. The psalter has marginal annotations made by the king, and astonishingly, the full 1540 book, complete with Henry's handwritten notes in the margins are available to view on the British Library's Virtual Books website, which is a thrill for those unable to see the manuscript in person.[64]

The image of William Somer with Henry in the psalter portrait appears to be an unhappy one, as most of Henry's old friends and acquaintances had, by this point, been executed, exiled or died of natural causes. Henry must have felt that there were few friends left he could safely trust or confide in, apart from his loyal fool, William Somer, who was always by his side. The image in the psalter of the lonely old king and his trusty fool is hauntingly sad. We can assume that William Somer had a unique, distinct, privileged and intimate friendship with Henry because they are depicted together, alone in this portrait. That Somer was Henry's sole listener as he played his harp, suggests much about the intimacy of their relationship.[65]

From the way that William Somer stands in the portrait, it could be argued that he suffered, like Richard III, from juvenile-onset scoliosis. William is depicted as being afflicted with a pronounced, higher shoulder and his leg appears to be dragging to one side as he tries to keep his balance. It is not clear from the portrait that William Somer suffered from a hunchback, which is different from scoliosis. Interestingly, however, hunchbacks were believed to have the gift of prophecy, and that is where we get the expression, 'I have a hunch'.

As we can see from the psalter portrait, we can assume that where the monarch presided, William Somer would not be far away. During Henry's reign, from the time Somer joined the court, William and the king had built a strong bond. William had developed a great friendship with the king, and they were said to be extremely close, which was evident because William called the king 'Harry', 'Hal', or 'Uncle', and he was the only person permitted to do so. Having risen in high favour with the king, William was allowed the freedom to speak his mind to the king, whose liberality with him is attested to by the accounts of the royal household.

William Somer always had access to the king. Erasmus said in his book, *In Praise of Folly*:

> Fools can provide a thing a prince is looking for—jokes, merriment and fun, wherever they go, they bring pleasure and entertainment, fun and laughter to everyone else, as if God had created them and given them the gift of relieving the sadness of life. Therefore, they are the favourite of kings. So much so, that many great rulers cannot eat a mouthful, or take a step, or last an hour without them, that they value fools a long way above the crab wise they continued to maintain for appearance's sake.[66]

Educated people of the Tudor age valued fools, for their honesty as oracles and sages, which allowed disabled people with learning disabilities the privilege to speak the truth to kings and nobles. Such intimacy awarded natural fools an unprecedented opportunity, at a time when, if anyone else had been so bold and honest, their words might have been construed as treasonous. They would have ended up in the Tower, on charges of dissension. Natural fools were thought to be uniquely placed to speak the truth because their innocence was said to give them a special relationship with God, and they were used as a conduit by God for the Holy Spirit. Erasmus wrote of such matters because he pointed out that Paul said, 'all men were fools before God, and the foolishness of God was wiser than men's wisdom.'[67]

However, Erasmus also pointed out that fools were not always wise in their discourse: 'We have all seen how an appropriate and well-timed joke can sometimes influence even grim tyrants ... The most violent tyrants put up with their clowns and fools, though these often made them the butt of open insults.'[68]

In religious terms, the disabled person or natural fool with learning disabilities was spiritually without blemish, because their disability meant that they were already suffering purgatory on earth; they also had a goodly character and simplicity of mind, which meant they were thought incapable of sin. As Erasmus had written, 'fools were conduits of the divine, who gave great pleasure to God because of their simple and good natures.'[69] It could be argued that allowing God to use natural fools as conduits for the Holy Spirit was the reason for the court fools' authority and favour in the Tudor period, and the reason why they were well cared for. Their clothes denoted this favour and were made from luxurious fabrics which set them apart from the usual uniforms of royal retainers. The only shocking thing about a fools' appearance was their shaven, bald heads, which may have been for a purely practical purpose, or for religious reasons, as it echoed the tonsures of the monks or priests, who left part of the top of their heads bare by shaving off their hair.

As Erasmus stated, a natural fools' folly was the behaviour of an innocent soul, who was a bearer of divinity. Like monks, in the soon to be dissolved monasteries, natural fools showed society, by their dress, and the way that the king and court treated them, that they were held in high esteem. Natural fools and disabled people had a unique status; ultimately admired because of their direct relationship with God. Some religious men and women believed these religious and spiritual ideas because the Bible stated in the New Testament, 1 Corinthians 1:27 that, 'God chose the foolish things of the world to shame the wise; God chose the weak things of the world to shame the strong'.[70]

The way a fool was dressed symbolised and reinforced ideas of status, as all court dress did in the Tudor period. Katherine, Countess of Devon, recorded in her household book of 24 October 1524:

A doz. points for Dick the Fool. A pair of shoes for Andrew of the kitchen, 5d. For 2 yards of "whyclyng" for two fools, and Andrew's doublet, 4d. For washing Dick the Fool's cloathing, 2d. Two loads of rushes, 2s. 4d. To a woman weeding in the garden, six days, 7d. A servant bringing two foxes to my Lady, 8d. For 28 stone of flocks for stuffing six mattresses, 18s. 8d.; for making same, 2s. 6d. 3 yards of canvas for bolsters, 12d. A quarter of porpoise, 4s. A ream of paper, 3s. Carriage to London of conger "bokhere" and "bak samen" (baked salmon ?), 12s. "For killing of a baran (?) hynd against Whitsuntide, for my Lady's grace, and for carriage of the same," 4s. Strawberries on 17th May, 4d. To a harper and a tumbler with the King's servants, 10s. Six yds. of white for the fool's coat, 6s. Making 2 fools' coats, 1s. For mending Dick and Mug and Kit's clothes, 4d. For my Lady and the household drinking at Trinity Chapel, 20 June, 2s. To buy two coats for Mug the fool when he went to London, 10s.[71]

This entry shows that nobility looked after disabled people within their own households, as well as at court.

King Henry also spared no expense on fools he owned, as we can see from the depictions in portraiture. Henry looked after young courtiers like Francis Weston, Will Brereton, and the musician Mark Smeaton, as well as his fool William Somer because he wanted to be a kind, and generous benefactor. William Somer appears many times, in the household accounts, for new clothes for 'William Somer, oure foole'. Henry's 'olde foole' Sexton or 'Patch' had grown too old and it was William who took Sexton's place. William's initial requirements for attending and living within the Tudor court included a fool's livery.

The king commissioned tailors to create an impressive wardrobe of clothes for William, as is recorded in the household accounts. There were two outfits documented as coats of green cloth. One lined with white crewel and one with green crewel. Dated in the accounts on 28 June 1535, there were two pairs of hose of blue cloth ordered. Henry wrote from Windsor Castle to the Lord Windsor, Keeper of the Great Wardrobe, to make a payment for robes, doublets for 'Wm. Somar, the King's fool'.[72]

William Somer had been commissioned to live within the confines of the Tudor court as a replacement for Sexton, and he had integrated his position not only through his strong bond with the king but also because of the clothing that the king commissioned the keeper of the Great Wardrobe to make for William; this reinforced his status within court hierarchy. A list of clothing includes:

A dubblette of wursteed, lined with canvas and coton ... a coote and a cappe of grene clothe, fringed with red crule, and lined with fryse ... a dublette of fustian, lyned with cotton and canvas ... a coote of grene clothe, with a hood of the same, fringed with white crule lyned with fryse and bokerham.[73]

The first order of clothing for William Somer in June 1535 represents his initial fitting out as a royal retainer and servant. By this time, William Somer had become ensconced in court life as a maintained, disabled person and 'innocent'.

There are more purchases for William in Cromwell's financial records of 28 January 1538, where there were records of a 'velvet purse for W. Sommer', however, there is no mention of anything to fill it, as William's expenses were met by the court. [74]

In 1544, William Somer was the recipient of a green cloth gown, three pairs of lined shoes at ten pence a pair and seven pairs of unlined shoes costing eight pence per pair. Then there were also two pairs of summer shoes, buskins at two shillings a pair and three pairs of winter boots at three shillings a pair. Henry would pay Sexton and Somer's keepers' regular money to make sure they were paid sufficiently to supply suitable clothing and quality food so that they ate properly, had their laundry cleaned and heads shaved.

Throughout his service as a retainer, in this elegant new apparel, William Somer's duty was to entertain and distract the king from his worldly care, and he seems to have done so admirably. In court society, thankfully, fools and disabled people were appreciated and were not always objects of curiosity and the butt of jokes, like they would become in the later Victorian era, where they were paraded as exhibits in freak shows. Nor were natural fools perceived as the folly of humanity and death; they were considered as spiritually untouchable, and outside the usual hierarchy of society. Natural fools were the last made first, as confirmed in the verses of 1 Corinthians, where the foolish things of this world were chosen by God to shame the world. Therefore, William Somer and other disabled people would influence their monarchs, because they could speak the truth, and held an essence of wisdom. As Erasmus said, 'No one would dream of hurting them. They [fools] are under the protection of the Gods and rightly held in honour by all.'[75]

Natural fools were cherished, well cared for, and valued for their directness and humour, as implied by their inclusion in Tudor family portraits, and they had gained a unique position in the noble and royal society of the Tudor court. Fools like Sexton, William Somer and Jayne Foole were loved and admired because they were often immune to Henry's royal temper since they were in the envious position of speaking their minds. Having someone at court considered an 'idiot' gave the said person an implicit license to talk back, which would have been unintentional; this was a symbolic check on the king's ego and that of other courtiers. Other courtiers would not have got away with such opportunities of expression, without falling foul of the monarch's temper. The appearance of the fool at court and in society, allowed a layman to turn everyday thinking on its head, just as Christmastide became turned upside down during festivities with the 'Lord of Misrule'.

The Lord of Misrule taking control of Christmas was one of the most significant features of the Christmastide festival, which was held on the Feast of the Epiphany and called the Feast of Fools. The Feast of Fools flourished in the cathedral towns of France and appeared in England no later than the fourteenth century. During the festival, the revellers engaged in the crowning of a mock-king, and for a brief period, the rigid medieval social order seemed to be turned upside-down. The Lord of Misrule was expected to keep up the pretence of ruling a mock kingdom, reigning in a decorous, yet harmless manner. In the time of Henry VII and Henry VIII, a Lord of Misrule was appointed annually at the court, and it seems that he was a descendant of the old traditional Christmas lord. The tradition of the Lord of Misrule continued until the death of Edward VI when the character and the culture make no more appearances at the English court.

However, there were times when William Somer turned things upside down in his unique way, and he did not correctly read Henry's mood. Robert Armin, a commentator and contemporary writer, repeated the tale of one incident in which 'the King upon a time being extreame melancholy & full of passion, all that Will Somers could do, wold not make him merry'.[76]

William Somer is then remembered as having staged a series of what is plainly, and probably deliberately, somewhat meaningless jests to gradually lure the king back into good humour. William Somer offered the king a brief, legitimate escape from responsibility, from the intellectual and emotional demands of ruling the country. His harmless banter, therefore, has had a valuable moral and social function.

However, William Somer did not always behave in front of the king in a Godly manner, and this opposing, opportunistic behaviour, paraded in innocence, is why William was a favourite with King Henry. William got away with farting in Henry's presence; William would pass wind, which would send the king into fits of laughter. He could get away with the bawdiest behaviour in front of the king, without being reprimanded. Henry suggested to Will, that because he had made him laugh so, he would be happy to grant him any reasonable thing. William thanked the king, saying that he needed nothing, but knew where to find Henry if he needed anything one day. Henry understood that William knew he could ask for anything when he was in need. This incident is retold, *In Fools and Jesters: With a reprint of Robert Armin's Nest of Ninnies*:

> Why qd Will it is a fart.
> At this, the King laught hartely, & was excéeding merry, and bids Will aske any reasonable thing, and he would graunt it.

> Thanks Harry saies he, now against I want I know where to find, for yet I néede no/thing, but one day I shall, for euery man sées his latter end, but knowes not his beginning.

> The King vnderstoode his meaning, and so pleasantly departed for that season, & Will laid him downe amongst the Spaniels to sléepe.[77]

It is alleged that William Somer had a hand in Wolsey's fall, but as we cannot pinpoint an exact date of the arrival of William Somer to Henry's court, it is difficult to know if Somer went to Wolsey's cellar to get some wine to drink and discovered casks filled with gold, which the king interpreted as Wolsey intending to use to the finance a rebellion against him. Wolsey would not remain chancellor forever, and in 1530, Thomas More eventually replaced him. Thomas More, too, maintained a natural fool, Henry Patenson, who did his best to persuade his master to acknowledge the royal supremacy and thereby save himself from execution. Patenson complained that he could not understand 'what aileth More' and proudly claimed that he had sworn the oath himself. We know that More rejected Patenson's wisdom, and when he could no longer care for Patenson, gave him to the Lord Mayor of London. Thomas More would eventually be beheaded for refusing to acknowledge Henry VIII as Supreme Head of the Church of England. No one remained in Henry's favour for long, except William Somer.

The most famous quip afforded to William Somer is by Thomas Wilson when in 1553, to illustrate paronomasia, he quotes William Somer in his 'Arte of Rhetorique' as follows:

William Somer, seeing much ado for account-making, and that the King's Majesty of most worthy memory, Henry the eighth, wanted money such as was due unto him: As please your grace (quoth he) you have so many fraud-iters, so many conveyers, and so many deceivers to get up your money, that they get all to themselves.[78]

These reported phrases are a pun on 'auditors, surveyors and receivers' which is both a joke and also a truth. Thomas Wilson notes that Somer 'should have said auditors, surveyors and receivers', however, by a clever interchange of letters, William Somer amused and condemned Henry's advisors and courtiers in the same breath. These examples of phrases quoted from William Somer impresses on the reader that his wit and humour is later compounded by other multiple anecdotes of wit and humour recorded in works published later, such as Will Somer's *Last Will and Testament*, Armin's *Foole upon Foole*, Samuel Rowley's *When You See Me, You Know Me*, or the anonymous, *A Pleasant History of the Life and Death of Will Summers*. Robert Armin emphasises William Somer's ability to use his 'merry prate' and aptitude for the spontaneous rhyme to enhance King Henry's wellbeing:

Few men were more beloved than was this Fool,
Whose merry prate kept with the King much rule.
When he was sad, the King and he could rhyme,
Thus, Will exiled sadness many a time.[79]

Historical evidence name-checks William Somer in a letter from Sir William Paget to Henry VIII in 1545, which credits William Somer again with a habit for wise and quotable sayings. When William Paget makes assurances to the French to advance a diplomatic matter, he quips, using one of William Somer's familiar phrases, that he has promised 'much more than he will abide by'. Even though most of the recollections of what William Somer said were recorded years after the events, it does not mean that they were inaccurate. William Somer was not alone in being praised for his humorous banter. Similar observations had been made of his predecessor Sexton. John Southworth, author of *Fools and Jesters at the English Court* says that these documents do not offer much in the way of history, but they all highlight William

Somer's use of his 'merry prate' and spontaneous rhymes to improve his master's state of mind. Other reports recorded imply he was less a wit, more a 'natural fool'.

It was William's verbal dexterity that caused the king to raise William Somer in such favour, which is why William appears in several portraits, commissioned by the king himself. Despite the affection the king or noble might have for them, the historian Suzannah Lipscomb, suggests that 'fools were possessions'. In our modern world, we would see this as a form of slavery, because under the law, fools could be seised from the general populace and brought to noble courts where they could be traded, sold and given as gifts to others. They could also be beaten for insolence if their jokes went too far and this was what happened to William Somer as King Henry was violent with him on at least one occasion. Sometimes, the sixteenth century's treatment of disabled people is not praiseworthy; there existed an incomprehensible and questionable disposition towards natural fools that raised them, as much as it disparaged them. Common idiots had generally been objects of amusement, dread and derision, seen as monstrous, evil and unfit to know God, as the Vulgate Bible's Psalm 52 proposed.[80] Psalm 52 reads as 'The fool says in his heart, There is no God'; however, I suggest this does not refer to a fool as in a disabled person, but a foolish person who has no wisdom.[81]

Robert Armin recalled how William Somer humiliated Thomas, who was a juggler to the king. William interrupted one of Thomas's performances when Thomas was carrying milk and a bread roll. William Somer asked the king for a spoon, and the king replied he had none, and Thomas told him to use his hands. Will then sang:

> This bit Harry I give to thee
> and this next bit must serve for me,
> Both which I'll eat apace.
> This bit Madam unto you,
> And this bit I my self eate now,
> And the rest upon thy face.[82]

William Somer threw the milk in Thomas' face and ran out. Thomas was never recorded as being present at court again.

Erasmus said:

> The fact is, kings do dislike the truth, but the outcome of this
> is extraordinary for my fools. They can speak truth and even
> open insults and be heard with positive pleasure; indeed, the
> words which would cost a wise man his life are surprisingly
> enjoyable when uttered by a clown. For truth has a genuine
> power to pleasure if it manages not to give offence, but this
> is something the gods have granted only to fools.[83]

This view of natural fools was upheld by the fact that the king was surrounded by 'yes' men. Fortunately, kings and nobles could rely on their fools to speak openly and honestly. Erasmus Desiderius writes *In Praise of Folly* that 'For if a man finds his happiness in pleasing princes and spending his time amongst those gilded and bejewelled godlike creatures, he'll learn that wisdom is no use at all to him, and is indeed decried above all by people like this.'[84] However, William Somer was known for his interventions with the king and the king did not decry Somer's wisdom.

There is evidence Somer could often change the king's mind. The king would grant what William craved, as in a chronicle relating to an oral history from 1540, Will interceded for a wealthy merchant, possibly his former employer called Richard Fermor. William Somer heard that Richard Fermor had been arrested and jailed for taking clothes and money to two imprisoned Catholic priests, who had spoken out against the Royal Supremacy. Richard Fermor had tried to help these two Catholic priests, Thomas Abel and Edward Powell and William wanted to help these men who would shortly be executed. His mission was to try and gain Richard Femor a pardon. William Somer was privileged, always having admission to the king, especially when the king was sick and melancholy, and near his end, Somer let fall some appropriate words, which caused the king to give orders towards restitution. William interceded on Richard Fermor's behalf and Henry granted Fermor a pardon.

After the king's death, some of Fermor's attained property was restored. This account suggests that Somer had the power to change the mercurial king's mind. And because of his foolishness, and the king's great affection for him, William did not suffer for siding with the lawbreakers. However, as noted previously, William Somer did occasionally overstep the mark as Ambassador Chapuys recorded that in 1535, a court fool nearly did suffer for his candour. In the State Papers, Chapuy's stated: 'Henry the other day nearly murdered his own fool, a simple and innocent man, because he happened to speak well in his presence of the Queen and Princess [Katharine of Aragon and Mary], and called the concubine "ribaude" [whore] and her daughter "bastard." He has now been banished from Court, and has gone to the Grand Esquire, who has sheltered and hidden him.'[85] The 'Grand Esquire' refers to Sir Nicholas Carew, Chief Esquire of the king. The writer Alison Weir goes as far as to say that Carew dared Somer to call Anne Boleyn and Elizabeth names, but that is not what Chapuys appears to say here. Chapuys just says that Carew sheltered Henry's fool.[86] This incident of banishment does suggest that even a natural fool could overstep the mark. Fortunately for William Somer, he managed to work his way back into the king's favour and maintain it for the rest of Henry's reign. The positive thing about Will's grave error was that it never resulted in his permanent exile from court.

However, Henry VIII never seemed to stay angry at Will Somer for long as the records suggest that as the reign progressed, only William could take Henry's mind from the incessant pain of his ulcerated leg, the cares of state and his growing ill-health and depression. Right until the end of the king's life, wherever Henry went, William Somer went too; from palace to palace, his every need was catered and provided for. At Christmas 1545, just a year before the king's death, the king and a small party of his usual companions and body servants were on their way from Westminster to celebrate the feast at Hampton Court. Included in this particular trip was a batch of sixteen horses that were ferried across the Thames. There were three mounts to carry the massively obese king, and one for his fool, as recorded in the privy accounts, 'On 24 Dec. the King removed from Westmester to Hampton Cowrtt on Christmas even, for 2 horses for my lord Hardbard 2d., 3 of the King's by John Dawson, 2 by Edmond, "Mr. Brownys servant of the quyrys," a horse of Mr. Awdley of the quyrys, "ij bottell horsse, a male horsse and Wyllyam Sommers' horse".' There is also an entry for William Somer for the purchase of a pair of spurs: 'Wm. Somer (a pair of spurs)', for his personal use.[87] Whatever William Somer did to deserve such treatment, and Henry's loyalty, William was considered important enough to have around, especially at Christmastide. This episode shows that disabled people integrated into a society not always known for its forgiveness and mercy, and stories retold of William Somer's life detail an intriguing part he played in stirring Henry's conscience, which reinforces William's reputation as someone the king could, and did confide in.

After Henry died in 1547, William Somer went on to serve at the court of Edward VI, however, it is unlikely that he was as close with Edward VI as he had been with his father. During the short reign of Edward VI, William was a part of the royal household, as it is recorded in the celebrations of 1550 that William Somer was provided with a painted costume where he would take part in the revels and celebrations of Christmastide and New Year.[88] In 1551, on Christmas Eve, William was at Greenwich Palace, cast as a fool-attendant in the train of George Ferrers, who had been appointed as the Lord of Misrule, and William was supplied with a gilded mace and chain, a 'sute of whighte and blewe bawdekyn, which was a brocaded silk, edged with 'redd satin' and a 'ffrocke of tauny silke stryped with gowlde, furred abowte the necke'.[89] On another occasion, William was asked to wear a 'harniss of paper boordes' which was a 'devise by the kinge for combat to be fought with Wylliam Somer'. King Edward asked William to make an appearance by royal command, and the king was involved in the planning, even if William did not take part.[90] This mock combat was an indication that fools such as Somer were not only appreciated for their wit but were expected to be physical, as part of their repertoire in this subsequent Tudor reign. The Tudor court was turning into an artificial tinsel world of entertainment, which would undoubtedly have made disabled people uncomfortable. By February of 1553, the fifteen-year-old king had become seriously ill, and by 6 July 1553, the teenager had died. William Somer attended the young king's funeral and the coronation of his successor, Mary Tudor.

Under Mary I, William Somer's role was mainly ceremonial, and being a sidekick to Jayne Foole.[91] However, it is interesting to note that William Somer must have been held in high regard by Mary I, because after the death of Henry VIII and his heir, Edward VI, William does appear in an interesting portrait of Queen Mary I pictured with the late Henry VIII. This is a posthumous 'Portrait of Henry VIII with Queen Mary and Will Somers the Jester,' by an unknown English artist, dated sixteenth century, and is now in the collection of the Sarah Campbell

Blaffer Foundation, Houston, Texas. The portrait was almost certainly dynastic, rather than sentimental, because, from the records, we know that Queen Mary had a difficult relationship with her father. After all, she had been forced to accept that her father's marriage to her mother was 'incestuous' and she was demoted from 'Princess' to bastard. Moreover, spiritually, her father's break with the Roman Catholic Church was abhorrent to her. Nonetheless, in this family portrait, they have been shown together. But here, there is no reference to Henry as a detested schismatic; he is in full Holbeinesque magnificence as King of England. With Mary by his side, the notion that she was indeed legitimate – and rightfully queen – is reinforced. William Somer is depicted as an older man in the painting and is shown wearing a skull cap. He appears to be grasping something, perhaps a staff, but this looks to have been painted out. The whole of the background is plain, and Somer's presence in this particular painting continues the tradition of how cherished he was by the former king and his heirs.

Warrants for the Great Wardrobe during Mary's reign were made for William Somer, who was supplied with elaborate clothing of 'a gowne of blue satten, the ground yellow stripping [striped] with a slight gold'. And a 'jerkin furred, with sleeves of same, furred with conie [rabbit]'.[92]

In the first year of her marriage, when Mary I married Philip of Spain in 1554, William was given 'twelve handkerchevers of Holland', of very fine linen, along with linen and knitted hose, 2 1/2 ounces of green silk 'employed upon a grene coat for hym' and three dozen green buttons. William was also to have a coat of blue damask, embroidered with blue and yellow silk, banded on the bottom hem with yellow velvet, which would show his liveried status. A gown of purple damask was to have three bands on the bottom of the hem, of the same material.[93] Clothes worn by William Somer on an ordinary day at court would have been a monogrammed livery embroidered with 'our letters', where three yards of red cloth were used 'to make hym a coate', and two of velvet to band the bottom of the hem. However, green would always remain the favourite colour for William's coats and gowns, because by wearing green fabric, natural fools such as William were displaying their subservience to their monarch, and their association with the court. William Somer's position was not sufficiently lowly enough for him to be required to wear the same livery of green and white like other servants, moreover, his position was not noble enough for him to be allowed to wear and follow the fashions of the Tudor court. The colour green also carried religious connotations, so to wear green fabrics represented Epiphany, symbolising nature and rebirth, two particularly apt characteristics embodied by a fool like William Somer.[94]

In October 1555, two more green coats were ordered from the Great Wardrobe for William, 'one garded with vellat, the other playne lined with cotton.'[95]

After twenty years at court, William Somer had never lost touch with his family, as his sister was given a new gown when she came to visit him: a plain dress of 'three yerdes of Russet Clothe to make a gowne for William Sommers his sister'.[96]

William was reputed to be the only man who made Mary laugh, apart from John Heywood.[97]

The accounts of Queen Mary indicate that as William Somer aged, Mary remained kind to him, and he remained a member of her court because, within a month of her approaching demise in 1558, the queen had ordered for:

> Willaim Somer our foole' a final bonanza of silks, velvets, linens, buttons, tassels , hose, and handkerchiefs, with 'two canvas doublets for him lined with Bockram ... a gowne of grene damaske garded with yellow vellat, and ... a jerkin of same damaske likewise garded with yellow Vellat.[98]

In 1559, Queen Elizabeth paid a bill incurred by Queen Mary, which included payments for clothes for William Somer and Jayne Foole. William Somer's last public event was the coronation of Elizabeth I, but he died shortly after on 15 June 1560, during her early reign. William Somer's death is recorded in the parish of St Leonards, Shoreditch, which is also the resting place of players and fools such as Richard Tarlton. A modern plaque in the church commemorates William's burial there. William's wit and wisdom was a blessing, on the most part to all that knew him, and perhaps that is why his memory lived on in the popular imagination after his death, and he had several works written about him. As late as 1676, a biography was published entitled *A Pleasant History of the Life and Death of Will Summers*:

> But this Will Summers was of an easie nature, and tractable disposition, who ... gained not only grace and favour from

his Majesty, but a general love of the Nobility; for he was no carry-tale, nor whisperer, nor flattering insinuator, to breed discord and dissension, but an honest, plain down-right, that would speak home without halting, and tell the truth of purpose to shame the Devil; so that his plainness mixt with a kind of facetiousness, and tartness with pleasantness made him very acceptable into the companies of all men.[99]

Although we have quotes of William Somer's puns written down during, and after his lifetime, it is significant that the closest we get to understanding who Will Somer was, and his status as a disabled person who was integrated within the Tudor court, is through the Accounts of the Great Wardrobe, and the items of clothing that were made and purchased for him. The changing clothing of William Somer challenges traditional notions that disabled people like William were clothed in motley or the parti-colours of their stage counterparts. As we can see from the records, court fools were instead clothed in luxurious fabrics such as silks, velvets and furs, showing that natural fools were honoured, yet, nevertheless considered demonstrably inferior to other courtiers in terms of their fashionableness, because they were frequently clothed in outdated styles to denote difference. By analysing household and wardrobe accounts from the court, we can examine the significance of a natural fools' clothing at the court, and the implications clothing had on a disabled person's status.[100]

William Somer was a higher calibre of natural fool than most, as he had managed to manoeuvre through the court of Henry VIII with barely a scratch, holding his own popularity in the face of Henry's ego for as long as he did. William also retained his popularity and strength of character through two highly contrasting and succeeding reigns. He was shrewd, kind and possessed a simplistic nature of a rare, and most valued kind.

Disabled people and natural fools embodied several contrasting characteristics as we have seen from the unique story of William Somer's life, and therefore fools like William occupied a prestigious position at the Tudor court. Simultaneously natural fools like Sexton, William Somer, and Jayne Foole were free, yet constrained, holy, yet naughty, truthful and illusory beings. Natural fools were disabled people who never truly fit into any of the social positions dictated by the deeply hierarchical court system. The 'natural fool' embodies many of the contracts? of the Tudor period towards disability. However, it is not a clear picture, and history is richer for it.

The difficulty of defining disabled people during the period has all too frequently relegated court fools to jesters in the footnotes of history. Disabled people such as natural fools are rarely studied explicitly and where natural fools are incorporated into broader histories of the Tudor period, they are often mentioned only in passing.[101] Up until recently, apart from the research of Suzannah Lipscomb, there has always been a reluctance to include disability history and the natural fool in broader histories, which is shocking since the Tudor period witnessed a zenith of foolery and disabled people lived within every echelon of Tudor society, especially those disabled people who made the Tudor court their home.

By Elizabeth's time, the professional, stage fool had become better known. Artificial fools such as Tarleton, Kempe and Armin had parts written for them, the latter two in Shakespeare's plays. However, we forget the solitary figure of the other natural fool in the portrait of 'The Family of Henry VIII', and that is the young woman wearing Dutch style clothing, sporting a shaved head, hidden beneath her linen coif and bonnet.

Like William Somer, Jayne Foole was a companion, rather than a pet, and she was brought to court during the tenure of Henry's second queen, Anne Boleyn. Jayne became the court fool to Queen Anne Boleyn first and later, and Mary I, when she was a princess and then later the queen. Before Edward VI and Mary's reigns, Jayne was cared for by Queen Catherine Parr. Jane was what John Southworth, in his book *Fools and Jesters at the English Court*, refers to as an 'innocent'. Jane was not a professional entertainer, but suffered from an intellectual disability, possibly what we now call Down syndrome, or she had a mental illness.[102] When Professor Suzannah Lipscomb was delivering a talk on court fools, she stated:

> Very little is known about Jayne; we do not know her full name, nor her age, or where she was born. However, there are some primary sources of her serving Queen Anne Boleyn, the Princess Mary and Queen Catherine Parr.[103]

Like the records of Jayne's contemporary, William Somer, Jayne's life is recorded in detail, through the records of clothes commissioned for her from the Accounts of the Great Wardrobe, and the Privy Purse expenses of the monarchs who owned her and cared for her. Understanding how disabled people dressed is vital to investigating the fluidity of their position at court and to scatter the myth that natural fools were poorly treated people, who were not loved, regarded or revered. However, there is one distinct account which does not involve Jayne's mode of dress; moreover, it magnifies Jayne Foole's vital role at court and her contribution to a major event during her time of service with Anne Boleyn. Jayne was originally a member of Anne Boleyn's household, but how early on she entered into Anne's household, is not recorded. However, when researching through the state papers of Henry VIII, there is a gem of a source which details the account of an incident on 1 June 1533, at Anne Boleyn's coronation, which gives a fascinating insight into the experience of Anne's fool on that day. When reading the account, we can just imagine Jayne getting very irate with the crowds, and saying exactly what was on her mind, as she defended her mistress, the Queen. Jayne did not mince her words when she stood up for Anne during the parade to Westminster, when many onlookers refused to wish Anne Boleyn well, and take their caps off their heads. Historian Eric Ives has argued that the source is unreliable as it is uncorroborated; other bloggers suggest the source is hostile and fictional, primarily if Chapuys, the Spanish ambassador wrote the account. Other historians suggest the source is incorrectly labelled; historian Lauren Mackay wrote about this in her book, *Inside the Tudor Court* where she states that the handwritten letter is not Chapuys, nor his secretary. It is in a packet of letters with no signature. [104]

The anonymous letter was biased, but it was not Chapuys account of the coronation. Lauren says:

> He was possibly playing down the spectacle for Charles V's sake, but he appears to have enjoyed some elements of the festivities, as he also reports that he was lavishly entertained at a banquet held on the German ambassador's barge where he wrote to de Granville, they drank a toast to the Emperor as the guns of the Tower fired. [105]

Chapuys was living it up on the German barge while it floated on the Thames. Even if he was not thrilled at the thought of Anne Boleyn's coronation, he was still there, being a part of it. He did write briefly about it but nothing to the extent of the anonymous letters. These accounts mostly described Anne's appearance negatively and are vehemently opposed to Anne Boleyn and the French, but it was not Chapuys that wrote them. It could be argued that the specifics on Jayne the Foole may be correct, but that does not mean it can be trusted one-hundred per cent. The source explains how, during the procession to Westminster, the crowd did not take their bonnets off to cheer for their new queen.

> Though it was customary to kneel, uncover, and cry "God save the King, God save the Queen," whenever they appeared in public, no one in London or the suburbs, not even women and children, did so on this occasion. One of the Queen's servants told the mayor to command the people to make the customary shouts, and was answered that he could not command people's hearts, and that even the King could not make them do so. Her fool, who has been to Jerusalem and speaks several languages, seeing the little honor they showed to her, cried out, "I think you have all scurvy heads, and dare not uncover".[106]

What is fascinating about this source however reliable or unreliable it might be, is that it shows what was expected: that the crowd would cry out to the queen to prove their fealty and loyalty, yet with Anne, this did not happen. There is a rumour that perpetuates today, which says the crowd were paid to lift their hats and shout out tributes to the queen. Jayne the Fool was thought to have Down syndrome, and this kind of disability would have heightened her awareness of what was happening, meaning she might easily have picked up on the atmosphere of the crowd, and as people with learning disabilities so often do, she spoke her mind against it.

Without permission, Jayne asked the Mayor to command the crowd to shout, but the Mayor replied that it was not down to him to change the minds of the people; he remarked that even if the king wanted to, he could not change their minds. Out of frustration, and loyalty to Anne Boleyn, Jayne told the crowd off in no uncertain terms, probably scowling and shaking her fist as she did. Her reprimand was direct, yet we do not know if Jayne's reprimand changed the behaviour of anyone amongst them.

The other illuminating point from the source is that the writer states that Jayne was well-travelled, as she had travelled to the holy city,

Jerusalem and that she was able to speak several other languages. It can be implied from this, that Jayne at some point, had been educated and had been in the care of other benefactors who could afford to travel. Perhaps she had been taken to the Holy Land for healing; maybe the family looking after her were trying to find a cure for her disability. There was no record of Anne commenting about Jayne, however, she did complain to her husband, the king, that after the parade, no one had shouted for her or removed their bonnets. Anne Boleyn also expressed her disdain for the crowds' ignorance on the day, because 'Her dress was covered with tongues pierced with nails, to show the treatment which those who spoke against her might expect.'[107]

Unfortunately, the account does not suggest specifically whether it was Jayne the Foole, but we could assume from the source that it might be Jayne who addressed the crowd with her retort. However, it is fascinating that this fool was well travelled, could speak several languages and be brazen enough to stand up for her mistress, which implies a feeling of loyalty between Queen Anne Boleyn and this natural fool. Anne Boleyn had taken this woman fool into her household, cared for her, paid for her upkeep and clothing, and no doubt treated the young woman with every respect she could; just as Henry, her husband, had done with William Somer.

Anne Boleyn cared for Jayne Foole right up unto the point she was unable to do so. In May 1536, from accounts of 'The Queen's Reckoning', there is a list of debts owed by Anne Boleyn at her death and we know that Anne Boleyn had ordered and commissioned '25 yds. of cadace fringe, morrey color, delivered to Skutt, her tailor, for a gown for her Grace's woman fool, and a green satin cap for her'.[108]

When Anne Boleyn's household was dissolved and dismissed, Princess Mary took Jayne in, and Jayne joined her household because Mary's Privy Purse expenses have frequent mentions of 'Jane the fole' from December 1537.[109] Mary paid for an assortment of things for her including to a groom called Hogman, for the stabling of Jayne's horse: 'Jane the fole hir horse.' And another for 'hosen and shoes', in December 1537.[110] In April 1538, there was an order for 'a yerde & a half of Damaske' and by July of 1538, the fabric had been used to make a 'gowne for Jane the Fole'.[111] Mary spoiled Jayne with expensive fabrics as Stopes notes that 'there is no distinction between the dress of Jane and that of the great ladies of Court', as Mary afforded her luxurious materials.[112] Mary also spared no expense in buying Jayne silk stockings, supposedly a new luxury reserved for Tudor nobility that were 'liberally given to the Court Fool', which suggests Mary was keen to see natural fools who belonged to her clothed in finery, even if such luxury could not often be seen.[113] Before the rise of natural fools like William Somer and Jayne Foole, fools before them were clothed to represent their position and to meet practical demands, now natural fools were adopted in a new kind of role as 'pets of the court'.[114]

While Mary was Jayne's keeper, Jayne became the wearer of an extensive and luxurious wardrobe of clothing. In a single order on 27 April 1540, Jayne was given:

> A Douche gowne ... of striped purple satten, a kirtle ... of striped silk lined with cotton, a Douche gowne ... of crimson satten striped with golde, a kyrtle ... of blew silk, a Dowche gowne ... of crimson striped satten, a kirtle of like crimson striped satten, a cloak ... of yellow cloth garded with grene clothe layde on with yellow, whippe lase, a douche gowne ... of blew damaske chequered, a kirtle ... of white satten fringed with copper silver, a kirtle ... of red vared sylke a petticoat ... of red cloth.[115]

Mary ordered clothes for Jayne, as if she was part of the nobility, as the use of silk or satin would have denoted someone of that rank. Mary also seems to have rejected ordering clothes in colours traditionally associated with folly, which were green and yellow. Only the cloak contained these colours, which indicates that while in the court, Jayne was well known. However, outside of court, Jayne's clothing would instantly distinguish her from other people and servants of the court. Moreover, the rich and exuberant colours on display in Jayne's wardrobe may have separated her in a crowd. However, if Jayne combined a multi-coloured array such as the yellow and green cloak with her blue gown, white kirtle and red petticoat, she would have been an extraordinary spectacle, with an eccentric and perhaps, old-fashioned silhouette. Thus, whilst the materials and fabrics used to make garments for Jayne may signify a rise in status, when considering the move in quality from motley to more luxurious fabrics, the use of colours would have ensured that Jayne was still a figure to ridicule, mock, and deride in her outlandish and eye-catching colour combinations, reinforcing her undefined position as motley had done under previous medieval monarchs.

Understanding how disabled people dressed is vital to investigating the fluidity of their position at court and to scatter the myth that natural fools were poorly treated people, who were not loved, regarded or revered. Another example of how clothing was used to re-affirm Jayne's status as a natural fool can be found in the style of her gowns. The entry, 'a Douche gowne...of striped purple satten,' stresses that her gowns were of the Dutch style, contrasting the French gown given to Lady Clifford at the close of the same entry. It is puzzling as to why Jayne wore Dutch style clothing, primarily as she was in Queen Anne's household originally, and we all know how Anne adored French fashions. Perhaps the Dutch style clothing Jayne wore was chosen for its simple lines and a practical form of dress, for a woman who probably had no care for the social status of dress. Wearing such a gaudy mix of colours and old-fashioned styles would have been humiliating for a Tudor noblewoman. Moreover, whilst the materials used to clothe Jayne were indicative of nobility, the clashing colours and unfashionable shaping and cut of the gowns would have ensured she was an object of derision, therefore, reaffirming her status as a natural fool.

Jayne often received the same clothes as Lucretia the Tumbler, as in the early 1540s Lucretia received identical items of clothing to Jayne. In December 1542, there is an order for a 'payr of Shoes for Jane & an other for lucrece'; and in January 1543, linen shifts are made for them both, which might suggest that Lucrece could have been a carer for Jayne for a short period of time.[116] John Southworth suggested that Lucretia was at some time Jayne's keeper or friend, and it is known that Lucretia and Jayne performed together. However, unlike Jayne, Lucretia was a trained entertainer with skills.

There were several payments to a barber in March and June of 1543, and September 1544 for her head to be shaved; where four pence were paid on each occasion. Professor Suzannah Lipscomb concluded that one of the reasons fools' heads were shaven, was because fools were essentially 'good' people, whose simplicity of character accounted for the natural fool's favoured position and authority.[117] Shaving the heads of natural fools demonstrated their divine status, as Suzannah Lipscomb proposes, 'echoing the tonsures of the religious'. It may too be contended that this was done out of mockery.[118]

of violet cloth, when she visited Elizabeth's court.[137] Thomasina could read and write because one of the queen's gifts to her was a 'penner' and inkhorn.[138] In 1580, together with John and Mary Scudamore, Thomasina paid a visit to Dr John Dee, the queen's astrologer, at Richmond. In the same year, she received a pair of knitting needles as a gift from the queen.

There is a painting which is said to include Thomasina in it, which hangs at Penshurst Place entitled 'La Volta', depicting Elizabethan courtiers leaping the risky steps of the contemporary dance, which was regarded as scandalous. Some art historians and curators at the National Portrait Gallery, London, and elsewhere, have suggested this is not Elizabeth I and Robert Dudley, Earl of Leicester, dancing together as is commonly thought but is often considered to represent the French court rather than the English. Lord De L'Isle, himself, has stated that the images of Robert Dudley and Queen Elizabeth are in dispute, as has art historian Sir Roy Strong. However, in 1973 an article in *Country Life* penned by Beryl Platts and entitled 'Pictorial Politics at Penshurst', gives a convincing argument against these assumptions. In the painting, the Duc D'Alencon has his arm around the lady in crimson, who is seated to the right of the picture, near the fireplace. She has her back to the viewer. The Duc D'Alencon, wearing light grey hose and a brown hat decorated with a feather, was betrothed to the queen. Sir Philip Sidney, Leicester's nephew, stands under the fireplace to the right and is pointing out the Duc's indiscretion to his uncle.[139]

'La Volta' is a family picture and as far as is known, has been owned by the Sidney family since it was painted. Although currently its provenance is uncertain, the very fact of the painting's existence argues that it was not known about at court. The feeling is that Elizabeth would certainly have had it destroyed as it depicts her not only smiling but also showing her ankles! Regarding the identification of the characters within the painting, it seems unlikely that anyone apart from Elizabeth herself would take centre-stage. We know, after all, that she regarded herself as the sun with all the planets revolving around her, and that the dance could be said to symbolise this. The National Gallery may have additional information,to suggest that 'La Volta' and the people within the depiction are not Elizabeth and Leicester but so far as the curators at Penshurst Place are concerned, the painting is of Elizabeth I dancing with her favourite, Robert Dudley, Earl of Leicester.

However, it is not the depiction of the dancing courtiers that is most interesting, but the dwarf, seated in the foreground to the left of the centre of the painting, who is dressed in black, facing the viewer, looking over her shoulder towards the dancers. It is an interesting addition to the painting. It looks like the participants in the painting are attending a celebration or party of some kind, where only adults are permitted. The 'La Volta' painting is an excellent visual source for someone with dwarfism in higher ranking nobility. The woman must certainly be a dwarf and is unlikely to be a child because there are no others in the image; looking elegant, the woman appears to be proportionate to a dwarf and as Thomasina is the only dwarf known to have been present at the court, among Elizabeth's women, it could be argued the depiction is almost certainly identifiable as Thomasina.

Jack Greene was the first fool to be mentioned in the state papers of Elizabeth in 1565, when breeches and hose were ordered for him:

> A payre of Hose of russet clothe for Jacke our said foule with lyninges of lynnen...for making a payre of slopes of fryse trimmed with red fringe ... a payre of stockings of grene cloth stiched upon with silke of sondry colors ... a payre of stockings of red clothe stiched alover with yellow silke and for making of a payre of stockings of grene clothe trimed with lace of silke of sondry collors with setting on of red sarceonet lined with red kersey all of our great wardrobe.[140]

During the same time, Hamond the cap maker was warranted:

> For the lyninge of ij hates with crimson taphata for our said foule with one plume of feathers: one for hate conteyninge xiiij fethers of diverse colours & for making and trimming the same faethers with silver spangles ...[141]

The commissions of clothing for Jack Greene suggest something of his status at court but tell us nothing of his character, or his role as a fool, however his decorated stockings suggest that he might have been a dancer. Fools were the first people to wear sloppes, which were large and voluminous breeches, which were later adopted by courtiers and players like Tarlton:

When Tarlton clown'd it in a pleasant vaine
With conceites did good opinions gaine
Upon the stage, his merry humours shop.
Clownes knew the Clowne, by his great clownish slop.
But now th'are gull'd, for present fashion says,
Dick Tarltons part, Gentleman's breeches plaies:
In every streete where any Gallant goes,
The swagg'ring Sloppe, is *Tarltons* clownish hose.[142]

Fools, whether as Suzannah Lipscomb categorises them as either natural or artificial, were, in instances such as this, the pioneers of Tudor fashion.

In the Spanish state papers in August 1565, there is an incident recorded of an intriguing encounter which took place between the queen and an unnamed natural fool belonging to the Earl of Leicester, which was described by the Spanish ambassador in London at the time, Guzman de Silva, in a despatch to his master King Philip:

> The next morning the earl of Leicester sent to ask if we would go and see the park, in doing which we punished three horses and saw a large quantity of game. We came round by the footpath leading to the riverside through the wood to where the Queen lodges, and when we came to her apartments Leicester's fool made so much noise calling her that she came undressed to the window. It was morning, and in an hour and a half she came down and walked for a long while talking with the Emperor's man and me about many different things.[143]

Guzman de Silva was accompanying the Imperial ambassador to Windsor Castle, where both men were to take leave of Elizabeth I. The Earl of Leicester had invited both ambassadors to view Windsor Park the morning after their arrival, 'in doing which we punished three horses and saw a large quantity of game'. When Leicester and the ambassadors arrived at Elizabeth's apartments, 'Leicester's fool made so much noise calling her that she came undressed to the window.'[144] And after keeping her visitors waiting for an hour and a half while she finished getting dressed and ready to receive them, came down to walk and talk with them.

219

The natural fool, such as the likes of William Somer, and Jayne Foole gave up their centre stage for a 'golden age' of folly in England, which occurred during the late-Elizabethan period when, ironically, the traditional, natural fool gave way to the comic actor or stage clown. Unlike her father before her, even though Elizabeth had learnt the art of fool keeping, and relying on natural fools for their sage honesty, blunt opinions and good humour, she had no such disabled person at court to turn to. The Elizabethan Tudor court may have been boiling over with ambition, status-mongering and plots a-plenty, but she had no natural fool to give her honest advice, except a group of 'Her Majesty's fools', more likely to be artificial fools, actors and mimicks, with no authentic wisdom to impart, except their ability to entertain. It seems that during this period the household fools were beginning to be eclipsed by the professional clown.

Her Majesty's Fools blur the lines between disability and entertainment, as they were not categorised as disabled people, therefore, a brief overview of these fools will suffice. The famous actor, comedian, and clown Richard Tarlton is sometimes described as jester to Queen Elizabeth.Historian Enid Welsford states that Tarlton, a man of humble origin, was a favourite of the queen. Both Enid Welsfsord and Thomas Fuller, who wrote the *History of the Worthies of England*, note that Elizabeth's famous fool had a unique ability to make Elizabeth laugh when she was in ill-humour.[145]

Other fools of Elizabeth's court were 'artificials', skilled and trained entertainers. John Pace, William Shenton, Lucretia the Tumbler, Robert Grene, Chester and Clod were the most famous of Elizabeth's artificial fools, entertaining her court with songs, stories, tumbling, juggling and impressions. As mentioned, of Queen Elizabeth's numerous fools, Richard Tarleton, son of a pig farmer, was the most significant. He was the first of the jesters not only to be permanently resident at court but also to have a career on stage as one of the queen's players. Tarleton remained high in royal favour and had regular access to Elizabeth.[146]

When Elizabeth I was in a serious mood, and out of good humour, Richard Tarlton could be in her company whenever he liked. Courtiers considered her highest favourites would, on occasion, go to Richard Tarleton before seeking an audience with the queen, as he would be their usher, preparing advantageous access to her. He told the queen 'more of her faults, than most of her chaplains and cured her melancholy better than all her physicians' much to the frustration of the nobles; however, Elizabeth appreciated him.[147]

Richard Tarlton is credited with originating the new and somewhat more sophisticated style of comic acting and clowning that became the standard in the late-sixteenth century and which later became associated with William Shakespeare's plays. William Kempe and Robert Armin were the most famous clowns in their day, and each was known for their unique talent. Kempe was noted for his Morris dancing and earned considerable notoriety for dancing a Morris dance from London to Norwich over nine days. Robert Armin, who was Tarlton's pupil, was an author and actor and is believed to have generated Shakespeare's interest in fool literature and court jesters. Tarlton was a member of the newly-formed theatre company, The Queen's Men, while Kempe and Armin became members of the Lord Chamberlain's men.

It is widely believed that the roles of Feste in *Twelfth Night*, Touchstone in *As You Like It* and the Fool in *King Lear* were written by Shakespeare for the talents of Robert Armin, while the roles of Dogberry in *Much Ado About Nothing*, and perhaps Bottom in *A Midsummer Night's Dream* were written with Kempe in mind. Welsford believes that the replacement of the motley fool by the stage clown in the late-sixteenth century was 'the natural result of the secular spirit of the times and the development of the professional theatre'.[148] The late Elizabethan and early Jacobean periods represent a golden age for folly and entertainment, as it was elevated to its highest representation by Shakespeare and it is for this reason that the fool survives in the twentieth century imagination. Late-sixteenth century accounts and historians have disagreed about the disability status of some of the court's most famous fools, as just after the Tudor dynasty ended, in 1616 Nicholas Breton defined a natural fool as one 'Abortive of wit, where Nature had more power than Reason.'[149]

With this quote, it is worth noting the revered status of natural fools and disabled people within the Tudor court, as they played a part at the court which was set apart from nobility and royalty, as well as the jugglers, jesters and artificial fools who entertained there.

These fascinating glimpses of 'natural fools' and disabled people at the Tudor court show people with learning disabilities played significant roles in the lives of the Tudor elite. In one form or another, fools created mayhem across European royal courts. Be it as a tumbler, juggler, trickster, jester or clown, every recorded culture had them, but unfortunately, thanks to Shakespeare and other writers of the period, it is the motley fool of the English medieval kings that remain uppermost in our minds. However, as we have learnt, natural fools and disabled people were not merely residing in court to amuse the monarch, they had other, more subtle duties, as we have understood, and their importance should not be underestimated. Their perceived lack of pride, their directness and their humour were valued as assets and woven into the fabric of court life, and disabled people held valued position within this elite Tudor society.

The natural fools in the Henry VIII family portrait discussed at the beginning of the chapter may not have been in the room at the time this family idyll was painted, which showed them on the periphery within it, but it is fascinating to see that they were shown as part of this royal family. Furthermore, it begs an interesting debate as to why disabled people such as William Somer and Jayne Foole were not excluded from the painting in the first place. Natural fools and disabled people were influential people, more than just the artificial, motley-dressed with bells on jester, because these disabled people held a privileged place and had unique qualities, and abilities to support, love, encourage, counsel, and bring entertainment, laughter, wisdom and wit. These characteristics gave them a divine status, and the favour was returned by a recognised importance and standing within the court of the different Tudor monarchs. William Somer and Jayne Fool may look down on us from this Tudor family painting, toying with us, convincing us they were just jesters. William Somer was not that much of a fool because Henry VIII used to listen to him, and take on board William's advice. To be an unauthorised advisor to a king is power. What kind of power is that? These natural fools were such close companions within the royal family, that their loyalty allowed them to be intimate companions to monarchs, allowing these fools to hold the hearts of the kings and queens they lived with. Moreover, natural fools juggle with our thoughts upending our preconceived ideas, flipping them upside down like the Lord of Misrule, turning our perceptions on their heads about disability history, and as historian Suzannah Lipscomb suggests, fools remove our conceptions that we, in the twenty-first century are so much better in the way we treat disabled people than they did in the early modern era.[150]

Conclusion

When reading Tudor history, one can often get a sense of being shown violent acts of cruelty where people fought and betrayed each other, invented new ways to torture and engage in revenge and bloodlust, and where the Tower of London and Tower Hill witnessed horrific beheadings. The rule of the Tudors does not leave you with a completely edifying legacy. Yet, despite, or perhaps because of all that, I have concluded that history, in general, was recorded more often by victorious, great men, rather than women, or minorities.

The trouble with mainstream history is that it has never particularly cared about the history of ordinary people, of women's history, of black history, and disability history until recently. Studying human relations and social history allows us to peer into the mirror of some ordinary yet extraordinary lives; a majority of everyday people who have often been overlooked, and whose voices have been long unheard. As disabled people took an unrecorded seat in great moments from history, their experiences were often ignored yet they have shaped or influenced our lives, and our world. History has not cared what disabled people have thought or felt; but disabled people's experiences of the world need to be recorded, now, and in the future, so that we can raise the profile of our narratives. It is by learning from disabled people's experiences that we can change the present and future experiences of disabled people, to be able to understand our community as fellow human beings, and make our lives better, and more importantly support us so our communities are free from prejudice, discrimination and inequality, and our lives are on a level playing-field with our able-bodied counterparts.

History offers us the opportunity to slide into another person's shoes and take them for a wander, even if those shoes might have callipers attached, or those feet mind need a walking stick to lean upon to gain a better balance, or those feet might be firmly fixed on the footrest of a wheelchair. Studying the life experience of disabled people both in the past and present gives us a risk-free opportunity to practise empathy and compassion, destroying the egotistic bubbles in which we protect ourselves, by reminding us that, for any type of human experience or emotion, we are not the first to undergo or feel it and we shall not be the last.

We become self-deluded if we ignore the histories of others; especially the ordinary histories of extraordinary minorities, which is just as important as learning about the kings or queens of England, and other histories we were taught at school. For far too long, voices of disabled people from the past have been left unheard and forgotten.

The Tudors' attitudes to disability were a juxtaposition of acceptance of impairment, as an everyday occurrence in the society in which they lived. Disability was thought by the Tudors to be an infliction of Satanic influence due to superstitions and religious beliefs or, perhaps the idea that disability came about from involvement in witchcraft. It is the acceptance of disability during the Tudor period that has compelled the writing of this book.

Most important of all, hearing these lost voices, and stories should remind us that generalisations about disability, as about everything else, condemn us to inaccuracy and lead to misunderstandings. Disability does not make us good or bad, pathetic or brave. It is just an element of what makes us human.

The Tudor era was an age before political correctness, and although some of the language used is robust, and not politically correct, attitudes were often surprisingly compassionate. Unlike today's damning treatment of the disabled community by the modern media, press, politicians and their imposing, dispassionate policies. I believe that the 'Great' in Britain should not continue to be imposed on our country from our imperialistic history of winning wars or territory, and gaining 'empires' but awarded because of how we treat people less fortunate than ourselves, at home, and abroad, each according to his ability, to each according to his need. The Tudors, and their treatment of disabled people, seem compassionate in the light of present political policies against the disabled and show us that they were sensitive to the considered needs of disabled people, trying to raise them and care for them as important and to be contributing members of Tudor society. Perhaps 'we' with our modern, twenty-first century outlook have been made 'fools' of by history in more ways than one.

Glossary of Disability Terms

What is fascinating about this sort of glossary is that these widely used terms to describe disabled people have been coined by non-disabled people.

Able-bodied – This term is used to describe someone who does not identify as having a disability. Some members of the disability community oppose its use because it implies that all people with disabilities lack 'able bodies' or the ability to use their bodies well. They may prefer 'non-disabled' or 'enabled' as being more accurate.

Ableism – is a system of oppression based on ability. Ableism is any attitude, action, or institutional practice backed by institutional power which subordinates people because of their perceived ability. It is any social relations, practice, or idea that presumes that all people are able-bodied. The mere presumption that everyone is able-bodied is effectively discriminatory in and of itself, often creating environments that are hostile to people with disabilities.

Abnormal/abnormality – is a word used to describe a condition that deviates from what is considered normal. It can be appropriate when used in a medical context, such as 'abnormal curvature of the spine' or an 'abnormal test result'. However, when used to describe an individual, 'abnormal' is widely viewed as derogatory. The phrase 'abnormal behaviour' reflects social-cultural standards and is open to different interpretations.

Afflicted with/stricken with/suffers from/victim of – terms that carry the assumption that a person with a disability is suffering or has a reduced quality of life. Not every person with a disability suffers, is a victim or is stricken.

Amputation/amputee – refers to the removal of a bodily extremity, usually during a surgical operation, for a variety of reasons. Amputee is the acceptable term for someone who has undergone an amputation. Some people have a physical characteristic that is not a result of an amputation.

Alms – charitable donations of food or money to the poor or those considered unable to look after themselves.

Almshouse – homes built, from the medieval period onwards, to shelter elderly, disabled or other people deemed unable to look after themselves (sometimes known as *Maison Dieu*).

Autism – a lifelong developmental disability that affects how a person communicates with and relates to other people, and how they make sense of the world around them.

Bedlam/Bethlem – famous names used by the public for the Royal Bethlehem Hospital in London, the first English institution for people with mental illness.

Birth defect – is defined as an imperfection or shortcoming. A birth defect is a physical or biochemical abnormality that is present at birth. Many people consider such terms offensive when describing a disability as they imply the person is deficient or inferior to others.

Blynde – early English word for blind.

Bridewell – formerly a type of hospital, first established in the sixteenth century for the improvement of the 'idle poor'; eventually became houses of correction for beggars and petty criminals.

City of London – The original walled city (known today as the square mile) around which the greater conurbation of London later grew; had its own system of government and was politically influential mainly from the medieval period to the eighteenth century.

Comfortable works – Church teaching of the medieval period which encouraged people to perform charitable tasks, to support and give alms to poor and disabled people as a means of speeding their passage to heaven.

Conglomerate asylum – a form of asylum consisting of different structures, without any real unity of style and often composed of buildings of widely varying ages.

County lunatic asylum – asylums built by counties across England to house 'pauper lunatics and idiots', meaning the mentally ill and learning disabled people unable to meet the costs of their care.

Court of Wards – a court established in the Tudor period which allocated responsibility for the affairs of 'lunatics' and 'natural fools'.

Cripple/creple – a term used to describe physically disabled people until the second half of the twentieth century; now used pejoratively or abusively.

Crooked/crookedness – an early English term to describe people seen as misshapen in their bodily form.

Deaff – old English word for deaf.

Deficient – see mental deficiency.

Deformed/deformity – is a condition in which part of the body does not have the typical or expected shape. Physical deformities can arise from a number of causes, including genetic mutations, various disorders, amputations and complications at birth. However, the word 'deformity' has a negative connotation when used about those living with disabilities.

Depression – is characterised by a loss of interest in activities, persistent fatigue, difficulty in concentrating and making decisions, persistent feelings of emptiness or hopelessness, and abnormal eating habits. Its proper name is 'major depressive disorder', psychotic depression (a combination of psychosis and depression), and postpartum depression (sometimes experienced by mothers after giving birth).

Developmental disabilities/disability – a group of conditions (that arise) due to an impairment in physical, learning, language or behaviour areas. These conditions begin during the developmental period of life, may impact day-to-day functioning and usually last throughout a person's lifetime. Developmental disabilities usually manifest before age 22, and those with such disabilities often require lifelong or extended individual support. Examples of developmental disabilities include autism spectrum disorder, cerebral palsy, hearing disabilities, intellectual disabilities and visual disabilities. A developmental disability can include a long-term physical or cognitive/intellectual disability or both.

Differently-abled – this term came into vogue in the 1990s as an alternative to 'disabled', 'handicapped' or 'mentally retarded'. Currently, it is not considered appropriate (and for many, never was). Some consider it condescending, offensive or simply a way of avoiding talking about disability. Others prefer it to 'disabled' because 'dis' means 'not', which means that 'disabled' means 'not able'. But particularly when it comes to referring to individuals, 'differently-abled' is problematic. As some advocates observe, we are all differently-abled.

Disabled access – the design features or adaptations of a building such as ramps, doors, toilets, etc. which mean that people with disabilities can enter and make use of it.

Disabled/disability – 'Disability' and 'disabled' generally describe functional limitations that affect one or more of the major life activities, including walking, lifting, learning and breathing. Various laws define disability differently, like the Equality Act 2010. This definition of disability also focuses on and promotes the concept of disability from the perspective of the social model rather than the traditional, antiquated medical model, which emphasises impairments and limitations and puts the onus on disabled people to be 'fixed' or adapt to societal barriers. Developed by disabled people, the social model regards disability as a socially constructed experience that identifies systemic barriers, negative attitudes and exclusion by society, purposely or inadvertently, as contributory factors in disabling people. The social model promotes the notion that while physical, sensory, intellectual, or psychological variations may cause individual functional limitation or impairments, these lead to disability only if society fails to take account of and include people regardless of their individual differences. The social model further recognises disability as a community and a culture.

Disabled people/people with disabilities – the phrase 'disabled people' is an example of identity-first language (in contrast to people-first language). It is the preferred terminology here in Great Britain, and the reason behind members of (some disability) groups' dislike for the application of people-first language to themselves is that they consider their disabilities to be inseparable parts of who they are. For example, they prefer to be referred to as 'autistic', 'blind' or 'disabled'.

Dissolution – the period mainly between 1533 and 1545 when England under Henry VIII broke with the church in Rome and 'dissolved' or plundered and shut down many religious buildings, including those which cared for the sick and the disabled.

Down syndrome – is a congenital condition caused by the presence of an extra full or partial copy of chromosome 21 in an individual's cell nuclei and is characterised by a range of physical and cognitive characteristics, of a chromosomal condition. Other terms commonly used to refer to people with Down syndrome include 'intellectually disabled', 'developmentally disabled' and a person who has a 'cognitive disability' or 'intellectual disability'. Down syndrome also can be referred to as Trisomy 21. Historically it was called 'mongoloidism', and people with it were called Mongoloids; this is now considered very offensive.

Dwarf/little person/midget/short stature – dwarfism is a medical or genetic condition that results in a stature below 4'10. Use of the word 'dwarf' is considered acceptable when referring to the genetic condition, but it is often considered offensive when used in a non-medical sense. The term 'midget' was used in the past to describe an unusually short and proportionate person. It is now widely considered derogatory.

Dumbe – early English word for a person unable to speak (modern equivalent is dumb); from the medieval period till the eighteenth century it signified that a person was deaf, as well as unable to speak.

Epilepsy – a neurological disorder which can cause loss of consciousness or convulsions; formerly known as 'falling sickness'. Epilepsy is a developmental disorder characterized by recurrent, unprovoked seizures. Epilepsy manifests differently in individuals: the severity of epileptic seizures, their occurrence rates and the emergence of other health problems differ from person to person. Epilepsy is most commonly treated with medication but also can include the use of medical devices, surgery, diet and emerging therapy methods. The difference between epilepsy and seizures is that seizures, abnormal movements or behaviour are due to unusual electrical activity in the brain, and are a symptom of epilepsy. But not all people who appear to have seizures have epilepsy, a group of related disorders characterised by a tendency for recurrent seizures.

Falling sickness – early English term for Epilepsy.

Fool/foolish – old English word usually used to denote a person we would recognise as having a learning disability today; sometimes used to indicate a mentally ill person; also, described people in the role of jester, but the distinction was made between 'artificial fools', people pretending to be foolish, and 'natural fools', people born 'foolish'.

Identity-first language – contrasts with people-first language. With identity-first language, the disability is mentioned first. For example, 'Down's syndrome girl' or 'autistic boy'. An example of people-first language is 'a girl with Down syndrome' or 'a boy with autism.' Generally speaking, people-first language is preferred, but in some cases – most notably in the Deaf community and among autistic people – identity-first language is preferred.

Idiocy/Idiot – in earlier forms of English used to describe 'dull-witted' people who were broadly equivalent to suffering from what we would define as learning disability, but also used in a broader sense to describe the labouring classes and the peasantry; today used pejoratively or abusively.

Impotent – in its early English sense referred to people considered unable to look after themselves for reasons of age, infirmity or disability; the 'impotent poor' were distinguished from the 'able-bodied' poor in Poor Law legislation.

Incurable – term used to describe mentally ill or learning disabled people whose condition is perceived to be permanent and who are therefore unable to 'recover'.

Injury/injuries – is commonly used to describe any harm, damage or impairment to an individual as the result of an accident or other event.

Innocent – early English word for a 'natural fool'; broadly a person we would recognise as having a learning disability today.

Insane – general term, still in use but not as widely as in the past, to denote mental illness; tends to be associated with criminal or highly irrational behaviour rather than lower-level illness.

Insane asylum/mental health hospital/psychiatric hospital – that cared for people with various mental illnesses, often for long periods of time, were once commonly referred to as insane asylums. The term has largely gone out of use and is now considered objectionable and inaccurate.

Institution – a building explicitly used for the separate care or treatment of specific groups of people, separated from mainstream society, and, usually, highly regulated in its operations.

Intellectual disabilities/intellectually disabled – is a disability involving 'significant limitations both in intellectual functioning (reasoning, learning, problem-solving) and in adaptive behaviour, which covers a range of everyday social and practical skills', and intellectual disabilities develop in individuals before the age of 18 and affect cognitive abilities.

Invalid – defines an invalid as 'a person made weak or disabled by illness or injury'. It is probably the oldest term for someone living with physical conditions that are considered seriously limiting. However, it is such a general term that it fails to accurately describe a person's condition and is now widely viewed as offensive in that it implies that a person lacks abilities.

Keeper – in the sixteenth and seventeenth centuries referred to any male carer, and did not imply any qualification.

Lame/lameness – early English term meaning limited use of one or more limb; applied to the restricted use of arms as well as legs.

Lazar House – an old term for a specialist institution housing lepers (now known as people with Hansen's disease); derived from the name of the Biblical character Lazarus.

Learning disability – the current terminology in use to describe the condition previously known as a mental handicap or mental deficiency; technically defined as 'a significant intellectual impairment and deficits in social functioning or adaptive behaviour (necessary everyday skills) which are present from childhood (Learning Disabilities the Fundamental Facts – The Foundation for People with Learning Disabilities, 2001).

Leper house/hospital – a medieval institution to house and care for people with leprosy (known today as Hansen's disease).

Lepre/lepra – medieval terms for leper and leprosy respectively.

Leprosy/leper – respectively, terms for the disease known today as Hansen's disease, and those who have the disease; a highly prevalent disabling condition in Europe in the medieval period.

Lesions – the general term for abnormalities in tissues of an organism, often caused by injury or disease; a common consequence of leprosy.

Lunatic/lunatick – early term to broadly describe the term mentally ill-used today; current usage is pejorative or abusive.

Maison Dieu – literally 'Godly house', an alternative term for an almshouse.

Mad doctor – eighteenth-century term to describe the proprietor or superintendent of a 'Madhouse'; mad doctors were not necessarily medically qualified.

Mariners – early English word for sailors.

Mental health – the state of a person's psychological wellbeing.

Mental illness – the accepted current terminology for people who have some disorder or 'abnormality' of the mind which affects their behaviour or ability to function; in the past often referred to as lunacy.

Mentally retarded – the terms 'mentally retarded,' 'retard' and 'mental retardation' were once common terms that are now considered outdated and offensive. According to the Oxford English Dictionary, it's derived from the Italian word ritardato, and the first definition of the adjective version is 'held back or in check; hindered, impeded; delayed, deferred.'

It's traced to religion in 1636 ('he to his long retarded Wrath gives wings'); to medicine in 1785 ('Polypus, sometimes obstructs the vagina, and gives retarded labour'). It also means 'characterised by deceleration or reduction in velocity,' as in a 1674 reference: 'When it hath passed ye vertex ye motion changeth its nature, & turneth from an equably accelerated into an equably retarded motion.' Actual references to retarded intelligence did not come until the turn of the 20th century, with the advent of the IQ test. Then numbers were assigned to words – not just 'mentally retarded', but also terms like an imbecile, idiot and moron.

Mobility – a person's ability to move around.

Mongoloid – was commonly used in the late 19th century to refer to people who had Down's syndrome, due to the similarity of some of the physical characteristics of the disorder to Eastern Asian people, who were called Mongoloid. It is considered highly derogatory to describe someone with Down's syndrome as being 'mongoloid.'

Natural – the shortened term for a natural fool.

Natural Fool – used from the medieval period until its usage died out in the eighteenth century to describe a person born with a lifelong mental impairment; used to make a distinction from 'lunatics', seen as people suffering a temporary impairment due to mental illness; also, distinguished from 'artificial fool', someone pretending to be a fool, such as a court jester.

Non-disabled – refers to someone who does not have a disability. Non-disabled is the preferred term when the context calls for a comparison between people with and without disabilities. Use 'non-disabled' or 'people without disabilities' instead of healthy, able-bodied, normal or whole.

Nurse – in the sixteenth and seventeenth centuries referred to any woman carer, and did not imply any qualification.

Ophthalmia – an infection causing inflammation of the eye, previously a significant cause of blindness but now treatable.

Patient/sick – characterising people with a disability as 'sick' or referring to them as 'patients' signals there is something unwell about them or that they are need of medical attention, when, in fact, that may not be the case.

Paralytic – early English word for paralysed.

Parish – a district for local government; of importance from the medieval period through to the nineteenth century, eventually replaced by provincial authority boundaries; initially defined by the area served by a church and priest.

Pauper – a person who did not have the means to support her or himself, or who received poor relief.

People-first language – avoids defining a person in term of his or her disability. In most cases, this entails placing the reference to the disability after a reference to a person, as in 'a person with a disability', or 'a person living with a disability', rather than 'the disabled person'. People-first language is not preferred by all people with disabilities. Specifically, some members of the autism and Deaf communities prefer identity-first language.

Poor Law – legislation designed to define English society's obligations and duties to the destitute, aged, sick or disabled people who were judged unable to look after themselves; contained punitive measures aimed at healthy poor people deemed 'idle' or unwilling to work; bean with a 1531 law under Henry VIII and culminated in the Poor Law Amendment Act of 1834.

Poor relief – from the sixteenth century, the use of parish or state funds to support impoverished, sick, aged or disabled people, as stipulated by the Poor Law; was given as cash (outdoor relief) to allow people to achieve a level of subsistence needed for survival, or in-kind (indoor assistance), such as a place in a workhouse; after the 1834 Poor Law Amendment Act, indoor relief was favoured over outdoor relief.

Purges – the practice widespread in early medicine, particularly in the eighteenth century, of removing blood or other fluids from a patient. Derived from the idea that the health of a person depended on the balance of four 'humours', and that purging restored balance when the body was out of alignment.

Purgatory – a Christian belief concerning a place of temporary suffering where people's earthly sins are cleansed before they ascend to heaven.

Quack doctor – a person pretending to have medical skills and promoting the sale of unproven or fraudulent medicinal remedies.

Raving – early English word used to describe people experiencing episodes of mental illness where they appeared to have no control of their emotions and to talk nonsensically.

Relief – see Poor relief.

Scrofula – the term used for lymphadenopathy of the neck, usually because of an infection in the lymph nodes, known as lymphadenitis.

Spastic – the word initially used to describe a person with cerebral palsy, but now only used in a pejorative or abusive sense.

Spital, Spytall – early English word for a hospital.

Sturdy – early English word meaning 'able-bodied' as in 'sturdy vagabond', meaning a beggar who has no disability or sickness preventing them from working.

Suffers from/victim of/afflicted with/stricken with – these terms carry the assumption that a person with a disability is suffering or has a reduced quality of life. Not every person with a disability suffers is a victim or is stricken.

Thaumaturgy – the capability of a magician or a saint to work magic or miracles.

Tom O'Bedlam – sixteenth or seventeenth century expression to describe a mentally ill beggar.

Trade Guild – associations of craftsmen in a trade, originating in the medieval period; their purpose was both to protect and regulate their trade and to care for their individual members, e.g. through the provision of almshouses.

Tubercular – having tuberculosis, an infectious disease of the lungs.

Ulcerations – open sores on the body, one of the symptoms of leprosy in the medieval period.

Vagabond – early English word for a beggar, tending to denote those who were perceived as 'idle', dangerous or criminal, as opposed to impotent beggars who were incapacitated in some way and not seen as hazardous.

Author's Note

My entrance into the world, according to my parents, was somewhat of a miracle. Born premature, at twenty-six weeks, and weighing only 2 lbs 2ozs meant little chance of survival in 1970; babies that small rarely survived. This early arrival meant I had been starved of oxygen, which led doctors to a diagnosis, six months later, of the neurological and physical disability, cerebral palsy. Moreover, because of this diagnosis, doctors advised my parents to eventually institutionalise me in a Shaftesbury Society boarding school for disabled children in 1973, so that I could have physiotherapy daily, and enjoy a basic education. However, I defied paediatric consultants, who said I would never walk, and that I would almost certainly be permanently in a wheelchair by the time I was ten years old. I resisted being assimilated; moreover, I stood up for the other disabled children at the school, who were more disabled than me, and I refused to be boxed in by social stigma and tradition. Despite my determination, I was told I would not achieve anything because of my physical limitations. My Mum disagreed with the consultants and doctors; she would always encourage me with my endeavours and repeatedly used to say, 'Use your disability to your advantage, rather than a disadvantage.' Mum was determined for me to live the most fulfilled life I could and fought against draconian, Victorian attitudes to get me into mainstream school by the time I was nine, where I struggled to be accepted by my non-disabled classmates. Waddling with a bent gait endeared me to some students who tried to sympathise, while others ridiculed me, and I became a target for bullies; there was no in-between.

Mainstream middle school was where my interest in history began when in 1979, in a lesson, our teacher explained the stories behind the wives of Henry VIII, 'divorced, beheaded, died, divorced, beheaded, survived'. Confounded by a monarch who could horrifically discard two of these women whom he had reputedly adored, and supposedly cherished, I became drawn into the narratives; how could Henry execute a couple of his wives? I suspect, like so many of the readers of this book, I became beguiled with Henry's second wife, Queen Anne Boleyn, reading the dramatic story of her fall, and authors like Jean Plaidy; this is where my fascination with the Tudors, and with history began.

To encourage my new found passion for the past, my Nan instilled in me the love of studying characters from history, and when I was a child, she enjoyed taking me to places of historical interest. I enjoyed wandering around stately homes such as Wilton House, Athelhampton House, Blenheim Palace, Kingston Lacy, and Longleat House imagining what the personalities of the owners of such palatial properties would have been like, how and why they lived their lives as they did, and what made them exceptional people to live in such luxury. These visits piqued an interest; if the rich and privileged lived in such houses and palaces, how different to this was the average persons' experience of life? I wondered how people with disabilities would have survived if they were not born into well-known, monied families who would have cared for them – what would have happened to someone like me if I had lived, and survived in the Tudor period?

It is with these deliberations that my understanding of history and humanities has developed over time. Later in life, after studying fashion, art, and teaching beauty therapy, I chose to study history at degree level, and qualified as a secondary school teacher, teaching both Fashion and History. To become a teacher in the United Kingdom, not only is a degree required, and a PCGE but preferably a Master's degree. Additionally, it is a requirement by the government that prospective teachers pass an accredited skills test in English, Maths and ICT. At school, I thought I was 'thick' at Maths; however, I finally got my GCSE equivalent in Maths through the Open University as part of my degree. However, after three attempts at the skills tests for Maths, and with one final chance of taking the qualification; if I failed it for the fourth time, I would not be able to become a teacher. Thankfully, the Open University sent me to be tested by an SEN assessor, so they could find out why I struggled so much with Maths. I passed the English first time, but achieving Maths was like trying to learn a foreign language.

Moreover, the outcomes of the SEN tests proved that not only did I struggle with number processes, but it also discovered that I had dyspraxia and dyscalculia, which are conditions linked to cognitive problems associated with cerebral palsy. So, not only have I been physically challenged all my life, but have had unseen learning disabilities, which I never knew I had and struggled with, a weakness at solving mathematical problems. As a teacher of history, I realised I also needed to increase my subject knowledge, to support my secondary school CPD. As teachers, we must constantly learn ourselves, which is why I recently completed a Post-Graduate Diploma in Humanities and History with the Open University. It seemed a natural progression to study disability and its history. With this study, for my Post-Graduate qualification, I decided to go on a journey of discovery, and research the lives of people with disabilities in the Victorian period. Disability history as a subject is considered taboo, but lately, it is becoming increasingly fashionable for academics to research. Furthermore, instances of disability are everywhere·in history. Once you begin looking for it, disability experience is conspicuously absent in the histories we write, which is why I wanted to add to the conversation. Moreover, my interest in disability history is as much a personal one, as an academic one, and one I hope to continue, if, and when, I begin a PhD.

To link both the Tudors and disability together seemed like a distinct development in my work, especially being disabled myself. I have always tried to be the exception to that rule, through all my achievements, and always encourage other disabled people to be the best they can be without limitation.

Moreover, my favourite period to study is the Tudors, so naturally, it is only right that I research this era of disability history. Old fashioned attitudes tend to project disabled people as unable to lead full lives and contribute to society.

The problem with studying disability history is the lack of primary accounts of disabled people so that we as historians are often limited to inference and conjecture in piecing together the experiences of people with specific challenges. To gain a clear perspective of disabled people during the Tudor period, visiting places of historical interest to the Tudors was important; this gave me a broader scope to inform my research. It is with thanks to Historic Royal Palaces for making it possible to wander around Her Majesty's Royal Palace and Fortress, the Tower of London, when all the public had been locked out; and I was able to soak up the atmosphere unhindered, which was an enormous privilege. It was an opportunity to wander around looking at paintings, tracing my fingers over the oak panelling and stone fireplaces, wishing I could be absorbed into them, to be able to observe history as it happened. It was imperative to visit the halls and walk the passageways in the palaces the Tudors once did because it informed my research, and my writing, which proved invaluable, especially when treading in the Tudors' footsteps at Hampton Court Palace, Penshurst Place, Hever Castle, and Berkeley Castle. I visualised events unfolding, just as they may have done long ago while exploring these sites and felt the traces of previous life experiences, imagining the whispers of those long-unheard voices, like Sexton, William Somer, and Jayne the Foole. It gave me an understanding of what might have been their most profound sentiments.

Another incredible experience was having the opportunity of being in the front row of The Aldwych Theatre, to watch Ben Miles in Dame Hilary Mantel's stage adaptions of both *Wolf Hall* and *Bring Up the Bodies*. I was fortunate as this was on the last night's performance when the author Hilary Mantel was in the audience – what an incredible experience that was. By sheer coincidence, it was Hilary Mantel who gave her honorary degree acceptance speech at my Open University, PGCE graduation ceremony where I was terrified I might trip up because I was physically tired and in pain, being the final graduate who walked across the stage at the Lighthouse, Poole, on October 2014.

As a disabled person in twenty-first century Britain, attitudes towards me and others with disabilities have been acquired over years by bringing a definition of 'disability', through political activism, which has been concluded through legislation. The legislation states that 'if a person has a physical or mental impairment that has a 'substantial' and 'long-term' negative effect on their ability to do normal daily activities as recorded under the Equality Act 2010 a person is considered disabled. Therefore, in this study, I have not restricted myself to those personalities who had physical challenges, such as being lame, crippled or those who were deaf or blind, moreover, I have also included those who had learning disabilities, conditions similar to Down syndrome, Aspergers Syndrome or Autism and those who were faced with the challenge of being unable to take part in everyday activities which were expected of them during the Tudor period. This sphere of study creates an opportunity for all sorts of issues to research such as melancholy, depression, infertility and deformity, anything that would have limited or stopped a Tudor from achieving what was expected of them in society.

In terms of language and terminology, I have kept as close to the terminology used to define disability during the period. There will, therefore, be the use of what might be considered out of date language, that on first glance some readers might be offended by. However, to explain the events and reasoning behind the history and some of the primary sources, it is essential to adhere as strictly as possible to the wording used at the time.

To answer the questions relating to disabilities, I have cited various primary sources, (the likes of which are sadly lacking because any form of disability was not widely recorded), secondary readings and previous arguments of fellow historians and writers in this book, to give an overview of disability history in the Tudor period.

When considering the evidence, the treatment of disabled people in Tudor society does tend to turn existing misconceptions on its head; especially when we consider and compare how our recent Conservative governments have been changing policies, to reduce the cost of disability to the state, and how these policy changes affect the way society perceives and treats disabled people today.

Acknowledgements

Disability and the Tudors: All the King's Fools is my first non-fiction book, and has been a very long time in writing. Disability history has been limping along, as a second-rate area of study until recently, and I have often heard authors suggest that writers should always 'write about what you know', and know about disability, and attitudes towards it in the modern-day, I do. The idea of this book was in the back of my mind whilst I was scouring the internet for publishers and agents to consider publishing my fictional series on Anne Boleyn, *Timeless Falcon*, when I stumbled across Pen and Sword's website, read their publishing manifesto and decided to take a chance on submitting an idea for 'Disability History'. After a few days, their commissioning editor from their History imprint got in touch, and Claire Hopkins had an encouraging conversation with me about how this book might materialise.

Firstly, it is entirely thanks to her inspirational guidance as my commissioning editor, without the assistance of any agent, that this book came into being. Claire has been a great encouragement, and I thank her for her unwavering enthusiasm; she had faith in me as an unknown historian and her subsequent support in considering my submission helped me bring the final work to fruition. Confirmation that my idea was travelling in the right direction, I went to hear Professor Lipscomb talk on court Fools at Hampton Court, and read about Peter Cooper's *All The King's Fools* production, performed at Hampton Court with disabled actors from The Misfits Theatre Company, where they collaborated with director Peter Cooper of Foolscap Productions and Past Pleasures, to bring disability history into the mainstream for visitors to the Palace. I'm grateful to them, because it gave me the conviction to keep going in writing this book. When I complete my PhD on disability history, which, funding permitted for a studentship, I hope my research will allow me to go even further in sourcing evidence of Tudor disability history, bringing further, fresh anecdotal stories to light. In that endeavour, I would like to thank Dr Rosamund Oates of the Manchester Metropolitan University for encouraging me to apply for a PhD.

Secondly, I also want to thank my editors, Dana Messer, Claire Hopkins and Sarah-Beth Watkins, who have meticulously supported me in transforming this book into its final incarnation. I would also like to thank Dr Lauren Mackay for her advice, and support in improving the initial manuscript, and for her insights into the Tudor period, and I am deeply indebted to them all for their creativity, insights and patience, with me as a new author.

Thirdly, thank you to writers such as Kyra Kramer for her insights into Henry VIII and his many ailments and thank you to Phil Roberts for his interview with me into the wounded sailors on board the Mary Rose. Fourthly, thank you to Dr David Starkey for having conversations, and afterwards emailing me in assisting me with information on Henry VIII. In particular, discussing with me the onset of Henry's lack of mobility and increasing disability in old-age, his ownership of three wheelchairs, and the revelation that Henry's privy chamber staff invented a kind of stairlift for his use at Whitehall Palace to assist moving the King easily up and downstairs. I would also like to thank Maria Hayward, Professor of Early Modern History, at the University of Southampton, who pointed me in the right direction, verifying my research on Henry VIII, his 'throne-type wheelchairs' and his stairlift.

I wish to thank and mention Philippa Langley, for her time, support and insights into the physical challenges of Richard III due to his scoliosis. Thank you to Viscount De L'Isle, Lady Middleton, Lucy McLeod and Gaye Jee from Penshurst Place, Kent for discussing evidence about the 'La Volta' painting of Elizabeth I and the Earl of Leicester. I would also like to thank Lucy Churchill for permission to use the images of her rendering and reconstruction of the 1534 medal to commemorate Anne Boleyn's coronation and second pregnancy. Thank you to Dr John Boneham, reference specialist of rare books at The British Library, in helping me find primary and secondary sources relevant to the period and to Dr Sean Cunningham, Head of Medieval Records at The National Archives, Kew for helping me find records and sources about some lesser-known disabled Tudors. Thank you to Broadstone library for supplying the bibliography required to help with my research. Finally, to Historic England Archives, the staff at the Louvre, HM Royal

Collection, and Bridgeman for images included in this publication. I am tremendously grateful to you all. I have given due credit and citation to historians, writers and researchers whose interpretations of the history have informed my work. Otherwise, the majority of inferences and conclusions have been my own while researching physically and intellectually disabled people of the Tudor period.

I would like to thank Jeffrey Salkilld, television and film producer, who allowed me to collaborate with him on a mini-documentary series project based on Jayne Foole, featuring actress Sarah Gordy as the protagonist; which without this book, I would never have had the experinece to be involved in. This book has been a labour of love, as well as an exciting opportunity to debut my research.

Special thanks go to family and friends, who have all encouraged me during the writing of this book. Thank you to Gina Clark from Tudor Dreams Historical Costumier, my best friend, and my rock of support, especially when at times I have been close to giving up in frustration – your encouragement is boundless. Finally I wish to thank my boys, Joshua and Lucas, who have trailed across the south of England over the past few years, staying at Hever Castle; visiting the Tower of London; Berkeley Castle; Sudeley Castle; and Hampton Court Palace on numerous occasions, absorbing my enthusiasm and interest in all things Tudor. You have been all been fantastic in so many ways.

Phillipa Vincent-Connolly
Poole, Dorset
November 2021

Bibliography

Primary Sources – Manuscript

BODLEIAN LIBRARY, OXFORD
Ashmole Manuscripts

MS Ashmole 213, fol. 110 – Medical and astrological papers of Dr Richard Napier (1559-1634)

BRITISH LIBRARY, LONDON
Cotton MSS

Nero C, x, ff.3 – Letter signed by five doctors, to Cromwell describing the queen's [Jane Seymour's] worsening condition; Hampton Court, 17 October 1537.

Titus B, i, f.551 – Proclamation declaring Henry VIII to be King of Ireland; 3 January 1542.

Titus D IV, ff. 2-14 – Poems on the coronation of King Henry VIII of England (1509–1547) and Queen Katherine of Aragon (d. 1536). by Thomas More, 1509

Vespasian A XII, f. 135r – John Rous describing Richard III.

Vespasian A XII, f. 137r – John Rous describing how Richard III defended himself during the Battle of Bosworth

Harley MSS

353, f.1 – Proclamation of the death of King Henry VIII and proclaiming his son Edward VI as King of England; London, 1 February 1547

1419 f.194v – Detail of a chair in Henry VIII's Inventory, covered with purple velvet, which has been referred to as a 'stairthrone'.

6,989, f.45 – Privy Council to Norfolk; Hampton Court, 23 February 1540.

Royal MSS

2A.XVI – The Psalter of Henry VIII, written and probably illuminated by John Mallard with Henry VIII depicted as the Biblical King David, 176ff; c.1540-1

Sloane MSS

1,017 – Collection of medical recipes, with, at **f.30v,** Henry's 'plaster' for Anne of Cleves

1,047 – Collection of recipes for ointments and nostrums devised by Henry VIII and four of his doctors

INNER TEMPLE LIBRARY

Petyt MS 538.47, fol.317 - Edward VI's 'Devise for the Succession'

LAMBETH PALACE LIBRARY, LONDON

Carew MSS 621, f.14 – Statement of the King's title to Ireland, listed as 1541

PARLIAMENTARY ARCHIVES, HOUSES OF PARLIAMENT, LONDON

Records of Parliament, Parliamentary Archives: GB-061

HL/PO/PU/1/1601/43Eliz1n2 – Poor Relief Act 1601

PIC/S/284 – Poor Law Amendment Act. [Parliamentary Archives, Original Act] 1601

PIC/S/285 – Poor Law Amendment Act. [Parliamentary Archives, Original Act] 1601

PIC/P/114 – Poor Law Amendment Act. [Parliamentary Archives, Original Act] 1601

THE NATIONAL ARCHIVES
KEW, SURREY

Exchequer
Treasury of the Receipt

E 23/4/1 – Henry's will, dated 30 December 1546

E36/231 – The Ordinances. Transcripts of the Eltham Ordinances, 17 Hen VIII; of increments of wages and allowances, 31-32 Hen VIII; of ordinances 31 Hen VIII; of orders of the Green Cloth, proclamations and other documents concerning the household and related concerns, Hen VIII-Eliz I, with list of contents

Court of Augmentations, Receipts and Payments Books

E 315/160 f.133v. – Household book of Sir Antony Denny, Keeper of the Palace of Whitehall; 34 Henry VIII – 2 Edward VI

PROB – Records of the Prerogative Court of Canterbury

Division within PROB - Wills and Letters of Administration

PROB 11 – Prerogative Court of Canterbury and related Probate Jurisdictions: Will Registers

PROB 11/12/74 – Will of Joane Frowik or Frowyk, Widow, 16 May 1500

Records of the Court of King's Bench and other courts, Crown Side Records

KB 8 – Court of King's Bench: Crown Side: Baga de Secretis - Roll and file of court of the Lord High Steward and peers. Principal defendants and charges: Queen Anne Boleyn, Sir George Boleyn Lord Rocheford, high treason, adultery and incest, 28 Hen VIII. 21 membranes. 1536 Apr 22-1537 Apr 21

Records of the Lord Chamberlain and Officers of the Royal Household

LC 2/2 – f.45, f.84v, ff.83, 77 – Wardrobe accounts for the funeral of Henry VIII, 1547

State Papers Domestic

SP 4/1 – List of documents issued under Henry's 'Dry Stamp', September 1545-January 1547

SP 1/100 f.60 – ff. 60, MC4301781136, – Petition of John Laurence, Cook to the Privy Council, 1535

Primary Accounts – Printed

An Acte for the Releife of the Poore, 43 Eliz 1 c 2. Poor Law Amendment Act. (Parliamentary Archives, Original Act, 1601 PIC/S/284 – Records of Parliament)

'APC'– Acts of the Privy Council, ns, vol. 1 1542-7, (John Roche Dasent, London, HMSO, 1890)

Anon., *A pleasant history of the life and death of Will Summers: And how hee came first to be known at court, and by what means he got to be King Henry the eighth's jester. With the entertainment that his cousen Patch, Cardinal Woolsey's fool, gave him at his Lords house, and how the hogsheads of gold were known by this means,* (London, printed for T[homas]. Vere, and J[ohn]. Wright, 1676)

Archives of St Bartholomew's Hospital [board of governors' minutes], Journal no. 2, (1567–86)

Armin, Robert, *Fool upon Fool,* (London, printed [by E. Allde] for William Ferbrand, dwelling neere Guild-hal gate ouer against the maiden-head, 1600)

Armin, Robert, *Fool upon Fool,* (London, printed [by W. White and S. Stafford] for William Ferbrand, dwelling in Popes-head Allie neare the Royall Exchange, 1605)

Armin, Robert, *The Two Maids of More-Clock,* (London, printed by N[icholas] O[kes] for Thomas Archer, and is to be sold in his shop in Popes-head Pallace, 1609)

Armin, Robert, *Fools and Jesters: With a reprint of Robert Armin's Nest of Ninnies, 1608,* (Adamant Media Corporation, 13 May 2004)

Boorde, Andrew, *The Breviary of Health,* (London, William Powell, 1552)

Boorde, Andrew, *Scoggin's Jests. The first and best part of Scoggin's jests: full of witty mirth and pleasant shifts, done by him in France, and other places: b eing a preseruatiue against melancholy. Gathered by Andrew Boord. Doctor of Physicke,* (London, printed [by Miles Flesher] for Francis Williams, 1626)

Bright, Timothie, *A Treatise of Melancholy,* (London, imprinted by Thomas Vautrollier [etc.], 1586)

CSP Spain – Calendar of Dispatches and State Papers, Spain
    Bergenroth, G.A., ed., *Calendar of State Papers, Spain,* Volume 2, 1509-1525, (London, HMSO, 1866)

CSP Ireland – Calendar of State Papers, Ireland
  Atkinson, E.G., ed., *Calendar of the State Papers, Ireland,* 1598–9 (1895) pp. 296-7
CSP Venice – Calendar of State Papers, Venice
  Brown, H.F., ed., *Calendar of the State Papers: Venice*, Volume 2. 1509-1519 (1867)
  Brown and Rawdon., eds., *Calendar of State Papers Relating To English Affairs in the Archives of Venice,* Volume 2, 1509-1519. (London, HMSO, 1867)
Caius, John. K., *A boke, or counseill against the disease commonly called the sweate, or sweating sicknesse*, (London, Richard Grafton, 1552)
Elyot, Thomas, Sir, *The castel of helth corrected and in some places augmented by the fyrste authour therof, Thomas Elyot knight, the pere of oure Lord 1541*, (London, In aedibus Thomae Bertheleti typis impress, 1541)
Foxe, John, *Acts & Monuments*, G. Townsend and S.R Cattley (eds), 8 Vols., (London, R B Seeley & W. Burnside, 1837-41)
Fuller, Thomas, *The History of Worthies in England*, (London, printed by J.G[rismond. W.L[eybourne]. And W.G[odbid]. For Thomas Williams, and are to be sold at the sign of the Bible in Little Britain, 1662)
Gerard, John, *The Herbal*, (London: by [Edm. Bollifant for [Bonham Norton and] John Norton, 1597)
Gifford, George, *Discourse of the subtill Practises of Devilles by Witches and Sorcerers*, (London, 1587). Sig. B2.
Hume, M.A.S., tr. *Chronicle of King Henry VIII of England*, (1889)
Letters and Papers, Foreign and Domestic, Henry VIII
  Brewer, J.S., ed, *Letters and Papers, Foreign and Domestic, Henry VIII*, (London, HMSO, 1920)
  Brewer, J.S., ed., *Letters and Papers, Foreign and Domestic, Henry VIII,* Volume 1, 1509-1514, (London, HMSO, 1920)
Gairdner, James., ed., *Letters and Papers, Foreign and Domestic, Henry VIII,* (London, HMSO, 1887)
Gairdner, James., ed,. *Letters and Papers, Foreign and Domestic, Henry VIII,* Volume 10, January-June 1536, (London, HMSO, 1887), pp. 12-26. [British History Online, accessed November 4, 2019]
Gairdner, James., ed., *Letters and Papers, Foreign and Domestic, Henry VIII,* (London, HMSO, 1891)

Gairdner, James., and Brodie, R H,. eds., *Letters and Papers, Foreign and Domestic, Henry VIII,* (London, HMSO, 1894)

Gairdner, James.,and Brodie, R H, eds., *Letters and Papers, Foreign and Domestic, Henry VIII,* Volume 18 Part 1, January-July 1543, (London, HMSO, 1901), pp. 480-489. [British History Online, accessed November 4, 2019]

"Edward III: January 1352", *Parliament Rolls of Medieval England*, Eds., Chris Given-Wilson, Paul Brand, Seymour Phillips, Mark Ormrod, Geoffrey Martin, Anne Curry, and Rosemary Horrox, (Woodbridge, Boydell & Brewer, 2005)

Giustinian, Sebastian, *Four years at the Court of Henry VIII: Selection of Despatches written by the Venetian Ambassador Sebastian Giustinian,* trans. Rawdon Brown, 2 vols, (London, Smith, Elder & Co., 1854)

Guicciardini, Francesco, *Dell'epitome dell'Historia d'Italia ... libri XX. Con diverse annotationi [by F. Sansovino] ... Et con i ritratti d'alquanti principi cavati dall'opera sua,* (Venetia, 1580).

Hall, Edward, *Hall's chronicle: containing the history of England, during the reign of Henry the Fourth, and the succeeding monarchs, to the end of the reign of Henry the Eighth, in which are particularly described the manners and customs of those periods. Carefully collated with the editions of 1548 and 1550,* (London, J.Johnson, 1809)

Hayward, Maria, ed., *The 1542 Inventory of Whitehall: The Palace and its Keeper*, 2 vols., (London, Society of Antiquaries of London, 2004)

Heywood, John, *The Proverbs and Epigrams of John Heywood (A. D. 1562),* (Printed for the Spenser society [by C. Simms and co.], 1867)

Heywood, Thomas, *An Apology for Actors*, (London, printed by Nicholas Okes, 1612), Sig. F4.

Holinshed, Raphael, *The Chronicles ([London]: Finished in Januarie 1587, and the 29 of the Queenes Majesties reigne, with the full continuation of the former years, at the expenses of John Harison, George Bishop, Rafe Newberie, Henrie Denham, and Thomas VVoodcocke. At London printed by Henry Denham in Aldergate street at the signe of the Starre,* (1587)

Holinshed, Raphael, *Chronicles of England, Scotland and Ireland*, 6 vols., (London, J.Johnson et al., 1808)

Journal of the House of Lords: Volume 1, 1509-1577. (London, HMSO, 1767-1830) pp.605-606

Journal d'un Bourgeois de Paris sous le Règne de François Premier (1515-1536)

Madden, Frederick, *Privy purse expenses of the Princess Mary, daughter of King Henry the Eighth, afterwards Queen Mary*, (RareBooksClub. com, 14 May 2012)

Madden, Frederick, *Privy purse expenses of the Princess Mary, daughter of King Henry the Eighth, afterwards Queen Mary, with a memoir of the princess, and notes by Frederick Madden*, (1831)

Nash, Thomas, *A pleasant Comedie [in prose and verse], called Summers last will and Testament*, (London, S. Stafford for W. Burre, 1600)

Nicolas, Nicholas Harris, Sir, ed., *Proceedings and Ordinances of the Privy Council of England*, Vol 7 (1540-2), (London, Commissioners of the Public Records, 1837)

Nicolas, Nicholas Harris, Sir, ed., *Privy Purse Expenses of Elizabeth of York: Wardrobe accounts of Edward the Fourth. With a Memoir of Elizabeth of York, and Notes*, (London, William Pickering, 1830)

Nicolas, Nicholas Harris, Sir, ed., *The Privy Purse Expenses of Henry VIII* (1529-1532)

Original Letters Illustrative of English History (11 vols. in 3 series, ed., Sir Henry Ellis, London, 1824, 1827, and 1846)

Perkins, W., *A Discourse of the Damned Art of Witchcraft; so farre forth as it is revealed in the Scriptures, and manifest by true Experience*, (Cambridge, 1608)

Perkins, William, *A Golden Chain*, (Cambridge, Printed by John Legatt [etc.], 1600), p.1027

Scot, Reginald, *Discoverie of Witchcraft*, (1584)

Stapleton, T., *The Life and Illustrious Martyrdom of Sir Thomas More, Formerly Lord Chancellor of England*, (Part III of "Tres Thomae," printed at Douai, 1588), translated, for the first time, into English by Philip E. Hallett, (Burns Oates & Washbourne Ltd, 1928)

Sylvester, Richard S. and Harding, Davis P., eds., *Two Early Tudor Lives: The Life and Death of Cardinal Wolsey by George Cavendish; The Life of Sir Thomas More by William Roper*, (Yale University Press, 1962)

The Roll of the Royal College of Physicians. See http:// www.rcplondon. ac.uk/history-heritage/Collegehistory-new/Munks%20Roll/Pages/ Munks-Roll.aspx

Tyndale, William, *The newe Testamēt as it was written, and caused to be writtē, by them which herde yt. To whom also oure saveoure Christ Jesus commanded that they shulde preache it unto al creatures*, translated into English by William Tyndale, assisted by his amanuensis William Roy, (Worms? printed by Peter Schoeffer? 1526?), British Library, General Reference Collection, C.188.a.17.

West, William, *Simboleography*, (1594)

Wilson, Thomas, *The art of rhetorique for the vse of all such as are studious of eloquence, set forth in English, by Thomas Wilson. 1553. Matrimonii encomium. English,* (England, George Robinson, 1553)

Secondary Sources

Adams, Francis, ed., *The Extant Works of Aretaeus, The Cappadocian. By Aretaeus*, (Boston, Milford House Inc. 1972, republication of the 1856 edition)

Abrams, Judith., *Judaism and Disability: Portrayals in Ancient Texts from the Tanach through the Bavli*, Illustrated Edition, (Gallaudet University Press, 2014)

Andrews, Jonathan, (2004). 'Napier, Richard (1559–1634), astrological physician and Church of England clergyman', *Oxford Dictionary of National Biography* [accessed 29 Oct. 2019]

Andrews, Jonathan, Porter, Roy, Tucker, Penny and Waddington, Keir, *The History of Bethlem*, (London, Routledge, 1997)

Anglo, Sydney, *Spectacle, Pageantry and Early Tudor Policy*, (Oxford, Clarendon Press, 1969)

Ankarloo, Bengt., Clark, Stuart., eds,. *Witchcraft and Magic in Europe: The Period of the Witch Trials*, (University of Pennsylvania Press, 2002)

Appleby, Jo, et al., (2015). 'Perimortem trauma in King Richard III: a skeletal analysis', *The Lancet*, Volume 385, Issue 9964, pp. 253–259

Arnold, Janet, *Queen Elizabeth's Wardrobe Unlock'd*, (London, Routledge, First edition, 1988)

Armstrong, C.A.J., ed., *The Usurpation of Richard the Third,* (Oxford, Second edition, 1969)

Bagguley, Paul., and Mann, Kirk, (1992). 'Idle, Thieving Bastards: Scholarly Representations of the Underclass', *Work, Employment and Society*, Volume 6, Number 1. pp.113-126

Bagwell, CE, "Respectful image": revenge of the barber surgeon, *Annals of Surgery*, 2005, Volume 241, pp. 872–8

Bailey, Brian, *Almshouses*, (Hale, First edition, 1988)

Barber, Nicola, *Medieval Medicine, Raintree Freestyle: Medicine Through the Ages,* (Raintree, Illustrated edition, 2019)

Barratt, C.R.B., *The History of the Society of Apothecaries of London*, (London, Elliot Stock, 1905)

Barratt N.R., (1973). 'King Henry VIII', *Annals Royal College of Surgeons of England*, Volume 52 pp.216-33

Barnes, Colin, *Disabled People in Britain and Discrimination: A Case for Anti-discrimination Legislation*, (University of California, C. Hurst & Co., 1991)

Billington, Sandra, *The Social History of the Fool*, (New York, St. Martin's Press, 1986)

Blanchard, Joël, *Philippe de Commynes: Mémoires*, (Paris, Fayard, 2006)

Blaug, Mark, (1963). 'The Myth of the Old Poor Law and the Making of the New', *The Journal of Economic History*, 23, no. 2 151–84. doi:10.1017/S0022050700103808.

Bloch, Marc, *The Royal Touch: sacred monarchy and scrofula in England and France*, (London, Routledge & Kegan Paul, 1973)

Bolland, Charlotte and Cooper, Tarny, *The Real Tudors: Kings and Queens Rediscovered*, (London, National Portrait Gallery, 2014)

Bonn, Robert, L., *Painting Life: The Art of Pieter Bruegel, the Elder*, (Syracuse University Press, 2007)

Borman, Tracy, 'James VI and I: the king who hunted witches', (History Extra: March 27 2019)

Borman, Tracy, *The Private Lives of the Tudors*, (London, Hodder & Stoughton, 2016)

Borman, Tracy, *Witches*, (London, Vintage, 2014)

Borradaile, H., 'Clowns and Fools of Shakespeare's Time', *Poet Lore*, 8 (January 1896)

Borsay, Anne, *Disability and Social Policy in Britain since 1750: A History of Exclusion,* (Palgrave, 2004)

Bottineau-Fuchs, Yves, *Georges Ier d'Amboise (1460–1510): Un Prélat Normand de la Renaissance*, (Editions des Falaises, 2005)

Brant, Sebastian, *The Ship of Fools*, trans. Edwin H. Zeydel, (New York, Columbia University Press, 1944)

Brantôme, Pierre de Bourdeille, seigneur de., *Corpus Historique Étampois*.

Brantôme, Pierre de Bourdeille, seigneur de., *Famous Women*, ([S.l.]: Humphreys, 1908)

Breverton, Terry, *Everything You Ever Wanted to Know About the Tudors But Were Afraid to Ask*, (Stroud, Amberley Publishing, Reprint edition 2015)

Brewer, Clifford, *The Death of Kings*, (London, Abson Books, 2000), pp.123-124

Brewster, Kaye, *Survey of Scottish Witchcraft,* (The University of Edinburgh, 2007)

Brogan, Stephen, *The Royal Touch in Early Modern England: Politics, Medicine and Sin*, (Woodbridge, Boydell and Brewer, NED - New edition, 2015)

Brunhölzl, (1999). 'Thoughts on the illness of Hermann von Reichenau (1019-1054)', *Sudhoffs Arch*, Volume 83 Issue 2 pp.239-43

Buckley, Richard, et al., (2013). 'The king in the car park: new light on the death and burial of Richard III in the Grey Friars church, Leicester in 1485', *Antiquity*, vol. 87, no. 336, (Cambridge University Press)

Burke, Peter, *Popular Culture in Early Modern Europe*, (Maurice Temple Smith Ltd, 1978)

Caius, J,K., *A boke, or counseill against the disease commonly called the sweate, or sweating sicknesse*, (New York, Scholars facsimiles & reprints, 1937)

Cameron, Kenneth Walter, *The background of John Heywood's "Witty and witless"; a study in early Tudor drama, together with a specialized bibliography of Heywood scholarship*, (Raleigh, N.C., Thistle Press, 1941)

Carpenter, Sarah, (2014). 'Laughing at Fools', *Theta*, vol. XI

Castiglione A., *A History of Medicine*, translated from the Italian by E.B. Krumbhaar, (New York, Alfred Knopf, 1941)

Chalmers, CR and Chaloner E.J., (2009). '500 Years Later Henry VIII, leg ulcers and the course of History', *Journal of the Royal Society of Medicine*, Vol 102: pp. 513–517

Chambers, Paul, *Bedlam: London's Hospital for the Mad*, (Ian Allen Publishing, 2009)

Clapton, J., 'Disability, Inclusion and the Christian Church', (Paper presented at Disability, Religion and Health Conference, Brisbane, October 18-20, 1996)

Clowes, William, (2015). 'A Prooved Practice for all Young Chirurgiens, 1588', *Bulletin of the Royal College of Surgeons of England*, pp. 25-27

Colewell, H.A., 'Andrew Borde and his Medicinal Works', *Middlesex Hospital Journal*, Volume 15, 1911), pp.25-43

Coleridge, Peter, *Disability, Liberty, and Development*, (Oxfam Publishing, 1993)

Cooper, Peet, *All The King's Fools*, (2011)

Croft, Pauline, (2004). 'Cecil, Robert, first earl of Salisbury (1563–1612), politician and courtier', *Oxford Dictionary of National Biography*

Crofton, Ian, *The Kings and Queens of England*, (Quercus Books, 2006)

Cummings, Bria.,*The Book of Common Prayer: The Texts of 1549, 1559, and 1662*, (OUP Oxford; Reprint edition, 2013)

Currie, Margaret, *The Letters of Martin Luther, Selected and Translated, 1908,* (Cornell University Library, 2009)

Davis, Lennard J., *Bending over Backwards: Disability, Dismodernism, and Other Difficult Positions*, (NYU Press, 2002)

Davis, Lennard J., *Enforcing Normalcy: Disability, Deafness, and the Body*, (Verso, 1995)

Davis, Norman, *Paston Letters and Papers of the Fifteenth Century: Part 1*, (Oxford University Press, 27 May 1971)

Dewhurst, J., (1984). 'The alleged Miscarriages of Catherine of Aragon and Anne Boleyn,' *Med. Hist.*, Vol 28, pp.49-56

Dewhurst, Kenneth, *Thomas Willis's Oxford Lectures*, (Sandford Publications,1980)

Devonald, G., (1963). 'Henry VIII', *Res Medica: Journal of the Royal Medical Society*, Volume 3, Number 4, pp.1-7

Doran, John, *The History of Court Fools*, (Richard Bentley, 1858);

Doran, Susan, and Durston, Christopher, *Princes, Pastors and People. The Church and Religion in England 1529-1689*, (London, Routledge, 1991)

Dureau, Jeanne-Marie, *Dictionnaire biographique des médecins en France au Moyen Age* (1979–1980)

Dyer, Alan D, (1978). 'Influence of Bubonic Plague in England 1500-1667', *Med. Hist.*, Vol 22 pp. 308-26

Ellis, Henry, *Original Letters Illustrative of English History*, First Series,Vol II, (London, 1825); Second series, Vol II (London 1827); Third Series, Vol III, (London, 1826)

Ellis, Henry, *Polydore Vergil's English History, from an early translation preserved among the mss. of the Old Royal Library in the British Museum / Polydorius Vergilius. Vol. 1, containing the first eight books comprising the period prior to the Norman Conquest / edited by Sir Henry Ellis.* (London, printed for the Camden Society by J. B. Nichols and son, 1884), pp. 226-7

Elton, G.R., (1953-4). 'An Early Tudor Poor Law', *History Review*, 6.

Elton, G.R., (1960). *Philanthropy in England, 1480–1660.* By W. K. Jordan. (London: George Allen and Unwin, 1959) pp.410. 42s. The Historical Journal, Volume 3, Issue 1, pp. 89-92

Elton, G.R., *The Tudor Constitution: Documents and Commentary,* (Cambridge University Press, 1982)

Erasmus, Desiderius, *In Praise of Folly*, (Grand Rapids, MI, Christian Classics Ethereal Library, University of Michigan Press,1958)

Erasmus, Desiderius, *In Praise of Folly*, (London, Penguin, new edition, 2004)

Everett Wood, Mary Anne, *Letters of Royal and Illustrious Ladies of Great Britain II*, (Henry Colborn, Great Malborough Street, 1846)

Feuillerat, A., ed., *Documents relating to the revels at Court in the time of King Edward VI and Queen Mary, (the Loseley Manuscripts),* (Louvain, 1914), p.49

Furdell, Elizabeth Lane, *The Royal Doctors 1485-1714: Medical Personnel at the Tudor and Stuarts Courts*, (Rochester, NY, Rochester University Press, 2001)

Freeling, George Henry, ed., *Newes from Scotland, declaring the damnable life and death of doctor Fian, a notable sorcerer, who was burned at Edenbrough in Ianuary last, 1591*, (Oxford University, 1816)

Fitzgerald, J., (1996). 'Geneticizing Disability: The Human Genome Project and the Commodification of self', paper presented at the Rehabilitation International Congress, Auckland, New Zealand

Fitzgerald, J., (1996). 'Reclaiming the Whole: Self, Spirit and society', paper presented at Disability Religion and Health Conference. Brisbane

Fontaine, C.R., (1994). 'Roundtable discussion: Women with Disabilities – A Challenge To Feminist Theology, *Journal of Feminist Studies in Religion*, 10(20), pp.99-134

Foreman, Paul, *The Cambridge Book of Magic: a Tudor necromancer's manual*, (Cambridge, Texts in Early Modern Magic, 2015)

Foucault, Michel, *Madness and Civilization: A History of Insanity in the Age of Reason*, (Abingdon, Routledge, 5th repr., 2005)

Fox, Julia, *Jane Boleyn: The Infamous Lady Rochford*, (W&N, 2009)

Fox, Julia, *Sister Queens: Katherine of Aragon and Juana Queen of Castile*, (W&N, 2012)

Frith, John, (2002). 'Syphillis: Its Early History and Treatment until Pencillin and the debate on its origins', *Jnl. Of Military & Vedterans Health* (Australian Military Med. Ass.), vol. 20, p.49-58

Fritz, Jean-Marc, *Le discours du fou au Moyen Age*, (University Press of France, digital reissue FeniXX, 1992)

Furdell, Elizabeth Lane, 'Boorde, Andrew c1490-1549, physician and author', *Oxford Dictionary of National Biography*, http://www.oxforddnb.com/view/article/2870 [accessed 16 October 2019]

Furdell, Elizabeth Lane, *The Royal Doctors, 1485–1714: medical personnel at the Tudor and Stuart courts*, (Rochester, NY, University of Rochester Press, 2001)

Gale, Thomas, *Certain Works of Chirurgerie. 1563*, (London, Rouland Hall Facsimile, Amsterdam and New York, Da Capo Press, 1971)

Génin, François, *Lettres de Marguerite d'Angoulême*, (Nabu Press, 2010)

Géoris, Michel, *Francois Ier. Magnifique*, (Editions France-Empire, 1998)

Goldsmith, Robert Hillis, *Wise Fools in Shakespeare* (East Lansing, Michigan, Michigan State University Press, 1955)

Goodman, Ruth, *How to be a Tudor: A Dawn-to-Dusk Guide to Everyday Life*, (London, Viking, 5 November 2015)

Gorman, James, 'Scientists Hint at Why Laughter Feels So Good', (New York Times, 2011) https://www.nytimes.com/2011/09/14/science/14laughter.html

Granger, James, *A biographical history of England from Egbert the Great to the revolution*, 5th edn, 1 (London, William Baynes & Son, 1824)

Griffin, Dustin H, *Satire: A critical Reintroduction*, (Lexington, The University Press of Kentucky, 1994)

Gritsch, Eric. W., *Martin - God's Court Jester*, (Sigler Pr; First Sigler Press edition, 1991)

Grueninger, Natalie, *Discovering Tudor London: A Journey Back in Time*, (London, The History Press, 2017)

Hall, Noliene, (1990). 'Henry Patenson: Sir Thomas More's Fool', *Moreana*, XXVII, 101-102

Hallett, A., *Almshouses*, (Princes Risborough, Shire Publications, 2004)

Hanham, Alison., *Richard III and his Early Historians, 1483–1535*, (Clarendon Press, Oxford, 1975)

Harris, Barbara J., *English Aristocratic Women, 1450–1550 Marriage and Family, Property and Careers*, (Oxford University Press, 2002)

Hart, Kelly, *The Mistresses of Henry VIII,* (The History Press, First edition, 2009)

Hart, Roger, *Witchcraft*, (London, Weyland Publishers Ltd, 1971)

Harward, Vernon, *The Dwarfs of Arthurian Romance and Celtic Tradition*, (E J. Brill, First edition, 1958)

Hayward, Maria, *Dress at the Court of Henry VIII*, (London, Maney Publishing, 2007)

Hanawalt, Barbara, A., *Growing Up in Medieval London – The Experience of Childhood in History*, (Oxford, Oxford University Press, 1993)

Hanawalt, Barbara, A., *The Ties that Bound: Peasant Families in Medieval England*, (Oxford, Oxford University Press, 1986)

Hazlitt, W.C., ed., *Shakespeare Jest-books: Reprints of the early and Very rare Jest-books Supposed to Have Been used by Shakespeare*, 3 Vols, I,II (London, Willis & Sotheran, 1864)

Herbert of Cherbury, Lord Edward., *Life and Raigne of King Henry the Eight*, (London, Thomas Whitaker, 1649) p.471

Herford, Charles E., *Studies in the Literary Relations of England and Germany in the Sixteenth Century*, (Abingdon, Frank Cass & Co. Ltd., 1966)

Higgins, P., *Making Disability: Exploring the social Transformation of Human Variation*, (Springfield Illinois, Charles C Thomas, 1992)

Hitchcock, Elsie, and P.E Hallet, with A.E. Reed., eds., *The Life of Sir Thomas More, sometimes Lord Chancellor of England*, (EETS, 1950)

Hodgart, Matthew, *Satire: Origins and Principles*, (New Brunswick, New Jersey, Transaction Publishers, 2010 reprint)

Hollen Lees, L., *The Solidarity of Strangers, The English Poor Laws and the People, 1700-1948*, (Cambridge, Cambridge University Press, 2006)

Hope Dodds, Madeline, and Dodds, Ruth, *The Pilgrimage of Grace, 1536-1537 V1: And the Exeter Conspiracy 1538*, (1915), (Literary Licensing, LLC, 7 Aug. 2014)

Howson, Brian, *Almshouses: A Social and Architectural History*, (The History Press, 2008)

Hudson, Geoffrey L., (2006). 'History of Disability: Early Modern West', *Encyclopedia of Disability*, Ed. Gary L. Albrecht. Vol. 1. (Thousand Oaks, SAGE Publications, Inc.)

Hughes, J.T., (2006). 'The Licensing of Medical Practitioners in Tudor England: Legislation enacted by Henry VIII', *Vesalius*, Volume XII, No 1, pp.4-11

Hutchinson, Robert, *Henry VIII, The Decline and Fall of a Tyrant*, (London, Orion Publising Group, 2019)

Hutchinson, Robert, *Young Henry: The Rise of Henry VIII*, (W&N, UK ed., Jan. 2012)

Hutton, Ronald, *The Witch: A History of Fear`, from Ancient Times to the Present*, (Yale University Press, 2017)

Ikram, Muhammad Q., Sajjad, Fazle H. & Salardini. Arash, (2016). 'The Head that Wears the Crown: Henry VIII and traumatic Brain Injury', *Jnl. Clinical Neuroscience*, Vol 16 pp. 16-19

Ishikawa, Naoko, *The English Clown: Prints in performance and performance in print*, (The Shakespeare Institute, Department of English, The University of Birmingham, January 2011)

Ives, E.W., (1972). 'Faction at the court of Henry VIII: the Fall of Anne Boleyn', *History*, LVII (No.190): 169

Ives, Eric, *The Life and Death of Anne Boleyn*, (Oxford, Wiley-Blackwell, 2005)

Ives, E. W., 'Henry VIII (1491–1547), king of England and Ireland', *Oxford Dictionary of National Biography,* (Oxford University Press, 3 Sep. 2004), [accessed 27 Oct. 2019]

Iyengar, Sujata, *Disability, Health, and Happiness in the Shakespearean Body (Routledge Studies in Shakespeare)*, (London, Routledge; First edition, 2015)

Jackson, Barry, (2008). 'Barber-Surgeons', *Journal of Medical Biography,*Volume 16, Issue 2, pp. 65-65

Jansen, S.L., *Dangerous talk and strange behavior: women and popular resistance to the reforms of Henry VIII*, (Basingstoke, Palgrave Macmillan, 1996)

James, R,R., (1937). 'The earliest list of surgeons to be licensed by the Bishop of London under the Act of 3 Henry VIII', *Janus*, 41, pp. 255-260

James, Susan. (2019). 'Jane, the Queen's Fool (fl. 1535–1558), court jester', *Oxford Dictionary of National Biography.* [accessed 6 Feb. 2020]

Jordan, W.K., *The Charities of London 1480-1660: The aspirations and the achievements of the urban society*, (Routledge, 2006)

Kenyon, Robert Lloyd, *The Gold Coins of England*, (London, Bernard Quaritch, 1884)

Keynes, M., (2005). 'The Personality and Health of King Henry VIII (1991-1547), A Medical Study', *Journal of Medical Biography*, Volume 13, pp.174-183

Khon, George C., *Encyclopaedia of Plaque and Pestilence from Ancient Times to the Present*, (New York, Infobase Publishing, third edition, 2011), p.228

Kincaid, A.N., ed., *The History of King Richard the Third*, (A. Sutton; New edition, 1979), p. 206

Knect, Robert, *The Valois: Kings of France 1328–1589*, (Hambledon Continuum; New edition, 2007)

Knowles, Elizabeth, *Oxford Dictionary of Quotations*, (Oxford, OUP, eigth edition, 2014)

Knudson, M.Margaret et al, 'Thromboembolism after Trauma: An Analysis of 1602 Episodes from the American College of Surgeons', National Trauma Databank, *Annals of Surgery*, 2004, Vol. 240, Issue 3

Köstlin, Julius, *Life of Luther*, (Nabu Press, 2012)

Kramer, Heinrich., *Malleus Maleficarum*, trans. by M. Summers, (Arrow Books, 1971)

Kybett, Susan Maclean, (1989). 'Henry VIII – A Malnourished King?', *History Today*, Volume 39

Lacroix, Paul, *Louis XII et Anne de Bretagne, Louis XII and Anne of Brittany. Chronicle of the history of France*, edited by Georges Hurtrel, (Paris, 1882)

Lamb, Angela L., Evans, Jane E., Buckley, Richard and Appleby, Jo., (2014). 'Multi-isotope analysis demonstrates significant lifestyle changes in King Richard III', *Journal of Archaeological Science*, Volume 50, pp. 559-565

Loades, David., ed., *The Papers of George Wyatt Esquire of Boxley Abbey in the county of Kent*, Camden Fourth Series, Volume 5, (London, Royal Historical Society, 1968)

Logan, Brian., 'Disability Is Deep in Comedy's DNA': Heritage Entertainment Develops Historical Accuracy at Hampton Court This Week, as Learning-disabled Actors Are to Play Tudor Court Jesters', *The Guardian*, 2011

Longmore, Paul K., *The New Disability History: American Perspectives (The History of Disability),* (New York, New York University Press, 2000)

Louda, Jiri., and MacLagan, Michael, *Lines of Succession: Heraldry of the Royal Families of Europe*, (London, Little, Brown and Company, 2nd edition, 1999), table 67.

Lippincott, H.F., (1975). 'King Lear and the Fools of Robert Armin', *Shakespeare Quarterly*, Vol. 26, No 3, p.243-253

Lipscomb, Suzannah, *1536: The Year That Changed Henry VIII*, (Lion Hudson, 2009)

Lipscomb, Suzannah, (August 2011). 'All The King's Fools', *History Today*, Volume 61, Issue 8

Lipscomb, Suzannah., *Hidden Killers of the Tudor Home* (2015 television series)

Lipscomb, Suzannah, 'Natural Fools at Henry VIII's Court', unpublished article, (2017)

Lipscomb, Suzannah, 'Playing The Fool', History Learning Talk, Hampton Court Palace, 23 May 2017

Lipscomb, Suzannah, (2017). 'The King's Fools - Disability in the Tudor Court', *Historic England*, https://historicengland.org.uk/research/inclusive-heritage/disability-history/1485-1660/disability-in-the-tudor-court/

Lipscomb, Suzannah, *'The King is Dead' The Last Will and Testament of Henry VIII*, (Head of Zeus, 2015)

Lipscomb, Suzannah, (2009). 'Who was Henry VIII?', *History Today*, Volume 59, pp.14–20

Lipscomb, Suzannah, *Witchcraft*, (Ladybird books, 2018)

Lisle, Leanda de., *The Sisters who would be Queen, The tragedy of Mary, Katherine and Lady Jane Grey*, (Harperpress, 2009)

Madden, Frederick, ed., *Privy Purse Expenses of the Princess Mary*, (London, 1831)

Madden, Frederick, ed., *Privy Purse Expenses of the Princess Mary*, (London, William Pickering, 1914)

Mackay, Lauren, *Inside the Tudor Court – Henry VIII and his Six Wives through the writings of the Spanish Ambassador, Eustace Chapuys*, (Stroud, Amberley, 2014)

MacLennan, Sir Hector, (1967). 'A Gynaecologist Looks at the Tudors', *Med Hist.*, Vol 11, pp.66-74

MacNalty, A.S., *Henry VIII: A Difficult Patient*, (London, Christopher Johnson, 1952)

MacNalty A.S., (1946). 'Sir Thomas More as a public health reformer', *Nature*, Volume 158, pp.732–5

Maltby, William, *The Reign of Charles V*, (European History in Perspective, 2002)

Mann, Jill, (1975). 'The Speculum Stultorum and the Nun's Priest's Tale', *The Chaucher Review*, Vol.9, No.3, p. 262-282

Marck, Robert de La,, Seigneur de Fleuranges, *Mémoires du Maréchal de Florange, dit le Jeune Adventureaux*, Volume 2, p. 148

Marshall, Peter, *1517: Martin Luther and the Invention of the Reformation*, (OUP Oxford; Illustrated edition, 2017)

Marshall, Peter, *Heretics and Believers: A History of the English Reformation*, (Yale University Press; Illustrated edition, reprint, 2018)

Marshall, Peter, *The Reformation: A Very Short Introduction* (OUP Oxford; Illustrated edition, 2009)

Marchant, Danielle, (2015). 'The Madness of Jane Boleyn', https://queenanneboleyn.com/2015/02/13/qab-guest-writer-the-madness-of-jane-boleyn-by-danielle-marchant/

Matarasso, Pauline, *Queen's Mate: Three women of power in France on the eve of the Renaissance*, (London, Routledge, First edition, 2001)

Mau, R., 'Dr. Martin Luther: Views on Disability', trans. by K. Ziebell, *The Caring Congregation*, 1983, Volume 4, Issue 3

Maundler, Peter, (1987). 'The Making of the New Poor Law Redivivus', *Past and Present*, 117

Maxwell-Stuart, P.G., *Malleus Maleficarum*, (Manchester University Press, 31 March, 2007)

McCabe, Richard A., (1981). 'Elizabethan Satire and the Bishops' Ban of 1599', *The Yearbook of English Studies*, Vol. 11, Literature and Its Audience, II Special Number, p.188-193

MacDonald, Michael, *Mystical Bedlam: Madness, Anxiety and Healing in Seventeenth-Century England (Cambridge Studies in the History of Medicine)*, (Cambridge, Cambridge University Press, 2009)

McIntosh, Marjorie Keniston, *Poor Relief in England, 1350–1600*, (Cambridge, Cambridge University Press, 2011)

Mead, Rebecca, (2008). 'The cross-eyed queen: dear diary dept', *The New Yorker*, Vol.84, Iss.23 (Proquest, August 4, 2008)

Menin, Nicolas, *An historical and chronological treatise of the anointing and coronation of the Kings and Queens of France ... To which is added an exact relation of the ceremony of the coronation of Louis XV. ... Faithfully done from the original French*, (London, 1727)

Merenda, P.F., (1987). 'Toward a Four-Factor Theory of Temperament and/or Personality', *Journal of Personality Assessment*, 51, pp.367–374

Metzler, Dr. Irina, *Fools and Idiots?: Intellectual disability in the Middle Ages (Disability History)*, (Manchester University Press, First edition, 2016)

Metzler, Dr. Irina, *Disability in Medieval Europe: Thinking about Physical Impairment in the High Middle Ages, c.1100–c.1400*, (Routledge, First edition, 2005)

Metzler, Dr. Irina, 'Medieval Culture', *Disability, Witches and the Middle Ages: Some Mythbusting*, (irinametzler.org, 2013)

Metzler, Dr. Irina, 'Medieval Culture', *Juristification and Medieval "Idiocy"*, (irinametzler.org, 2016), https://irinametzler.org/2016/06/23/juristification-and-medieval-idiocy/. [accessed 21 October 2018]

Midelfort, H.C.E., *A History of Madness in Sixteenth-Century Germany*, (Stanford UP, 1999)

Miles, M., 'Disability in an Eastern Religious Context: Historical Perspectives', (National Library of Medicine, Disability and Society, 1995, Vol 10, Issue 1, pp. 49-70

Miles, M., (2001). 'Martin Luther and Childhood Disability in 16th Century Germany: What did he write? What did he say?', *Journal of Religion, Disability and Health*, The Haworth Press, Inc., Binghampton, NY 13904-1580, Volume 5, Issue 4, pp. 5-36

Miller, C.H., Bradner, L., Lynch, C. A., and Oliver, R. P., eds., *Epigram 19, in volume 3.2, Latin Poems, of The Complete Works of St. Thomas More*, (Yale University Press, 1984)

More, Cresacre, *The Life of Sir Thomas More*, (London, W Pickering, 1828)

More, Thomas, *The confutation of Tyndale's answer, The Confutation of Tyndale's Answer, Books 5 – 9*, Made by Sir Thomas More, Knight Lord Chancellor of England, Page and line numbers correspond to The Complete Works of St. Thomas More (Yale University Press), volume 8.2. (Spelling standardized, punctuation modernized by Mary Gottschalk), (CTMS, 2013)

Mount, Toni, *Medieval Medicine: Its Mysteries and Science*, (Stroud, Amberley Publishing; Illustrated edition, 2016)

Mount, Toni, *The Medieval Housewife & Other Women of the Middle Ages*, (Stroud, Amberley Publishing, 2014)

Muir, Edward, *Ritual in Early Modern Europe*, (Cambridge, Cambridge University Press, 1997)

Multiple Contributors, *A Pleasant History of the Life and Death of Will Summers: How he Came First to be Known at Court, and by What Means he got to be King Henry the Eighth's Jester*, (Gale ECCO, Print Editions, 20 April 2018)

Mulryne, J.R., 'Somer, William (d.1559), court fool', *Oxford Dictionary of National Biography*, http://www.oxforddnb.com/view/article26029 [accessed 16 October 2019]

Murray, I. G., 'Clowes, William (1543/4–1604), surgeon', *Oxford Dictionary of National Biography*, [accessed 16 September 2019]

Nash, et al., *Archaeologia or Miscellaneous Tracts relating to Antiquity*, Vol. IX 9, (Society of Antiquaries of London, London, printed by J Nichols, 1789)

Nielsen, Kim E., *A Disability History of the United States (Revisioning American History Book 2)*, (Beacon Press, 2013)

Nolan, Michael, *A treatise of the Laws for the Relief and Settlement of the Poor*, (New York, Garland, 1805, reprint 1978)

Norman, P., ed., *Decrees of the Ecumenical Councils*, Volume 1, (London, Sheed & Ward and Washington DC, Georgetown University Press, 1990)

Nutton, Vivian, (2004). 'Caius, John (1510–1573), scholar and physician', *Oxford Dictionary of National Biography*, [accessed 31 Oct. 2019]

Nutton, Vivian, (2004). 'Linacre, Thomas (c. 1460–1524), humanist scholar and physician', *Oxford Dictionary of National Biography*, [accessed 4 Nov. 2019]

O'Brien, Gerald, *Framing the Moron: The Social Construction of feeble-mindedness in the American eugenic era (Disability History)*, Manchester University Press, 2013)

O'Brien, Zoie, 'Is this why you lost PIP? Disability activists claim DWP assessments ignore mobility rule', *Express Newspaper*, (Sunday, 26 February 2017)

Page, William, 'Hospitals: St John the Baptist, Redcliffe,' *A History of the County of Somerset: Volume 2*, (London: Victoria County

History, 1911), pp. 160-161. British History Online [accessed October 26, 2019]

Parker, K.T., *The Drawings of Hans Holbein in the Collection of H.M. the King at Windsor Castle*, (Phaidon Press, 1945)

Paster, Gail Kern, *The Body Embarrassed: Drama and the Disciplines of Shame in early Modern drama*, (Ithaca, N.Y., Cornell University Press, 1993)

Patterson, Annabel, *Reading Holinshed's "Chronicles"*, (Chicago, University of Chicago Press, 1994)

Pelling, Margaret, and Webster, Charles 'Medical Practitioners', in C. Webster, ed., *Health, Medicine, and Mortality in the Sixteenth Century,* Cambridge Monographs on the History of Medicine, (1979)

Percy, George, and Wingfield, *The Founding of Jamestown: Percy's Discourse of Virginia, Wingfield's Discourse of Virginia, 1607 1619*, (1907, reprint 2010)

Porter, Linda, *Mary Tudor: The First Queen*, (London, Piatkus Books, 2009)

Porter, Roy, *A Social History of Madness, Stories Of The Insane (Phoenix Giants)*, (W&N, second revised edition, 2 Jan. 1996)

Porter, Roy, *The Greatest Benefit to Mankind: A Medical History of Humanity*, (Fontana Press, 1997)

Poynter, F.N.L., 'The Influence of government legislation on Medical Practice in Britain', in *The Evolution of Medical Practice in Britain*, edited by F.N.L Poynter (London, Pitman Medical, 1961)

Prandoni, Dr Paolo., Susan R. Kahn., (2009). 'Post-thrombotic Syndrome: Prevalence Prognostication and Need for Progress', *British Journal of Haematology,* Vol 145, Issue 3, pp. 269-438

Psillos, Stathis and Curd, Martin, *The Routledge companion to philosophy of science*, (London, Routledge, 2010)

P, T. W., (1827). 'Buffoons' and 'my lord mayor's fool.', *The Mirror of literature, amusement, and instruction,* Nov.1822-June 1847, Volume 9, No.250 pp. 266-7. [Proquest accessed 16 Sep. 2019]

Peltier, Lennard, F., *The Origins of Orthopedics*, (Norman Pub, 1993)

Rawcliffe, Carole, *Tudor Health Reform. The Form and Function of Medieval Hospitals*, (2011)

Rawcliffe, Carole, *Leprosy in Medieval England*, (London, Boydell Press, 2009)

Rembis, Michael, *The Oxford Handbook of Disability History*, Oxford Handbooks, (OUP.COM, 2018)

Richardson, Douglas, *Magna Carta Ancestry: A Study in Colonial and Medieval Families, ed. Kimball G. Everingham, Volume IV*, (second ed., 2011)

Roberts, Phil., *The Mary Rose in a Nutshell*, (Lucar, MadeGlobal Publishing, 2016)

Rolleston, J.D., (1934). 'Venereal Disease in Literature', *British Journal of Venereal Diseases*, vol 10, p.147

Rose, Elliot, *Cases of Conscience: Alternatives open to Recusants and Puritans under Elizabeth I and James I*, (New York, Cambridge University Press, 1975)

Rous, John, *Historia Regum Angliae*, translated in Hanham, *Richard III and his Early Historians 1483-1535* (1975), pp. 120-121

Row-Heyveld, Lindsey, (2009). 'The Lying'st Knave in Christendom: The Development of Disability in the False Miracle of St Alban's', *Disability Studies Quarterly*, Volume 29

Rowlands, J., 'A Portrait Drawing by Hans Holbein the Younger', *British Museum Yearbook*, (London, British Museum, 1997)

Rowlands, John, (1979). 'Review of Holbein and the Court of Henty VIII', *Master Drawings*, XVII XVII (No.1): pp.53-56

Rowlands, John and Starkey, David, (1983). 'An Old Tradition Reasserted: Holbein's Portrait of Queen Anne Boleyn', *The Burlington Magazine*, vol. 125 (no. 959): pp.88-92

Russell, Gareth, *Young, Damned and Fair. The Life and Tragedy of Catherine Howard at the Court of Henry VIII*, (William Collins, 11 Jan. 2018)

Samman, N., 'The Henrician Court during Wolsey's ascendancy C.1514-1529', unpublished PhD thesis, (University of Wales, 1988)

Sander, L., *Hysteria Beyond Freud*, (University of California Press, 1993)

Sander, Nicholas, *Rise and Growth of the Anglican Schism*, (Burns and Oates, 1887)

Sander, Nicholas, *Rise and Growth of the Anglican Schism (De Origine ac Progressu Schismatis Anglicani, Rome, 1585)*, ed. and trans. David Lewis, (London, 1877)

Screti, Zoe, 'A Motley to the View': The Clothing of Court Fools in Tudor England', *Midlands Historical Review*, Vol. 2 (2018), ISSN 2516-8568.

Sergeant, P.W., *The Life of Anne Boleyn*, (Kessinger Publishing Co, 1923, Illustrated edition, 2005)

Schauer, Margery S., and Schauer, Frederick, (1980). 'Law as the Engine of State: The Trial of Anne Boleyn', *William & Mary Law Review*, Volume 22:49 Issue 1. Article 3

Schirmer, Walter Franz and Lydgate John, *A Study in the Culture of the XVth Century*, (Great Britain, Meuthuen and Co. Ltd., 1961)

Schweik, Susan M., *The Ugly Laws, (The History of Disability)*, (NYU Press, 2010)

Sexton, John P., *The Ashgate Research Companion to Medieval Studies*, (Taylor & Francis Group, 2018)

Shrewbury, J.F.D., (1952) 'Henry VIII: A Medical Study', *Journal of the History of Medicine and Allied Sciences*, Volume 7

Simkin, John., *Poverty in Tudor England*, (Spartacus Educational Publishers Ltd. 1997-2016)

Slack, Paul, *Poverty and Policy in Tudor and Stuart England: A Synthesis of work on the period up to 1712*, (London, Longman, 1988)

Slack, Paul, *The English Poor Law 1531-1782*, (Exeter College, Oxford, Macmillan Education, 1990)

Slack, Paul, *The English Poor Law 1531–1782*, (Cambridge University Press, 1990)

Soberton, Sylvia Barbara, *Golden Age Ladies: Women Who Shaped the Courts of Henry VIII and Francis I*, (CreateSpace Independent Publishing Platform, 4 May 2016)

Southworth, John, *Fools and Jesters at the English Court*, (Sutton, 1998)

Spicker, Paul, *The Origins of Modern Welfare: Juan Luis Vives, De Subventione Pauperum, and City of Ypres*, (Peter Lang AG, Internationaler Verlag der Wissenschaften (1608), 2010)

Starkey, David, (1998).'The inventory of King Henry VIII', transcript edited by., transcribed by Philip Ward, assistant editor., and indexed by Alasdair Hawkyard, *Society of Antiquaries* MS 129 and British Library MS Harley 1419. [Vol. I], (London, Harvey Miller Publishers for the Society of Antiquaries of London)

Starkey David, and Doran, Susan, eds., *Henry VIII: Man and Monarch*, (London, British Library Publishing, 2009)

Starkey, David, 'A Monarchy of Misfits?', Wimborne Literary Festival, The Allendale Centre, Sat 18th May, 2019, 7:30pm, Wimborne Minster, Dorset.

Starkey, David, 'Henry VIII used his very own 'stairthrone' when the steps became too much', *Mail Online*, (Daily Mail, News Article, 1138522, 7 February 2009)

Statues of the Realm, 3, 31-32, (London, Printed by the Command of George III, 1817)

Stearns, Helen, (1937). 'The Date of Skelton's Bowge of Court', *Modern Language Notes*, Vol. 52, No.8, p.572-574

Stopes, C., (1905). 'Jane, the Queen's Fool', *The Athenaeum*, 4059, pp. 200-220

Stopes, C., *Shakespeare's Eenvironment*, (London, G. Bell, 1914)

Striker, Henri-Jacques, *A History of Disability*, translated by William Sayers. (University of Michigan Press, 1999)

Strickland, Agnes, *Lives of the Queen's of England from the Norman Conquest*, 6 Vols, (London, Bell and Daldy, 1866)

Skultans, Vieda., *English Madness: Ideas on Insanity, 1580-1890*, (Routledge & Kegan Paul Books; First edition, 6 Dec. 1979), p.20

Swain, Barbara, *Fools and Folly during the Middle Ages and the Renaissance*, (Folcroft Library Editions, 1976)

Tallis, Nicola, *Crown of Blood: The Deadly Inheritance of Lady Jane Grey*, (London, Michael O'Mara, 2016)

Thomas, Keith, *Religion and the Decline of Magic: Studies in Popular Beliefs in Sixteenth and Seventeenth-Century England*, (London, Penguin, New edition, 30 January 2003)

Thompson, C,J,S., 'King Henry as an apothecary', Chapter XIV, in *The Mystery and Art of the Apothecary*, (London: John Lane, The Bodley Head, 1929)

Thornley, I.D., 'The Act of Treasons, 1352', *The Journal of the Historical Association*, Volume 6, 1921-1922

Thurley, Simon, *Houses of Power, The Places that Shaped the Tudor World*, (London, Bantam Press, 2017)

Tierney, Brian, *Medieval Poor-Law: A Sketch of Canonical Theory and its Application in England*, (Berkeley, University of California Press, 1959)

Turner, David M., *Social History of Disabilities and Deformity: Bodies, Images and Experiences*, Routledge Studies in the Social History of Medicine Book, (London, Routledge, First edition, 2006)

Turner, William Henry, *Calendar of charters and rolls preserved in the Bodleian Library*, (Oxford, Clarendon Press, 1878)

Tittler, Robert and Jones, Norman, *A Companion to Tudor Britain*, (Oxford, Wiley-Blackwell, an imprint of John Wiley & Sons Ltd, 2009)

Tyson, Donal., *The Demonology of King James I: Includes the Original Text of Daemonologie and News from Scotland*, (Llewellyn Publications, annotated edition, 8 April 2011)

Watt, Diane, (2004). 'Barton, Elizabeth [called the Holy Maid of Kent, the Nun of Kent] (c. 1506–1534), Benedictine nun and visionary', *Oxford Dictionary of National Biography*, [accessed 28 Oct. 2019]

Watt, D., (2015). 'Mary, the Physician: Women Religion and Medicine in the Middle Ages', *Medicine, Religion and Gender in Medieval Culture*, (University of Surrey, D S Brewer), pp.27-44

Wardroper, John, *Jest upon Jest: A Selection from the Jestbooks and Collections of Merry Tales published from the of Richard III to George III*, (London:Routledge & Kegan Paul, 1970)

Warkany, J., *History of Teratology*, (John Wiley and Sons, 1975)

Weir, Alison, *Henry VIII, King and Court*, (Vintage, 2008)

Weir. Alison, *The Six Wives of Henry VIII*, (Vintage, 1991)

Wellcome Trust History, 'Engaging Lives', *Historic Royal Palaces and the Medical Humanities*, 50 (Summer, 2012)

Wellman, Kathleen, *Queens and Mistress of Renaissance France*, (Yale University Press, June 2013)

Welsford, Enid, *The Fool: His Social and Literary History*, (London, Faber and Faber, 1935)

Welsford, Enid., *The Fool: His Social and Literary History*, (Faber & Faber; First paperback edition, 1968)

Wendell, S., (1989). 'Toward a Feminist Theory of Disability', in Bequart Holmes, H and Purdy, L.M., eds., *Feminist Perspectives in Medical Ethics*, (Bloomington and Indianapolis, Indian University Press)

Westfall, Suzanne, (2001). 'The boy who would be king: court revels of King Edward VI, 1547-1553', *Comparative Drama*, vol. 35, no. 3, p. 271+. [accessed 13 Nov. 2019]

Whitelock, Anna, 'Playing the Fool', *BBC History Magazine*, (2011)

Wiles, David, *Shakespeare's Clown: Actor and Text in the Elizabethan Playhouse*, (Cambridge, Cambridge University Press, 1987)

Williams, P., *Life in Tudor England*, (London, BT Batsford, 1964)

Wilson, J.R., (2017). 'The Trouble with Disability in Shakespeare Studies', *Disability Studies Quarterly*, Volume 37, No 2

Woodward, G.W.O., *The Dissolution of the Monasteries*, (Pitkin Publishing reprinted edition 1 Aug. 1985)

Wriothesley, Charles., *A chronicle of England during the reigns of the Tudors, from A.D. 1485 to 1559*, Issue 20, (London, Camden Society, 1875)

Wyatt, George, *The Life of Anne Boleigne*, edited by D. M. Loades. (London, Royal Historical Society, 1968)

Wyatt, George, *Extracts from the Life of the Virtuous, Christian and Renowned Queen Anne Boleigne*, published privately, 1817, and publicly as an appendix to vol. 2 of S. W. Singer's edition of George Cavendish's *The Life of Cardinal Wolsey*, (London, 1825)

Young, S., *The Annals of the Barber-Surgeons of London*, (London, Blades, East and Blades, 1890)

Zall, P.M., ed., *A Hundred Merry Tales and Other English Jestbooks of the Fifteenth and Sixteenth Centuries*, (Lincoln, University of Nebraska Press, 1963), p.156

Zeydel, Edwin Hermann., ed., *The Ship of Fools*, (New York, Columbia University Press, 1962)

Website Sources

AMPC: Amplified Bible, Classic Edition, https://www.bible.com/bible/8/1CO.1.25.AMPC

BBC, 'Princess Eugenie to have spine op.'. (BBC News, Health, 4 October 2002). http://news.bbc.co.uk/1/hi/health/2298741.stm [retrieved 28 Oct 2019]

BBC History Magazine, Playing the Fool, www.annawhitelock.co.uk/jesters [retrieved 11 Nov 2019]

Bernard GINESTE [ed], "Pierre Bontemps: Claude de France (marble orante, circa 1550)," in Corpus Étampois, http://www.corpusetampois.com/cae-16-bontemps-claude.html, May 2003 [accessed 18/02/2021]

Bernard GINESTE [ed], "Quicherat: Claude de France (engraving after a contemporary portrait, 1875)", in Corpus Étampois, http://www.corpusetampois.com/cae-19-quicherat-claude.html, May 2003. [accessed 18/02/2021]

Bernard GINESTE [ed], "Brantôme: Vie de Claude de France,"in Corpus Étampois, http://www.corpusetampois.com/che-16-brantome-claudedefrance1.html, May 2003 [accessed 18/02/2021]

Borman, Tracy., James I and Witchcraft, (TudorTimes.co.uk: January 2015) [accessed 15/09/2019]

British History Online. http://www.british-history.ac.uk/letters-papers-hen8/vol1/pp55-71

British History Online. http://www.british-history.ac.uk/letters-papers-hen8/vol3/pp136-148

British History Online. http://www.british-history.ac.uk/letters-papers-hen8/vol12/no2/pp335-345

Davies, 2012, Benefit cheats: David Turner on 'history of distrust of disability. https://www.bbc.com/news/uk-wales-17067379

https://digitalarchive.parliament.uk/PIC/S/284

'Elizabethan Era Colours and Meanings', http://www.elizabethanenglandlife.com/elizabethan-era-colors-and-meanings.html, [accessed 21 February 2020]

Equality Act 2010 c. 15, Part 2, Chapter 1, Section 6. (www.legislation.gov.uk) [accessed 13/06/2019]

http://www.documentacatholicaomnia.eu/03d/1466-1536,_Erasmus_Roterodamus,_In_Praise_Of_Folly,_EN.pdf

Ekstrand, D, W., The Four Human Temperaments, The Transformed Soul, Additional Studies, http://www.thetransformedsoul.com/additional-studies/miscellaneous-studies/the-four-human-temperaments, (2012) {accessed 18/02/2021]

Gairdner, James., ed., *Letters and Papers, Foreign and Domestic, Henry VIII, Volume 6, 1533*, Henry VIII: November 1533, 11-20 British History Online (London, 1882), pp. 562-578. http://www.british-history.ac.uk/letters-papers-hen8/vol6/pp562-578 [accessed 28 October 2019]

Art Historian/Author/Adviser specialising in connoisseurship, documentary & scientific research for rediscovery & restitution of masterpieces by the great masters of art history for 5 Decades https://graemecameron.wixsite.com/graeme [accessed 01/01/2021]

Heywood, John., The Play of the Weather, Printed by WILLIAM RASTELL, (4 September 2010). The Play of the Weather Script, Staging the Henrician Court, bringing early modern drama to life, http://stagingthehenriciancourt.brookes.ac.uk/resources/play_of_the_weather_script.html

House of Lords Journal Volume 1: 20 March 1563." Journal of the House of Lords: Volume 1, 1509-1577. London: His Majesty's

Stationery Office, 1767-1830. 605-606. British History Online. Web. 15 September 2019). http://www.british-history.ac.uk/lords-jrnl/vol1/pp605-606

Independent assessment services delivered by ATOS, www.mypipassessment.co.uk/what-we-do/, 2018. [accessed 8 August 2018]

Lipscomb, Suzannah., *Suzannah Lipscomb on The Tudors,* Audio (HistoryHit.TV, 2019), https://tv.historyhit.com/watch/24028617

Mental Illness in the 16th and 17th Centuries, Historic-England.org.uk (2016)

Metzler, Dr. Irina., Medieval Culture, Juristification and Medieval "Idiocy", (irinametzler.org. 2016), https://irinametzler.org/2016/06/23/ juristification-and-medieval-idiocy/. [accessed 21 October 2018]

Richard III Society website (2017), http://www.richardiii.net/ index.php. [accessed 21 October 2018]

Roger, Euan., Living with leprosy in late medieval England, blog. nationalarchives.gov.uk, Thursday 5 December 2019.

Royal National Orthopaedic Hospital, Princess Eugenie's story, https://www.rnohcharity.org/the-appeal/princess-eugenie-s-story [accessed 28 Oct 2019]

Shakespeare, William., King Lear. Act 1, Scene 4. From Amanda Mabillard. http://www.shakespeare-online.com/ [accessed 26 Oct 2019]

Shakespeare, William., Speech: "Now is the winter of our discontent" *Poetry Foundation* (Chigaco, 2019), https://www.poetryfoundation.org/poems/56973/speech-now-is-the-winter-of-our-discontent

Endnotes

Introduction

1. Definition 1: "disable, *v.*", in *Oxford English Dictionary*, second ed. (Oxford, Oxford University Press, 1989), OED Online.
2. Definition 2: "disability, *n.*", in *Oxford English Dictionary*, second ed. (Oxford, Oxford University Press, 1989), OED Online.
3. Definition 3: "disabled, *adj.* and *n.*," in *Oxford English Dictionary*, second ed. (Oxford, Oxford University Press, 1989), OED Online. These data points come from research by J. Wilson using *Early English Books Online* (eebo.chadwyck.com). When you keyword search for 'deformity', 'disability', 'deformed', and 'disabled' with the date limited to 1564–1616, *EEBO* automatically searches for variant spellings, e.g. defourmed or deformyd, etc.
4. Wilson, J.R., (2017). 'The Trouble with Disability in Shakespeare Studies', *Disability Studies Quarterly*, Volume 37, No 2
5. (Equality Act 2010 c. 15, Part 2, Chapter 1, Section 6. (www. legislation.gov.uk) [accessed 13 June 2019]
6. A 'fool' was considered deficient in judgement or sense, one who acts or behaves stupidly, a silly person, a simpleton. (In Biblical times the use applied to vicious or impious persons.) In Modern English, the word has a much stronger sense than it had at an earlier period as it now implies insulting with contempt which does not, in the same degree, belong to any of its synonyms, or the derivative 'foolish'. Cf. French sot.
7. Maltby, William, *The Reign of Charles V* (European History in Perspective, 2002)
8. Buckley, Richard, et al., (2013). 'The king in the car park: new light on the death and burial of Richard III in the Grey Friars church, Leicester in 1485', *Antiquity*, vol. 87, no. 336, (Cambridge University Press) pp.253-259

9. Henry VIII: July 1519, 16-29. *Letters and Papers, Foreign and Domestic, Henry VIII, Volume 3, 1519-1523*, Ed. J S Brewer. (London: HMSO, 1867) pp.136-148. British History Online [accessed 4 September 2019]

10. Giustinian, Sebastian, *Four years at the Court of Henry VIII: Selection of Despatches written by the Venetian Ambassador Sebastian Giustinian*, trans. Rawdon Brown, 2 vols, (London, Smith, Elder & Co., 1854) p.312. Hall, *Chronicle*, f.2v; CSP, Ven, iii, 918, 1287. "Venice: October 1519." *Calendar of State Papers Relating To English Affairs in the Archives of Venice,* Volume 2, 1509-1519. Ed. Rawdon Brown. (London: HMSO, 1867) pp.556-565. British History Online [accessed 4 September 2019]

11. Lipscomb, Suzannah, *1536: The Year That Changed Henry VIII*, (Lion Hudson, 2009) p.29

12. Hans Holbein, Cartoon Showing Henry VIII, 1537 (ink wash on paper sheets mounted on canvas), 257.8 x 137.1cm, National Portrait Gallery, London.

13. See figure 1 in the images section of this book of The Walker – Henry VIII, artist unknown, painted between 1537 and 1562? (oil on six oak panels, 238.2 x 134.2 cm), The Board of Trustees of NMGM, The Walker, Liverpool, no.1033

14. Bolland, Charlotte and Cooper, Tarnya, *The Real Tudors: Kings and Queens Rediscovered*, (London, National Portrait Gallery, 2014) p.26

15. Ibid pp.50, 52, 53, 55

16. The Family of Henry VIII c. 1545, Oil on canvas, 144.5 x 355.9 cm (support, canvas/panel/strexternal) British School, 16th century, RCIN 405796.

17. Striker, Henri-Jacques, *A History of Disability*, translated by William Sayers. (University of Michigan Press, 1999) p.67

18. Hanawalt, Barbara, A., *The Ties that Bound: Peasant Families in Medieval England*, (Oxford, Oxford University Press, 1986)

19. We have evidence of Will being able to change Henry VIII's mind. Erasmus mentions foolishness: the freedom to speak the truth. *In the Praise of Folly*, Erasmus suggests that people cannot speak the truth, and also serve demons. Erasmus, Desiderius, *In Praise of Folly*, (Grand Rapids, MI: Christian Classics Ethereal Library: University of Michigan Press, 1958),p.21. Online copy

created 9 July 2000. http://www.documentacatholicaomnia. eu/03d/1466-1536,_Erasmus_Roterodamus,_In_Praise_Of_ Folly,_EN.pdf

20. Ibid.

21. Armin, Robert, *Fools and Jesters: With a reprint of Robert Armin's Nest of Ninnies, 1608*, (Adamant Media Corporation, 13 May 2004)

22. "Henry VIII: October 1537, 21-25." *Letters and Papers, Foreign and Domestic, Henry VIII*, Volume 12 Part 2, June-December 1537. Ed. James Gairdner. (London: HMSO, 1891) pp.335-345. British History Online [accessed 5 September 2019]

23. The Bible, in 1 Corinthians i.25, appeared to suggest that God spoke through a natural fools' foolishness. The Amplified Bible, Classic addition states in 1 Corinthians 1:25 - [This is] because the foolish thing [that has its source in] God is wiser than men, and the weak thing [that springs] from God is stronger than men.

24. Erasmus, Desiderius. *In Praise of Folly*, (Grand Rapids, MI, Christian Classics Ethereal Library, University of Michigan Press,1958), p.21.Online copy created 9 July 2000. http:// www.documentacatholicaomnia.eu/03d/1466-1536,_Erasmus_ Roterodamus,_In_Praise_Of_Folly,_EN.pdf

25. Figure 6, Lockey, Rowland. 1593 and 1594. Thomas More and Family. Nostell Priory.

26. Woodward, G.W.O. *The Dissolution of the Monasteries*, (Pitkin Publishing, reprinted Edition (1 Aug. 1985), p.24

27. Elton, G.R., *The Tudor Constitution: Documents and Commentary*, (Cambridge University Press, 7 October 1982)

28. Mead, Rebecca, (2008). 'The cross-eyed queen: dear diary dept', *The New Yorker*, Vol.84, Iss.23 (Proquest, August 4, 2008)

Chapter One – Everyday Life in the Community

1. Le Goff, Jacques, *Medieval Civilisation 1400-1500*, trans., J. Burrow, (Oxford, Blackwell, 1988) p.240

2. For discussions on the carnivalesque see: Peter Burke, *Popular Culture in Early Modern Europe*; Edward Muir, *Ritual in Early Modern Europe*.

3. Bonn, Robert, L., *Painting Life: The Art of Pieter Bruegel the Elder*, (Syracuse University Press, 2007)
4. Metzler, Dr Irina., Medieval Culture, Juristification and Medieval "Idiocy", (irinametzler.org. 2016), [accessed 21 October 2018]
5. Ibid.
6. Dewhurst, Kenneth, *Thomas Willis's Oxford Lectures*, (Sandford Publications,1980) p.160
7. Metzler, Dr Irina., Medieval Culture, Juristification and Medieval "Idiocy", (irinametzler.org. 2016), [accessed 21 October 2018]
8. Tittler, Robert and Jones, Norman, *A Companion to Tudor Britain*, (Wiley-Blackwell, an imprint of John Wiley & Sons Ltd, 2009), p.369
9. Metzler, Irina, *Disability in Medieval Europe: Thinking about Physical Impairment in the High Middle Ages, c.1100–c.1400*, (London, 2006)
10. Roberts, Phil., *The Mary Rose in a Nutshell*, (Lucar, MadeGlobal Publishing, 2016)
11. Interview with Phil Roberts, 2017; author of The Mary Rose in a Nutshell.
12. Ibid.
13. Ibid.
14. Ibid.
15. Ibid.
16. Ibid.
17. Roberts, Phil., *The Mary Rose in a Nutshell*, (Lucar, MadeGlobal Publishing, 2016)
18. Percy, George, and Wingfield, *The Founding of Jamestown: Percy's Discourse of Virginia, Wingfield's Discourse of Virginia, 1607 1619*, (1907, reprint 2010)
19. Murray, I. G., 'Clowes, William (1543/4–1604), surgeon', *Oxford Dictionary of National Biography*, [accessed 16 September 2019]
20. Journal no. 2, 1567–86, Archives of St Bartholomew's Hospital [board of governors' minutes]
21. Clowes, William., 'A Prooved Practice for all Young Chirurgiens, 1588', *Bulletin of the Royal College of Surgeons of England*, (2015), pp. 25-27
22. Murray, I. G., 'Clowes, William (1543/4–1604), surgeon', *Oxford Dictionary of National Biography*, [accessed 16 September 2019]

23. Clowes, William., 'A prooved practice for all young chirurgiens, 1588', *Bulletin of the Royal College of Surgeons of England*, Vol. 83 No. 5. (RCS Bulletin, 2001)

24. Atkinson, E. G. ed., *Calendar of the State Papers, Ireland, 1598–9*, (1895), pp. 296-7

25. Green, M. A. Everett., ed., *Calendar of the State Papers, Domestic, 1598–1601*, (1869), p. 13

26. Elizabeth I, c.4; 39 Elizabeth I, c.21; 43 Elizabeth I, c.3; H.M.C Salisbury, iv. 298

27. Slack, Paul, *The English Poor Law 1531–1782*, (Cambridge University Press,1990), p.16

28. Barnes, Colin, *Disabled People in Britain and Discrimination. A Case for Anti-discrimination Legislation*, (University of California: C. Hurst & Co., 1991)

29. Gairdner, James and Brodie, R.H., eds. 'Letters and Papers: April 1539, 1-5', *Letters and Papers, Foreign and Domestic, Henry VIII*, Volume 14 Part 1, January-July 1539. (London, HMSO, 1894). pp. 330-348. British History Online [accessed 16 September 2019]

30. From notes, I had taken when I attended Suzannah Lipscomb's talk, 'Playing The Fool'. History Learning Talk, Hampton Court Palace, 23 May 2017

31. P. T. W., (1827). 'Buffoons' and 'my lord mayor's fool', *The Mirror of literature, amusement, and instruction,* Nov.1822-June 1847, Volume 9, No.250, pp. 266-7. [Proquest accessed 16 Sep. 2019]

32. Hall, Noliene, (1990). 'Henry Patenson: Sir Thomas More's Fool', *Moreana*, XXVII, 101-102, pp.75-86

33. In her [Margaret's] next repair to her father in the Tower, she showed him a letter she had previously received from Alice. And what communication was thereupon between her father and her, ye shall perceive by an answer here following (as written to the lady Alington). But whether this answer were written by Sir Thos. More in his daughter Roper's name, or by herself, it is not certainly known.

34. "Henry VIII: August 1534, 26-31", in *Letters and Papers, Foreign and Domestic, Henry VIII*, Volume 7, 1534, ed. James Gairdner (London: HMSO, 1883), pp.421-433. British History Online [accessed 16 February 2020]

35. 'Familia Thomæ Mori' published by Christian von Mechel, after Hans Holbein the Younger; etching, 1787 (1530), 15 in. x 18 in. (380 mm x 456 mm) plate size. (National Portrait Gallery, London, 2017)—see plate 5 in the illustrations section of this book.

36. Thomas More had an original way of seeing things, and the most compelling proof of Thomas More's wit and warmth is his masterpiece, Utopia. Anyone who dreams of an idealistic world should revere More, because, in this 1516 book, he created the very idea of utopianism, and went so far as to name it as such. His imaginary island somewhere in the Americas was not all it seems, however. Utopia is concurrently a serious discussion of the ideal society, which, according to More, would be what we would recognise today as communism, and a text that mocks itself. More introduces jokes that undercut the book's clear message and the result is a complex intellectual balancing of ideas' stemming from the need to create a better society. See Thomas Stapleton, *The Life and Illustrious Martyrdom of Sir Thomas More*, trans. by Philip E. Hallett (2010)

37. See the print of 'Sir Thomas More and his Family' by Rowland Lockey, after Hans Holbein, the Younger (1593), from Nostell Priory, West Yorkshire, in the images section of the book.

38. *The Life of Sir Thomas More*, sometimes Lord Chancellor of England, edited by Elsie Vaughn Hitchcock, and P.E. Hallet, with A. E. Reed, EETS (1950), p.208; Anderegg, *Life of Sir Thomas More* (1972); Thomas More, 'The Confutation', pp.900-901. For the Bruges context of Patenson's 'Proclamation' see also G. Marc'hadour, 'Thomas More dans l'histoire de Bruges', *Moreana*, XXV, p. 110. Thomas More, *The Life of Sir Thomas More* (1828)

39. Lipscomb, Suzannah, 'Playing The Fool'. History Learning Talk, Hampton Court Palace, 23 May 2017   .

40. Cameron, Kenneth Walter, *The background of John Heywood's "Witty and witless"; a study in early Tudor drama, together with a specialized bibliography of Heywood scholarship*, (Raleigh, N.C., Thistle Press, 1941)

41. More, Thomas, *The Confutation of Tyndale's Answer*, p.900

42. Lipscomb, Suzannah, 'Playing the Fool.' History Learning Talk, Hampton Court Palace, 23 May 2017

43. Ibid.

44. Ibid.

45. Stapleton, T., *The Life and Illustrious Martyrdom of Sir Thomas More, Formerly Lord Chancellor of England*, (Part III of "Tres Thomae," printed at Douai, 1588), translated, for the first time, into English by Philip E. Hallett, (Burns Oates & Washbourne Ltd, 1928) p.90

46. Cited by Bernuth, p. 251: 'sondern ihnen viel mehr alles gutes und liebes bezeigen | sie auffnehmen | Herbergen | Kleiden | Speisen... sie schutzen | beschirmen und verteidigen | auch im Tod nicht verlassen.' Armin, *Foole Vpon Foole, or Six Sortes of Sottes*, (1600)

47. Welsford, Enid, *The Fool: His Social and Literary History*, (1968), p. 204

48. Augsburg 1490, Plate in Hodgart, Matthew., Satire Origins and Principles. p.96

49. Hodgart, Matthew, *Satire Origins and Principles*, p.96-97

50. Classic studies of this sort are Enid Welford's *The Fool: His Social and Literary History*, (London: Faber and Faber, 1935) and David Wiles's *Shakespeare's Clown: Actor and Text in the Elizabethan Playhouse*, (Cambridge: Cambridge University Press, 1987)

51. Ishikawa, Naoko, *The English Clown: Prints in performance and performance in print*, (The Shakespeare Institute, Department of English, The University of Birmingham, January 2011) p.14

52. 'disable, v.', *Oxford English Dictionary*, 2nd ed. (1989)

53. All references to Shakespeare's works are to *The Riverside Shakespeare* (1997)

54. 1609 was at least twenty-four years before the OED's first recorded usage of the adjective 'disabled' in the medical sense. For the seventeenth-century instance of 'the disable', see Philip Vincent, *The Lamentations of Germany*, (1638). In 1638 appeared 'The Lamentations of Germany, wherein, as in a Glasse, we may behold her miserable condition'. This was composed by Dr Vincent, a theologian from London who speaks of his travels in Southern Germany around 1633–5. He was besieged in Heidelberg by the Spaniards and gives a horrible description of the extremities to which the town was reduced, and the excesses of the soldiery engaged in the war. Dr Vincent was censured and warned against practising medicine, 6 September 1639. See Margaret Pelling and Francis White, 'Physicians and Irregular Medical Practitioners

in London 1550–1640', Database (2004): https://www.british-history.ac.uk/no-series/london-physicians/1550-1640.   [accessed 21 October 2018]

55. Ishikawa, Naoko, *The English Clown: Prints in performance and performance in print*, (The Shakespeare Institute, Department of English, The University of Birmingham, January 2011) p.18

56. Ibid. p.23

57. Howleglas is a collection of German roguish jester stories. Three copies of the original book are known to exist, each being of a different impression, and each being more or less imperfect. The copies do not differ in any material respect; the variations being merely in the spelling, and in the correction of misprints. They are all in small quarto and in black letter. Two of the copies are in the British Museum. Ouvry, Frederi., *Howleglas* (Classic Reprint) (Forgotten Books, 8 Feb. 2019)

58. Zall, P.M., ed., *A Hundred Merry Tales and Other English Jestbooks of the Fifteenth and Sixteenth Centuries*, (Lincoln, University of Nebraska Press, 1963), p.156

59. Bright, Timothie, *A Treatise of Melancholy*, (London, imprinted by Thomas Vautrollier [etc.], 1586)

60. Heywood, Thomas, *An Apology for Actors*, (Londo, printed by Nicholas Okes, 1612. Sig. F4.

61. Ishikawa, Naoko, *The English Clown: Prints in performance and performance in print*, (The Shakespeare Institute, Department of English, The University of Birmingham, January 2011) p.58

62. Perkins, William, *A Golden Chain*, (Cambridge, Printed by John Legatt [etc.], 1600), p.1027

63. All quotations from the 1626 *Scoggin's Jests* are from Boorde's edition (published in 1626), Boorde, *Scoggin's Jests*, Tale 41, p.50

64. Goldsmith, Robert Hillis, *Wise Fools in Shakespeare*, (East Lansing, Michigan: Michigan State University Press, 1955), p.7

65. Davis, Lennard J., *Bending over Backwards: Disability, Dismodernism, and Other Difficult Positions*, (2002), pp. 50-52; Davis, Lennard J., *Enforcing Normalcy: Disability, Deafness, and the Body* (Verso, 1995)

66. Ishikawa, Naoko, *The English Clown: Prints in performance and performance in print*, (The Shakespeare Institute, Department of English, The University of Birmingham, January 2011) p.184

67. Ibid. p.205
68. Ibid. p.213
69. These data points come from research by J. Wilson using Early English Books Online (eebo.chadwyck.com). When you keyword search for 'deformity', 'disability', 'deformed', and 'disabled' with the date limited to 1564–1616, EEBO automatically searches for variant spellings, e.g. defourmed or deformyd, etc.
70. For example, in *The Merchant of Venice* Bassanio 'disabled' his estate by living beyond his means. Shakespeare, *The Merchant of Venice*, 1.1123
71. Iyengar, Sujata, *Disability, Health, and Happiness in the Shakespearean Body (Routledge Studies in Shakespeare)*, (London, Routledge; 1st edition, 2015)
72. Warkany, J., *History of Teratology*, (1975), pp. 3-45; Peltier, Lennard F., *The Origins of Orthopedics*, (1993), pp.20-40
73. Row-Heyveld, L., *The Lying'st Knave in Christendom: The Development of Disability in the False Miracle of St Alban's*, (2009)
74. 'stigmatic, adj. and n.', in OED
75. Richard III Society website (2017), http://www.richardiii.net/index.php. [accessed 21 October 2018]
76. Shakespeare, *Richard III*, I.i.18-27. Shakespeare, William, Speech: "Now is the winter of our discontent" Poetry Foundation (Chigaco, 2019), https://www.poetryfoundation.org/poems/56973/speech-now-is-the-winter-of-our-discontent
77. Shakespeare, William; *Richard III*, I.i.18-27.

Chapter Two – Tudor Laws and Disability

1. Hollen Lees, L., *The Solidarity of Strangers, The English Poor Laws and the People, 1700-1948*, (Cambridge, Cambridge University Press, 2006) p.19
2. More, Thomas, *Utopia*, translator, Dominic Baker-Smith, (Penguin Classics 27 Feb. 2020)
3. Hale, Matthew, *A Discourse Touching Provision for the Poor (1683)*, pp.2-3
4. McIntosh, Marjorie Keniston, *Poor Relief in England, 1350–1600*, (Cambridge, Cambridge University Press, 2011) pp.1-36

5. Slack, Paul, *The English Poor Law 1531-1782*, (Exeter College, Oxford, Macmillan Education, 1990) pp.11-12

6. Slack, Paul, *Poverty and Policy in Tudor and Stuart England: A Synthesis of work on the period up to 1712*, (London, Longman, 1988) pp.27-29

7. Slack, Paul, *The English Poor Law 1531-1782*, (Exeter College, Oxford, Macmillan Education, 1990) p.12

8. Tierney, Brian, *Medieval Poor-Law: A Sketch of Canonical Theory and its Application in England*, (Berkeley, University of California Press. 1959)

9. Elton, G.R., (1953-4). 'An Early Tudor Poor Law', *History Review*, 6, pp.55-67

10. Ibid.

11. Jordan, W.K., *Philanthropy in England 1480-1660*, (1959)

12. Ibid.

13. McIntosh, Marjorie Keniston, *Poor Relief in England, 1350–1600*, (Cambridge, Cambridge University Press, 2011) pp.1-36

14. Blaug, Mark, 'The Myth of the Old Poor Law and the Making of the New', *The Journal of Economic History*, 23, no. 2 (1963): 151–84. doi:10.1017/S0022050700103808.

15. Simkin, John, *Poverty in Tudor England*, (Spartacus Educational Publishers Ltd. 1997-2016)

16. Slack, Paul, *The English Poor Law 1531-1782*, (Exeter College, Oxford, Macmillan Education, 1990)

17. Tittler, Robert and Jones, Norman, *A Companion to Tudor Britain*, (Wiley-Blackwell, an imprint of John Wiley & Sons Ltd, 2009)

18. Elton, G.R., (1953-4). 'An Early Tudor Poor Law', *History Review*, 6, pp.55-67

19. The only surviving copy of Cromwell's original Poor Law is a primary source is MS Royal 18 CVI at the British Library and written in a fine, faint pencil mark.

20. Elton, G.R., (1953-4). 'An Early Tudor Poor Law', *History Review*, 6, pp.55-67

21. Hollen Lees, L., *The Solidarity of Strangers, The English Poor Laws and the People, 1700-1948*, (Cambridge, Cambridge University Press, 2006) p.19

22. Slack, Paul, *The English Poor Law 1531-1782*, (Exeter College, Oxford, Macmillan Education, 1990)

23. Blanchard, Ian, (1970). 'Population Change, Enclosure, and the Early Tudor Economy', *Economic History Review*, 23.3

24. Simkin, John, *Poverty in Tudor England*, (Spartacus Educational Publishers Ltd. 1997-2016)

25. Slack, Paul, *The English Poor Law 1531-1782*, (Exeter College, Oxford, Macmillan Education, 1990)

26. Ibid.

27. Barnes, Colin, *Disabled People in Britain and Discrimination. A Case for Anti-discrimination Legislation*, (University of California, C. Hurst & Co., 1991)

28. Ibid.

29. Slack, Paul, *The English Poor Law 1531-1782*, (Exeter College, Oxford, Macmillan Education, 1990)

30. Simkin, John, *Poverty in Tudor England*, (Spartacus Educational Publishers Ltd. 1997-2016)

31. Tittler, Robert and Jones, Norman, *A Companion to Tudor Britain*, (Wiley-Blackwell, an imprint of John Wiley & Sons Ltd, 2009)

32. Ibid.

33. Ibid.

34. Slack, Paul, *The English Poor Law 1531-1782*, (Exeter College, Oxford, Macmillan Education, 1990)

35. Simkin, John, *Poverty in Tudor England*, (Spartacus Educational Publishers Ltd. 1997-2016)

36. Ibid.

37. Slack, Paul, *The English Poor Law 1531-1782*, (Exeter College, Oxford, Macmillan Education, 1990) pp. 9,24, 42, 51-54

38. Ibid.

39. Ibid.

40. Ibid. pp.9, 24, 42, 51-54

41. Ibid. pp.9, 24, 42, 51-54

42. Ibid. pp.9, 10, 12, 15, 19

43. Ibid. pp.9, 10, 12, 15, 19

44. Ibid. pp.4, 7-8, 11, 36, 42

45. Grueninger, Natalie, *Discovering Tudor London: A Journey Back in Time*, (London, The History Press, 2017)

46. Slack, Paul, *The English Poor Law 1531-1782*, (Exeter College, Oxford, Macmillan Education, 1990)

47. Tittler, Robert and Jones, Norman, *A Companion to Tudor Britain*, (Wiley-Blackwell, an imprint of John Wiley & Sons Ltd, 2009)

48. Ibid.

49. Ibid.

50. Reginae Elizabethae Anno 43 Chapter 2; An Acte for the Releife of the Poore, (43 Eliz. I c. 2), Parliamentary Archives: GB-061, 57. 1671 – Lists of documents of the House of Commons, marked "In a bag, Anno 13 Eliz. 1571, 1572; "18 Eliz. 1575" (6 pages).

51. Impotent – in its early English sense referred to people considered unable to look after themselves for reasons of age, infirmity or disability. The 'impotent poor' were distinguished from the 'able bodied' poor in poor law legislation.

52. Slack, Paul, *The English Poor Law 1531-1782*, (Exeter College, Oxford, Macmillan Education, 1990) pp. 35, 37, 40

53. Slack, Paul, *The English Poor Law 1531-1782*, (Exeter College, Oxford, Macmillan Education, 1990)

54. 39 Elizabeth, c 2; see Michael Nolan, *A treatise of the Laws for the Relief and Settlement of the Poor*, (New York, Garland, 1805; reprint 1978), 2:385

55. Slack, Paul, *Poverty and Policy in Tudor and Stuart England*, (London, Longman, 1988), pp.22-7, 130

56. 13 & 14 Charles II, c 12

57. Maundler, Peter, 'The Making of the New Poor Law Redivivus', *Past and Present* 117 (1987) p.133

58. Slack, Paul, *The English Poor Law 1531-1782*, (Exeter College, Oxford, Macmillan Education, 1990) p.48

59. Ibid.

60. The Act can be viewed on the parliamentary digital archives https://digitalarchive.parliament.uk/PIC/S/284; Reginae Elizabethae Anno 43 Chapter 2; An Acte for the Releife of the Poore, 43 Eliz 1 c 2.

61. Spicker, P., (2019). 'British Social Policy 1601-1948', *An introduction to Social Policy*, http://spicker.uk/social-policy/history.htm, obtained on 22 October 2019.

62. Davies, (2012). 'Benefit cheats: David Turner on history of distrust of disability', https://www.bbc.com/news/uk-wales-17067379

63. The system became law in 1597/8, but the Act that consolidated the system dates from 1601.

64. Bagguley, Paul, and Mann, Kirk, (1992). 'Idle, Thieving Bastards: Scholarly Representations of the Underclass', *Work, Employment and Society*, 6 pp.113–26

Chapter Three – Superstition and Disability

1. Goodman, Ruth, *How to Be a Tudor: A Dawn-to-Dusk Guide to Everyday Life*, (London, Viking, 2015)

2. Lipscomb, Suzannah, *Witchcraft: A Ladybird Expert Book*, Series 117, (London, Penguin Random House, 2018), p.8

3. Psillos, Stathis, and Curd, Martin., *The Routledge companion to philosophy of science*, (London, Routledge. 2010), pp.129-38

4. Young, Francis, *Magic as a Political Crime in Medieval and Early Modern England - A History of Sorcery and Treason*, (London, I.B Tauris, 2017)

5. *Journal of the House of Lords:* Volume 1, 1509-1577, (London, HMSO, 1767-1830. pp.605-606.) British History Online. [accessed 15 September 2019]

6. Young, Francis, *Magic as a Political Crime in Medieval and Early Modern England - A History of Sorcery and Treason*, (London: I.B Tauris, 2017)

7. Lipscomb, Suzannah, *Witchcraft: A Ladybird Expert Book*, Series 117, (London, Penguin Random House, 2018), p.8

8. Borman, Tracy, *Witches*, (Vintage, 2 October 2014), p.6

9. Gifford, George, *Discourse of the subtill Practises of Devilles by Witches and Sorcerers*, (London,1587). Sig. B2.

10. Perkins, W., *A Discourse of the Damned Art of Witchcraft; so farre forth as it is revealed in the Scriptures, and manifest by true Experience*, (Cambridge, 1608). Sig. A2v.

11. West, William, *Simboleography*, (1594), cited in Hart, pp.20-1. A juggler was someone who cured diseases with spells or charms.

12. Hutton, Ronald, *The Witch: A History of Fear`, from Ancient Times to the Present*, (Yale University Press, August 2017), definitions, p.ix.

13. Breverton, Terry, *Everything You Ever Wanted to Know About the Tudors But Were Afraid to Ask*, (Stroud, Amberley Publishing, reprint edition 15 Nov. 2015)
14. Barnes, Colin, *Disabled People in Britain and Discrimination. A Case for Anti-discrimination Legislation*, (University of California: C. Hurst & Co., 1991)
15. Bloch, Marc, *The Royal Touch: sacred monarchy and scrofula in England and France*, (London, Routledge & Kegan Paul, 1973), p.54
16. Brogan, Stephen, *The Royal Touch in Early Modern England: Politics, Medicine and Sin*, NED - New edition, (Woodbridge, Boydell and Brewer, 2015), pp. 23–44
17. Bloch, Marc, *The Royal Touch: sacred monarchy and scrofula in England and France*, (London, Routledge & Kegan Paul, 1973), p.73
18. See image in figure section entitled 'Queen Mary I touching the neck of a boy for the King's evil (scrofula)'.
19. Brogan, Stephen, 'The Tudors: Revival and Reform of Royal Therapeutics, 1485–1603', *The Royal Touch in Early Modern England: Politics, Medicine and Sin*, NED - New edition, (Woodbridge, Boydell and Brewer, 2015), pp.45–66
20. Bloch, Marc, *The Royal Touch: sacred monarchy and scrofula in England and France*, (London, Routledge & Kegan Paul, 1973), p.3
21. Kenyon, Robert Lloyd, *The Gold Coins of England*, (London, 1884), p.89
22. Bloch, Marc, *The Royal Touch: sacred monarchy and scrofula in England and France*, (London, Routledge & Kegan Paul, 1973), p.95
23. Metzler, Dr. Irina, 'Medieval Culture', *Disability, Witches and the Middle Ages: Some Mythbusting*, (irinametzler.org, 2013)
24. Ibid.
25. Freeling, George Henry, ed., *Newes from Scotland, declaring the damnable life and death of doctor Fian, a notable sorcerer, who was burned at Edenbrough in Ianuary last, 1591*, (Oxford University, 1816)
26. Tyson, Donald, *The Demonology of King James I: Includes the Original Text of Daemonologie and News from Scotland*, (Llewellyn Publications; annotated edition, 8 April 2011)

27. Ibid.
28. Metzler, Dr. Irina, 'Medieval Culture', *Disability, Witches and the Middle Ages: Some Mythbusting*, (irinametzler.org, 2013)
29. "Henry VIII: January 1536, 26-31", in *Letters and Papers, Foreign and Domestic, Henry VIII*, Volume 10, January-June 1536, ed. James Gairdner, (London, HMSO, 1887), pp.64-81. British History Online. [accessed 6 December 2019]
30. KB 8 - Court of King's Bench: Crown Side: Baga de Secretis - Roll and file of court of the Lord High Steward and peers. Principal defendants and charges: Queen Anne Boleyn, Sir George Boleyn Lord Rocheford, high treason, adultery and incest, 28 Hen VIII. 21 membranes. 1536 Apr 22-1537 Apr 21
31. Schauer, Margery S., and Schauer, Frederick, (1980). 'Law as the Engine of State: The Trial of Anne Boleyn', *William & Mary Law Review*, Volume 22:49 Issue 1. Article 3, p.66
32. Hudson, Geoffrey L., (2006). "History of Disability: Early Modern West", *Encyclopedia of Disability*, ed. Gary L. Albrecht, Vol. 1. (Thousand Oaks, SAGE Publications, Inc.), pp.3-4
33. Ibid.
34. Barnes, Colin, *Disabled People in Britain and Discrimination. A Case for Anti-discrimination Legislation*, (University of California, C. Hurst & Co., 1991)
35. Maxwell-Stuart, P.G., *Malleus Maleficarum*, (Manchester University Press, 31 March 2007)
36. Thomas, (1977). As cited in Colin Barnes, *Disabled People in Britain and Discrimination. A Case for Anti-discrimination Legislation*, (University of California, C. Hurst & Co., 1991), pp.80-1

Chapter Four – Religion, Reformation and Disability

1. Marshall, Peter, *Heretics and Believers: A History of the English Reformation*, (reprint, 2018)
2. Marshall, Peter, *The Reformation: A Very Short Introduction*, (2009)
3. Doran, Susan, and Durston, Christopher, *Princes, Pastors and People. The Church and Religion in England 1529-1689*, (London, Routledge, 1991), p.1

4. Marshall, Peter, *The Reformation: A Very Short Introduction*, (2009)
5. Ibid.
6. Doran, Susan, and Durston, Christopher, *Princes, Pastors and People. The Church and Religion in England 1529-1689*, (London, Routledge, 1991), p.3
7. Marshall, Peter, *Heretics and Believers: A History of the English Reformation*, (reprint, 2018)
8. Cummings, Brian, *The Book of Common Prayer: The Texts of 1549, 1559, and 1662*, (reprint, 2013)
9. Knowles, Elizabeth, *Oxford Dictionary of Quotations*, (2014)
10. Watt, Mary, *The Physician: Women Religion and Medicine in the Middle Ages*, (2015)
11. Barnes, Colin, *Disabled People in Britain and Discrimination. A Case for Anti-discrimination Legislation*, (University of California, C. Hurst & Co., 1991)
12. Abrams, Judith, *Judaism and Disability: Portrayals in Ancient Texts from the Tanach through the Bavli*, (1998)
13. Fritz, Jean-Marc, *Le discours du fou au Moyen Age*, (1992), p. 371; Irina Metzler, *Disability in Medieval Europe: Thinking about Physical Impairment in the High Middle Ages, c.1100–c.1400*, (2005), pp. 53-55
14. Marshall, Peter, *1517: Martin Luther and the Invention of the Reformation*, (2017)
15. Ibid.
16. Hitchcock, Elsie, and P.E Hallet, with A.E. Reed., eds., *The Life of Sir Thomas More, sometimes Lord Chancellor of England*, (EETS, 1950) pp.165-6
17. STC 10898
18. Metzler, Dr Irina, *Disability in Medieval Europe: Thinking about Physical Impairment in the High Middle Ages, c.1100–c.1400*, (2005)
19. Ibid.
20. Coleridge, Peter, *Disability, Liberty, and Development*, (1993), pp.45-46
21. Köstlin, Julius, *Life of Luther*, (1905)
22. Mau, R., 'Dr. Martin Luther: Views on Disability', trans. by K. Ziebell, *The Caring Congregation*, 1983, Volume 4, Issue 3
23. Gritsch, Eric. W., *Martin - God's Court Jester*, (1983), pp. 154-158

24. LW 49: 158
25. Currie, Margaret, *The Letters of Martin Luther, Selected and Translated*, (1908), pp.300, 481
26. LW 49: 158
27. LW 54: 22, ftn. 57
28. Currie, Margaret, *The Letters of Martin Luther, Selected and Translated*, (1908), p.309
29. Kramer, Henrich., *Malleus Maleficarum*, p. 4, 5
30. Ibid. p.197
31. Ibid. p.297
32. Midelfort, H. C. Erik, *A History of Madness in Sixteenth-Century Germany*, (1999), p. 55, ftn 139
33. Metzler, Dr Irina, *Disability in Medieval Europe: Thinking about Physical Impairment in the High Middle Ages, c.1100–c.1400*, (2005) pp. 53-55
34. Midelfort, H. C. Erik, *A History of Madness in Sixteenth-Century Germany*, (1999), p. 71, ftn. 139
35. Fritz, Jean-Marc, *Le discours du fou au Moyen Age*, (1992), p.371
36. On the twelfth-century writer Al-Gawzi who compiled 'Stories about Idiots and Sots', and differentiated idiocy, as a permanent, innate condition, from madness and folly see Dols, 1992; also Zakharia, 1995.
37. Augustine, IV 1, transl. (1872), pp. 32-33
38. Ibid.
39. Swain, Barbara, *Fools and Folly during the Middle Ages and the Renaissance*, (1932), p. 8
40. *In Praise of Folly* was published in 1511 and was very influential with the Tudor court.

Chapter Five – Almshouses and Hospitals

1. Grueninger, Natalie, *Discovering Tudor London. A Journey Back in Time*, (London:,The History Press, 2017)
2. Rawcliffe, Carole, *Tudor Health Reform. The Form and Function of Medieval Hospitals*, (2011)
3. For those of our readers who are also etymologists, I'm using a 2662 page edition of a Webster's International Dictionary as a

reference source—the word 'alms' also has historical roots in the Greek and French languages.

4. Leprosy now known as people with Hansen's disease.

5. Hallett, Anna, *Almshouses*, (2004); Howson, Brian, *Almshouses: A Social and Architectural History*, (2008), p. 5. See figure 6 of an exterior view from the north-east showing the former Maison Dieu alms-house; Bailey, Brian, *Almshouses*, (1988); *Howson, Almshouses: A Social and Architectural History*, (2008)

6. Rawcliffe, Carole, *Tudor Health Reform. The Form and Function of Medieval Hospitals*, (2011)This is because hospital buildings were (and are) not seen as necessary as the medieval castles and monasteries, which have been preserved under the auspices of the National Trust and English Heritage. Picturesque ruins do survive, but give us no idea as to their original size or function.

7. Rawcliffe, Carole, *Tudor Health Reform. The Form and Function of Medieval Hospitals*, (2011)

8. See images section within this book.

9. Rawcliffe, Carole, *Tudor Health Reform. The Form and Function of Medieval Hospitals*, (2011)

10. Ibid.

11. Mount, Toni, *The Medieval Housewife & Other Women of the Middle Ages*, (2015); Mount, Toni, *Medieval Medicine: Its Mysteries and Science*, (2016)

12. 'Item I bequeath to any lazour, be it man or woman being at time of my decease in the lazerhouse[s] of St Giles beside Holborn, Newenton [Newington] Green, the Loke beyond St George's bar, Hammersmith and Knightsbridge for to pray for my soul'. The National Archives, Catalogue reference, PROB 11/12/74 - Will of Joane Frowik or Frowyk, Widow, 16 May 1500.

13. Rawcliffe, Carole, *Tudor Health Reform. The Form and Function of Medieval Hospitals*, (2011)

14. Roger, Euan, 'Living with leprosy in late medieval England', blog. nationalarchives.gov.uk, [accessed 5 December 2019]

15. Hallett, Anna, *Almshouses*, (Princes Risborough, Shire Publications, 2004), p.46

16. Rawcliffe, Carole, *Tudor Health Reform. The Form and Function of Medieval Hospitals*, (2011)

17. Ibid.

18. Ibid.
19. Page, William, ed., 'Hospitals: St John the Baptist, Redcliffe', in *A History of the County of Somerset*, Volume 2, (London: VCH, 1911), pp.160-161. British History Online, [accessed 26 October 2019]
20. Rawcliffe, Carole, *Tudor Health Reform. The Form and Function of Medieval Hospitals*, (2011)
21. Ibid.
22. Ibid.
23. Hallett, Anna, *Almshouses*, (Princes Risborough, Shire Publications, 2004), p.7
24. Rawcliffe, Carole, *Tudor Health Reform. The Form and Function of Medieval Hospitals*, (2011)
25. Ibid.
26. Ibid.
27. Chambers, Paul, *Bedlam: London's Hospital for the Mad*, (2009), p. 18
28. Ibid.
29. Stevenson, Christine, 'The Architecture of Bethlem at Moorfield', eds., Andrews, Jonathan, Porter, Roy, Tucker, Penny and Waddington, Keir, *The History of Bethlem*, (London, Routledge, 1997)
30. Ibid. p.234
31. Chambers, Paul, *Bedlam: London's Hospital for the Mad*, (2009), p.27
32. Stevenson, Christine, 'The Architecture of Bethlem at Moorfield', eds., Andrews, Jonathan, Porter, Roy, Tucker, Penny and Waddington, Keir, *The History of Bethlem*, (London, Routledge, 1997), p.233
33. Chambers, Paul, *Bedlam: London's Hospital for the Mad*, (2009)
34. Stevenson, Christine, 'The Architecture of Bethlem at Moorfield', eds., Andrews, Jonathan, Porter, Roy, Tucker, Penny and Waddington, Keir, *The History of Bethlem*, (London, Routledge, 1997), p.234
35. Lipscomb, Suzannah, 'Playing The Fool'. History Learning Talk, Hampton Court Palace, 23 May 2017
36. Ekstrand, D.W., *The Four Human Temperaments*, (2012); P. F. Merenda, 'Toward a Four-Factor Theory of Temperament and/

or Personality', *Journal of Personality Assessment*, 51, (1987): pp.367–374

37. Ekstrand, D, W., *The Four Human Temperaments*, (2012)
38. Ibid.
39. Stevenson, Christine, 'The Architecture of Bethlem at Moorfield', eds., Andrews, Jonathan, Porter, Roy, Tucker, Penny and Waddington, Keir, *The History of Bethlem*, (London, Routledge, 1997), p.234

Chapter Six – Physicians, Surgeons, Barber-surgeons, Healers

1. Williams, P., *Life in Tudor England*, (London: BT Batsford, 1964), pp.100-119
2. Quoted in Williams, P., *Life in Tudor England*, (London: BT Batsford, 1964), p.104
3. Statement attributed to Erasmus. Entry on John Colet. Trapp, J. B. "Colet, John (1467–1519), dean of St Paul's and founder of St Paul's School", *Oxford Dictionary of National Biography*. (Oxford: 23 Sep. 2004), [accessed 27 Oct. 2019]
4. The doctrine of the four elements was formulated by Empedocles (504-443 BC) of Agrigentum in Sicily in Italy. The concept of the four humours was known to Hippocrates but arose from Babylonian and Egyptian ideas of physiology. See Castiglione A., *A History of Medicine,* translated from the Italian by E.B. Krumbhaar. (New York, Alfred Knopf, 1941), pp.140-141 and 159-164
5. Ibid.
6. Barber, Nicola, *Medieval Medicine*, (2012), p. 13
7. Pelling, Margaret, and Webster, Charles 'Medical Practitioners', in C. Webster, ed., *Health, Medicine, and Mortality in the Sixteenth Century* (1979), p. 183
8. Boorde, Andrew, *The Breviary of Health*, (London, William Powell, 1552). See also, Colewell, H.A., 'Andrew Borde and his Medicinal Works,' *Middlesex Hospital Journal*, Volume 15, 1911, pp.25-43
9. Norman, P., ed., *Decrees of the Ecumenical Councils*, Volume 1, (London, Sheed & Ward and Washington DC, Georgetown University Press, 1990), p.244

10. Young, S., *The Annals of the Barber-Surgeons of London*, (London, Blades, East and Blades, 1890)

11. Barratt, C,R,B., *The History of the Society of Apothecaries of London*, (London, Elliot Stock, 1905)

12. Lady Mary Brandon, 2 June 1510–d.c. 1540/1544; Roy Porter, *The Greatest Benefit to Mankind: A Medical History of Humanity*, (1997), p.178

13. In October 2002, the twelve-year-old Eugenie underwent back surgery in London at the Royal National Orthopaedic Hospital to correct her condition, where two 12-inch titanium rods were put in her back. The Princess made a full recovery and was not expected to undergo any further surgery. Royal National Orthopaedic Hospital, Princess Eugenie's story, https://www.rnohcharity.org/the-appeal/princess-eugenie-s-story [retrieved 28 Oct 2019]

14. Watt, Diane, (2004). 'Barton, Elizabeth [called the Holy Maid of Kent, the Nun of Kent] (c. 1506–1534), Benedictine nun and visionary', *Oxford Dictionary of National Biography*, [accessed 28 Oct. 2019]

15. Knight, Kevin, 'Elizabeth Barton', (New-Advent.com, 2012)

16. Hart, Kelly, *The Mistresses of Henry VIII*, (2009), p. 27

17. Gairdner, James., ed., *Letters and Papers, Foreign and Domestic, Henry VIII*, Volume 6, 1533, Henry VIII: November 1533, 11-20, (London, HMSO, 1882), pp. 562-578, [accessed 28 October 2019]

18. Lefkowitz, Mary, *Woman's Life in Greece and Rome: A Source Book in Translation*, (2005), pp. 247-249

19. Sander, L., *Hysteria Beyond Freud*, (1993), pp. 3–90

20. Adams, Francis, ed., *The Extant Works of Aretaeus, The Cappadocian. By Aretaeus*, (Boston, Milford House Inc. 1972, republication of the 1856 edition)

21. Ibid.

22. Skultans, Vieda, *English Madness: Ideas on Insanity, 1580-1890*, (Routledge & Kegan Paul Books; First edition, 6 Dec. 1979), p.20

23. 'Mental Illness in the 16th and 17th Centuries', Historic-England.org.uk (2016)

24. Ibid.

25. Porter, Roy, *A Social History of Madness, Stories Of The Insane (Phoenix Giants)*, (W&N, 2nd Revised edition, 2 Jan. 1996), p. 13

26. Lipscomb, Suzannah, 'Playing The Fool'. History Learning Talk, Hampton Court Palace, 23 May 2017

27. I will use the terms 'leprosy' and 'leper' within their medieval contexts; this is following the vocabulary used within Carole Rawcliffe's *Leprosy in Medieval England*, (London, Boydell Press, 2009), pp.11-12. As Carole Rawcliffe argues, to describe medieval lepers as 'sufferers from Hansen's disease' is both anachronistic and misleading, and instead we need to engage with these figures in their own historical context.

28. Hallett, A., *Almshouses*, (Princes Risborough, Shire Publications, 2004)

29. Gale, Thomas, *Certain Works of Chirurgerie. 1563*, (London: Rouland Hall Facsimile, Amsterdam and New York, Da Capo Press, 1971)

30. Porter, Roy, *A Social History of Madness, Stories Of The Insane (Phoenix Giants)*, (W&N, 2nd Revised edition, 2 Jan. 1996), p. 13

31. MacDonald, Michael, *Mystical Bedlam: Madness, Anxiety and Healing in Seventeenth-Century England*, (Cambridge University Press, 1983)

32. Andrews, Jonathan, (2004). 'Napier, Richard (1559–1634), astrological physician and Church of England clergyman', *Oxford Dictionary of National Biography*. [accessed 29 Oct. 2019]

33. Bodl. Oxf., MS Ashmole 213, fol. 110.

34. Andrews, Jonathan, (2004). 'Napier, Richard (1559–1634), astrological physician and Church of England clergyman', *Oxford Dictionary of National Biography*. [accessed 29 Oct. 2019]

35. MacDonald, Michael, *Mystical Bedlam: Madness, Anxiety and Healing in Seventeenth-Century England*, (Cambridge University Press, 1983)

Chapter Seven – The Health of a King and his Decline into Disability

1. Ives, E. W., 'Henry VIII (1491–1547), king of England and Ireland', *Oxford Dictionary of National Biography*, (Oxford University Press, 3 Sep. 2004), [accessed 27 Oct. 2019]

2. Poynter, F.N.L., 'The Influence of government legislation on Medical Practice in Britain', in *The Evolution of Medical Practice in Britain*, edited by F.N.L Poynter (London, Pitman Medical, 1961), pp.5-15

3. Thompson, C,J,S., 'King Henry as an apothecary', Chapter XIV, in *The Mystery and Art of the Apothecary*, (London: John Lane, The Bodley Head, 1929), pp.168-178

4. Grueninger, Natalie, *Discovering Tudor London: A Journey Back in Time*, (London, The History Press, 2017); Goodman, Ruth, *How to Be a Tudor: A Dawn-to-Dusk Guide to Everyday Life*, (London, Viking, 5 November 2015)

5. Hughes, J.T., (2006). 'The Licensing of Medical Practitioners in Tudor England: Legislation enacted by Henry VIII', *Vesalius*, Volume XII, No 1, pp.4–11

6. Grueninger, Natalie, *Discovering Tudor London: A Journey Back in Time*, (London, The History Press, 2017); Goodman, Ruth, *How to Be a Tudor: A Dawn-to-Dusk Guide to Everyday Life*, (London, Viking, 5 November 2015)

7. Nutton, Vivian, (2004). 'Caius, John (1510–1573), scholar and physician', *Oxford Dictionary of National Biography*, [accessed 31 Oct. 2019]

8. Caius, J, K., *A boke, or counseill against the disease commonly called the sweate or sweating sicknesse*, (London, Richard Grafton, 1552)

9. Khon, George C., *Encyclopaedia of Plaque and Pestilence from Ancient Times to the Present*, 3rd edition (New York, Infobase Publishing, 2011), p.228

10. Dyer, Alan D., 'Influence of Bubonic Plague in England 1500-1667', *Med. Hist.*, Vol 22 (1978), p.309

11. Samman, N., 'The Henrician Court during Wolsey's ascendancy C.1514-1529', (unpublished PhD Thesis, University of Wales, 1988)

12. Wellcome Trust History, 'Engaging Lives', *Historic Royal Palaces and the Medical Humanities*, 50 (Summer, 2012): pp.2-3

13. Pelling, Margaret, and Webster, Charles 'Medical Practitioners', in C. Webster, ed., *Health, Medicine, and Mortality in the Sixteenth Century* (1979), p. 183

14. MacNalty, A.S., *Henry VIII: A Difficult Patient*, (London, Christopher Johnson, 1952)
15. Keynes, M., (2005). 'The Personality and Health of King Henry VIII (1991-1547), A Medical Study', *Journal of Medical Biography*, Volume 13, pp.174-183. In an appendix, the author lists Henry's attention to medical care; Chalmers, CR and Chaloner E.J., (2009). '500 Years Later Henry VIII, leg ulcers and the course of History', *Journal of the Royal Society of Medicine*, Vol 102: pp. 513–517
16. Extracts from the Ordinances of Eltham, copied in the 1660s from the 1526 original. The National Archives, London, E 36/231.
17. The Ordinances. (London, The National Archives, E36/231)
18. Wellcome Trust History, 'Engaging Lives', *Historic Royal Palaces and the Medical Humanities*, 50 (Summer, 2012), pp. 2-3
19. Thurley, Simon, *Houses of Power, The Places that Shaped the Tudor World*, (London, Bantam Press, 2017), p.169
20. Ibid. p.383
21. Ibid. p.383
22. Professor Suzannah Lipscomb has discussed the hazards and hidden dangers surrounding the household killers of the era: Suzannah Lipscomb, Hidden Killers of the Tudor Home (2015 television series).
23. Pelling, M., *Barbers and Barber-Surgeons: An Occupational Group in an English Provincial Town, 1550–1640*, (1981)
24. The Ordinances. (London: The National Archives, E36/231)
25. Ibid.
26. Borman, Tracy, *The Private Lives of the Tudors*, (London, Hodder & Stoughton, 2016)
27. Lipscomb, Suzannah, Hidden Killers of the Tudor Home (2015)
28. Chalmers, CR and Chaloner E.J., (2009). '500 Years Later Henry VIII, leg ulcers and the course of History', *Journal of the Royal Society of Medicine*, Vol 102: pp. 513–517
29. The text is in Statutes of the Realm, 3, 31-32, (London, printed by the Command of George III, 1817)
30. Council of practice differed in parishes from that in London, where the Company of Surgeons and College of Physicians were dominant.
31. James, R, R., (1937). 'The earliest list of surgeons to be licensed by the bishop of London', *Janus*, 41 pp.255–60

32. Statues of the Realm, 3, pp.213-214, (London, printed by the Command of George III, 1817)

33. Statues of the Realm, 3, p.793, (London, printed by the Command of George III, 1817)

34. Statues of the Realm, 3, pp. 794-796, (London, printed by the Command of George III, 1817)

35. See figure 11, within the images section, King Henry VIII and the Barber-Surgeons. The Holbein portrait is an oil on 11/12 oak panels, in a late seventeenth-century gadrooned giltwood frame.

36. The Holbein | THE WORSHIPFUL COMPANY OF BARBERS. https://barberscompany.org/the-holbein /; Jackson, Barry, *Barber-Surgeons*, (2008)

37. Moore, Norman, and I. G. Murray. 'Vicary, Thomas (d. 1561), surgeon', *Oxford Dictionary of National Biography*, 23 Sep. 2004, [accessed 31 Oct. 2019]

38. Ibid.

39. The book had 1,484 pages.

40. Brown, H.F., ed., *Calendar of the State Papers: Venice*, Volume 2. 1509-1519 (1867), pp.242-246

41. "Henry VIII: July 1509", *Letters and Papers, Foreign and Domestic, Henry VIII*, Volume 1, 1509-1514, ed. J S Brewer. (London, HMSO, 1920) pp.55-71. British History Online. [accessed 4 September 2019]

42. Miller, C.H., Bradner, L., Lynch, C. A., and Oliver, R. P., eds., *Epigram 19, in volume 3.2, Latin Poems, of The Complete Works of St. Thomas More*, (Yale University Press, 1984) pp.100-113. Thomas More, *Poems on the coronation of King Henry VIII of England, (1509–1547) and Queen Katherine of Aragon (d. 1536)*, Cotton MS Titus D IV, ff. 2-14: 1509. Hall, Edward, *Hall's Chronicle*, pp.507-510

43. Crofton, Ian, *The Kings and Queens of England*, (Quercus Books, 2006), p.128

44. "Venice: October 1519", in *Calendar of State Papers Relating To English Affairs in the Archives of Venice*, Volume 2, 1509-1519, ed. Rawdon Brown (London, HMSO, 1867), pp.556-565. [accessed 3 December, 2019]

45. Hall, Edward, *Hall's Chronicle: containing the history of England, during the reign of Henry the Fourth, and the succeeding monarchs,*

to the end of the reign of Henry the Eighth, in which are particularly described the manners and customs of those periods. Carefully collated with the editions of 1548 and 1550, (London, J.Johnson, 1809)

46. MacNalty, A.S., *Henry VIII: A Difficult Patient*, (London, Christopher Johnson, 1952)

47. Hutchinson, Robert, *Henry VIII, The Decline and Fall of a Tyrant*, (London, Orion Publishing Group, 2019), p.14

48. Hutchinson, Robert, *Young Henry: The Rise of Henry VIII*, (W&N, UK ed., Jan. 2012), p. 187

49. "Henry VIII: April 1515, 16-30", in *Letters and Papers, Foreign and Domestic, Henry VIII*, Volume 2, 1515-1518, ed. J S Brewer (London, HMSO, 1864), pp.104-118. British History Online, [accessed 4 December, 2019]

50. "Venice: May 1515", in *Calendar of State Papers Relating To English Affairs in the Archives of Venice*, Volume 2, 1509-1519, ed. Rawdon Brown (London, HMSO, 1867), pp.242-246. British History Online, [accessed 4 December, 2019]

51. "Venice: June 1515", in *Calendar of State Papers Relating To English Affairs in the Archives of Venice*, Volume 2, 1509-1519, ed. Rawdon Brown (London, HMSO, 1867), pp.246-251. British History Online, [accessed 4 December, 2019]

52. "Henry VIII: May 1521, 11-20", in *Letters and Papers, Foreign and Domestic, Henry VIII*, Volume 3, 1519-1523, ed. J S Brewer (London, HMSO, 1867), pp. 485-516. British History Online, [accessed 4 December, 2019]

53. Giustinian, Sebastian, *Four years at the Court of Henry VIII: Selection of Despatches written by the Venetian Ambassador Sebastian Giustinian*, trans. Rawdon Brown, 2 vols, (London, Smith, Elder & Co., 1854)

54. "Venice: October 1519", in *Calendar of State Papers Relating To English Affairs in the Archives of Venice*, Volume 2, 1509-1519, ed. Rawdon Brown (London, HMSO, 1867), pp.556-565. [accessed 3 December, 2019]

55. Hall, Edward, *Hall's Chronicle: containing the history of England, during the reign of Henry the Fourth, and the succeeding monarchs, to the end of the reign of Henry the Eighth, in which are particularly described the manners and customs of those periods. Carefully collated with the editions of 1548 and 1550*, (London, J.Johnson, 1809), p.674

56. Ibid. p.697
57. Barratt N.R., (1973). 'King Henry VIII', *Annals Royal College of Surgeons of England*, Volume 52, p.231
58. Ibid.
59. Erasmus, Desiderius, *Opus Epistolarum*, ed. P.S. and H.M. Allen., 11 Vols, VIII, 2143, (Oxford, 1906-470), p.129
60. Doran, Susan, and Durston, Christopher, *Princes, Pastors and People. The Church and Religion in England 1529-1689*, (London, Routledge, 1991), p.1
61. Ibid.
62. "Henry VIII: January 1511", in *Letters and Papers, Foreign and Domestic, Henry VIII*, Volume 1, 1509-1514, ed., J S Brewer (London, HMSO, 1920), pp. 369-377. [accessed 3 December, 2019]
63. Ibid.
64. Ibid.
65. "Henry VIII: February 1516, 16-29", in *Letters and Papers, Foreign and Domestic, Henry VIII*, Volume 2, 1515-1518, ed., J S Brewer (London, HMSO, 1864), pp. 429-447. [accessed 3 December 2019]
66. "Henry VIII: September 1533, 1-10", in *Letters and Papers, Foreign and Domestic, Henry VIII*, Volume 6, 1533, ed., James Gairdner (London, HMSO, 1882), pp. 449-466. [accessed 3 December 2019]
67. Dewhurst, J., 'The alleged Miscarriages of Catherine of Aragon and Anne Boleyn,' *Med. Hist.*, Vol 28, (1984), pp.49-56
68. "Henry VIII: February 1536, 6-10", in *Letters and Papers, Foreign and Domestic, Henry VIII*, Volume 10, January-June 1536, ed., James Gairdner (London, HMSO, 1887), 98-108. British History Online [accessed 3 December 2019]
69. "Spain: January 1536, 21-31,", in *Calendar of State Papers, Spain*, Volume 5 Part 2, 1536-1538, ed., Pascual de Gayangos (London, HMSO, 1888), pp.11-29. [accessed 3 December 2019.
70. Hutchinson, Robert, *Henry VIII The Decline and Fall of a Tyrant*, p.10
71. Frith, John, 'Syphilis: Its Early History and Treatment until Penicillin and the debate on its origins', *Jnl. Of Military & Veterans Health* (Australian Military Med. Ass.), vol. 20 (2002), p.50
72. The name syphilis was applied to the disease in 1530 by the Italian doctor Girolamo Fracastoro. The medical profession first

used the term in the nineteenth century. See Crosby, *The Early History of Syphilis*, p.219

73. Rolleston, J.D., (1934). 'Venereal Disease in Literature', *British Journal of Venereal Diseases*, vol 10, p.147

74. Hutchinson, Robert, *Henry VIII, The Decline and Fall of a Tyrant*, (London, Orion Publising Group, 2019), p.242

75. "Henry VIII: March 1536, 1-10", in *Letters and Papers, Foreign and Domestic, Henry VIII*, Volume 10, January-June 1536, ed., James Gairdner (London, HMSO, 1887), pp.161-181. British History Online [accessed 13 December 2019]

76. Hall, Edward, *Hall's Chronicle: containing the history of England, during the reign of Henry the Fourth, and the succeeding monarchs, to the end of the reign of Henry the Eighth, in which are particularly described the manners and customs of those periods. Carefully collated with the editions of 1548 and 1550*, (London. J.Johnson, 1809), p.33

77. "Henry VIII: January 1536, 26-31", in *Letters and Papers, Foreign and Domestic, Henry VIII*, Volume 10, January-June 1536, ed., James Gairdner (London, HMSO, 1887), pp.64-81. British History Online [accessed 13 December 2019]

78. Lipscomb, Suzannah, *1536: The Year That Changed Henry VIII*, (Lion Hudson, 2009), p.26

79. Lipscomb, Suzannah. *1536: The Year That Changed Henry VIII*, (Lion Hudson, 2009), p.26; Chamberlin, *The Private Character*; Scarisbrick, *Henry VIII*, p.485

80. "Henry VIII: April 1537, 26-30", in *Letters and Papers, Foreign and Domestic, Henry VIII*, Volume 12 Part 1, January-May 1537, ed., James Gairdner (London, HMSO, 1890), pp. 477-516. British History Online [accessed 1 January 2020]

81. "Henry VIII: June 1537, 11-20", in *Letters and Papers, Foreign and Domestic, Henry VIII*, Volume 12 Part 2, June-December 1537, ed., James Gairdner (London, HMSO, 1891), pp. 25-42. British History Online [accessed 1 January 2020]

82. Chalmers, CR and Chaloner E.J., (2009). '500 Years Later Henry VIII, leg ulcers and the course of History', *Journal of the Royal Society of Medicine*, Vol 102: p.516

83. Hope Dodds, Madeline, and Dodds, Ruth, *The Pilgrimage of Grace, 1536-1537 V1: And the Exeter Conspiracy 1538*, (1915), (Literary Licensing, LLC, 7 Aug. 2014)

84. MacLennan, Sir Hector, 'A Gynaecologist Looks at the Tudors', *Med. Hist.*, Vol.11 (1967), p.69

85. "Henry VIII: May 1538, 10-15", in *Letters and Papers, Foreign and Domestic, Henry VIII*, Volume 13 Part 1, January-July 1538, ed., James Gairdner (London, HMSO, 1892), pp.354-372. British History Online [accessed 2 January 2020]

86. "Letters and Papers: May 1539, 11-15", in *Letters and Papers, Foreign and Domestic, Henry VIII*, Volume 14 Part 1, January-July 1539, eds., James Gairdner and R H Brodie (London, HMSO, 1894), pp. 442-449. [accessed 2 January 2020]

87. Hutchinson, Robert, *Henry VIII The Decline and Fall of a Tyrant*, p.3

88. "Henry VIII: December 1540, 21-25", in *Letters and Papers, Foreign and Domestic, Henry VIII*, Volume 16, 1540-1541, eds., James Gairdner and R H Brodie (London, HMSO, 1898), pp.156-162. British History Online [accessed 2 January 2020]

89. "Henry VIII: December 1540, 21-25", in *Letters and Papers, Foreign and Domestic, Henry VIII*, Volume 16, 1540-1541, eds., James Gairdner and R H Brodie (London, HMSO, 1898), pp.156-162. British History Online [accessed 2 January 2020]

90. Hayward, Maria (ed.), *The 1542 Inventory of Whitehall: The Palace and its Keeper*, 2 vols., (London, Society of Antiquaries of London, 2004), items 1,214, 1,232-3. pp.119-120

91. 6,989, f.45 – Privy Council to Norfolk; Hampton Court, 23 February 1540.

92. BL, Harleian MS 6,989, f.45.

93. Nicholas, Sir Harris, ed., *Proceedings and Ordinances of the Privy Council of England*, 1540-2, Vol 7, (London, Commissioners of the Public Records, 1837)

94. BL, Royal MS 2A.XVI, f.63v, and a copy of this image can be found in the plate section of this book.

95. Hutchinson, Robert, *Henry VIII, The Decline and Fall of a Tyrant*, (London, Orion Publishing Group, 2019), p.244

96. Brewer, Clifford, *The Death of Kings*, (London, Abson Books, 2000), pp.123-124

97. Ikram, Muhammad Q., Sajjad, Fazle H. & Salardini. Arash, (2016). 'The Head that Wears the Crown: Henry VIII and traumatic Brain Injury', *Jnl. Clinical Neuroscience*, Vol 16 pp. 16-19

98. BL, Royal MS 2A.XVI, f.63v, and a copy of this image can be found in the plate section of this book.

99. Multiple Contributors, *A Pleasant History of the Life and Death of Will Summers: How he Came First to be Known at Court, and by What Means he got to be King Henry the Eighth's Jester*, (Gale ECCO, Print Editions, 20 April 2018)

100. Bright, Timothie, *A Treatise of Melancholy*, (London, imprinted by Thomas Vautrollier [etc.], 1586)

101. Erasmus, Desiderius, *In Praise of Folly*, (Grand Rapids, MI, Christian Classics Ethereal Library, University of Michigan Press, 1958)

102. MacNalty AS., *Henry VIII: A Difficult Patient*, (London, Christopher Johnson Publishers, 1952)

103. BL, Sloane MS 1,047 – Collection of recipes for ointments and nostrums devised by Henry VIII and four of his doctors

104. "Henry VIII: March 1541, 1-10", in *Letters and Papers, Foreign and Domestic, Henry VIII*, Volume 16, 1540-1541, eds., James Gairdner and R H Brodie (London, HMSO, 1898), pp.282-289. British History Online [accessed 2 January 2020]

105. Ibid.

106. "Henry VIII: May 1544, 16-20", in *Letters and Papers, Foreign and Domestic, Henry VIII*, Volume 19 Part 1, January-July 1544, eds., James Gairdner and R H Brodie (London, HMSO, 1903), pp.318-338. British History Online [accessed 14 December 2019]

107. "Henry VIII: January 1547, 30-31", in *Letters and Papers, Foreign and Domestic, Henry VIII*, Volume 21 Part 2, September 1546-January 1547, eds., James Gairdner and R H Brodie (London: HMSO, 1910), pp.388-453. British History Online [accessed 13 December 2019]

108. TNA, SP 4/1 – List of documents issued under Henry's 'Dry Stamp', September 1545-January 1547.

109. Suzannah Lipscomb on The Tudors, Audio (HistoryHit.TV, 2019), https://tv.historyhit.com/watch/24028617

110. TNA, E 315/160 f.133v. – Household book of Sir Antony Denny, Keeper of the Palace of Whitehall; 34 Henry VIII – 2 Edward VI."Henry VIII: October 1546, 6-10", in *Letters and Papers, Foreign and Domestic, Henry VIII*, Volume 21 Part 2, September 1546-January 1547, eds., James Gairdner and

R H Brodie (London, HMSO, 1910), pp.108-121. British History Online [accessed 13 December 2019]

111. Hayward, Maria (ed.), *The 1542 Inventory of Whitehall: The Palace and its Keeper*, 2 vols, (London, Society of Antiquaries of London, 2004), p.263

112. Starkey, David., 'A Monarchy of Misfits', Wimborne Literary Festival, The Allendale Centre, Wimborne Minster, Dorset, 18 May 2019, 7.30 pm. https://www.wimborneliteraryfestival.co.uk/

113. Harley MS, 1419 f.194v - Detail of a chair in Henry VIII's Inventory, covered with purple velvet, which has been referred to as a 'stairthrone' (British Library).

114. Lipscomb, Suzannah, *The King is Dead' The Last Will and Testament of Henry VIII*, (Head of Zeus, 2015), p.19

115. *Acts of the Privy Council,* Vol 2 1547-1550, p.18, "Pages 1-26", in *Acts of the Privy Council of England* Volume 2, 1547-1550, ed. John Roche Dasent (London, HMSO, 1890), pp.1-25. British History Online [accessed 14 December 2019]

116. Hayward, Maria (ed.), *The 1542 Inventory of Whitehall: The Palace and its Keeper*, vol 1, (London, Society of Antiquaries of London, 2004), pp. 31-32

117. Furdell, Elizabeth Lane, *The Royal Doctors 1485-1714: Medical Personnel at the Tudor and Stuarts Courts*, (Rochester, NY, Rochester University Press, 2001), p.28

118. The National Archives, Records of the Lord Chamberlain and Officers of the Royal Household, LC 2/2 – f.84v, ff.83, 77 - Wardrobe accounts for the funeral of Henry VIII. 1547.

119. The National Archives, Records of the Lord Chamberlain and Officers of the Royal Household, LC 2/2 – f.45 – Wardrobe Accounts for the funeral of Henry VIII. 1547.

120. Strickland, Agnes, *Lives of the Queens of England from the Norman Conquest*, Vol 3, (London, Bell and Daldy, 1866), p.255

121. Ibid. p.298

Chapter Eight – Disabled People in High Places

1. Vespasian A XII, f. 137r – John Rous describing how Richard III defended himself during the Battle of Bosworth, Manuscript, British Library.

2. Croft, Pauline, "Cecil, Robert, first earl of Salisbury (1563–1612), politician and courtier," *Oxford Dictionary of National Biography*. 23 Sep. 2004

3. Shakespeare, William, *King Richard III*, Act 1 scene 1

4. Gairdner, James, *History of the Life and Reign of Richard the Third*, 1898, p.5

5. Kincaid, A.N. ed., *The History of King Richard the Third*, (1979), p. 206

6. Armstrong, C.A.J., ed., *The Usurpation of Richard the Third*, (Oxford, 2nd edn, 1969), pp.136-8

7. Rous, John, *Historia Regum Anglie*, Cotton MS, Vespasian A XII, f. 135r - Manuscript, (4th quarter of the 15th century British Library)

8. *Historia Regum Angliae*, written towards the end of Rous' life, i.e. after 1485; Hanham, Alison, *Richard III and his Early Historians, 1483–1535*, (Oxford, Clarendon Press, 1975), pp.120-121, which contains a useful full-length translation of this extract from Cotton MS Vespasian A XII on Richard III's reign.

9. Ellis, Henry, *Polydore Vergil's English History*, from an early translation preserved among the ms. of the Old Royal Library in the British Museum / Polydorius Vergilius. Vol. 1, containing the first eight books comprising the period before the Norman Conquest / edited by Sir Henry Ellis. (London: printed for the Camden Society by J. B. Nichols and Son, 1884), pp. 226-7

10. Appleby, Jo, et al., (2015). 'Perimortem trauma in King Richard III: a skeletal analysis', *The Lancet*, Volume 385, Issue 9964, pp. 253–259

11. Lamb, Angela L., Evans, Jane E., Buckley, Richard and Appleby, Jo., (2014). 'Multi-isotope analysis demonstrates significant lifestyle changes in King Richard III', *Journal of Archaeological Science*, Volume 50, pp. 559-565

12. Blanchard, Joël, *Mémoires*, trans. Philippe de Commynes, (Paris: Fayard, 2006), pp. 299-300

13. Ibid.

14. Philippe Tourault, Anne de Bretagne, Perrin, p. 255: a declaration dated 30 April 1501 at Lyon and never published, declared null and void any marriage contract of Claude of France with other princes than the future François I (1990)

15. Marck, Robert de La, Seigneur de Fleuranges, *Mémoires du Maréchal de Florange, dit le Jeune Adventureaux*, Volume 2, p.158

16. Guicciardini, Francesco, *Dell'epitome dell' Historia d'Italia ... Libri XX. Con diverse annotationi [by F. Sansovino] ... Et con i ritratti d'alquanti principi cavati dall'opera sua.* (Venetia, 1580)

17. Holinshed, Raphael, *Holinshed's Chronicles of England, Scotland and Ireland*, Volume 3, p. 611

18. Soberton, Sylvia Barbara., *Golden Age Ladies: Women Who Shaped the Courts of Henry VIII and Francis I*, (CreateSpace Independent Publishing Platform, 4 May 2016), pp.56, 57, 117

19. Lacroix, Paul, *Louis XII et Anne de Bretagne, Louis XII and Anne of Brittany. Chronicle of the history of France*, edited by Georges Hurtrel, (Paris, 1882), p.306

20. Menin, Nicolas, *[An historical and chronological treatise of the anointing and coronation of the Kings and Queens of France ... To which is added an exact relation of the ceremony of the coronation of Louis XV. ... Faithfully done from the original French.]*, (London, 1727)

21. NHS Choices - A Squint, also called Strabismus, is where the eyes point in different directions (NHS England, 2017)

22. Gunton, 'Strabismus', Primary Care (2015)

23. Online Etymology Dictionary (2001–2017)

24. Géoris, Michel, *Francois Ier. Magnifique*, (Editions France-Empire, 1998) p. 20

25. "Henry VIII: June 1515, 16-30", in *Letters and Papers, Foreign and Domestic, Henry VIII*, Volume 2, 1515-1518, ed. J S Brewer (London, HMSO, 1864), pp.162-174. [accessed 19 November 2019]

26. Soberton, Sylvia Barbara., *Golden Age Ladies: Women Who Shaped the Courts of Henry VIII and Francis I*, (CreateSpace Independent Publishing Platform, 4 May 2016), p.58

27. Wellman, Kathleen, *Queens and Mistress of Renaissance France*, (Yale University Press, June 2013)

28. Matarasso, Pauline, *Queen's Mate: Three women of power in France on the eve of the Renaissance*, (2001)

29. Soberton, Sylvia Barbara., *Golden Age Ladies: Women Who Shaped the Courts of Henry VIII and Francis I*, (CreateSpace Independent Publishing Platform, 4 May 2016), p.102

30. Marck, Robert de La, Seigneur de Fleuranges, *Mémoires du Maréchal de Florange, dit le Jeune Adventureaux*, Volume 2, p.148

31. *Journal d'un Bourgeois de Paris sous le Règne de François Premier* (1515-1536), p. 206-207

32. Soberton, Sylvia Barbara., *Golden Age Ladies: Women Who Shaped the Courts of Henry VIII and Francis I*, (CreateSpace Independent Publishing Platform, 4 May 2016), p.104

33. Génin, François, *Lettres de Marguerite d'Angoulême*, (Nabu Press, 29 Aug. 2010), pp. 166-167

34. Brantôme, *Corpus Historique Étampois*

35. Extract from *Corpus Historique Étampois*: Brantôme - Vie de Claude de France -Vie des Dames illustres- entre 1590 et 1614 (in French) [retrieved 19 November 2019]

36. Sylvester, Richard S. and Harding, Davis P., eds., *Two Early Tudor Lives: The Life and Death of Cardinal Wolsey by George Cavendish; The Life of Sir Thomas More by William Roper*, (Yale University Press, 1962), p. 120. "Introduction, Section 5", in *Letters and Papers, Foreign and Domestic, Henry VIII*, Volume 4, 1524-1530, ed. J S Brewer, (London, HMSO, 1875), ccxxv-cclxxxv. British History Online [accessed 29 January 2020]

37. "Capillo nigro", says Saunders, f. 16 b.

38. Brown's Ven. Cal. IV. p. 365., "Introduction, Section 5", in *Letters and Papers, Foreign and Domestic, Henry VIII*, Volume 4, 1524-1530, ed. J S Brewer, (London, HMSO, 1875), ccxxv-cclxxxv. British History Online [accessed 29 January 2020]

39. See various download options at archive.org Medallic illustrations of the history of Great Britain and Ireland to the death of George II. Vol I, (1885)

40. Churchill Lucy., 'My work and the things that inspire me', Blog (2012). Lucychurchill.wordpress.com

41. The thyroid is a butterfly-shaped gland located at the base of the neck, just below an Adam's apple.

42. On goitres see NHS England (England, 2017)

43. Rowlands, John., 'A Portrait Drawing by Hans Holbein the Younger', (1977), pp. 231-237, Starkey, David., 'Holbein's Irish Sitter?' (1981), pp. 100-101

44. See figure 19 in the images section of this book.

45. "Introduction, Section 5", in *Letters and Papers, Foreign and Domestic, Henry VIII*, Volume 4, 1524-1530, ed. J S Brewer (London, HMSO, 1875), ccxxv-cclxxxv. British History Online [accessed 29 January 2020]

46. Rowlands, John, 'An Old Tradition Reasserted: Holbein's Portrait of Queen Anne Boleyn' (1983), pp. 88-92, Parker, *The Drawings of Hans Holbein in the Collection of H.M. the King at Windsor Castle*, (1945)

47. Rowlands, John, 'Review of Holbein and the Court of Henty VIII, Master Drawings' (1979)

48. Ibid.

49. KB 8 - Court of King's Bench: Crown Side: Baga de Secretis - Roll and file of court of the Lord High Steward and peers. Principal defendants and charges: Queen Anne Boleyn, Sir George Boleyn Lord Rocheford, high treason, adultery and incest, 28 Hen VIII. 21 membranes. 1536 Apr 22-1537 Apr 21; Ives, Eric, 'Faction at the Court of Henry VIII: the Fall of Anne Boleyn' (1972), pp. 169

50. Sylvester, Richard S. and Harding, Davis P., eds., *Two Early Tudor Lives: The Life and Death of Cardinal Wolsey by George Cavendish; The Life of Sir Thomas More by William Roper,* (Yale University Press, 1962), pp. 183-84

51. Parker, K.T., *The Drawings of Hans Holbein in the Collection of H.M. the King at Windsor Castle*, (Phaidon Press, 1945), p. 22

52. Ibid.

53. Cited in Sydney Anglo, *Spectacle, Pageantry and Early Tudor Policy*, (Oxford, Clarendon Press, 1969), p. 259. John Rowlands, 'Review of Holbein and the Court of Henty VIII, *Master Drawings*, XVII No.1, (New York 1979), pp.53-56

54. Sander, Nicholas, *Rise and Growth of the Anglican Schism* (1887), p.25

55. KB 8 - Court of King's Bench: Crown Side: Baga de Secretis - Roll and file of court of the Lord High Steward and peers. Principal defendants and charges: Queen Anne Boleyn, Sir George Boleyn Lord Rocheford, high treason, adultery and incest, 28 Hen VIII. 21 membranes. 1536 Apr 22-1537 Apr 21

56. Nicholas Sander in the *New Advent Catholic Encyclopaedia*

57. Elliot, Rose, *Cases of Conscience: Alternatives open to Recusants and Puritans under Elizabeth I and James I*, (New York, Cambridge University Press, 1975), p. 47

58. *Calendar of State Papers, Venice*, Volume 4, pp. 355-368. *Sanuto Diaries*, v. lvii, pp. 279, 824

59. Simon Grynée quoted in P. W. Sergeant, *The Life of Anne Boleyn*, (1923), p.129

60. "Henry VIII: June 1533, 1-5", in *Letters and Papers, Foreign and Domestic, Henry VIII*, Volume 6, 1533, ed. James Gairdner (London, HMSO, 1882), pp.262-275. British History Online [accessed 30 January 2020]

61. Gardiner, *Letters and Papers*, Volume 6, pp. 262-275. R. T. 145. No. 5, 37. 585. Coronation of Anne Boleyn. Fr., pp. 7. From a catalogue of papers at Brussels, now lost.

62. Weir, Alison, *The Six Wives of Henry VIII*, (1991), p. 151

63. Heywood, John, *The Play of the Weather*, printed by William Rastell, (4 September 2010). http://stagingthehenriciancourt. brookes.ac.uk/resources/play_of_the_weather_script.html

64. "Introduction, Section 5", in *Letters and Papers, Foreign and Domestic, Henry VIII*, Volume 4, 1524-1530, ed. J S Brewer, (London, HMSO, 1875), ccxxv-cclxxxv. British History Online [accessed 30 January 2020]

65. Ibid.

66. Bell, D. C., *Notices of the historical persons buried in the Chapel of St. Peter ad Vincula, in the tower of London: With an account of the discovery of the supposed remains of Queen Anne Boleyn*, (1877), p. 26

67. Loades, David, ed., *The Papers of George Wyatt Esquire of Boxley Abbey in the county of Kent*, Camden Fourth Series, Volume 5, (London, Royal Historical Society, 1968)

68. Wyatt, George, *Extracts from the Life of the Virtuous, Christian and Renowned Queen Anne Boleigne*, published privately, 1817, and publicly as an appendix to vol. 2 of S. W. Singer's edition of George Cavendish's *The Life of Cardinal Wolsey*, (London, 1825)

69. For information on Graeme Cameron's research on the Anne Boleyn Crown of England's Personal Portrait 1536, Whitehall Palace, London, refer to his twitter feed @GraemeCameron2 and his website https://graemecameron.wixsite.com/graeme. All information cited with Graeme's kind permission.

70. Fox, Julia, *Jane Boleyn, The True Story of the Infamous Lady Rochford*, (2009)

71. Russell, Gareth, *Young, Damned and Fair. The Life and Tragedy of Catherine Howard at the Court of Henry VIII*, (William Collins, 11 Jan. 2018)

72. Weir, Alison, *Henry VIII, King and Court*, (Vintage, 2008)

73. Russell, Gareth, 'February 13th 1542: The Execution of Catherine Howard and Jane Boleyn'.

74. Marchant, Danielle, 'The Madness of Jane Boleyn', (2015)

75. Fox, Julia, *Jane Boleyn: The True Story of the Infamous Lady Rochford*, (2009)

76. Russell, Gareth, 'February 13th 1542: The Execution of Catherine Howard and Jane Boleyn'.

77. Fox, Julia, *Jane Boleyn: The True Story of Infamous Lady Rochford*, p. 295

78. John Laurence, cook, to the Lords of the Council, Document Ref.: SP 1/100 f.60 Folio Numbers: ff. 60 Date: 1535 Source Archive: The National Archives of the UK, Gale, Document Number: MC4301781136 State Papers Online, Gale and Star Chamber miscellaneous (STAC 10), Date: 1535 Source Archive: The National Archives of the UK, both plates of this document are within the images section of this book.

79. It is highly probable that Mary Grey was named after Princess Mary, having been born after the princess had been restored to the line of the succession.

80. Tallis, Nicola, *Crown of Blood: The Deadly Inheritance of Lady Jane Grey*, (Michael O'Mara, 2016), pp. 39-40

81. Lisle, Leanda de, *The Sisters who would be Queen, The tragedy of Mary, Katherine and Lady Jane Grey*, (Harperpress, 2009), p.14

82. Ibid. p.41

83. Skidmore, Chris, *Edward VI*, (2009), p.248

84. Inner Temple Library, Petyt MS 538.47 fol.317, Edward VI's "Devise for the Succession"

85. Doran, Susan, (2004). "Keys [née Grey], Lady Mary (1545?–1578), noblewoman", *Oxford Dictionary of National Biography* [accessed 16 Jan. 2020]

86. Ibid.

Chapter Nine – Disability in the Tudor Court

1. "Henry VIII: Miscellaneous, 1535", in *Letters and Papers, Foreign and Domestic, Henry VIII,* Volume 9, August-December 1535, ed. James Gairdner (London, HMSO, 1886), pp.367-402. British History Online [accessed 15 February 2020]

2. James Gairdner, and Brodie, R H (eds.) "Letters and Papers: April 1539, 1-5", *Letters and Papers, Foreign and Domestic, Henry VIII,* Volume 14 Part 1, January-July 1539. (London, HMSO, 1894), pp. 330-348. British History Online. [accessed 16 September 2019]

3. Lipscomb, Suzannah, 'All the King's Fools', *History Today,* Volume 61, Issue 8, (August 2011)

4. Lipscomb, Suzannah, 'All The King's Fools', *History Today,* Volume 61, Issue 8, (August 2011); Lipscomb, Suzannah, 'Playing The Fool'. History Learning Talk, Hampton Court Palace, 23 May 2017

5. Bright, Timothie, *A Treatise of Melancholy,* (London, imprinted by Thomas Vautrollier [etc.], 1586)

6. Cooper, Peet, *All the Kings Fools,* (2011). https://www.allthekingsfools.co.uk/

7. Ibid.

8. "Spelthorne Hundred: Hampton Court Palace, pictures", in *A History of the County of Middlesex: Volume 2, General; Ashford, East Bedfont With Hatton, Feltham, Hampton With Hampton Wick, Hanworth, Laleham, Littleton,* ed. William Page (London: VCH, 1911), pp.379-380. British History Online [accessed 15 February 2020]

9. Mulryne, J. R., (2004). "Somer [Sommers], William (d. 1559), court fool", *Oxford Dictionary of National Biography* [accessed 16 October 2019]; Lipscomb, Suzannah, 'All the King's Fools', *History Today,* Volume 61, Issue 8, (August 2011)

10. James, Susan, (2019). "Jane, the Queen's Fool (fl. 1535–1558), court jester", *Oxford Dictionary of National Biography* [accessed 6 Feb. 2020]

11. See Figure 12 in the images section.

12. The history of fools has been well documented in Welsford, Billington and Southworth.

13. The history of fools has been well documented in Welsford, Billington and Southworth. Lipscomb, Suzannah, 'Playing The Fool'. History Learning Talk, Hampton Court Palace, 23 May 2017; Whitelock, Anna, Playing the fool: Tudor Jesters', (2008)

14. Lipscomb, Suzannah, 'Playing The Fool'. History Learning Talk, Hampton Court Palace, 23 May 2017

15. Gorman, James, 'Why Laughter Feels So Good', (New York Times, September 13, 2011)

16. Lipscomb, Suzannah, 'Playing The Fool'. History Learning Talk, Hampton Court Palace, 23 May 2017

17. Elyot, Thomas. Sir., *The castel of helth corrected and in some places augmented by the fyrste authour therof, Thomas Elyot knight, the pere of oure Lord 1541,* (London: In aedibus Thomae Bertheleti typis impress, 1541)

18. Ibid.

19. Southworth, John, *Fools and Jesters at the English Court,* (2011), p. 76

20. Ibid. p. 81

21. Ibid. pp. 78-80

22. "Inquisitions Post Mortem, Henry VII, Entries 601-650", in *Calendar of Inquisitions Post Mortem,* Series 2, Volume 3, Henry VII, (London, HMSO, 1955), eds., Cyril Flower, M. C. B. Dawes and A. C. Wood, pp.356-371. British History Online [accessed 15 February 2020]

23. "Inquisitions Post Mortem, Henry VII, Appendix I: 972-1021", in *Calendar of Inquisitions Post Mortem,* Series 2, Volume 3, Henry VII, (London, HMSO, 1955), eds., Cyril Flower, M. C. B. Dawes and A. C. Wood, pp.501-521. British History Online [accessed 16 February 2020]

24. "Inquisitions Post Mortem, Henry VII, Entries 751-800", in *Calendar of Inquisitions Post Mortem,* Series 2, Volume 3, Henry VII, (London, HMSO, 1955), eds., Cyril Flower, M. C. B. Dawes and A. C. Wood, pp.406-425. British History Online [accessed 15 February 2020]

25. Nicolas, Nicholas Harris, Sir, ed., *Privy Purse Expenses of Elizabeth of York: Wardrobe accounts of Edward the Fourth. With a Memoir of Elizabeth of York, and Notes,* (London, William Pickering, 1830) pp. 37-38

26. Lipscomb, Suzannah, 'All The King's Fools', *History Today*, Volume 61, Issue 8, (August 2011)

27. The history of fools has been well documented in Welsford, Billington and Southworth; Lipscomb, Suzannah, 'Playing The Fool'. History Learning Talk, Hampton Court Palace, 23 May 2017

28. Southworth, John, *Fools and Jesters at the English Court*, (Sutton, 1998), p. 81

29. Ibid. p. 83

30. Nicolas, Nicholas Harris, Sir, ed., *Privy Purse Expenses of Elizabeth of York: Wardrobe accounts of Edward the Fourth. With a Memoir of Elizabeth of York, and Notes*, (London, William Pickering, 1830)

31. Southworth, John, *Fools and Jesters at the English Court*, (Sutton, 1998)

32. "Henry VIII: December 1509", in *Letters and Papers, Foreign and Domestic, Henry VIII*, Volume 1, 1509-1514, ed. J S Brewer (London, HMSO, 1920), pp.127-144. British History Online [accessed 15 February 2020]

33. Motley - a woollen fabric of mixed colours made in England between the fourteenth and seventeenth centuries. A garment made of motley fabric, namely a woollen fabric of mixed colours made in England between fourteenth and seventeenth centuries, especially the characteristic dress of the professional fool company. Apparel Search Glossary M (2017), p. 3

34. Lipscomb, Suzannah, 'Playing The Fool'. History Learning Talk, Hampton Court Palace, 23 May 2017

35. Ibid.

36. Though Armin elsewhere ambiguously refers to another artificial jester or fool in the court.

37. Lipscomb, Suzannah, 'Playing The Fool'. History Learning Talk, Hampton Court Palace, 23 May 2017

38. Ibid.

39. Porter, Roy, *A Social History of Madness, Stories Of The Insane*, (Phoenix Giants) (W&N; 2nd Revised edition, 2 Jan. 1996)

40. Cameron, Kenneth Walter, *The background of John Heywood's "Witty and witless"; a study in early Tudor drama, together with A specialized bibliography of Heywood scholarship*, (Raleigh, N.C.: Thistle Press. 1941)

41. Carpenter, Sarah, (2014). 'Laughing at Fools', *Theta*, vol. XI, pp.3 22

42. Nicolas, Nicholas Harris, Sir, ed., *Privy Purse Expenses of Elizabeth of York: Wardrobe accounts of Edward the Fourth. With a Memoir of Elizabeth of York, and Notes*, (London, William Pickering, 1830), *Original Letters Illustrative of English History* (11 vols. in 3 series, ed., Sir Henry Ellis, (London, 1824, 1827, and 1846)

43. Lipscomb, Suzannah, 'All The King's Fools', *History Today*, Volume 61, Issue 8, (August 2011)

44. Armin, Robert, *Fool upon Fool*, (London, printed [by E. Allde] for William Ferbrand, dwelling neere Guild-hal gate ouer against the maiden-head, 1600)

45. *Letters and Papers, Foreign and Domestic, of the Reign of Henry VIII*, Volume 4, (HMSO, 1875)

46. Sylvester, Richard S. and Harding, Davis P., eds., *Two Early Tudor Lives: The Life and Death of Cardinal Wolsey by George Cavendish; The Life of Sir Thomas More by William Roper*, (Yale University Press, 1962)

47. Ibid.

48. Ibid.

49. Heywood, John, *The Proverbs and Epigrams of John Heywood (A. D. 1562)*, (Printed for the Spenser society [by C. Simms and co.] 1867), p. 106

50. Ibid.

51. Sylvester, Richard S. and Harding, Davis P., eds., *Two Early Tudor Lives: The Life and Death of Cardinal Wolsey by George Cavendish; The Life of Sir Thomas More by William Roper*, (Yale University Press, 1962)

52. Lipscomb, Suzannah, 'The King's Fools - Disability in the Tudor Court', (Historic England, 2017)

53. Ibid.

54. Ibid.

55. Ibid.

56. Ibid.

57. "Henry VIII: January 1536, 26-31", in *Letters and Papers, Foreign and Domestic, Henry VIII*, Volume 10, January-June 1536, ed. James Gairdner (London, HMSO, 1887), pp.64-81. British History Online [accessed 15 February 2020]

58. "Spain: July 1535, 1-31", in *Calendar of State Papers, Spain*, Volume 5 Part 1, 1534-1535, ed. Pascual de Gayangos (London,

HMSO, 1886), pp.507-523. British History Online [accessed 16 February 2020]

59. "Henry VIII: January 1536, 26-31", in *Letters and Papers, Foreign and Domestic, Henry VIII,* Volume 10, January-June 1536, ed. James Gairdner (London, HMSO, 1887), pp.64-81. British History Online [accessed 16 February 2020]

60. Granger, James, *A biographical history of England from Egbert the Great to the revolution,*(5th edition, 1824), p.149

61. Mulryne, J. R, (2004). "Somer [Sommers], William (d. 1559), court fool", *Oxford Dictionary of National Biography* [accessed 16 October 2019]

62. Walford, Edward, "Greenwich", in *Old and New London*: Volume 6, (London, Cassell, Petter & Galpin, 1878), pp.164-176. British History Online [accessed 16 February 2020]

63. Royal 2 A.XVI, f. 63v – The Psalter of Henry VIII, written and probably illuminated by John Mallard with Henry VIII depicted as the Biblical King David, 176ff; c.1540-1

64. http://www.bl.uk/manuscripts/FullDisplay.aspx?ref=Royal_MS_2_A_XVI

65. Royal MSS, 2A.XVI – f. 63v, Henry VIII and his court jester William Sommers (Psalm 52); See this image in the plates section of this book.

66. Erasmus, Desiderius. *In Praise of Folly*, (Grand Rapids, MI, Christian Classics Ethereal Library, University of Michigan Press, 1958)

67. AMPC: Amplified Bible, Classic Edition, https://www.bible.com/bible/8/1CO.1.25.AMPC

68. Erasmus, Desiderius. *In Praise of Folly,* (Grand Rapids, MI, Christian Classics Ethereal Library, University of Michigan Press, 1958)

69. Ibid.

70. 1 Corinthians 1:27. https://biblehub.com/1_corinthians/1-27.htm

71. "Henry VIII: October 1524, 21-25", in *Letters and Papers, Foreign and Domestic, Henry VIII*, Volume 4, 1524-1530, ed. J S Brewer (London, HMSO, 1875), pp.332-346. British History Online [accessed 16 February 2020]

72. "Henry VIII: June 1535, 22-30", in *Letters and Papers, Foreign and Domestic, Henry VIII*, Volume 8, January-July 1535, ed. James

Gairdner (London: HMSO, 1885), pp.356-379. British History Online [accessed 16 February 2020]

73. Nash, et al., *Archaeologia or Miscellaneous Tracts relating to Antiquity*, Vol. IX 9, (Society of Antiquaries of London, London, printed by J Nichols, 1789) p.249; also in *Letters and Papers Foreign and Domestic, Henry VIII,* VIII, pp.366-7

74. "Letters and Papers: Miscellaneous, 1539", in *Letters and Papers, Foreign and Domestic, Henry VIII*, Volume 14 Part 2, August-December 1539, eds. James Gairdner and R H Brodie (London, HMSO, 1895), pp.303-358. British History Online [accessed 19 February 2020]

75. Erasmus, Desiderius, In Praise of Folly, (Grand Rapids, MI, Christian Classics Ethereal Library, University of Michigan Press, 1958)

76. Armin, R., Lippincott, H. Frederick., *A Shakespeare jestbook, Robert Armin's Foole upon foole (1600): a critical, old-spelling edition*, (Salzburg, Austria: Institut für Englische Sprache und Literatur, Universität Salzburg, 1973)

77. Armin, Robert, *'A Nest of Ninnies'*, in *The Collected Works of Robert Armin*, 2 Vols, I ed., J.P. Feather, (New York, Johnson Reprint, 1972)

78. Wilson, Thomas, *Arte of Rhetorique*, 1590, ed. G.H. Mair (Oxford 1909), p.201 William Somer was a true eccentric who was one of those rare people who could turn a phrase, with his amiable wit and amusement.

79. Armin, R., Lippincott, H. Frederick., *A Shakespeare jestbook, Robert Armin's Foole upon foole (1600): a critical, old-spelling edition*, (Salzburg, Austria: Institut für Englische Sprache und Literatur, Universität Salzburg, 1973)

80. Lipscomb, Suzannah, 'All The King's Fools', *History Today*, Volume 61, Issue 8, (August 2011)

81. Southworth, John, *Fools and Jesters at the English Court*, (Sutton, 1998), p.95

82. Armin, R., Lippincott, H. Frederick., *A Shakespeare jestbook, Robert Armin's Foole upon foole (1600): a critical, old-spelling edition*, (Salzburg, Austria: Institut für Englische Sprache und Literatur, Universität Salzburg, 1973)

83. Erasmus, Desiderius., *In Praise of Folly*, (Penguin, edition, 22 April 2004)

84. Ibid.
85. "Spain: July 1535, 1-31", in *Calendar of State Papers, Spain,* Volume 5 Part 1, 1534-1535, ed. Pascual de Gayangos (London, HMSO, 1886), pp.507-523. British History Online [accessed 16 February 2020]
86. Weir, Alison, *Henry VIII, King and Court,* (Vintage, 2008).p.365
87. "Henry VIII: January 1547, 30-31", in *Letters and Papers, Foreign and Domestic, Henry VIII,* Volume 21 Part 2, September 1546-January 1547, ed. James Gairdner and R H Brodie (London, HMSO, 1910), pp.388-453. British History Online [accessed 20 February 2020]
88. *Documents relating to the revels at Court in the time of King Edward VI and Queen Mary, The Loseley Manuscripts,* ed. A. Feuillerat (Louvain, 1914), p.49
89. Harward, Vernon, *The Dwarfs of Arthurian Romance and Celtic Tradition,* (E J. Brill; 1st edition, 1958), (n.4) p.25
90. Davis, Norman, *Paston Letters and Papers of the Fifteenth Century,* Part 1: Pt. 1, (Oxford University Press, 27 May 1971), p.539
91. Southworth, John, *Fools and Jesters at the English Court,* (Sutton, 1998), p.99
92. Stopes, C.C, 'Jane, the Queen's Fool', *The Athenaeum,* 4059 (August, 1905), p. 210
93. Stopes, C. C., *Shakespeare's Environment,* (London: G. Bell, 1914), pp 260-263. Citing manuscripts in the British Library.
94. 'Elizabethan Era Colours and Meanings', http://www.elizabethanenglandlife.com/elizabethan-era-colors-and-meanings.html, [accessed 21 February 2020]
95. Turner, William Henry., ed., *Calendar of charters and rolls preserved in the Bodleian Library,* (Oxford Clarendon Press, 1878), pp. XVIII – XIX
96. Stopes, C. C., *Shakespeare's Environment,* (London: G. Bell, 1914), (n.20), p.266
97. Southworth, John, *Fools and Jesters at the English Court,* (Sutton, 1998), p.100
98. Stopes (n.20), p.266
99. *A Pleasant History of the Life and Death of Will Summers* (1676)
100. Screti, Zoe, 'A Motley to the View': The Clothing of Court Fools in Tudor England', *Midlands Historical Review,* Vol. 2 (2018), ISSN 2516-8568.

101. Porter, Linda, *Mary Tudor: The First Queen*, (London, 2010) p.1518; Lisle, L. de *Tudor: The Family Story*, (London, 2013) pp.101, 327

102. Lipscomb, Suzannah, 'Playing The Fool'. History Learning Talk, Hampton Court Palace, 23 May 2017

103. Ibid.

104. Mackay, Lauren, *Inside the Tudor Court – Henry VIII and his Six Wives through the writings of the Spanish Ambassador, Eustace Chapuys*, (Amberley, 2014)

105. Ibid. p. 101

106. "Henry VIII: June 1533, 1-5", in *Letters and Papers, Foreign and Domestic, Henry VIII*, Volume 6, 1533, ed. James Gairdner (London, HMSO, 1882), 262-275. British History Online [accessed 21 February 2020]

107. Ibid.

108. "Henry VIII: May 1536, 16-20", in *Letters and Papers, Foreign and Domestic, Henry VIII*, Volume 10, January-June 1536, ed. James Gairdner (London, HMSO, 1887), pp.371-391. British History Online [accessed 21 February 2020]

109. Madden, Frederick, ed., *Privy Purse Expenses of the Princess Mary*, (London, 1831)

110. Ibid. pp.48, 50

111. Ibid. pp.64, 73

112. Stopes, C.C, 'Jane, the Queen's Fool', *The Athenaeum*, 4059, (August, 1905), p.209

113. Ibid. p.210

114. Richardson, E., 'Two Court Fools by Frans Floris', *Bulletin of the Detroit Institute of Arts of the City of Detroit*, 18 (May 1939), p. 2

115. Stopes, C.C, 'Jane, the Queen's Fool', *The Athenaeum*, 4059, (August, 1905), p. 210

116. Madden, Frederick, ed., *Privy Purse Expenses of the Princess Mary*, (London, William Pickering, 1914), p.93

117. Lipscomb, Suzannah, 'All The King's Fools', *History Today*, Volume 61, Issue 8, (August 2011)

118. Ibid.

119. Borradaile, H., 'Clowns and Fools of Shakespeare's Time', *Poet Lore*, 8 (January 1896) p. 212

120. Madden, F., *Privy Purse Expenses of the Princess Mary*, (London, 1831) pp.150, 161-162, 164

121. Cranefield, P., 'A Seventeenth-Century View of Mental Deficiency and Schizophrenia' and Willis,Thomas on 'Stupidity or Foolishness', *Bulletin of the History of Medicine*, 35 (1961), p. 305

122. Lipscomb, Suzannah, 'Playing The Fool'. History Learning Talk, Hampton Court Palace, 23 May 2017

123. Madden, Frederick, ed., *Privy Purse Expenses of the Princess Mary*, (London, William Pickering, 1914)

124. Madden, Frederick, *Privy Purse Expenses of the Princess Mary*, (London, 1831), pp. 130-131

125. Madden, Frederick, *Privy purse expenses of the Princess Mary*, (London, 1831), pp.123

126. "Henry VIII: November 1544, 26-30", in *Letters and Papers, Foreign and Domestic, Henry VIII*, Volume 19 Part 2, August-December 1544, ed. James Gairdner and R H Brodie (London, HMSO, 1905), pp.396-421. British History Online [accessed 22 February 2020]

127. Southworth, John, *Fools and Jesters at the English Court*, (Sutton, 1998), p.133

128. "Henry VIII: June 1546, 21-30", in *Letters and Papers, Foreign and Domestic, Henry VIII*, Volume 21 Part 1, January-August 1546, ed. James Gairdner and R H Brodie (London, HMSO, 1908), pp.546-582. British History Online [accessed 22 February 2020]

129. Southworth, John, *Fools and Jesters at the English Court*, (Sutton, 1998), p.134

130. "Queen Mary - Volume 4: July 1554", in *Calendar of State Papers Domestic: Edward VI, Mary and Elizabeth*, 1547-80, ed. Robert Lemon (London, HMSO, 1856), p.63. British History Online [accessed 22 February 2020]

131. *Calendar of Charters and Rolls in the Bodleian Library*, ed. WH. Turner (Oxford, 1878), p.xviii; C. Stopes. p.265

132. Southworth, John, *Fools and Jesters at the English Court*, (Sutton, 1998), p.153

133. Stopes, C.C., 'Jane, the Queen's Fool', *The Athenaeum*, 4059 (August, 1905), p.266

134. Stopes, p.268, citing Chequer Accounts, 6 Mary, 427 (18)

135. Madden, Frederick, ed., *Privy Purse Expenses of the Princess Mary*, (London, William Pickering, 1914), pp. 59, 177

136. Arnold, Janet, *Queen Elizabeth's Wardrobe Unlock'd*, (1988), p.171

137. Southworth, John, *Fools and Jesters at the English Court*, (Sutton, 1998), p.141

138. Ibid.

139. See Figure 16 in the image section.

140. Arnold, Janet, *Queen Elizabeth's Wardrobe Unlock'd*, (1988), (n.4), p.201

141. Ibid.

142. Arnold, Janet, *Queen Elizabeth's Wardrobe Unlock'd*, (1988), p.206. Arnold quoting The Letting of Humours Blood in the Head-Vaine (1600). Epigram 30, sig. C2V.

143. "Simancas: August 1565", in *Calendar of State Papers, Spain (Simancas)*, Volume 1, 1558-1567, ed. Martin A S Hume (London, HMSO, 1892), pp.458-470. British History Online [accessed 23 February 2020]

144. Ibid.

145. Thomson, Peter, (2004). "Tarlton, Richard (d. 1588), actor and clown", *Oxford Dictionary of National Biography* [accessed 6 Feb. 2020]

146. Fuller, Thomas, *The History of Worthies in England*, (London: printed by J.G[rismond. W.L[eybourne]. And W.G[odbid]. For Thomas Williams, and are to be sold at the sign of the Bible in Little Britain, 1662)

147. Ibid.

148. Welsford, Enid, *The Fool: His Social and Literary History*, (1968)

149. Lipscomb, Suzannah, 'Natural Fools at Henry VIII's Court', unpublished article (2017)

150. Lipscomb, Suzannah, 'Playing The Fool'. History Learning Talk, Hampton Court Palace, 23 May 2017

Index